WHEN TITANS CLASHED

WHEN TITANS CLASHED

How the Red Army Stopped Hitler

DAVID M. GLANTZ
JONATHAN M. HOUSE

Maps by Darin Grauberger and George F. McCleary, Jr.

Birlinn

This edition published in 2000 by
Birlinn Limited
8 Canongate Venture
5 New Street
Edinburgh
EH8 8BH

www.birlinn.co.uk

ISBN 1 84158 049 X

British Library Cataloguing-in-Publication Data
A catalogue record for this book is available from the British Library

Printed and bound by
Creative Print and Design, Ebbw Vale

In memory of an able historian and fine friend,
Colonel Paul Adair, British Army Retired,
who worked so hard to reveal the human dimension of
the War on the Eastern Front

Contents

Maps and Illustrations

ILLUSTRATIONS (PHOTO INSERT)

"Under the banner of Lenin, forward to victory!" (poster, 1941)
"The Motherland calls!" (poster, 1941)
Chiefs of the Red Army
Marshal of the Soviet Union G. K. Zhukov, *Stavka* representative,
    Western and 1st Belorussian Front commander

Acknowledgments

The authors owe a special debt to historians who have long struggled to unearth the truths of the German-Soviet war, among them a host of Russian military historians who have had to contend with the awesome task of conducting historical research and writing within stifling and rigid ideological constraints. It is indeed remarkable, and a testament to their doggedness and skill, that so many have succeeded in determining and revealing truth despite formidable obstacles. Among Western military historians, Malcolm MacIntosh and John Erickson stand colossal in their field. Their massive contributions in the study of the Red Army served as inspiration and models for this work, and their contributions have well endured the test of time. Earl F. Ziemke, Albert Seaton, and many others who have worked from primarily German archival materials on the War in the East deserve similar recognition, as do numerous German veterans who have written memoirs about a war against a shadowy enemy.

Above all, the authors acknowledge the millions of Soviet and German soldiers who fought, suffered, and died in this titanic and brutal struggle. Their sacrifice demands that this story be told.

Finally, heartfelt thanks go to the able editors of the University Press of Kansas and to Mary Ann Glantz, who were instrumental in putting this book into presentable form.

Theater of Operations

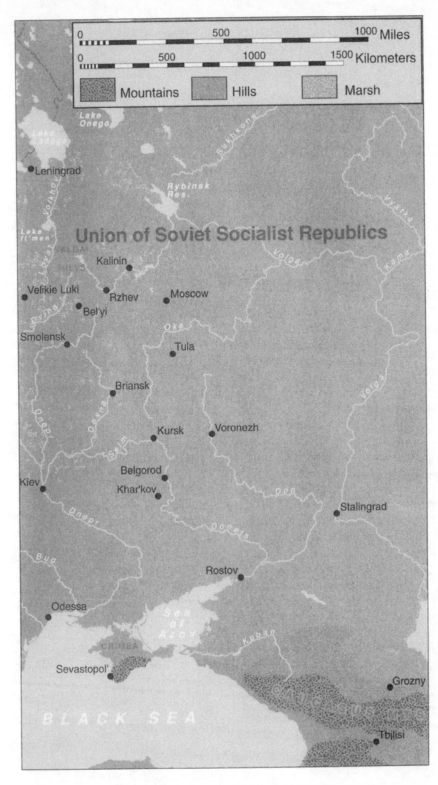

Theater of Operations (continued)

Introduction

The Union of Soviet Socialist Republics has passed from the world scene. Appropriately enough, its death throes in August 1991, like its birth in 1917, were marked by the refusal of the armed forces to repress opponents of the conservative government in power. With this demise, the intensive Cold War study of Soviet history and institutions may seem irrelevant.

Yet the decline and death of the USSR has provided historians with unprecedented sources and opportunities to integrate Soviet experience into the broader history of Russia and Europe as a whole. These sources and opportunities are particularly significant in regard to a seemingly familiar topic—the Soviet defeat of National Socialist Germany in World War II.

For decades, both popular and official historians in the West presented the Soviet-German struggle largely from the German point of view.[1] As a practical matter, German archives and memoirs have been readily available as sources about this struggle since the 1950s, whereas their Soviet equivalents were obscured by difficulties of ideology, access, and language. Even when published in translation, most popular Soviet accounts of the war were filled with obligatory communist rhetoric that made their factual assertions appear to be so much propaganda. Westerners quite naturally viewed with suspicion the many detailed Russian-language accounts of the war and the few Western studies that relied on them.

Consciously or unconsciously, however, German accounts were often just as biased as their Soviet counterparts, warping our understanding of the titanic struggle that occurred on what the Germans taught us to call the "Eastern Front." German officers such as Field Marshal Erich von Manstein and Major General F. W. von Mellenthin wrote about the war in Russia based primarily on their experiences during 1941–1943, when the Red Army was still recovering from the purges of the 1930s and the surprise of the German invasion. The senior German commanders of 1944–1945, the period of the greatest Soviet triumphs, left few memoirs.[2] If they escaped capture or death, they were loath to dwell on the series of defeats they suffered at the hands of their opponents. Thus our view of Soviet military capabilities and performance was twisted by an error equivalent to evaluating American war performance based on the American defeats immediately after Pearl Harbor.

1

The Soviets themselves, however, devoted enormous energy to the study of their "Great Patriotic War." Even today, with the USSR gone, virtually all former Soviet officers and officers of the Soviet Union's former allies view military affairs through the prism of 1941–1945. The idea of military history as a Marxist science produced a remarkably frank and open Soviet literature about the war. Once Premier N. S. Khrushchev began to de-Stalinize official history in the late 1950s, World War II Soviet commanders at all levels felt free to publish their memoirs of the war. Such memoirs were subject to considerable censorship and deliberately avoided certain embarassing political and military topics. With these memoirs appeared a host of detailed operational studies necessary for the proper education of future Soviet military leaders. Moreover, few Soviet military writers, including senior commanders, had full access to surviving archival war records. Within these constraints, however, these publications were frequently honest, largely accurate regarding place, time, and event (although not always consequence), and even critical about many of those wartime decisions they were permitted to describe.

In recent years, the gradual Soviet collapse has led to increasing frankness on economic, political, diplomatic, and military matters, including publication of many documents, as well as extensive, yet still limited, access to Soviet archives and archival products. While these recent disclosures were naturally subject to censorship before they were published, many of the extensive military documents have been released in full and without editing. The authenticity and accuracy of these works can now be verified by comparing them with the many archival materials that fell into German hands in wartime and into Western hands in the postwar years. In the absence of complete access to Soviet participants and archival records, this body of recent archival publications and disclosures still represents a considerable advance in our understanding of the war. When compared with the more traditional accounts of the Eastern Front derived from German sources, these archival materials allow us to develop a far more complete synthesis of that war.

This book summarizes ongoing research and reinterpretations of the Soviet-German conflict based on newly released Soviet archival studies. Because the bulk of new sources are Soviet, this study emphasizes the Soviet side as much as previous histories exaggerated the German version of events. What emerges is an intensely human story of leadership errors, military adaptation under the pressures of war, disruption and suffering on a gigantic scale, and incredible endurance by both German and Soviet citizens. An understanding of this story is essential for historians to correct some mistaken generalizations about World War II.

PRELUDE
1918–1941

CHAPTER 1

The Red Army, 1918–1939

RUSSIAN CIVIL WAR, 1918–1921

One of the ironies of Russian history is that, having seized power in Petrograd by undermining military discipline and civil authority, the Bolsheviks owed their survival to strong armed forces. The shock troops of the October 1917 revolution were militant soldiers and sailors, but, even with the addition of the armed workers of the Red Guard, these forces were inadequate to face the threats to the infant Soviet state.

From every direction, both foreign enemies and so-called White Russian forces menaced the new government. With the Imperial Russian Army exhausted by three years of world war and dissolved by mutiny, nothing stood between the new government and the victorious German Army. In March 1918, German forces dictated an armistice and then roamed at will over western Russia. Even after they were defeated in Western Europe in November 1918, the Germans supported the breakaway Baltic states of Latvia, Lithuania, and Estonia, as well as a separatist movement in the Ukraine. Once the Bolshevik government signed the armistice with Germany, its former allies also intervened in an effort to reverse the revolution and bring Russia back into the World War. To support the White troops, American and British soldiers landed at Archangel'sk and Murmansk in the north, while additional British and French forces operated in Odessa, Crimea, and the Caucasus region. In Siberia, the highly professional Czech Army, composed of former Russian prisoners of war who had enlisted to fight against Austria–Hungary, dominated the railroad line in support of the Whites. Japanese and American troops spread westward to Irkutsk in Siberia from the Pacific port of Vladivostok.

The result was the Russian Civil War of 1918–1921, a formative experience for both the Soviet state and its Red Army. During 1918 and 1919, V. I. Lenin and his commissar for military affairs, L. D. Trotsky, used the railroad lines to shuttle their limited reserves from place to place, staving off defeat time after time. This became known as echelon war, in which large forces were shifted by railroad (echelon) to reinforce successively threatened fronts. Some infantry divisions were shifted between fronts as many as five times in the course of the war. This experience gave all

5

participants an abiding sense of the need for strategic reserves and forces arrayed in great depth.[1]

Necessity forced Lenin to declare "War Communism," a system of extreme requisitions and political repression. In order to create effective military forces, the new government had to conscript men of all social backgrounds and accept the services of thousands of former Imperial officers. In turn, the need to ensure the political loyalty of such "military experts" led to the institution of a political commissar for each unit who had to approve all actions of the nominal commander.

Ultimately the new government triumphed. In early 1920, the Czech commander in Siberia turned over to the Soviets the self-appointed White Russian leader, Admiral A. V. Kolchak, in return for unrestricted passage out of the country. Later that same year, the Red Army repulsed a Polish invasion in support of the Ukrainian separatists, but was itself halted by "the miracle along the Vistula" just short of Warsaw. For years thereafter, the leaders of the Red Army engaged in bitter recriminations concerning the responsibility for this defeat. Despite the Polish setback, by 17 November 1920 the last White Russians had been driven from the Crimea. After a few actions in Turkestan and the Far East, the war was over.

In the process, the first generation of Soviet military commanders had developed a unique view of warfare. Unlike the positional, trench-warfare battles of the World War, the Russian Civil War was characterized by vast distances defended by relatively small numbers of troops. Under these circumstances, Soviet commanders tried to integrate all tactical operations into an overall campaign plan, aiming for objectives deep in the enemy's rear. The two keys to victory proved to be concentration of superior forces to overwhelm the enemy at a particular point, and then rapid maneuvers such as flank movements, penetrations, and encirclements to destroy the thinly spread enemy. The prerequisite for such maneuvers was a highly mobile offensive force, which in the Civil War relied on armored railroad trains and cars and, especially, horse cavalry formations. The elite of the Red Army, Marshal S. M. Budenny's 1st Cavalry Army, produced a generation of officers who believed passionately in the value of mobility and maneuver and soon embraced mechanized forces as the weapon of choice.[2]

RISE OF THE DEEP OPERATION, 1922–1937

In the immediate postwar era, the chaotic state of the Soviet economy precluded the expense of a large standing army, and by 1925 the Red Army had been reduced to 562,000 men—one tenth of its peak wartime strength.

Cavalry and some border district rifle divisions remained at reduced size, while the majority of surviving divisions retained only a fraction of their required strength. These divisions relied for wartime strength on reservists drawn from particular territorial regions. The system adopted in 1924–1925, combining regular-cadre formations with territorial-militia forces, was supposed to produce almost 140 divisions in wartime, but its peacetime capability was extremely limited.[3]

In an era of retrenchment, one of the few sources of funds and equipment for weapons experimentation was the secret Soviet-German military collaboration agreements. The two former enemies shared both a fear of Poland and a desire to circumvent the restrictions placed on them by the western allies of the World War. The Treaty of Versailles (1919) forbade Germany to possess tanks, poison gas, and aircraft, but, for a decade after 1921, the German army and government provided funds and technical assistance to produce and test such weapons in the Soviet Union. Both sides gained the opportunity to test equipment they could not otherwise have produced, but the actual number of such weapons was relatively small.[4]

Soviet-German cooperation included exchanging observers for military exercises, but, in retrospect, the two armies developed their military doctrines and theories almost independently. During the 1920s, the experience of the Civil War led Soviet military writers to review all their concepts for waging war. The former tsarist officer A. A. Svechin led the strategic debate, while M. V. Frunze tried to formulate a uniform military doctrine[5] appropriate to a socialist state.

Perhaps most important, the brilliant Civil War commander M. N. Tukhachevsky and the military theorist V. K. Triandafillov developed a strategic theory of successive operations based on the Soviet military failure against Poland in 1920 and the failed German offensives against France in 1918. Put simply, they believed that modern armies were too large and resilient to be defeated in one cataclysmic battle. Instead, the attacker would have to fight a series of offensive battles, each followed by a rapid exploitation into the enemy rear and then another battle when the defender reorganized his forces.[6]

To place these battles in a common strategic context, Soviet soldiers began to think of a new level of warfare, midway between the tactics of individual battles and the strategy of an entire war. This intermediate level became known as Operational Art (*operativnaia iskusstva*). Operational Art may be thought of as the realm of senior commanders who plan and coordinate operations of large formations within the context of a strategic operation or an entire campaign, that is, a series of actions culminating in the achievement of a strategic objective. In 1927, Svechin summarized this theoretical structure: "Tactics make the steps from which operational leaps are assembled, strategy points out the path."[7]

During the late 1920s and early 1930s, Soviet theorists perfected the tactical concept of Deep Battle (*glubokii boi*). They planned to use new technology, especially tanks and aircraft, to penetrate the elaborate defense systems developed during the World War. Surfaced as a concept in the *Field Regulations of 1929*, deep battle found full expression in the *Instructions on Deep Battle* published in 1935.

By 1936, accelerated technological change led, in turn, to the larger concept of the Deep Operation (*glubokaia operatsiia*). Instead of planning to penetrate the enemy in a single, tactical, deep battle, Tukhachevsky and other theorists projected penetrations and exploitations out to an operational depth of 100 kilometers or more. The essence of such a deep operation was to use the most modern weapons available to neutralize simultaneously all the enemy's defenses to the maximum possible depth and then to exploit so rapidly that the defender would be unable to reorganize in time. In the words of A. I. Egorov, "The principal and basic task of military art is to prevent the formation of a firm front [by the defending enemy], imparting a destructive striking force and a rapid tempo to operations."[8]

Initially, Tukhachevsky and the other theorists intended to accomplish this using the weapons of the Russian Civil War–infantry, artillery, and cavalry formations supplemented by armored cars. In that form, Tukhachevsky's tactics would differ little from those of other armies. During and immediately after the World War, most Western armies viewed the tank primarily as a support weapon to assist the infantry in penetrating prepared enemy defenses. Soviet operational and tactical theory evolved rapidly, however, and, by the early 1930s, Red theorists included the entire spectrum of mechanized forces functioning (at least in theory) as a sophisticated combined-arms team. Infantry, led by tanks and supported by artillery and engineers, would penetrate the enemy's defenses, while other artillery and aircraft struck deeper into the enemy rear, to be followed by large, independent airborne and armored formations. To accomplish this, tanks would be organized into three different echelons: some tanks would lead the infantry penetration; others would conduct short-range exploitations of that breakthrough; and still others, operating in large combined-arms mechanized formations, would lead the pursuit and encirclement of the beaten enemy.[9] These concepts, which appeared in print as early as 1929, were codified into the Red Army's *Provisional Field Regulations of 1936*.

The idea of a deep, mechanized operation was unusual but not unique for its time. Military theory in all major armies evolved in the same general direction, using varying degrees of mechanization to penetrate enemy defenses and thereby defeat or avoid the stalemate of trench warfare. What was unprecedented about the Soviet concept was the official sanction it received from the Soviet dictator I. V. Stalin, who geared a large proportion of his five-year economic development plans to provide the industrial capacity and production needed to implement that concept. Given the shortcomings of Russian industry during the World War and the belief that the Communist Revolution remained vulnerable to capitalist attack, it was natural that Stalin should give a high priority to the development of a munitions industry.

This effort bore fruit in a surprisingly short time. With the exception of a few experimental vehicles, the Soviet Union did not produce its first domestic tank, the MS-1, based on the design of the American-made Walter Christie, until 1929. Four years later, Russian factories were turning out 3,000 tanks and other armored vehicles per year. Similar rapid growth occurred in aircraft, artillery, and other armaments.[10]

This official sanction and a generous supply of equipment were the bases for a steady growth in mechanized force structure. The first experimental tank regiment had been formed in Moscow in 1927, using 60 foreign-built tanks.[11] Three years later, in May 1930, the first experimental mechanized brigade appeared, composed of armored, motorized infantry, artillery, and reconnaissance units.[12]

The development of the Deep Operation called for more and larger mechanized formations in order to penetrate enemy defenses and then maintain the momentum of a rapid exploitation. On 9 March 1932, a special commission of the People's Commissariat of Defense recommended creation of armored forces of all sizes to perform specific combat functions at every level of command. Each rifle (infantry) division of 12,500 men (18,000 in wartime) would include a single tank battalion (57 light tanks), and each cavalry division a mechanized regiment (64 light tanks). Tank brigades formed the general reserve force for each rifle corps and army, and separate mechanized corps, acting as the "mobile group" of Civil War days, would conduct exploitations deep into the enemy's rear areas. These corps, each composed of two tank and one rifle brigade, were in fact slightly larger than a Western division. Each such brigade integrated the different combined arms—tanks, motorized infantry, artillery, engineers, and antiaircraft guns.[13]

The Soviets formed their first two mechanized corps in the fall of 1932, three years before Germany created its first panzer divisions. Over the next several years, the number and complexity of armored, mechanized, and airborne formations grew steadily. Airborne forces, in particular, were elite units, composed in large part of dedicated Communists who had learned to parachute in the Komsomol youth organization.

Large-scale exercises tested the theory of combined mechanized and airborne offensives. At the same time, the rest of the Red Army gradually shifted to regular-cadre composition, eliminating the mixed territorial-cadre system. By 1 June 1938, the Red Army was a full-time force of 1.5 million men.[14]

Of course, Soviet mechanization was not perfect. Just as in prewar Germany, the majority of tanks produced in Russia were very lightly armored, relying on speed for protection. Radio communication, a necessity for battlefield maneuvering, was notoriously unreliable. The mechanized corps proved so large and unwieldy that in 1935 its authorized size was temporarily reduced. Because the average Soviet soldier of the period lacked experience as a driver or mechanic, the equipment broke down and wore out at a rapid pace. In retrospect, some Soviet historians have admitted that the emphasis on mechanized, offensive warfare caused the Red Army to neglect planning and training for the defensive, at least at the operational level. Left undisturbed, the Soviet "tankists" would have required several more years to work out such problems.

Nevertheless, in the mid-1930s, the Soviet Union led the world in production, planning, and fielding of mechanized forces. Perhaps most important, the Red Army was well ahead of its German counterparts in both theoretical concepts and practical experience of mechanized warfare. In Germany, Heinz Guderian and other armored weapons theorists received only limited support from civil and military leaders—panzer units were as much a part of Hitler's diplomatic bluff as they were a real instrument of warfare, and their use was not integrated into official German doctrine. Tank production took a back seat to aircraft for the new German Air Force, and those tanks that were produced were often assigned to infantry support units and other organizations outside Guderian's control. At the same time, the German Army as a whole was only just beginning to expand beyond the severe limits dictated by the Treaty of Versailles. In short, had the Germans and Soviets fought in the mid-1930s, the Red Army would have had a considerable advantage over its opponent.

AN ARMY IN DISARRAY, 1937–1939

By 1939, that advantage had disappeared, and the Red Army was in disarray. Of the many causes of this change, the most serious was Stalin's purge of the Soviet leadership. Beginning in 1934, he systematically eliminated any potential competitors for power throughout the Soviet government. By 1937, only the Red Army remained untouched.

I. V. Stalin had always loved the Red Army but suspected its professional leadership. During the Civil War, Stalin had served as a political officer on various fronts. In the process, he developed a deep suspicion of professional soldiers (his cavalry cronies excepted), especially the ex-tsarist military experts who helped run the Red Army but, on occasion, betrayed it. Stalin was quick to blame professionals, including M. N. Tukhachevsky and A. I. Egorov, for every setback, conveniently evading his own share of responsibility for the Soviet Civil War defeat in front of Warsaw.

Once peace returned, Stalin remained uncomfortable with innovative theorists such as Tukhachevsky. Like his fellow-dictator Adolf Hitler, Stalin valued loyalty, orthodoxy, and intellectual subservience. Independent ideas disturbed him. His only close military associate, Defense Commissar K. E. Voroshilov, encouraged Stalin's prejudices in this regard. Voroshilov was an unimaginative crony who executed orders without question. He himself resented Tukhachevsky's intellectual brilliance because it highlighted his own limited abilities as a commander. As a result, Voroshilov eagerly repeated rumors of a military conspiracy centered around Tukhachevsky. Tukhachevsky's past service under Trotsky and his previous extended visit to Germany provided some shreds of fact to support allegations that he was a Trotskyite or German spy. On 27 May 1937, Marshal Tukhachevsky and a number of his colleagues were arrested.[15]

What was unusual about the army purges was that they began without the public show trials that had accompanied all previous steps in Stalin's reign of terror. All the court martial proceedings were secret and hasty. One loyal officer, E. B. Gamarnik, committed suicide rather than serve on the board that tried Tukhachevsky, but other senior officers, including Marshals S. M. Budenny and V. K. Bliukher, participated willingly. On 12 June 1937, Voroshilov simply announced the execution of Deputy Defense Commissar Tukhachevsky, the commanders of two military districts, and six other high-ranking colleagues.

For the next four years, right up to the German invasion, Soviet officers disappeared with alarming frequency. Of an estimated 75,000 to 80,000 officers in the armed forces, at least 30,000 were imprisoned or executed. They included three out of five marshals; all 11 deputy defense commissars; all commanders of military districts; the commanders and chiefs of staff of both the Navy and the Air Force; 14 of 16 army commanders; 60 of 67 corps commanders; 136 of 199 division commanders; 221 of 397 brigade commanders; and 50 percent of all regimental commanders.[16] Another 10,000 officers were dismissed from the service in disgrace.

Stalin's basis for identifying traitors was tenuous at best. Few, if any, of the commanders convicted had committed identifiable crimes. The only consistent criterion appeared to be elimination of all senior leaders who did not owe their careers to Stalin and who, therefore, might pose a challenge to his authority. Of those imprisoned, 15 percent were later rehabilitated for war service, some leaving prison camp directly to command a division or larger unit. Perhaps the most famous former prisoner was K. K. Rokossovsky, who ended the war as a marshal of the Soviet Union commanding a *front*. The purges were still continuing when war engulfed the Soviet Union in 1941.

In 1937–1939, however, the rehabilitation of purged figures was well in the future. An entire generation of commanders, government administrators, and factory managers was decimated. Younger men, often lacking the experience or training, found themselves thrust into high command. In 1938, for example, then-Major S. S. Biriuzov reported to the 30th Irkutsk Rifle Division after completing staff officer training. He found that the commander, political commissar, chief of staff, and all but one primary staff officer of the division had been arrested, leaving him as division commander, a position that called for at least three ranks higher and ten more years of experience than he possessed.[17] Stars fell on the Voroshilov General Staff Academy class of 1937. The class graduated a year ahead of schedule and included such future luminaries as A. M. Vasilevsky, A. I. Antonov, and M. V. Zakharov, who were thrust precipitously into high staff and command positions.[18] Training and maintenance naturally suffered, paving the way for the disastrous performance of the Red Army in 1939–1942. Moreover, although Deep Battle and the Deep Operation remained official operational concepts of the Red Army, the sudden death of Tukhachevsky threw both concepts and the mechanized force structure into ill repute. Many of Tukhachevsky's theoretical writings were recalled from public circulation and destroyed.[19]

The Spanish Civil War (1936–1939), that great dress rehearsal for World War II, further slowed the development of Soviet arms. A limited number of Soviet tanks and tankers participated on the Republican side, just as the Germans and Italians provided equipment and men to support Francisco Franco. The Soviets suffered a number of setbacks. Their tanks were too lightly armored; they had improvised crews that often could not communicate with the Spanish-speaking infantry they supported; and in combat, the tanks tended to outrun the accompanying foot soldiers, which allowed the Fascist defenders to destroy the tanks with relative ease. D. G. Pavlov, chief of armored forces and one of the most senior Soviet officers to serve in Spain, returned home with an extremely pessimistic attitude. He concluded that the new mechanized formations were too large and clumsy to control, too vulnerable to artillery fire, and would have great difficulty penetrating prepared enemy defenses in order to conduct deep operations.

In short, armor could not attack independently but had to be integrated with combined-arms functions.[20]

In retrospect, other armies had similar difficulties with mechanization in the later 1930s. Except in France, all nations produced tanks that were inadequately armored and tended to use armor as independent, cavalry-reconnaissance units rather than in close cooperation with the other combat arms. Certainly German and Italian tankers experienced similar problems in Spain. In the Soviet case, however, the weaknesses described by Pavlov added fuel to the fires of indecision and suspicion started by the Great Purge.

In July 1939, a special commission convened in response to these criticisms reviewed the entire question of armored force organization. The commission was chaired by one of Stalin's cronies, Assistant Defense Commissar G. I. Kulik, and included such surviving famous names of the Russian Civil War as Marshals S. M. Budenny and S. K. Timoskenko. Few experienced armor officers or younger advocates of Tukhachevsky's ideas were allowed to participate in the commission's study. In August, the commission reached a compromise that directed the removal of the motorized infantry elements from tank corps (the name given to mechanized corps in 1938) and tank brigades, reducing such units to an infantry-support role. The Kulik Commission did authorize the creation of four new motorized divisions that closely resembled the German panzer division of the day and could be used either as a mobile group for a limited penetration or as part of a larger cavalry-mechanized group for a deeper, *front*-level exploitation. Although the tank corps were formally ordered abolished by 15 January 1940, two of them survived in practice. Overall, Soviet mechanized concepts and force structure had regressed to a far more primitive, less ambitious stage than they had reached in 1936.[21]

LAKE KHASAN AND KHALKIN-GOL

The last portion of the Red Army to feel the brunt of the great purges was in Siberia and the Far East, where distance from Moscow combined with an external threat to limit the disorganizing effects of Stalin's bloodbath. The Japanese incursions into Manchuria in 1931 and into China proper six years later brought Moscow and Tokyo into an undeclared conflict that flared twice in the late 1930s. The Soviet government reacted strongly to these challenges in a successful, if costly, effort to deter Japan from open war.

During July and August 1938, the two powers repeatedly clashed over possession of a narrow spit of land at Lake Khasan, seventy miles southeast of Vladivostok. On 11 August, the hard-pressed Japanese asked for an armistice, eventually withdrawing after suffering 526 killed and 900 wounded. The Soviet performance was characterized by frontal attacks and poor combined-arms coordination, resulting in 792 Soviet troups dead or missing and 2,752 wounded.[22]

Undeterred, the Japanese chose a remote area on the Khalkhin-Gol, the river between Outer Mongolia and the Japanese satellite state of Manchukuo, or Manchuria, to next test the Soviets' will. In May 1939, the Japanese occupied the area around the village of Nomonhan, hoping to challenge Soviet strength in an area where poor roads would restrict the size of forces that could be brought to bear. After an initial rebuff, however, command of the Soviet forces went to Corps Commander (*Komkor*) G. K. Zhukov, one of Tukhachevsky's most brilliant disciples. Undetected by the Japanese, Zhukov massed 57,000 men, 498 tanks, and 385 armored cars organized into three rifle divisions, two tank brigades, three armored car brigades, one machine gun brigade, and an airborne brigade. At 0545 hours on Sunday, 20 August 1939, he struck. A recently mobilized territorial division bogged down in front of the Japanese defenses, but, at the same time, Soviet mobile forces moved around both flanks and encircled most of the Japanese troops. A Japanese attempt to break out of the trap failed on 27 August. On 15 September the Japanese signed an agreement in Moscow to end the undeclared war. The brief operation cost the Soviets 7,974 killed and 15,251 wounded and the Japanese 61,000 killed, wounded, or captured.[23]

Khalkhin-Gol had two major results. First, the Japanese government decided that it had seriously underestimated the Soviets, and Tokyo looked elsewhere for new spheres of influence. This contributed to the ultimate conflict with the United States, but it also secured the Soviet back door throughout World War II as Japan refrained from joining Hitler's attack on the Soviet Union. Secondly, Zhukov began his meteoric rise, taking with him many of his subordinates, who later became prominent wartime commanders. For example, Zhukov's chief of staff at Khalkhin-Gol, S. I. Bogdanov, later commanded 2d Guards Tank Army, one of the elite mechanized formations that defeated Germany.

Khalkhin-Gol demonstrated the viability of Soviet theory and force structure, but it was the one bright spot in an otherwise dismal picture. One week after Zhukov's victory, the German Army invaded Poland, beginning the campaign that brought Germany and the Soviet Union into direct contact and conflict in Eastern Europe. The Red Army was woefully unprepared for the challenge.

CHAPTER 2

Armed Truce, 1939–1941

MOLOTOV-RIBBENTROP PACT

Conflict between Germany and the Soviet Union seemed inevitable from the moment that Adolf Hitler came to power in 1933. Hitler had gained office in part by depicting himself and his political party as the only bulwark against the spread of international Communism. Apart from the ideological rivalry between National Socialism and Marxist Communism, the two states were natural geopolitical competitors. The Russian experience of constant invasion from the west motivated any government in Moscow to seek buffer states in central and eastern Europe. Similarly, German power politics and Nazi ideology regarded German dominance of the same region as an inevitable part of national resurgence.

Secret German-Soviet military cooperation ended by mutual consent within months of Hitler's accession to power. The two regimes fought by proxy in the Spanish Civil War, sending "volunteers" and equipment to help the opposing sides. Russian bombers even damaged a German warship off the coast of Spain in 1938. Meanwhile, Moscow condemned each successive German demand for more land in central Europe.

Yet I. S. Stalin was reluctant to fight Hitler without allies. In the late 1930s, the Soviet economy was just beginning to recover from previous conflicts and internal purges. Moreover, Stalin had no desire to fight a war that would weaken the young socialist state while eliminating the German threat to the capitalist West. M. M. Litvinov, the Soviet commissar for foreign affairs, campaigned vainly for collective security in response to German aggression. The 1938 Munich crisis that began the dismemberment of Czechoslovakia convinced Stalin that Britain and France were unlikely to take effective action against Hitler and would willingly sacrifice the Soviet Union if the opportunity arose. Although the Soviet Union conducted a partial mobilization of its armed forces to intimidate Germany and impress its erstwhile allies, Moscow was not even invited to the Munich conference.[1]

After lengthy diplomatic negotiations, British and French military representatives finally came to Moscow in August 1939, ostensibly to discuss specific plans for combined actions. Both the junior rank of these representatives and the limited military forces that Great Britain could pledge confirmed Soviet skepticism about the seriousness of these negotiations. The talks ultimately foundered on the question of troop transit rights through Poland. The Soviet negotiator, Marshal Voroshilov, naturally insisted that Red Army forces be allowed to enter Poland in order to join in a combined response to any further German aggression. It is unclear whether this was a sincere Soviet proposal or a test of Western resolve. In either event, the Polish strongman, Colonel Joseph Beck, was understandably opposed to such passage rights, suspecting his former enemy of territorial ambitions. King Carol II of Rumania was equally opposed to Soviet passage across his territory. In desperation, on 22 August the French negotiator unilaterally pledged that Warsaw would permit such transit in wartime.

By this time Stalin had decided that he would gain more by compromising with Hitler than he could expect from his divided and uncertain Western partners. On 3 May 1939, Litvinov had been replaced by V. I. Molotov. This was a clear signal that Moscow was departing from its policy of collective security against Hitler, and, in the ensuing months, the two enemies negotiated a trade and finance agreement. The Germans were initially suspicious of Soviet overtures, which occurred while negotiations continued with the British and French representatives. As the Polish crisis intensified, however, Hitler reconsidered. Both dictators felt that they were running out of time; Hitler wanted a free hand to dispose of Poland quickly, while Stalin did not wish to be pulled into a premature war without reliable allies. On 20 August 1939, Hitler sent Stalin a message asking that the Soviet leadership receive the German Foreign Minister, Joachim von Ribbentrop, not later than 23 August. Ribbentrop flew to Moscow and quickly finalized a nonaggression agreement that was announced to a stunned continent on 24 August.[2]

The Molotov-Ribbentrop Pact publicly promised friendship and mutual nonaggression but secretly divided eastern Europe into spheres of influence. Germany would occupy western and central Poland. In return, the Soviet Union would have the dominant position in the Baltic states and would control Poland east of the San and Bug Rivers. Neither side expected this agreement to last indefinitely, and the pact did not prevent Germany's ally Japan from challenging the Soviet Union in Asia, as described in chapter 1. Still, Berlin and Moscow were freed of their immediate concerns about a two-front conflict and could focus on digesting their allotted spoils before resuming their long-term antagonism.

POLAND AND THE BALTIC STATES

Despite this agreement, the rapid German conquest of Poland in September 1939 was an unpleasant shock to Moscow. Unlike Czechoslovakia, Poland was ready to fight dismemberment, and Soviet analysts had expected the struggle to continue for months. Within the first two weeks of war, however, the Polish collapse was evident.

The Soviet government had to scramble to assemble its own forces, both to assert its claims to eastern Poland and to protect itself against German treachery. On 5 September 1939, Moscow began to recall reservists to active duty and soon thereafter implemented universal conscription.[3] This partial mobilization seriously disrupted Soviet industry by taking one million skilled workers away from the factories on short notice; the result was a significant production shortfall in 1940. Meanwhile, the Ukrainian and Belorussian Military Districts were placed on a wartime footing as *fronts*, roughly equivalent to army group headquarters.

On 14 September, Molotov notified the Germans that the Red Army would intervene in its designated area of Poland, and three days later Soviet troops crossed the border. Because of the hurried mobilization, most army units had not yet reached their assembly areas. Instead, each *front* formed a mobile group comprising cavalry and mechanized units.[4] These mobile groups, in true Soviet fashion, were expected to penetrate the weak Polish border defenses and move rapidly to the western boundary of the allotted Soviet sphere.

Even these selected units were hamstrung by improvised logistics, especially fuel shortages. For example, A. I. Eremenko experienced repeated difficulties as commander of the Belorussian Front's 6th Cavalry Corps. His forward detachment, composed of a tank regiment and a motorized rifle battalion, penetrated almost 100 kilometers on the first day. In an attempt to continue this advance, Eremenko had to siphon fuel from one third of his vehicles to keep the other two thirds moving. By the time he encountered the Germans at Bialystok, Eremenko had to obtain an emergency fuel resupply by airlift.[5]

Such logistical difficulties were compounded by the resistance of the dying Polish state. Polish forces inflicted losses on the Red Army totaling 996 killed and 2,002 wounded, and a few skirmishes developed between the Soviets and the Germans as well.[6] Soviet leaders later insisted that the ethnic Ukrainians and Belorussians of eastern Poland had welcomed them with open arms. By the end of October, people's meetings in the region had requested union with the Ukrainian and Belorussian Socialist Republics, and the new territory was absorbed into the USSR. It is undoubtedly true that some of these people preferred Soviet annexation to German domination, although the Polish military leadership did not share such sentiments. During the spring of 1940, 14,500 captured Polish officers, cadets, and sergeants were executed and buried in mass graves at Katyn and other sites inside the Soviet Union. Although Moscow later blamed the German invaders, this massacre was the work of Stalin and the NKVD.[7]

The Red Army did not receive even this mixed welcome in the Baltic States, where Stalin was eager to implement the Molotov-Ribbentrop Pact. Between 28 September and 10 October 1939, Moscow forced Estonia, Latvia, and Lithuania to sign mutual assistance agreements. The three governments agreed to permit Soviet naval, air, and coast artillery bases on their territories. They also promised to support each other in case of attack and not to participate in alliances directed against the Soviet Union or other signatories. In exchange, Moscow returned the city of Vilnius from Polish to Lithuanian control.[8]

Preoccupied with redeploying its forces to face Britain and France, Germany was in no position to support the Baltic countries even if it had been willing to void the Molotov-Ribbentrop Pact. However, the Baltic national governments continued their traditional economic ties with Germany and attempted to improve their defenses against Moscow. Numerous minor incidents erupted between the local populace and the Soviet forces.

Even this limited Baltic independence did not survive for long. On 14 June 1940, Stalin issued an ultimatum to the Lithuanian government. He demanded the dismissal and prosecution of two anti-Soviet ministers accused of "provocative actions" against the Soviet garrisons as well as full occupation of major Lithuanian cities by the Red Army. Twenty-four hours later, the Soviet Union occupied Lithuania and issued similar ultimatums to Latvia and Estonia. Local Communists formed Soviet-backed governments that immediately requested admittance as republics of the Soviet Union. By August 1940, all three republics had been absorbed, and the main Soviet naval base was transferred to the ice-free port of Tallin.[9]

In June 1940, Moscow moved to fulfill the remaining terms of the secret Molotov-Ribbentrop accords, pressuring the Rumanian government to give Bessarabia to the Soviet Union. When the Rumanians refused, Stalin formed a Southern Front under Zhukov's command from the Kiev Special and Odessa Military District forces. Between 28 and 30 June, Southern Front's 9th Army, under the command of Major General I. V. Boldin and assisted by airborne assaults on key Rumanian objectives, invaded Bessarabia and forcibly incorporated the territory into the Soviet Union.[10]

FIRST FINNISH WAR

These annexations occurred only after a frustrating conflict with Finland in 1939–1940. In October 1939, the Soviet government had asked Finland for a number of concessions, including the strategic islands of Koivisto and

Hogland on the water approaches to Leningrad, border adjustments in the far north, and cession of land on the Karelian Isthmus. The latter was a 50-mile-wide swampy area between the Gulf of Finland and Lake Ladoga on the most direct route from Finland to Leningrad. Finland had fortified the isthmus as the so-called Mannerheim Line, named for the Finnish military commander and hero of the Russian Civil War; the Soviet demand meant abandoning these defenses. In addition to these outright territorial changes, Moscow also wanted a 30-year lease on the Hango peninsula in southwestern Finland. In return, the Soviets offered undeveloped land north of Lake Ladoga.

From 14 October to 3 November 1939, Finnish representatives attempted to bargain in Moscow, offering to surrender one of the islands and part of the disputed border regions. Ultimately Molotov broke off the negotiations when the Finns refused to lease Hango. On 26 November, the Soviets created a border incident and demanded that Finnish troops pull back 15 miles from the frontier. Two days later Moscow abrogated its nonaggression treaty with Helsinki and broke diplomatic relations on 29 November. The Soviet attack began the following day.

In anticipation of a Soviet attack, the Finnish government had gradually mobilized its forces to the equivalent of 14 divisions. Six divisions were dedicated to the Mannerheim Line, which consisted of a lightly defended forward area along the border followed by two belts of field fortifications, barbed wire, and minefields. These defenses were tied in with the various rivers and other water obstacles on the isthmus. Only in the center of the isthmus, where no river existed for a 20-mile stretch around the town of Summa, did the Finns have significant concrete pillboxes and gun emplacements. Finnish forces and defenses were far thinner in the rest of the country, relying on the remote and almost impassable terrain to limit the size of any invasion force. The entire Finnish Army, although well trained for arctic warfare, was short on heavy weapons and ammunition. A Finnish infantry division, for example, had 3,000 fewer troops and less than one third the artillery authorized to its Soviet equivalent.[11] The country possessed perhaps 100 armored vehicles and 400 obsolete aircraft. Unlike the Soviets, the Finns lacked a major industrial base to support prolonged warfare, and their geographic isolation made it difficult to import munitions in any large quantities.

Despite these weaknesses, the Finnish armed forces were at least prepared for a winter war, whereas their opponents were rushed into an ill-prepared offensive. Just as in the Polish campaign in September, Stalin ordered the Red Army to invade Finland after a painfully short preparation period. In order to do this, divisions from the Ukrainian Military District, where the weather was mild by Russian standards, were abruptly redeployed to conduct a winter campaign in near-arctic latitudes. The hasty movement meant that few, if any, Soviet units had adequate intelligence or terrain information about Finland. The Red Army had no detailed information about the Mannerheim Line and advanced blindly into its defenses. Moreover, although Leningrad itself was a major industrial center and transportation hub, communications north of the city were tenuous at best. Soviet commanders had to operate on a logistical shoestring, with only a single railroad line to supply their forces.

Like the Finns, the Leningrad Military District forces, under the command of Army Commander 1st Rank K. A. Meretskov, concentrated their main effort in the Karelian Isthmus. V. F. Iakovlev's 120,000-man 7th Army deployed two corps (five infantry divisions and two tank brigades) in its first attack echelon, three infantry divisions in second echelon, and one rifle division and a tank corps in reserve to reinforce and exploit the anticipated breakthrough. Although their efforts north of Lake Ladoga were far more modest, the Soviets still outweighed the Finns in numbers of soldiers and equipment. The 8th Army deployed five infantry divisions just north of the lake, and an additional five divisions were spread out along the Finnish border as far as Murmansk in the north. Perhaps the greatest threat was posed by the 9th Army, whose three divisions were aimed at the narrow neck of Finland near the town of Suomussalmi. If this thrust succeeded, it could reach the Gulf of Bothnia and cut the country in two.[12]

The initial assault on 30 November was hurried and amateurish. After a brief bombardment, 7th Army pushed across the border, driving back the weak Finnish covering forces but showing little understanding of the terrain or the problems of coordinating infantry, artillery, and armor. Moscow promptly recognized a puppet Finnish Democratic Government established in the border village of Terjoki and apparently planned to annex the entire country through this facade of legality. By 12 December 7th Army had come up against the first defensive belt of the Mannerheim Line, protecting the town of Viipuri (Vyborg). Four days later, Iakovlev launched his main attack, concentrating on the fortified area of Summa in the mistaken belief that this was the weakest point. Even had they achieved a breakthrough, Iakovlev's reserve units were not concentrated to exploit it.

Despite suicidal bravery on the part of the troops, everything possible went wrong. The Soviet attacks became totally stereotyped and predictable. Every afternoon at about 1500 hours the artillery would fire for 30 minutes at the general area of the Finnish positions, without specific targets. When weather permitted, the Red Air Force joined the attack, but its efforts were scattered across the entire front, lacking in direction and generally ineffectual. Soviet engineers had difficulty breaching the anti-tank obstacles in front of Summa, and Soviet tanks became entangled in those obstacles. Most of the tanks were too lightly armored to face Finnish antitank weapons, and they became separated from their protecting infantry. When Iakovlev switched to night attacks later in the month, the Finnish commanders responded with massed machine-gun fire and searchlights. By 20 December, Moscow was forced to cancel the offensive in the isthmus. The Soviet troops were more effective on the defensive, quickly halting a four-division Finnish counterattack launched on 23 December, but the defeat was apparent.[13]

Soviet attacks farther north were equally ineffective. In the extreme North, the 104th Rifle Division achieved a modest success against limited resistance, but this was more than offset by the dismal Soviet performance at Suomussalmi. On 7 December 1939, the 44th Rifle Division (from Kiev) attacked from the east and the 163d Rifle Division from the north. The 44th Rifle Division reached Suomussalmi on 9 December, but heavy snow and abnormally cold weather confined the division to the single hard-surfaced road leading from the border to the town. As a result, this Ukrainian division was strung out and vulnerable, an ideal target for Finnish 9th Infantry Division, which had several battalions equipped with skis. A Finnish counterattack on 11 December drove the 44th Rifle Division out of Suomussalmi. The Finns established road obstacles that broke the division up into small fragments. They then conducted ambushes and hit and run attacks that gradually destroyed the isolated Ukrainian units. Virtually the entire 44th Rifle Division was eventually destroyed, and its personnel were killed or captured. When the 163d Rifle Division attempted to close the pincers by attacking from the north, it, too, was cut off. The survivors retreated eastward across a frozen lake, leaving most of their guns, tanks, and trucks behind. Both divisions virtually ceased to exist.[14]

The first response from Moscow, in typical Stalinist style, was to seek scapegoats. L. Z. Mekhlis, a senior political commissar who had been instrumental in the later stages of the Great Purges, arrived in 9th Army to investigate the disaster at Suomussalmi. On his orders, the commander of the 44th Division was shot out of hand, and dozens of senior officers were replaced.[15] Such measures were hardly designed to encourage initiative on the part of other commanders.

More generally, however, the Red Army completely overhauled its command structure and tactics before launching a renewed attack. One of the surviving senior commanders of the Civil War, S. K. Timoshenko, became commander of a Northwestern Front to control operations against the Mannerheim Line. The 7th Army received a new commander, Meretskov (removed from command of the entire operation), and two additional rifle corps. More important, 7th Army was assigned a much narrower frontage on which to attack, with the new 13th Army moved in beside it, on the eastern side of the isthmus. The Red Army's senior official for mobile operations, D. G. Pavlov, assembled a special mobile group composed of a rifle corps, a cavalry corps, and a tank brigade. His mission was to advance across the ice around the southwestern end of the Finnish defenses to seize Viipuri. The entire Soviet force received intensive training in winter operations and conducted elaborate exercises on penetrating fixed fortifications. Special assault groups were organized, each consisting of a rifle platoon, a machine gun platoon, three tanks, snipers, engineers, and dedicated artillery. A limited number of new KV-1 heavy tanks was brought in, and the Red artillery was reinforced and reorganized.

All these preparations had to be completed under severe time constraints in order to renew the offensive while cold, clear winter weather still kept the ground frozen and permitted close air support. In early February, reconnaissance units began limited attacks to locate the main Finnish defenses. Then, on 12 February 1940, the Red Army launched an offensive unlike any of its previous efforts. The artillery fire was not only heavier but far more accurate, stunning the Finnish defenders with repeated direct hits on their defensive positions. The infantry advanced in a dispersed formation behind an artillery barrage that moved forward slowly, denying the Finns the easy targets of previous battles. Where possible, the Soviet assault detachments outflanked enemy positions to attack from the side and rear.

After two-and-a-half days of ferocious fighting, Soviet 50th Rifle Corps broke into the first defensive line in the critical Summa sector. Three tank brigades began to widen the penetration, and the outnumbered Finns had no choice but to fall back on their second defensive line, covering the city of Viipuri. A major snowstorm on 21 February halted operations for three days, but Timoshenko used the time to replace his leading rifle divisions with fresh troops from the second echelon. On 24 February, Pavlov's mobile group moved across the ice to seize the island of Koivisto and prepared to continue its advance around the Finnish southern flank.

Beginning on 28 February, 12 Soviet divisions and 5 tank brigades attacked the second defensive belt. After four days the attackers entered the suburbs of Viipuri, while Pavlov's mobile group attacked southwest of the city, cutting off its main road to Helsinki. In desperation, the defenders counterattacked Pavlov's mobile group and flooded the countryside around Viipuri. The Soviet infantry and engineers waded through chest-deep, ice-cold water to continue clearing the city, which was largely deserted.

The Finns could do no more, and on 9 March, General Heinrichs, the commander of the Finnish forces in the isthmus, admitted that his troops were at the end of their endurance. An armistice took effect on 13 March. Moscow failed to achieve outright annexation of Finland but gained far more territory than it had originally demanded.

The cost was out of all proportion to the gains, however. In human terms, Molotov admitted that 48,745 Red Army soldiers had died, and another 158,000 had been wounded.[16] The Soviet Union was expelled from the League of Nations for its aggression, further isolating it diplomatically and militarily. The Finnish War's effects on the Russo-German relationship were equally severe. The bumbling, hesitant Soviet military performance undoubtedly encouraged Hitler and his commanders to believe that the Soviet Union was incapable of defending itself. The belated efforts of Britain and France to reinforce the Finns by invading Scandinavia contributed to Hitler's decision to invade Norway in April 1940, putting German troops uncomfortably close to Soviet territory.

In general, Soviet actions in the Baltic States irritated and disturbed the German government, even if they were within the letter of the Molotov-Ribbentrop Pact. This sense of concern was increased in late June 1940, when Moscow forced Rumania to cede two provinces, Bessarabia and Northern Bukovina, in the area that is now Moldova. These last seizures appeared to threaten the German petroleum supplies in Rumania. The truce between Berlin and Moscow was deteriorating rapidly.

REFORMS OF 1940

The failures in Finland led to a searching reexamination and reform effort in the Soviet armed forces. The government's first actions contributed greatly to the authority and prestige of its professional officers. Conventional general-officer ranks, which had been suppressed for years, were reintroduced, and numerous senior officers received awards and promotions. Meanwhile the hated political commissars, who had regained their power as co-commanders during the Great Purges, were again reduced to a subordinate position, restoring that unity of command that had often been lacking in the Finnish campaign. In October 1940, a new, draconian code of military justice gave commanders much of the authority that tsarist officers had once enjoyed.

The senior leadership of the Red Army paid for its errors. Stalin decided that Voroshilov's performance had been inadequate during both the Finnish War and the undeclared struggle with Japan. In May 1940, Marshal S. K. Timoshenko became defense commissar, with Voroshilov relegated to the honorary titles of deputy chairman of the Council of Ministers and chairman of the USSR Defense Committee. General B. M. Shaposhnikov, whose warnings about the strength of the Finns had been ignored, also lost his post as chief of staff, being replaced by K. A. Meretskov.[17]

Voroshilov's dismissal opened the way for a revival of Soviet mechanized forces. In this regard, the German successes in conquering France and the Low Countries during the spring of 1940 reinforced the negative Soviet experience of large-scale operations in Finland and, more important, alarmed the Soviet High Command. The new chief of the Main Armored Directorate, Lieutenant General Ia. N. Fedorenko, persuaded Timoshenko and Stalin to reverse the Kulik Commission's decision on abolishing large mechanized formations. On 6 July 1940, the Council of Ministers authorized creation of eight new mechanized corps. These formations were much larger than previous so-called corps, each one consisting of two tank and one motorized rifle divisions for a total of 1,031 tanks and 36,080 troops. In February 1941, the War Commissariat decided to activate 21 additional mechanized corps, for a total of 29. Additional separate tank and motorized rifle divisions were also authorized.[18]

While Marshal S. M. Budenny headed a commission to review the tactical lessons of Finland, Defense Commissar Timoshenko toured the country, conducting a series of major training exercises and winnowing out inadequate commanders. The successful leaders of Khalkhin-Gol and the second Finnish offensive moved into senior command positions throughout the army. G. K. Zhukov, the victor at Khalkhin-Gol and in Bessarabia, succeeded Timoshenko as commander of the critical Kiev Special Military District, and then, in January 1941, was appointed chief of the General Staff. A division commander in Finland, Colonel General M. P. Kirponos was promoted in June 1940 to command the Leningrad Military District and, in February 1941, the Kiev Special Military District, where in June 1941 he would demonstrate more courage than skill. Meretskov went from command of 7th Army on the Karelian Isthmus to chief of the General Staff, until he was replaced by Zhukov in January 1941. In the long run, these and numerous other command changes would have benefited the Red Army, but the immediate effect of such wholesale shifts was considerable personal turmoil and inefficiency. The General Staff had three different chiefs—Shaposhnikov, Meretskov, and Zhukov—in eight months. By June 1941, 75 percent of all officers had been in their current positions for less than one year.[19]

At the end of December 1940, a group of senior Red Army and Air Force commanders assembled in Moscow for a conference and war game.[20] A series of frank discussions illuminated the conceptual disunity of the officer corps. Lieutenant General P. L. Romanenko, commander of 1st Mechanized Corps and a veteran of the Spanish and Finnish Wars, criticized even Zhukov's views as too timid and, in essence, called for a return to M. N. Tukhachevsky's operational concepts. Romanenko argued that the rapid German victory in France was possible only because the Germans had assembled entire mobile armies comprising mechanized and airborne corps supported by artillery and air elements. When it came time to discuss the resources to implement mechanized concepts, however, Stalin intervened to support Marshal Kulik and the other more conservative officers. As a result, the new mechanized corps remained the largest mobile formation in the Red Army. Even these corps did not receive the logistical priority necessary to complete their formation and training.[21]

The Moscow conference also brought one more painful round of personnel shifts. In a map exercise and war game conducted at the end of the conference, Zhukov as commander of the "Blue" (enemy) side decisively defeated the "Red" (Soviet) side in one of the two games. Stalin unexpectedly summoned the participants to the Kremlin for an immediate review of the exercise. Caught off guard, the chief of the General Staff, Meretskov, stumbled through his summary. Stalin, probably already looking for an excuse to replace him, fired Meretskov immediately and replaced him with Zhukov. In the ensuing days, commanders from military district down to division level were again reshuffled in an apparent attempt to place some experienced officers in Siberia in case of a two-front war with Japan and Germany. Thus Red Army commanders began 1941 with yet another reminder of the precarious nature of their positions and even of their personal survival.[22]

SOVIET PREPARATIONS FOR WAR

Soviet war planning since 1935 had focused on the twin threats posed by Nazi Germany and Japan. Strategic plans developed in November 1938 under the auspices of the chief of the General Staff, Colonel General B. M. Shaposhnikov, considered both threats but identified the Western Theater of war as the priority. The geographic reality of the Pripiat' Marshes posed a particular problem to planners since the marshes divided the theater in half.[23] The question was whether German planners would focus their strategic attention north of the Pripiat' into Belorussia or south of the marshes into the Ukraine.[24]

In 1938 Shaposhnikov's plan postulated defense against both variants. After the partition of Poland in 1939, the General Staff revised its strategic plans to accord with the increasing German threat. Developed by Major

General A. M. Vasilevsky, deputy chief of the General Staff Operations Directorate, the July 1940 plan postulated a probable German thrust into Belorussia along the Minsk-Smolensk axis. Mobilization measures were adjusted to fit this plan. When Meretskov became chief of the General Staff in August 1940, another reevaluation took place. With Stalin taking an active role, the October 1940 war plan shifted strategic emphasis from the northwestern to the southwestern axis, probably because of Stalin's concern for the economically vital Ukraine. He was also influenced by a "Kiev" faction formed around Zhukov, then-commander of the Kiev Special Military District. Yet another adjustment of mobilization plans was now required.

The January 1941 Moscow war game was designed to validate the October plan. The war game, which exercised both defensive and counter-offensive scenarios, indicated, to Stalin's consternation, that the General Staff had overestimated Soviet defensive capabilities and underestimated German offensive potential.[25] In the months after the war game, the General Staff again revised its mobilization plans and probably held new war games to develop a sounder defensive strategy against what appeared to be an ever-increasing likelihood of future German attack. Fragmentary evidence exists of this frenetic planning as the Soviet military press focused attention on hitherto neglected defensive themes.

By April 1941, Soviet-German relations were deteriorating, and Soviet intelligence began detecting German offensive preparations.[26] As indications of future German attack increased during the ensuing months, Stalin and Soviet diplomats postured as if peace reigned supreme. Despite this pacific political stance, in April 1941 Stalin implemented readiness measures of a "special threatening period of war" [*osoboe ugrozhaemyi voennyi period*], a special readiness state that was to be implemented only when war was imminent. In the context of spring 1941, this meant partial mobilization while diplomacy focused on the maintenance of peace. The dichotomy between Stalin's frantic desire for peace (at least in 1941) and his desire to undertake prudent defensive measures to stave off defeat if war occurred produced confusion and paved the way for the catastrophic defeat of the Red Army in 1941. Virtually simultaneously, the Soviets initiated partial internal mobilization while prohibiting their most ready forces in the border military districts from undertaking measures vital for their own survival.

Between April and June 1941, the Soviets accelerated the process of "creeping up to war"—which had in reality been under way since 1937—by conducting a concealed strategic deployment (mobilization) of forces. From April 26 through May 10, the Trans-Baikal, Ural, and Siberian Military Districts and Far Eastern Front dispatched forces to the border military districts. On 13 May, the General Staff ordered 28 rifle divisions and the headquarters of four armies (16th, 19th, 21st, and 22d) to move from interior districts to border districts, and a fifth army to assemble near Moscow.[27] This mobilization was to be complete by 10 July. From late May to early June, the General Staff called up 800,000 reservists to fill out 100 cadre divisions and numerous fortified regions.[28]

Despite these prudent efforts, the Soviet Union was not ready for war in June 1941, nor did it intend, as some have contended, to launch a preventative war.[29] Although the General Staff had expended more than three years in developing defensive plans and intelligence agencies had provided enough information to give clear warning, Soviet forces were poorly arrayed, trained, and equipped, and the Soviet political leadership was paralyzed by its fixation on maintaining peace, at least until 1942. Hope clouded reality, and both the Red Army and the Soviet people would pay the price.

CHAPTER 3

Opposing Armies, 1941

THE GERMAN ARMY

In many ways, the German Army of 1941 was at the height of its power, although it was by no means invincible. Traditionally, the German officer corps had prided itself on its doctrine, a unity of training and thought that allowed junior officers to exercise their initiative because they understood their commander's intentions and knew how their peers in adjacent units would react to the same situation. During the late 1930s, this doctrinal unity had been disrupted by disagreements about the correct employment of armor. The victories of 1940 in the Low Countries and France had vindicated the minority of younger German theorists who believed in mechanized warfare, even if some senior commanders retained more traditional views. The panzer (armored) forces had demonstrated the concept of massing mobile, offensive power to break into and through an enemy's defenses on a narrow portion of the front and then exploit to the rear, disrupting logistics and command echelons while seeking to encircle large portions of the enemy army. The encircling force would then defend in two directions, inward and outward, to prevent enemy troops from breaking into or out of the trap.

The 1940 campaigns had already shown, however, that the enemy often escaped from such encirclements. In theory, panzer divisions would be followed closely by motorized infantry divisions that would provide the manpower to seal this encirclement and compel its surrender, freeing the spearheads for further exploitation. In practice, Germany never had enough motor vehicles to equip more than a small number of its infantry troops. The vast majority of the German Army throughout World War II consisted of foot-mobile infantry and horse-drawn artillery and supplies, sometimes forcing the mechanized and motorized spearheads to pause while their supporting units caught up by forced marches.

The key organization of this offensive doctrine was the panzer or armored division. In order to satisfy Hitler's desire to create more such units for the Russian operation, the number of tanks in both existing and new armored divisions was reduced during the winter of 1940–1941. The 1941 panzer divisions had only two to three tank battalions each, for an authorized strength of 150 to 202 tanks per division. In practice, the average number of operational tanks was probably 125. In addition to these tanks, the division contained five infantry battalions, four mounted in trucks and one on motorcycles. Very few of these motorized infantry units were equipped with armored personnel carriers, and it is not surprising that the majority of casualties fell among the infantry. The panzer division also included armored reconnaissance and engineer battalions, and three artillery battalions equipped with guns towed behind trucks or tractors. These elements, together with communications, antitank and antiaircraft units, roughly totaled 17,000 men. Motorized infantry divisions were slightly smaller, generally having only one tank battalion, seven motorized infantry battalions, and three or four artillery battalions.[1] The first four Waffen (combat) SS divisions began the Eastern war with an organization identical to that of regular army motorized infantry divisions, although they later evolved into lavishly equipped panzer divisions.

Typically, a 1941 motorized (panzer) corps consisted of two panzer divisions and one motorized infantry division.[2] In turn, two to four motorized corps formed a panzer group, an organization that in several instances was redesignated a panzer army in the course of the 1941 campaign. In most cases the redesignation occurred when conventional infantry corps were added to the panzer group.

The battles of 1939–1940 had rarely forced the Germans to defend against a deliberate attack; therefore, German defensive doctrine remained largely that of 1918. This remarkably effective doctrine relied upon infantry units that created elaborate defenses in depth, with the bulk of forces held in reserve rather than placed in the front line. When the enemy attacked, the forward elements were allowed to fall back while preparing rapid counterattacks to eject the intruder. This doctrine rested on three assumptions, all of which were rapidly invalidated in Russia: that sufficient German infantry would be available to establish a defense in depth, that the main enemy attack would be by dismounted infantry, and that German commanders would be permitted to select their own positions and conduct a flexible defense as the local situation required. To accomplish this defense, the typical German infantry division of 15,000 men consisted of three regiments with three infantry battalions each, plus four horse-drawn artillery regiments. The primary antitank weapon remained the tiny 37mm antitank gun, which had already proven inadequate against French and British heavy armor. In most divisions only the 100mm or 105mm medium-artillery battalion and the famous 88mm antiaircraft guns were effective against such tanks.[3]

Germany's main weaknesses lay in the field of logistics. The vast expanse of the Soviet Union included only 40,000 miles of hard-surfaced, all-weather roads and 51,000 miles of railroads. These railroads were of a wider gauge than those found in Germany. As they advanced eastward, the Germans converted captured railbeds to their own gauge, but for much of 1941 all supplies moving by rail to the forward area had to be transferred onto whatever Soviet-gauge rolling stock the Germans could capture.[4] Moreover, the mechanized forces lacked the maintenance capacity for a long campaign. Tanks and other armored vehicles are complex devices that, in contrast to ordinary automobiles, require extensive maintenance and suffer frequent mechanical failures. The fact that German tank designs underwent a never-ending series of modifications meant that each tank battalion and company had a variety of models with noninterchangeable parts. Spare parts and trained maintenance personnel were always in scarce supply, with many major repairs requiring that the vehicle be returned to the factory in Germany. Even the relatively limited distances involved in the Polish Campaign of 1939 had posed such a strain on German armor that an entire corps was immobilized for maintenance overhaul by the end of the campaign.[5] Many of the units that attacked the Soviet Union in June 1941 had already participated in the Balkan campaign that spring; they had certainly had time to repair their equipment between these two operations, but their supply of parts and tank treads must have been depleted even before they entered the vast Russian plain.

Perhaps the fundamental logistical weakness was the German economy, which had not yet been mobilized for war. Throughout the war, Germany's lack of petroleum and other raw materials limited production and transportation. By June 1941, the German industrial economy was already dependent on three million foreign workers, and the labor shortage became more acute with each new draft of conscripts for the army. As in the previous campaigns, Hitler was banking on a quick victory rather than preparing for a prolonged struggle. In fact, he was already looking beyond the 1941 campaign, planning to create new mechanized and air formations for follow-on operations in North Africa and Asia Minor. Hitler dedicated virtually all new weapons production to such future plans, leaving the forces in the east chronically short of materiel. The Wehrmacht had to win a quick victory or none at all.[6]

OPERATION BARBAROSSA

To achieve this quick victory, the Germans planned to destroy the bulk of Soviet forces in a series of encirclements near the new Soviet-Polish frontier. In light of later recriminations concerning the changing objectives of the campaign, it is worth reviewing Hitler's original plan. Although contingency planning began in the summer of 1940, Directive 21, "Fall [Case or Operation] Barbarossa," was not issued until 18 December 1940. Hitler's intention was clearly focused on the Red Army rather than on any specific terrain or political objective:

> The mass of the [Red] army stationed in Western Russia is to be destroyed in bold operations involving deep penetrations by armored spearheads, and the withdrawal of elements capable of combat into the extensive Russian land spaces is to be prevented.
>
> By means of rapid pursuit a line is then to be reached from beyond which the Russian air force will no longer be capable of attacking the German home territories.[7]

In a conference two weeks earlier, Hitler had remarked that, in comparison to the goal of destroying the Soviet armed forces, "Moscow [is] of no great importance."[8] Of course, Hitler and his advisers confidently expected that the communist regime in Russia would collapse, recreating the chaos of 1918. In doing so, they underestimated both Stalin's control over the people and the Soviet capability to generate replacement units almost as rapidly as their first-line troops were destroyed. It was only later in 1941, when neither the Red Army nor the Soviet government showed signs of quitting, that the Germans began to focus on Moscow as a means of knocking their opponents out of the war before winter.

To destroy the Red Army, Hitler massed at least 152 German divisions, including 19 panzer and 15 motorized infantry divisions, in the East. (See Table 3-1.) In terms of equipment, the German forces included an estimated 3,350 tanks, 7,200 artillery pieces, and 2,770 aircraft. These units were seconded by 14 Finnish divisions in the North and 14 brigade-sized Rumanian divisions in the south. Overall control of the Eastern Theater lay with the Army High Command, or *Oberkommando des Heeres (OKH)*.[9] These forces were divided into an Army of Norway in the far north and three army groups—North, Center, and South—from the Baltic to the Black Sea. A German air fleet supported each of these four commands. The main effort, including two of the four panzer groups (Second and Third), was allocated to Army Group Center under Field Marshal Fedor von Bock. These two panzer groups were supposed to meet at Minsk to create the first major encirclement of the campaign. Thus, the mass of German offensive power was located north of the Pripiat' Marshes, the nearly impassable ground that effectively divided the theater into northern and southern regions.

To some extent, German planners hoped that the lack of roads and railroads would actually work to their advantage, making it impossible for

Table 3-1. Order of Battle, June 1941

Germany	Soviet Union

Army of Norway
    (Col. Gen. Nikolaus von Falkenhorst
	Northern Front
	    (Col. Gen. M. M. Popov)

Finnish Army	7th Army
Army Group North	14th Army
(Fld. Marshal Wilhelm von Leeb)	23d Army
Sixteenth Army	1st & 10th Mechanized Corps
Eighteenth Army	Northwestern Front
Fourth Panzer Group	(Col. Gen. F. I. Kuznetsov)
Army Group Center	8th Army
(Fld. Marshal Fedor von Bock)	11th Army
Fourth Army	27th Army (400 km east)
Ninth Army	3d & 12th Mechanized Corps
Second Panzer Group	5th Airborne Corps
Third Panzer Group	Western Front
Army Group South	(Gen. D. G. Pavlov)
(Fld. Marshal Gerd von Rundstedt)	3d Army
Sixth Army	4th Army
Eleventh Army	10th Army
Seventeenth Army	13th Army
Third Rumanian Army	6th, 11th, 13th, 14th, 17th, & 20th Mechanized Corps
Fourth Rumanian Army	4th Airborne Corps

	Southwestern Front
	    (Col. Gen. M. P. Kirponos)
	    5th Army
	    6th Army
	    12th Army
	    26th Army
	    4th, 8th, 9th, 15th, 16th, 19th,
	        22d, & 24th Mechanized Corps
	    1st Airborne Corps

	Southern Front (formed 25 June)
	    (Gen. I. V. Tiulenev)
	    9th Army
	    18th Army
	    2d & 18th Mechanized Corps
	    3d Airborne Corps

	Stavka Reserve (still deploying)
	    16th, 19th, 20th, 21st, 22d, &
	        24th Armies
	    5th, 7th, 25th, & 26th Mechanized Corps

the mass of Soviet troops to retreat eastward before they were surrounded. Later events proved that the German intelligence analysts had over-emphasized the degree to which the Red Army was concentrated in the forward area, in part due to deliberate Soviet deceptive measures to deter German attack by portraying greater strength forward than was the actual case. In particular, these analysts were totally unaware of the reserve group of armies being formed east of the Dnepr River.[10] Beyond the initial frontier battles, the projected advances of the three German army groups led in diverging directions, toward Leningrad (Army Group North), Moscow (Army Group Center), and Kiev (Army Group South.) Thus, from its inception, Operation Barbarossa contained the danger of dissipating the German effort in a vain attempt to seize everything simultaneously.

THE RED ARMY

As described in the previous two chapters, the Red Army of 1941 was in serious disarray. Although its strategy was now defensive, its official operational concepts remained the offensive, deep-operational theory of M. N. Tukhachevsky and V. K. Triandafillov. Like the Germans, the Soviets had neglected the development of detailed defensive concepts and procedures, at least at operational (army) levels of command and planning.

The purges had produced a severe shortage of trained commanders and staff officers able to implement official concepts. The army contained a sprinkling of qualified leaders from the Japanese and Finnish campaigns but lacked both the experience and the self-confidence of the veteran *Wehrmacht* officer corps. In contrast to the German belief in subordinate initiative, Red Army officers had learned that any show of independent judgment was hazardous to their personal health. Some, like G. K. Zhukov, were willing to accept these risks and be justified by their results, but many other officers preferred to apply the textbook solution, without regard to the local situation or the terrain. In addition, to avoid the fatal error of losing territory, on both the offensive and the defensive, Soviet forces were often distributed evenly across the front, as well as in great depth, instead of concentrating in areas where they would be most needed.

The troops were also handicapped by the political requirement to defend every inch of the existing frontier. One of the scenarios that Stalin feared in 1941 was a German provocation, a seizure of some small salient of Soviet territory instead of an all-out invasion. This concern reinforced the tendency to plan a continuous, frontal defense along the border rather than the type of fluid battle maneuver that had made the Red Army so effective during the Civil War. The prewar defenses of the old Polish-Soviet frontier had been partially abandoned and somewhat stripped of land mines, barbed wire, and guns in order to build 20 new fortified regions in the territories occupied in 1939, the so-called Special Military Districts. Despite belated efforts in spring 1941, these new defenses were far from complete when the Germans attacked. Forward rifle forces were garrisoned as much as 80 kilometers away from the frontier. To avoid any provocation to the Germans, the actual border was thinly manned by NKVD security troops, and the forward Soviet defenses were in many instances overrun before they could be manned on 22 June.

The Soviet defenders shared many of the logistical problems of their opponents but had the inestimable advantage of fighting on their own familiar terrain. Long before the hardships of the Russian winter arrived, the Soviet soldier had shown his ability to continue living and fighting with far fewer supplies than other soldiers would require. As the battle rolled eastward across European Russia, the Soviet supply lines became steadily shorter and easier to support, while the Germans were faced with ever-lengthening lines of communication and the problems of dealing with millions of prisoners and captured civilians. One qualification to this generalization, of course, is that much of the Soviet Union's essential war industry was located west of Moscow. Fifteen hundred factories had to be packed up hastily and transferred eastward to the Urals before the Germans arrived. Key mineral resources were abandoned in the process. This inevitably caused an enormous disruption in wartime production during 1941. In addition, forward Soviet supply depots were overrun by the rapid German advance before their contents could be distributed to the troops.[11]

Soviet military organization reflected the shortcomings of its concepts and leadership. The Red Army had no equivalent to the panzer group or panzer army that could accomplish a large-scale, independent penetration mission into the enemy's rear echelons. As described in chapter 2, the largest Soviet armored formation in 1941 was the mechanized corps, a rigid structure that contrasted unfavorably with the easily reorganized German motorized corps. Each mechanized corps was centered around two tank divisions, each authorized 10,940 men and 375 tanks organized in two tank regiments, one motorized infantry regiment, and battalions of reconnaissance, antitank, antiaircraft, engineer, and signal troops. Such divisions were imbalanced, with far more tanks than other combat arms elements, although, to compensate for this, mechanized corps also included a motorized infantry division and various support units, for an authorized total of 36,080 men.[12]

Most of the available Soviet mechanized corps were scattered in separate garrisons, with the divisions of a corps often separated by up to 100 kilometers. In addition, some of these mechanized corps were subordinated to different rifle army headquarters, where they were supposed to provide the reserve force for local counterattacks in support of the army's front-line rifle corps. Others were designated to take part in major counterthrusts under *front* control. Thus, the mechanized units were dispersed, both in terms of location and command structure, making it difficult to concentrate them for army or *front* counterstrokes. Although they were supposed to be available to engage in independent, deep operations, their dispersion and poor logistical structure made such operations almost impossible.

The actual strength of these corps varied widely. Some had a considerable amount of equipment; the 3d Mechanized Corps in Lithuania possessed 460 tanks, of which 109 were the new KV-1 and T-34 designs. Other corps, especially those farther away from the frontier, were considerably weaker.[13] In the Western Front's 4th Army, for example, 14th Mechanized Corps had only 520 aging T-26 light tanks, instead of its authorized complement of 1,031 medium and heavy tanks. Draconian factory discipline could only do so much to make up for past neglect in weapons production. The Southwestern Front's 19th Mechanized Corps had only 280 of its authorized tanks, all but 11 of them obsolete models. Moreover, this corps was expected to use requisitioned civilian trucks for its wheeled transportation; when the war actually began, the motorized rifle regiments in its two tank divisions had to march 120 miles on foot to do battle, slowing the movement of the available tanks.[14] As new equipment became available from the production lines, it was distributed to select corps in the forward area; however, the paucity of new machines (1,861) was such that even full-strength mechanized corps included a hodgepodge of different vehicles.[15] This complicated maintenance to an enormous extent. In addition, Soviet formations remained notoriously weak in radio communications and logistical support, making coordinated maneuver under the chaotic conditions of the surprise German invasion almost impossible.

Soviet infantry organization was superficially similar to that of the Germans, with each rifle division authorized 14,483 men organized into three rifle regiments of three battalions each plus two artillery regiments and supporting services. Three rifle divisions were grouped into a rifle corps, with two or three rifle corps and one mechanized corps generally composing a field army. In practice, however, the Red Army was woefully understrength, with most divisions numbering 8,000 or less, even before the German onslaught.[16] In late May 1941, the Soviet government attempted to remedy this problem by calling up 800,000 additional reservists and accelerating the graduation of various military schools. These additional personnel were just joining their units when the attack came.

A 1941 field army was supposed to have three rifle corps, each with five divisions, plus a mechanized corps and several separate artillery regiments. In practice, many of these armies had only 6 to 10 divisions organized in two rifle corps, with an incomplete mechanized corps and little maintenance support.

In the short-term struggle that Hitler planned, Germany had clear qualitative and even quantitative advantages over the Soviet Union. If the first onslaught failed to knock out the communist regime, however, that regime had the potential to overwhelm Germany. In addition to the large Soviet forces that could be transferred from Siberia and the Far East to Europe, the 1941 Red Army was just beginning to field a new generation of tanks (T-34 mediums and KV heavies) that were markedly superior to all current and projected German vehicles. At the time, most German armored units were equipped with Mark III and Mark IV medium tanks, dependable second-generation vehicles that were more than a match for lightly armored opponents like the Soviet T-26. In 1941, Germany was in the process of rearming all Mark IIIs with a medium-velocity 50mm main gun, while the Mark IVs still retained a low-velocity 75mm gun. The velocity of these weapons was at least as important as the size of the shell because high velocity was necessary for effective armor penetration. Neither German weapon could penetrate the thick frontal armor of the T-34 medium tanks and KV-1 heavy tanks that were just coming off the assembly lines in Russia.

Compared to the German tanks, the T-34 was heavier (26.5 tons to the Mark IV's 25), faster (31 mph to the Mark IV's 24), and better armed, carrying a 76mm high-velocity gun. The 47.5-ton KV-1 tank, also equipped with a 76mm gun, was invulnerable to almost any German weapon except the famous 88mm gun. Few Soviet tanks, however, had radios, and this made command and control in combat difficult, if not impossible. Considering the puny antitank weapons available to most German infantry units, these two new Soviet tanks were a nightmare waiting to happen. After unusual manufacturing delays in 1940, 1,861 T-34s and KV-1s had been produced by 22 June 1941.[17] These new tanks were distributed primarily to five mechanized corps in the border military districts, over half going to 4th Mechanized Corps in the Kiev Special Military District and 6th in the Western Special Military District. The remainder (100 each) went to 3d, 8th, and 15th Mechanized Corps. The overall paucity of new tanks in other corps and the logistical and training shortcomings in the corps that possessed them further reduced their combat effectiveness.[18] Where the Germans encountered them in large numbers, however, the tanks caused understandable consternation.

AIR FORCES

The strengths and weaknesses of the German and Soviet air forces largely paralleled that of their ground forces. The 2,770 Luftwaffe aircraft deployed to support "Operation Barbarossa" represented 65 percent of Germany's first-line strength. To avoid telegraphing German intentions, many of these aircraft had remained in the West, continuing the air attacks on Britain until a few weeks before the offensive. The Messerschmitt Bf-109f fighter was a superb design, but the other German aircraft were rapidly approaching obsolescence. In particular, the famous Ju-87 Stuka dive bomber could survive only in an environment where the enemy air force was helpless. The initial German air attacks ensured this situation in the first few months but could not do so indefinitely. The primary German bombers, the Dornier-17 and Ju-88, had already proved inadequate in both range and bomb capacity during the Battle of Britain, and the Ju-52 transport, although a remarkably durable and versatile aircraft, was similarly restricted in range and carrying capacity.

German industry had not made good the losses of the Battle of Britain; Germany actually had 200 fewer bombers in 1941 than in the previous spring. Similarly, the May 1941 airborne invasion of Crete had devastated German parachute formations and air transport units; 146 Ju-52s had been shot down, and another 150 were seriously damaged.[19] With such shortages, and operating out of improvised forward airfields, the German pilots would be hard put to provide effective air superiority or offensive air strikes over the vast expanse of European Russia. The famous Luftwaffe was basically a tactical air force, suitable for supporting a short-term ground offensive but not for conducting a deep and effective air campaign.

The Red Air Force posed little immediate threat to the Luftwaffe. Although its estimated 9,576 combat aircraft made it the largest air force in the world, its equipment, like that of the Red Army, was obsolescent and suffering from prolonged use. The Great Purges had struck aircraft manufacturers and designers as well as military commanders, ending the Soviet lead in aeronautics. At least one designer was shot for sabotage when an experimental aircraft crashed, and many other engineers were put to work in prison design shops. To put it mildly, such sanctions did not encourage innovative design solutions.[20]

Newer aircraft, such as the swift MiG-3 fighter and the excellent Il-2 *Sturmovik* ground-attack airplane, were in some ways superior to their German counterparts. But these aircraft were just entering service in spring 1941, and many units had a mixture of old and new equipment. Transition training to qualify the pilots to fly the new aircraft proceeded at a snail's pace because Red Air Force commanders feared that any training accidents would lead to their arrest for "sabotage." On 12 April 1941, Timoshenko and Zhukov complained to Stalin that training accidents were destroying two or three aircraft each day and demanded the removal of several senior air force officers. At the time of the German attack, many Soviet fighter pilots in the forward area had as few as four hours' experience in their aircraft.[21] The changeover to new equipment was so confused that numerous Soviet pilots had not become familiar with the appearance of new Soviet bombers and erroneously fired on their own aircraft on 22 June.

The occupation of eastern Poland in 1939 had made forward Red Air Force units as vulnerable as their Red Army counterparts. The Japanese and Finnish conflicts had given some senior air force officers a false sense of their own superiority, and they insisted on massing their aircraft in the new territories, from which they expected to launch huge air offensives in the event of war. Relatively few airfields were operational in the forward area, with many being torn up for expansion in spring 1941. The few available airfields lacked revetments and antiaircraft defenses to protect the crowded parking aprons.

Soviet air units were divided between a number of different commands: some air divisions supported specific ground armies or *fronts*, others were directly subordinate to the General Staff, and still others were dedicated to the regional air defense of the homeland. In the context of the chaotic opening campaign, where tenuous communications and chains of command evaporated, such divisions made it difficult to bring coordinated air power to bear at key points. Few Soviet aircraft had radios in 1941.

Perhaps most significantly, the Red Air Force, like the Red Army, suffered from severe deficiencies in leadership at all levels. Three successive air force commanders had disappeared during the purges, leaving inexperienced officers in most commands. Both in Spain and in the opening battles of 1941, Red Air Force tactics tended to be very rigid. Throughout the disastrous summer of 1941, Soviet bombers stubbornly attacked at an altitude of 8,000 feet, too high to ensure accurate bombing but low enough for German fighters to locate and attack them. Despite the bravery of individual Soviet fighter pilots who repeatedly rammed German aircraft, their combat formations were too defensive to be effective against their dogfighting opponents.

SOVIET PLANNING

Despite the weaknesses of the Red Army and Air Force, Soviet military planners hoped that they would halt any German offensive short of the Dnepr River line and then shift rapidly to a strategic counteroffensive.

In July 1940, Chief of Staff B. M. Shaposhnikov approved Major General A. M. Vasilevsky's war plan. Vasilevsky's plan assumed an attack by Germany, supported by Italy, Finland, Rumania, and possibly Hungary and Japan. The total enemy force would be 270 divisions, of which 233 would be massed along the Soviet Union's new western borders. Vasilevsky assumed that the main German effort—123 infantry divisions and 10 panzer divisions—would be focused north of the Pripiat' Marshes, with objectives in the direction of Minsk, Moscow, and Leningrad. He therefore planned to put the bulk of Red Army forces in the same region.[22]

Defense Commissar S. K. Timoshenko rejected this plan, probably because he anticipated Stalin's objections. When K. A. Meretskov became chief of staff in August 1940, he had Vasilevsky and the rest of the General Staff draw up a new plan. The second draft provided for two variants, concentrating the bulk of Soviet forces either north or south of the Pripiat' Marshes, depending on the political situation. On 5 October, Stalin reviewed this draft. He did not openly reject the northern option but remarked that Hitler's most likely goals were the grain of the Ukraine and the coal and other minerals of the Donbas region. The General Staff therefore presented a new plan, approved on 14 October 1940, which shifted the basic orientation of forces to the southwest (see Map 2). With minor modifications, this plan became the basis for Mobilization Plan (MP) 41.

MP-41 called for 171 divisions to be arrayed in three successive belts, or operational echelons, along the new frontier.[23] The first echelon was intended as a light covering force, and each of its 57 rifle divisions had up to 70 kilometers of frontier to defend. The next two echelons contained much larger concentrations of troops, with 52 and 62 rifle divisions, respectively, and most of the 20 mechanized corps in European Russia. All of these formations belonged in peacetime to the various military districts of the western Soviet Union; in the event of war, these districts would be transformed into five army group headquarters called *fronts*. Because these *fronts* were based on peacetime boundaries, they did not correspond directly to the three German army groups. Thus, for example, the Leningrad Military District became the Northern Front, with defense responsibilities both northward toward Finland and westward toward German Army Group North.

Behind the five forward *fronts*, a completely separate group of five field armies was in the process of forming a second strategic echelon behind the original three belts. This Reserve Front was assembling along the line of the Dnepr and Dvina Rivers. Their force concentration was typical of the Soviet principle of echeloning forces in great depths; it was virtually invisible to German intelligence prior to hostilities. Both the

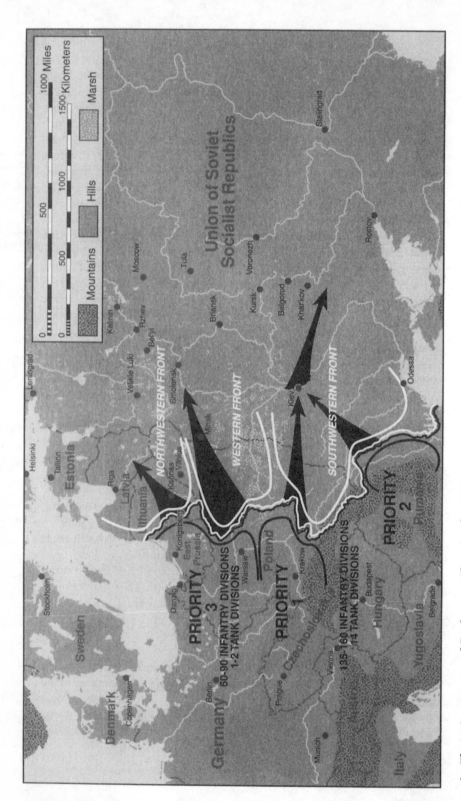

2. *Threat Assessment and Deployment Plan, October 1941*

Reserve Front and significant elements of forward units had only begun to deploy forward in late April. As in so many other respects, the German attack on 22 June caught the Soviets in transition.

The Soviet defenders had fundamentally misestimated the situation, not only by concentrating forces so far forward but also by expecting the main enemy thrust south of the Pripiat' Marshes. During the 1960s, when it was fashionable to blame Stalin for all the failures of the Soviet war effort, various memoirs alleged that Stalin had overruled his military advisers in this regard. Yet, in the long run, Stalin was correct to insist that Hitler was interested in economic resources. His commanders apparently agreed with his decisions, if only because they expected to use their forces in the southwest to counterattack into the flank of any German invasion in the north. Even Zhukov did not change the basic concept when he became chief of staff in February 1941. Thus the Red Army was off-balance, concentrated in the southwest, while the main German mechanized forces advanced in the north.[24]

As the tension increased in 1941, Zhukov tried to persuade Stalin of the need for a preemptive attack. The new chief of staff wrote a "Report on the Plan of Strategic Deployment of Armed Forces of the Soviet Union to the Chairman of the Council of People's Commissars on 15 May 1941" and convinced Timoshenko to co-sign the document. In this hand-written proposal, Zhukov argued for an immediate offensive, using 152 divisions to destroy the estimated 100 German divisions assembling in Poland. The Southwestern Front would attack across southern Poland to separate Germany from her southern allies, while the Western Front would grapple with the main German force and capture Warsaw. Given the many problems that the Red Army was experiencing at the time, such an attack would have been a desperate gamble. Stalin was probably justified in ignoring Zhukov's proposal.[25]

INDICATIONS AND WARNING

There remains the puzzling question of how the 1941 German attack achieved such overwhelming political and military surprise. In retrospect, there were ample indications of impending hostilities.[26] Communist railway workers in Sweden, resistance fighters in Poland, and numerous other agents reported the massive buildup of forces in the east. German high-altitude reconnaissance aircraft flew over Soviet territory on more than 300 occasions, prompting repeated diplomatic protests but little defensive action. German espionage agents and German-backed Ukrainian guerrillas infested the western Soviet Union in the spring of 1941. Beginning on

16 June, the German Embassy in Moscow evacuated all nonessential personnel, and by 21 June no German merchant ship remained in Soviet-controlled ports.

At first glance, it is easy to accept the standard interpretation that Stalin's obstinate blindness was responsible for the debacle. He is often cited as a classic example of a leader who ignored evidence of an opponent's *capability* to attack because he doubted the *intention* to attack. Undoubtedly, Stalin was guilty of wishful thinking, of hoping to delay war for at least another year in order to complete the reorganization of his armed forces. He worked at a fever pitch throughout the spring of 1941, trying desperately to improve the Soviet Union's defensive posture while seeking to delay the inevitable confrontation.

There were numerous additional reasons for Stalin's reluctance to believe in an immediate German offensive. First, the Soviets feared that Germany's other enemies, especially Great Britain and the Polish resistance, would provide misleading information in order to involve Moscow in the war. Similarly, the Soviet leaders were concerned that excessive troop concentrations or preparedness in the forward area might provoke Hitler, either by accident or as a pretext for some limited German action such as seizure of border lands and demands for more economic aid. Stalin was not, after all, the first European leader to misunderstand Hitler, to believe him to be "too rational" to provoke a new conflict in the East before he had defeated Britain in the West. Certainly Hitler's own logic for the attack—that he had to knock the Soviet Union out of the war to eliminate Britain's last hope of assistance—was incredibly convoluted.

This Soviet fear of provoking, or being provoked by, a rational German opponent goes far to explain the repeated orders that were issued forbidding Soviet troops to fire, even at obvious border violators and reconnaissance aircraft. It also helps explain the Soviets' scrupulous compliance with existing economic agreements with Germany. Stalin apparently hoped that by providing Hitler with scarce materials vital to the German economy he would remove one incentive for immediate hostilities. Thus in the 18 months prior to the German invasion, the Soviet Union shipped two million tons of petroleum products, 140,000 tons of manganese, 26,000 tons of chromium, and a host of other supplies to Germany.[27] The last freight trains rumbled across the border only hours before the German attack.

There were also institutional reasons for the failure of Soviet intelligence to predict Hitler's plan. The Great Purges had decimated Soviet intelligence operations as well as the military command structure. Only the military intelligence service, the GRU, remained essentially intact, and the GRU chief, Lieutenant General F. I. Golikov, had apparently succumbed to German deception efforts. Golikov duly reported indications of German preparations, but he labeled all such reports as doubtful while emphasizing indications of continued German restraint. Other intelligence officials were so afraid of provoking Stalin or Hitler that their reports were slanted against the likelihood of war.[28]

German deception operations also contributed to Soviet hesitation. First, the planned invasion of Britain, Operation Sealion, was continued as a cover story for Operation Barbarossa. The German High Command (*Oberkommando des Wehrmacht,* or OKW) confidentially informed its Soviet counterpart that the troop buildup in the east was actually a deception aimed at British intelligence and that Germany needed to practice for Sealion in a region beyond the range of British bombers and reconnaissance aircraft. In a June 1941 newspaper article, Propaganda Minister Joseph Goebbels "leaked" disinformation that a British invasion was imminent. Goebbels then ostentatiously had the newspaper withdrawn from circulation and put himself in simulated disgrace for his "mistake."

Hitler directed that the German troop concentration be portrayed as a defensive precaution against possible Soviet attack, again encouraging the Soviets to avoid any threatening troop movements. A host of other German deceptions suggested impending operations from Sweden to Gibraltar. Then, in May 1941, the German Foreign Ministry and OKW encouraged rumors that Berlin might demand changes in Soviet policy or economic aid. This led many Soviet commanders to believe that any attack would be preceded by a German ultimatum or some other diplomatic warning.

The German invasion of Yugoslavia and Greece during April and May 1941 also helped conceal Operation Barbarossa. This invasion not only provided a plausible explanation for much of the German buildup in the East but also caused a series of delays in the attack on Russia itself. Thus intelligence agents who correctly reported the original target date of 15 May 1941 were discredited when that day passed without incident. By late June, so many warnings had proved false that they no longer had a strong impact on Stalin and his advisers.

Viewed in this context, the Soviet strategic surprise is much more comprehensible. Among myriad conflicting signals, identifying an imminent threat was difficult at best. Late on the evening of 21 June, Stalin approved a confused warning message to his commanders.[29] Unfortunately, the archaic communications system failed to notify many headquarters prior to the first German attacks. Only the naval bases and the Odessa Military District were sufficiently remote to react in time.

Some commanders risked Stalin's displeasure by taking their own precautions. Colonel General M. P. Kirponos of the Kiev Special Military

District maintained close liaison with NKVD border troops and alerted his units when the Germans massed at the border. Such initiative was the exception rather than the rule.

In retrospect, the most serious Soviet failure was neither strategic surprise nor tactical surprise, but institutional surprise. In June 1941, the Red Army and Air Force were in transition, changing their organization, leadership, equipment, training, troop dispositions, and defensive plans. Had Hitler attacked four years earlier or even one year later, the Soviet armed forces would have been more than a match for the Wehrmacht. Whether by coincidence or instinct, however, the German dictator invaded at a time when his own armed forces were still close to their peak while his arch enemy was most vulnerable. It was this institutional surprise that was most responsible for the catastrophic Soviet defeats of 1941.

CONCLUSION

For the Soviets, the 1930s was a decade of alternating hope and frustration. Faced with growing political and military threats from Germany in the West and Japan in the East and the Western powers' equally disturbing apathy, the Soviet Union felt isolated on the international stage. Diplomatically Moscow promoted global disarmament, while internally it reformed, modernized, and expanded its military establishment. Soviet formulation of advanced strategic, operational, and tactical fighting concepts in the early 1930s was accompanied after 1935 by a steady expansion of its armed forces, an expansion that continued unabated until June 1941. This peacetime mobilization made the Soviet armed forces the largest in the world.

Size did not equate with capability, however. What the Soviets would call "internal contradictions" negated the progress of Soviet arms and undermined the Soviet state's ability to counter external threats. Foremost among these contradictions was Stalin's paranoia, which impelled him to stifle original thought within the military and inexorably bend the military to his will. The bloodletting that ensued tore the brain from the Red Army, smashed its morale, stifled any spark of original thought, and left a magnificent hollow military establishment, ripe for catastrophic defeat.

Less apparent was the political contradiction inherent in the nature of the Soviet state. Communist absolutism placed a premium on the role of force in international politics and encouraged its military leaders to study war in scientific fashion to formulate advanced military concepts in the service of the all-powerful state. Yet the abject obedience required of the officer corps to the Party, and hence to the state, conditioned passive acceptance by the officer corps of the bloodletting that ensued. Just as political leaders like N. I. Bukharin admitted to false crimes against the state for the "greater good," so military leaders also served or perished at the whim of Stalin.

These contradictions undermined the Red Army's ability to serve the state effectively and condemned to failure any attempts to reform. In the end only unprecedented crisis and abject defeat in war would impel successful reform. It is to the credit of the emasculated officer corps that, when this defeat came, the surviving officers had a sufficient legacy from the enlightened days of the early 1930s to allow them to overcome institutional constraints and lead the Red Army to victory.

FIRST PERIOD OF WAR
JUNE 1941–NOVEMBER 1942

CHAPTER 4

German Onslaught

> Enemy aviation has complete air dominance; during the day Minsk was subjected to many bombardments in waves numbering from 8 to 50 airplanes. There are large fires and destruction in the city. *Front* headquarters and *Front* air forces building were severely damaged by direct bomb hits.
>
> *Operational Report No. 5, Western Front Headquarters, 24 June 1941* [1]

CONFUSION

Shortly after 0300 hours on the morning of 22 June 1941, 30 hand-picked Luftwaffe bomber crews crossed the Soviet frontier at high altitude. In groups of three, these bombers struck 10 major Soviet air bases precisely at 0315 hours, the time when a brief artillery bombardment signaled the start of the ground war. As soon as the sun rose, the Luftwaffe followed up this attack with a force of 500 bombers, 270 dive bombers, and 480 fighters to hit 66 Soviet airfields in the forward areas.[2] The Red Air Force lost over 1,200 aircraft in the first morning of the war. Throughout the next few days, the Luftwaffe had undisputed air supremacy, and all Soviet troop and rail movements received relentless attention (see Map 3).

The initial ground advance met little resistance in most areas. Some border posts were overrun almost before the NKVD border guards could assemble, whereas in other areas those troops and forces of local fortified regions fought to their last rounds, delaying the Germans for a few hours while the Red Army hurried forward to its defensive positions. Only the citadel of Brest held out until 12 July.

Organization and command differentiate armies from mobs, and, for the Red Army, both organization and command dissolved rapidly. Even before the first air strikes, Brandenburger special operations troops in Red Army uniforms had parachuted or infiltrated into the Soviet rear areas. There they set about cutting telephone lines, seizing key bridges, and spreading alarm and confusion. In the area of the main German effort, north of the Pripiat' Marshes, the headquarters of Lieutenant General A. A. Korobkov's 4th Army was never able to establish communications with headquarters above and below it. Two other army headquarters belonging

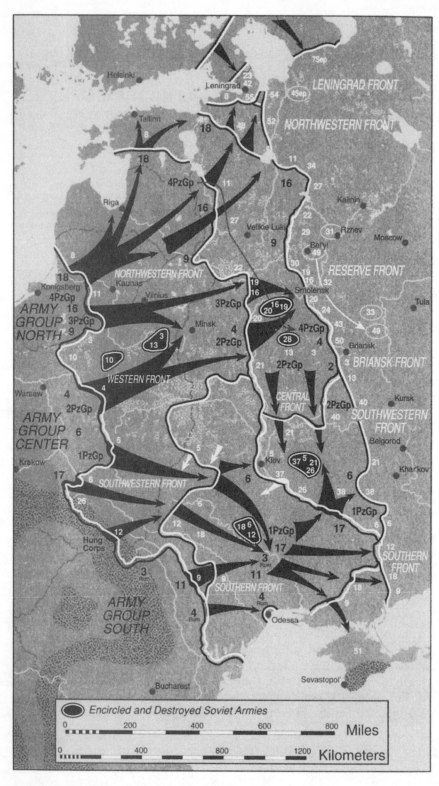

3. *Summer–Fall Campaign (1), 22 June–30 September 1941*

to the Western Front, Lieutenant General V. I. Kuznetsov's 3d and Lieutenant General K. D. Golubev's 10th Armies, were in tenuous radio communications with the *front* commander, but they were hardly more functional as command elements. On the first day of the war, Lieutenant General I.V. Boldin, Western Front chief of operations, flew through a swarm of hostile German planes to 10th Army headquarters outside Bialystok. The headquarters consisted of two tents in a small wood alongside an airstrip, where the Army commander, Golubev, attempted to counter the Germans despite shattered telephones, constant radio jamming, and total confusion. On 23 June, Golubev tried in vain to launch a counterattack with his few available forces in accordance with prewar plans, but within days 10th Army ceased to exist except as fugitives seeking to break out of German encirclements.[3]

Besides the sheer force and speed of the German advance, the greatest difficulty the defenders experienced was lack of detailed information about the current situation at the front. The reality was far worse than anyone in Moscow believed, resulting in a series of impossible orders to counterattack with units that had ceased to exist. On the evening of 22 June, Stalin and Defense Commissar S. K. Timoshenko issued Directive No. 3 for a general counteroffensive against the Germans, and in the next several days they stubbornly insisted the forward *fronts* implement this directive. In many cases subordinate commanders passed on these orders even though they knew the real situation, simply because those subordinates feared retribution for refusing to obey. After several days the enormity of the initial defeat became obvious to all. Even then, however, the General Staff in Moscow was hard pressed to get accurate, timely reports from the front. Staff officers were sent out to patrol the forward area and report back each evening. On numerous occasions the staff called Communist Party chiefs in various villages and collectives to determine the extent of the German advance.[4]

THE FIRST STRIKES

North of the Pripiat' Marshes, the initial German thrusts succeeded rapidly. Led by Fourth Panzer Group, Army Group North swept rapidly through Lithuania and into Latvia. After a few anxious moments dealing with the first T-34 and KV tanks they encountered near Raseinai, Fourth Panzer Group's XXXXI Panzer Corps bypassed the tank divisions of Soviet 3d and 12th Mechanized Corps, who were defeated by lack of coordination, fuel, and ammunition more than by enemy action.[5] Virtually all of the Soviet mechanized corps lost 90 percent of their strength during the first week of war.[6]

Fourth Panzer Group's other spearhead, LVI Panzer Corps, encountered little organized opposition, reached the Dvina River, and seized several bridges intact. Despite the suicidal gallantry of Soviet bomber pilots, those bridges remained in operation, although the Germans paused here for six days (26 June–2 July) to allow the rest of their forces to catch up.[7]

In Army Group Center, Third Panzer Group pressed eastward along the vulnerable boundary line between the Northwestern and Western Fronts, easily outflanking the latter's 3d Army, and reached Vilnius by the evening of 23 June. The Western Front commander, Lieutenant General D. G. Pavlov, was badly rattled, but on 24 June he attempted to organize a counteroffensive under his operations officer, Lieutenant General Boldin. General Boldin was given nominal control of 6th and 11th Mechanized Corps and 6th Cavalry Corps and ordered to attack northward, toward Grodno, to prevent an encirclement of the exposed Soviet units around Bialystok. Without effective communications, air cover, logistical support, and sufficient modern tanks, this effort was doomed from the start. Soviet commanders encountered the standard German response to mechanized counterattacks: the leading German units gave ground quickly, luring the enemy tanks into antitank guns that always followed immediately behind the spearhead. By the end of 25 June, 6th Cavalry Corps had suffered more than 50 percent casualties (mostly from air attack), and one tank division was out of ammunition. Another division could muster only 3 tanks, 12 armored carriers, and 40 trucks.[8]

Boldin's diversion allowed many units to escape from the Bialystok area eastward toward Minsk, but the relief was only temporary. With Third Panzer Group penetrating toward Minsk on the north flank of Soviet Western Front and Second Panzer Group advancing parallel to it in the south, Pavlov had to pull back. On the night of 25 to 26 June, he attempted a general disengagement to withdraw behind the Shchara River at Slonim. Not all units received the order to withdraw, and most were unable to break contact. Pavlov's *front* had already lost much of its fuel and motor transportation, so that the troops withdrew on foot, under constant German air attack. En route, the headquarters of Lieutenant General F.N. Remezov's 13th Army, which was in the process of deploying forward into *front* second echelon, was ambushed by leading German elements who captured various classified reports. With numerous bridges over the Shchara River destroyed, 10th Army was unable to get most of its units across.

On 26 June, a panicked Pavlov signaled Moscow that "up to 1,000 tanks [of Third Panzer Group] are enveloping Minsk from the northwest; . . . there is no way to oppose them."[9] A final effort near Slutsk by elements of

20th Mechanized Corps and 4th Airborne Corps failed to halt the advancing Germans. By 30 June, Second and Third Panzer Groups had closed their pincers around a huge pocket west of Minsk containing much of 10th, 3d, and 13th Armies. The Western Front had virtually ceased to exist as an organized force; it is not surprising that Pavlov was executed soon thereafter.[10] His immediate successor, Colonel General A. I. Eremenko, had no time to organize the defense of the Berezina River east of Minsk, and the German armored spearheads pushed onward across the Berezina toward the Dnepr in early July.

Even in this first fantastic encirclement, where the Germans destroyed or swallowed up over 417,000 Soviet soldiers, there were flaws in the German victory.[11] As usual, they found it very difficult to assemble sufficient forces to actually seal off the encircled Soviets, and thus large numbers of soldiers escaped, leaving their heavy equipment behind. Hitler was afraid that the panzer groups would advance too far, so he ordered that they pause while the encirclement was eliminated. This, of course, was precisely the kind of conservative hesitation that would allow the Red Army time to regroup. General Franz Halder, chief of OKH, the German Army High Command, was reduced to hoping that Heinz Guderian, commander of Second Panzer Group, would continue the advance on his own initiative! Halder also noticed that Soviet troops generally fought to the death and that German intelligence had misidentified numerous large Red Army units. All this boded ill for the future.[12]

COUNTERATTACKS IN THE SOUTHWEST

The Germans had much less initial success south of the Pripiat' Marshes. The River Bug ran along much of the common border in this area, hampering the initial attack and giving the NKVD and Red Army troops precious minutes to react. More important, as remarked in chapter 3, the Southwestern Front commander, Colonel General M. P. Kirponos, had kept in close contact with the border guards in the days prior to the invasion, moving his forces smoothly through the various stages of alert. Because of the prewar Soviet belief that any German attack would focus on the Ukraine, Kirponos was blessed with a relative wealth of mechanized formations to counter First Panzer Group. None of his mechanized corps were fully equipped or trained, but they gave a much better account of themselves than their counterparts in the Western Front.[13]

Once across the Bug River, the leading divisions of First Panzer Group lunged eastward through the forward positions of the Soviet 5th Army, followed closely by infantry units of German Sixth Army. General Kirponos received Directive No. 3 on the night of 22 June, but his units were still assembling from garrisons as much as 400 kilometers away and had to move forward under German air interdiction. Kirponos was forced to commit his forces piecemeal, often in hasty attacks from the march that struck the flanks of the German penetration.

On 23 June, the two tank divisions of Major General I. I. Karpezo's 15th Mechanized Corps attacked northward into the German right flank in an attempt to relieve the encircled 124th Rifle Division near Miliatin. The motorized division of this corps had been left behind for lack of trucks, a common problem throughout this period. Swampy ground and German air strikes slowed the advance of the two tank divisions, and the German 197th Infantry Division established a strong antitank defense on its open flank. The handful of T-34 tanks in this attack gave the Germans a momentary fright, but by evening the 11th Panzer Division had resumed its advance to the east, leaving the 197th to hold the Soviets off.

The next day, 24 June, Lieutenant General M. I. Potapov of Soviet 5th Army attempted a more elaborate attack on the other, northern flank of the German advance near Voinitsa. Despite poor coordination with supporting infantry and artillery, 22d Mechanized Corps halted and bloodied German 14th Panzer and 198th Infantry Divisions. The mechanized corps commander, Major General S. M. Kondrusev, died in the first fighting. After 36 hours of confused struggle, on 25 June 14th Panzer Division outflanked the Soviets and raced eastward to the Styr River. This forced Potopov to cut short the attack and to withdraw to avoid being outflanked.

Thus by 26 June, Colonel General Ewald von Kleist's First Panzer Group had crossed the Styr River, beaten off two limited attacks on its flanks, and positioned itself for pursuit through Rovno to Kiev, the industrial and political center of the Ukraine. But by this time, Kirponos had been able to assemble significant mechanized forces. Unfortunately, the three rifle corps slated for a counteroffensive still had not arrived, and thus four incomplete mechanized corps attacked without support. As before, Potapov's 5th Army was supposed to coordinate the northern flank attacks, this time by Major General K. K. Rokossovsky's 9th and Major General N. V. Feklenko's 19th Mechanized Corps. Both corps' motorized infantry divisions lacked transport and could not accompany them forward. In the south, Kirponos's chief of armored troops, Major General R. N. Morgunov, was to coordinate the 15th and 8th Mechanized Corps. Both flanks received air support, but in this as in many other cases Potapov's staff proved too inexperienced to coordinate effective support for the attacking tankers.

On 26 June, 8th Mechanized Corps drove German 57th Infantry Division back 10 kilometers. That night, however, 8th Corps received orders to press forward to Dubno, directly into the center of German strength. A mobile group built around Colonel I. V. Vasil'ev's 34th Tank Division attempted to do so on 27 June, but the divided corps was surrounded and severely mauled by German air, artillery, and armor. The remnants of 8th Mechanized Corps managed to break out and escape eastward on 1 July. The neighboring 15th Mechanized Corps was again stymied by air attacks and swamps, and it accomplished little. On the northern flank, the two tank divisions of 19th Mechanized Corps had also tried to advance on 26 June, but ran directly into the attacking 13th and 11th Panzer Divisions, which knocked them back to Rovno.

Major General K. K. Rokossovsky, commander of 9th Mechanized Corps, had only a limited view of the battlefield, but it was obvious to him that the counteroffensive order was unrealistic. He dutifully attempted to attack on 27 June, but lost contact with 19th Mechanized Corps and suffered significant losses among his obsolete light tanks. When ordered to renew the attack the next day, he chose instead to take up defensive positions and ambush the leading task force of 13th Panzer Division en route to Rovno. For perhaps the first time in the war, the German Army ran into the massed fire of Soviet artillery and suffered severe losses. After two days of escalating German air and ground attacks, Rokossovsky was ordered to fall back.

This fierce if unsuccessful Soviet counteroffensive delayed Army Group South for at least a week, helping to create the situation that later tempted Hitler to redirect part of Army Group Center away from Moscow in order to secure the Ukraine. The border battles in the Ukraine also demonstrated that German armor was not invincible and gave future commanders like Rokossovsky their first expensive but useful lessons in mechanized warfare.[14]

HEARTS AND MINDS

The German plan for quick victory was based in part on the assumption that large portions of the Soviet population would welcome liberation from Stalinism. This assumption appeared justified in the first euphoria of the German onslaught. Most Latvians and Lithuanians, as well as significant numbers of Ukrainians and other subject nationalities, were at least cooperative if not enthusiastic about the change of regimes. Regardless of nationality, many older residents of European Russia remembered the hard but bearable and "correct" German occupation of 1917–1919 and were inclined to wait on events rather than abandon their homes to become refugees. Taking no chances, the Moscow government uprooted a half-million ethnic Germans of the Volga-German Autonomous Soviet Republic and shipped them farther east.

From the very start, however, German occupation policy appeared deliberately intended to alienate the populace. Prior to the invasion, OKW issued two orders based on the flimsy excuse that Moscow had not signed the Geneva and Hague accords on the law of war. The "Commissar Order" declared that Soviet political officers were not prisoners of war and should be shot out of hand. A second order specified that, in the event that a German soldier committed offenses against civilians or prisoners, disciplinary action was optional, at the discretion of the unit commander.[15]

Several senior German commanders refused to publish these orders and protested them to their superiors. In their memoirs, most of these German officers later insisted that the Wehrmacht never implemented such policies and that atrocities were largely the work of SS, genocidal Einsatzkommando units, and other Nazi Party occupation forces who followed behind the army.

Such protests were undoubtedly sincere, but, in practice, German soldiers were far from innocent. The senior, professional officers were often out of touch with their subordinates. Both the company-grade officers and the rank and file had come of age under the Nazi regime, and, consciously or unconsciously, reflected Nazi attitudes. One analysis of three combat divisions in 1941 indicates that 29 percent of the officers were Nazi Party members, and that these officers, who had a higher education and social status than their peers, set the tone of those divisions.[16]

A large portion of the Wehrmacht regarded the Soviet people as bumbling and potentially treacherous subhumans. In itself this is by no means a unique psychological failing. Soldiers feel the need to dehumanize or demonize their opponents in order to overcome their natural reluctance to kill, and atrocities have all too frequently ensued. In dealing with Soviet prisoners and civilians, however, this unofficial German attitude produced widespread instances of brutality and murder. Quite apart from the moral implications of such conduct, the German behavior served to alienate potential allies and to spark widespread resistance.

The most obvious explanation for the German brutality was the horror of the Eastern Front itself, where German troops suffered heavy casualties while they were isolated from society and surrounded by a hostile populace and terrain. In fact, however, the German troops engaged in atrocities almost from the start of the war. Long before the Nazi Party forces arrived in a given region, the first troops to enter a Russian town frequently executed several people in an attempt to deter any resistance. The Commissar Order was often interpreted to mean the execution of anyone identified as a Communist Party member or anyone who appeared to be Jewish, since Nazi propaganda held that many Communists were Jewish. The troops frequently shot such people out of hand, even when ordered to turn them over to the Nazi security services for interrogation. Other prisoners were forced to clear land mines or engage in similar actions considered too dangerous for German troops.[17]

The unspeakable genocide of European Jews has attracted worldwide attention. What is often overlooked in the horror of this crime is the related brutality of German policies toward the non-Jewish, Slavic population. The sheer scale of these crimes makes it difficult to arrive at accurate estimates of the cost. Almost three million Russians, Belorussians, and Ukrainians were enslaved as forced laborers in Germany under conditions that frequently resulted in death or permanent injury. In addition, at least 3,300,000 Soviet prisoners of war died in German hands through starvation, disease, and exposure. This represented 58 percent of the total number of Soviet soldiers captured by the Germans.[18] Regardless of which troops guarded them, those prisoners were the moral responsibility of the German Army that captured them. In fact, in 1941 the German Army made so little provision for the huge mass of prisoners that many of those who survived the act of surrender died in a matter of months for lack of food and shelter. Once winter approached, the poorly equipped German soldiers often deprived their prisoners of coats and boots.

Paradoxically, Germany's need for laborers actually improved the lot of the prisoners and detainees in late 1941. As potential slave workers, the hapless prisoners finally had value to their captors. Even then, however, the racist attitude of the German troops caused additional suffering en route to Germany. Several commanders attempted to march their prisoners across the vast expanse of the newly conquered territories to avoid "infecting" German railroad cars with such "sub humans." Small wonder, then, that German industry received little help from slave laborers until 1942.[19]

For the populace that was left on the land in the occupied territories, German policies of systematic expropriation of food and raw materials often condemned the inhabitants to slow death. By some accounts, the Rumanian occupation of the southwestern Soviet Union was even harsher.

In the face of such barbaric treatment, even Soviet citizens who actively collaborated were unlikely to feel any loyalty to the occupiers. In 1941 there were few effective guerrilla units in the German rear except for a small number of bypassed Red Army soldiers. As the war progressed, however, the partisan threat to the German occupiers in Russia became second only to that in Yugoslavia. In turn, the bitter struggle of partisan warfare called forth even greater brutality on the part of the Germans seeking to eradicate the unseen foe. All this being said, from the very start, the Red Army responded in kind.

SMOLENSK

On 3 July, General Franz Halder, the head of OKH, noted in his diary that "the objective to shatter the bulk of the Russian Army this [western] side of the Dvina and Dnepr [Rivers] has been accomplished . . . east of [these rivers] we would encounter nothing more than partial forces. . . . It is thus probably no overstatement to say that the Russian Campaign has been won in the space of two weeks.[20]

German forces had destroyed the forward elements of the Western Front and severely mauled those of the Southwestern and Northwestern Fronts. They stood on the Dvina and Dnepr Rivers, ready to resume their exploitation once supplies, infantry support, and Hitler's nerve had caught up to the victorious panzer groups. Many German commanders must have felt, like Halder, that the war was won, whereas the struggle had only begun.

The steps by which the Red Army recovered from surprise attack and prepared for the next series of defensive battles are described in the next chapter, as part of the general Soviet response. For the moment, it is sufficient to note that the Dnepr River was guarded not just by the remnants of the Western Front but also by the five armies of Marshal S. M. Budenny's Reserve Front that had begun moving into the area in late May. Stalin had placed Timoshenko in command of Western Front and transferred four of the reserve armies, the 19th, 20th, 21st, and 22d, to that command. The fifth such army, Lieutenant General M. F. Lukin's weak 16th, defended Smolensk, the next major city on the road from Minsk to Moscow.[21] This desperate move sacrificed the original plan of using these forces as a strategic counteroffensive force. To restore the lost strategic depth, while other armies were mobilizing, two of the first wave of armies mobilized in wartime, the 24th and 28th, concentrated around Viaz'ma and Spas-Demensk east of Smolensk covering the approaches to Moscow.[22]

All these formations had shortages in tanks, communications, antitank weapons, and antiaircraft guns. Senior commanders were changed on almost a daily basis. These formations had received little opportunity to prepare for battle, resulting in an uneven performance. Still, the Germans had no knowledge of the existence of these forces until they bumped into them. The result was a series of poorly coordinated but intense struggles around Smolensk during July and August 1941 that stopped the German forces in their tracks for the first time in the war.

Lieutenant General P. A. Kurochkin's 20th Army attempted to slow the German advance to the Dnepr as early as 6 July, when his 5th and 7th Mechanized Corps sacrificed themselves by frontally attacking the spearhead of the German advance near Lepel'. By attacking prepared German

7th Panzer Division antitank defenses without sufficient reconnaissance and without proper infantry-armor cooperation, the two corps were decimated.[23] The real struggle began during 10 to 11 July, when Guderian's Second Panzer Group crossed the Dnepr to begin the next phase of operations. Guderian's immediate opponent was the 13th Army, which had only just escaped from the Minsk pocket. The 13th Army included only four weak rifle divisions, had no armor, and presented little resistance. By 13 July, Guderian's XXXXVI Panzer Corps had passed north of Mogilev and his XXIV Panzer Corps had crossed to the south, encircling 61st Rifle and 20th Mechanized Corps of 13th Army in Mogilev. These corps continued to resist for another two weeks (until 26 July), but that resistance did not halt the German exploitation.[24] Similarly, Lieutenant General I. S. Konev's 19th Army literally counterattacked as it dismounted from railroad trains on 11–13 July, making a vain effort to retake the Vitebsk salient from the Germans. By the evening of 13 July, Guderian's 29th Motorized Infantry Division was only 11 miles from Smolensk, and 19th Army had almost dissolved.[25]

That same day, twenty divisions of Colonel General F. I. Kuznetsov's 21st Army, supported by the surviving elements of 3d Army, struck the southern flank of Second Panzer Group and the arriving infantry of the German Second Army.[26] In four days, 20th Army also launched a series of bloody but inconclusive assaults near Vitebsk. The 21st Army's counterstroke, accompanied by a deep cavalry advance into the German rear south of Bobruisk, appears to have been part of an overall attempt to implement the Soviet prewar general defense plan. This plan apparently called for a series of concerted counterstrokes along the entire front after the German forces had reached or were attempting to breach Soviet defenses along the line of the Dnepr River. Accordingly, while Kuznetsov delivered his thrust toward Bobruisk against Guderian's southern flank, Soviet 11th and 48th Armies struck German Army Group North's armored spearheads near Stol'btsy, east of Pskov. Meanwhile Potapov's 5th Army, supported by its remaining armor, struck Army Group South's armored vanguard near Korosten', west of Kiev.

Because of the failure of these various counterattacks, the coordinated nature of this effort went unnoticed by the Germans and postwar historians alike. Once these initial efforts had failed, at Moscow's insistence all three Soviet *front* commanders sought new opportunities to implement the plan. This was most apparent in the south, where Kirponos struck repeatedly in ensuing days against the Germans near Korosten', but to no avail.

Guderian refused to be distracted by 20th Army's counterattack, although it tied up most of his forces. On 24 July, after much shuffling of units, 18th Panzer Division joined with 29th Motorized Division to continue the advance. By themselves, however, these two divisions were too weak to link up with Colonel General Hermann Hoth's Third Panzer Group and envelop Smolensk. Even before this attack, the 18th Panzer Division's commander had remarked that the heavy casualties must stop "if we do not intend to win ourselves to death."[27] Hoth's armor of Third Panzer Group had advanced parallel to Guderian but further to the north via Polotsk and Vitebsk. By permitting his forces to become diverted with Ninth Army's advance toward Velikie Luki, Hoth's spearheads belatedly reached the area east of Smolensk on 14 July. Meanwhile, after three days of house-to-house fighting, Soviet 16th Army was forced out of the city. The fact that 18th Panzer Division had only 12 tanks still in operation bore mute witness to the ferocity of the fighting and the debilitating effect on German panzer forces unsupported by infantry divisions.

At this point the question of sealing encircled enemy units again preoccupied the German leadership. Generals Guderian and Hoth wanted to continue the advance on Moscow, and, to this end, Guderian sent 29th Motorized Division to secure a bridgehead on the eastern bank of the Dvina River at El'na. By contrast, the Army Group Center Commander, Field Marshal Guenther von Kluge, and Hitler's own staff wanted to destroy as many of the newly located Soviet units as possible. Because of the violent Soviet attacks on the flanks of the two panzer groups, Guderian believed that he had enough force available to hold El'na or seal up the 16th Army east of Smolensk, but not both.

While the Germans hesitated, Timoshenko filled the gap in his defenses in an effort to prevent encirclement of 16th Army or further exploitation to the east. Rokossovsky, who had been reassigned to Western Front headquarters to command 16th Army after the border battles in the southwest, was sent on 17 July to hold the Dnepr River crossing around Iartsevo against Third Panzer Group. He assembled a motley collection of shattered units and stragglers around the cadres of the 38th Rifle and 101st Tank Divisions, the latter reduced to only 40 obsolete tanks.[28] Despite constant Luftwaffe airstrikes, Rokossovsky's scratch force halted 7th Panzer Division from 18 to 23 July and then counterattacked the following day.

Beginning 21 July, operational groups formed from newly deployed 29th, 30th, 28th, and 24th Armies attacked German positions around Smolensk from Bel'yi in the north through Iartsevo to Roslavl' in the south to free the encircled 16th and 20th Armies.[29] This hastily conducted series of Soviet counterstrokes placed immense pressure on overextended German panzer units and caused frightful casualties on both sides, but in the end they failed due to bad coordination, weak fire support, and an almost total lack of logistical support. On 31 July, Guderian's XXIV Panzer Corps struck back at the most successful of the attacking Soviet groups (Group

Kachalov) and within days destroyed it, paving the way for future German operations eastward or to the south against the northern flank of Soviet forces defending Kiev.

The 20th Army's surviving units had also counterattacked on 23 July, but their flanks were unsecured, inviting encirclement. Elements of Third Panzer Group (XXXIX Panzer Corps) and Second Panzer Group (XXXXVII Panzer Corps) finally linked up east of Smolensk on 27 July, surrounding large portions of 16th, 19th, and 20th Armies. Under Lieutenant General P.A. Kurochkin of 20th Army, these Soviet forces broke out to the east a few days later, assisted by the strenuous Soviet counterstrokes north, east, and south of Smolensk. Third Panzer Group once again attempted to break through Rokossovsky's positions at Iartsevo at the end of the month, but Soviet artillery and a few KV-1 tanks stopped the 7th and 20th Panzer Divisions almost immediately.[30] As a vivid illustration of increasingly tenacious Soviet resistance along the Smolensk-Moscow axis, beginning on 30 August, Soviet forces delivered incessant blows against the Germans' El'na bridgehead, finally forcing them to relinquish the position by 8 September.

In September, in part because of the growing Soviet resistance on the Moscow axis, the main German effort turned south to clear the Ukraine, as will be discussed in chapter 6. The Germans did not renew their attacks east from Smolensk for a month. As a result, the magnitude of the Soviet defensive success at Smolensk was not immediately apparent to senior German commanders and received little coverage in their memoirs. By contrast, this limited victory gave the Red Army a great morale boost and a precious month to reorganize for the defense of Moscow. The momentum of the Blitzkrieg was slipping away, not only because of the hesitation of the German high command but also because of the stubborn resistance of Soviet troops.[31]

CHAPTER 5

Soviet Response

The German invasion forced the Soviet regime to do far more than redeploy the five armies of its Reserve Front. During the first weeks of the war, Moscow made fundamental changes in its command and control, unit organization, and military industrial plant. In the crisis, the Soviets temporarily abandoned many of their prewar doctrinal concepts, making the first of many painful but effective adjustments to the reality of modern war.

COMMAND AND CONTROL

During the first six weeks, the nomenclature and organization of the Soviet Union's national command structure underwent frequent changes, most of which had little practical effect on the day-to-day conduct of the war.[1] On 23 June, the War Commissariat's wartime staff, equivalent to a national security council, was activated as the Main Command Headquarters (*Stavka Glavnogo Komandovaniia*); this council was chaired by War Commissar S. K. Timoshenko and included Stalin, V. I. Molotov, and the most senior commanders such as G. K. Zhukov and S. M. Budenny. After a bewildering series of changes in name and membership, the council emerged on 8 August as the Supreme High Command (*Stavka Verkhnogo Glavnokomandovaniia*, or *Stavka VGK*,) with Stalin as titular commander-in-chief. In practice the term *Stavka* was used loosely to describe both the Supreme High Command council itself and the General Staff that served that council. In theory, the State Committee for Defense (*Gosudarstvennyi Komitet Oborony*, or GKO) was the highest body, overseeing *Stavka VGK* as well as the General Staff. A separate Air Force Command (*Komanduiushii VVS Krasnoi Armii*) was also established to sort out the wreckage of the Red Air Force.[2]

In reality, however, there was no strong central control during the first days of the war. Stalin withdrew from public view and even from the day-to-day conduct of the war, apparently in shock. Late on 22 June, the day of the invasion, Premier/Foreign Minister Y. M. Molotov made a halting, plaintive radio address, announcing the German attack but apparently still unwilling to believe that total war had begun. Not until 3 July did

Stalin himself address the nation, making a strong radio speech that called for guerrilla resistance and for the destruction or evacuation of anything useful to the invader. Already in this speech, Stalin began to stress Russian nationalism instead of loyalty to the Soviet state, an emphasis that the regime continued throughout the war.

While Stalin and Molotov faltered, their principal military advisers fanned out from the capital as soon as the war began in a desperate attempt to learn what was happening and bring some modicum of control to the situation. Timoshenko, Zhukov, A. M. Vasilevsky, Budenny, and others traveled extensively, visiting numerous headquarters during the first few days. Eventually a rough system was evolved in which the ailing Marshal B. M. Shaposhnikov served (until his health gave way) as *Stavka* chief of staff in Moscow, while the other senior commanders who enjoyed Stalin's trust acted as theater commanders or trouble-shooters, changing location frequently to provide government-level emphasis to crisis areas.

Part of this new system was the creation on 10 July of three theater-level, multi-*front* strategic commands known as Main Commands of Directions (*Glavnye komandovaniia napravlenii*).[3] These commands were designed to provide unity of control for all *fronts* and other forces operating along a single strategic direction or axis. Originally, they were headed by Marshal K. E. Voroshilov (Northwestern Direction, including Baltic and Northern Fleets), Marshal Timoshenko (Western Direction), and Marshal Budenny (Southwestern Direction, including the Black Sea Fleet). When Timoshenko assumed direct control of the Western Front at the end of July, Lieutenant General V. D. Sokolovsky nominally became head of the Western Direction. The political officers or "members of council" for the three directions were three future leaders of the Communist Party, A. A. Zhdanov, N. A. Bulganin, and N. S. Khrushchev, respectively. In practice, Stalin and the *Stavka* frequently bypassed the three directions to give orders directly to subordinate headquarters. This layer of command proved to be superfluous and ineffective and was eliminated during 1942.

In the best Stalinist tradition, the initial defeats brought renewed authority to the political commissars, who assumed coequal status with force commanders and chiefs of staff. While many career soldiers were released from prison to help fight the invaders, others took their places in a general atmosphere of suspicion.[4] D. K. Pavlov was not the only commander to face summary execution. Many soldiers who escaped from German encirclements returned to Soviet lines only to find themselves disarmed, arrested, and interrogated by NKVD "rear security" units looking for cowardice and sabotage. In addition, 95,000 civilian members of the Communist Party and Communist Youth Organization (KOMSOMOL) were mobilized at the end of June; some of these went into specially formed shock units, while others were expected to reinforce the dedication of the surviving Red Army units.[5]

This renewal of Communist Party influence and terror in the army was unnecessary, since virtually all soldiers were doing their utmost without such threats. The moving force behind this party involvement was the sinister L. Z. Mekhlis, who became head of the army's Main Political Administration on 23 June. Voroshilov, Zhukov, and most of the career military officers despised Mekhlis for his role in the Great Purges and resisted any effort by high-level political commissars to meddle in the conduct of the war. Ultimately, however, Mekhlis himself fell victim to his own system, as we shall see.

Many of the initial Soviet defeats were the direct results of the inexperience of the surviving Soviet officer corps. Field commanders lacked the practical experience and confidence to adjust to the tactical situation and tended to apply stereotyped solutions, such as distributing their subordinate units according to textbook diagrams without regard to the actual terrain. The result was forces that were not focused and concentrated on the most likely avenues of German advance and that attacked and defended in such a stylized, predictable manner that the experienced Germans found it easy to counter and avoid Soviet blows.[6]

Headquarters at every level lacked trained staff officers to coordinate maneuvers, fire support, and logistics. The border battles in the Ukraine were typical, with field army headquarters that proved incapable of coordinating simultaneous attacks by more than one mechanized corps and unable to direct the few available aircraft to provide effective support to the ground units. There were exceptions, of course, but the overall performance of the Red Army hierarchy was so poor that it contributed to the confusion caused by the surprise attack. Small wonder that both German and Western military observers concluded that the Red Army was on the verge of final disintegration.

Soviet staffs also lacked effective communications to control their subordinates and report the situation to their superiors. Once German infiltrators and air strikes hamstrung the fixed telephone network, many headquarters were unable to communicate at all. Even the military district headquarters, which upon mobilization became *front* commands, were short of long-range radio equipment and skilled radio operators. Existing Soviet codes were so cumbersome that commanders often transmitted their messages "in the clear," providing ample tactical intelligence for the German radio-intercept units.

In other words, the Red Army had too many headquarters for the available trained staff officers and communications. Moreover, the initial defeats caused the average strength of divisions, corps, and field armies to decline so catastrophically that the remnants no longer justified the elaborate hierarchy of headquarters left in command. This, plus a general shortage of specialized weapons, such as tanks and antitank weapons, suggested that the organizational structure of the Red Army required a drastic simplification.

REORGANIZATION

It is a tribute to the wisdom of the senior Red Army leadership that they were able to conceive of and execute such a reorganization at a time when the German advance placed them in a state of perpetual reaction to crisis. By going back to basic, simpler organizations, the Red Army leaders temporarily abandoned their prewar concepts but saved the force, which they gradually rebuilt over the next two years.

Stavka Circular 01, dated 15 July 1941, began this reorganization and truncation of force structure.[7] Field commanders received instructions to eliminate the corps level of command, evolving to a smaller field army that had only five or six rifle divisions plus two or three tank brigades, one or two light cavalry divisions, and several attached artillery regiments of the High Command reserve.[8] This allowed the more experienced army commanders and staffs to have direct control over rifle divisions. Those divisions were also simplified, giving up many of the specialized antitank, antiaircraft, armor, and field artillery units included in peacetime division establishments. Such equipment was in desperately short supply, and the new system centralized all specialized assets so that army commanders could allocate them to support the most threatened subordinate units. In the process the authorized strength of a rifle division was reduced from 14,500 to just under 11,000. The authorized number of artillery pieces in the division was reduced to 24, while the number of trucks dropped by 64 percent. The actual strength of most divisions was much lower, and, as time passed, many of these weakened units were redesignated as separate brigades. In fall 1941 and early 1942, the *Stavka* formed about 170 rifle brigades, in lieu of new rifle divisions. These demi-divisions of 4,400 men, consisting of three rifle and various support battalions subordinate directly to brigade headquarters, were significantly easier for inexperienced Soviet commanders to control.

The 15 July circular also abolished mechanized corps, which seemed particularly superfluous given the current shortage of skilled commanders and modern tanks. Most motorized rifle divisions in these corps were redesignated as the normal rifle divisions that they in fact were. The surviving tank divisions were retained on the books at a reduced authorization of 217 tanks each. Some of the original, higher-numbered reserve tank divisions that had not yet seen combat were split to produce more armored units of this new pattern.[9] Virtually all such tank units were subordinated to rifle army commanders. In fact, tanks were so scarce in summer and fall 1941 that the largest new armored organizations formed during this period were tank brigades. Some of these brigades had as few as 50 newly produced tanks, with minimal maintenance and other support. For the moment, therefore, the Red Army had abandoned its previous concept of large mechanized units, placing all the surviving tanks in an infantry-support role.[10]

The same circular also directed a massive expansion of cavalry units, creating 30 new light cavalry divisions of 3,447 horsemen each. Later in the year, this total rose to 82 such divisions, but because of high losses the divisions were integrated into the cavalry corps by late December. Apparently Civil War commanders like Budenny were attempting to recover the mobility of that era without regard to the vulnerability of the horses on the battlefield. German accounts tended to ridicule cavalry units as hopeless anachronisms. Still, given the shortage of transportation of all types, the Soviet commanders felt they had no choice. During the winter of 1941–1942, when all mechanized units were immobilized by cold and snow, the horse cavalry divisions (and newly created ski battalions and brigades) proved effective in the long-range, guerrilla warfare role that Stalin and Budenny had envisaged.

Just as independent operations for mechanized forces were sacrificed, so the Red Air Force abolished its Strategic Long-Range Aviation command temporarily. Tactical air units were reorganized into regiments of only 30, rather than 60, aircraft.[11]

Organization was easier to change than tactical judgment. Soviet commanders from Stalin down displayed a strange mixture of astuteness and clumsiness well into 1942. Most of the great changes in Soviet operational and tactical concepts and practice did not occur until 1942–1943, but during the crisis of 1941, the *Stavka* began the first steps in this process. Many of the instructions issued at the time seem absurdly simple, underlining the inexperience of the commanders to whom they were addressed. In July, an "Artillery Defense Order" directed the creation of integrated antitank regions along the most likely avenues of German mechanized advance.[12] Commanders were forbidden to distribute the available guns evenly across their defensive front. In August, the *Stavka* formally criticized commanders who had established a thinly spread defense without depth or antitank defenses. Creating such depth was easier said than done when so many units were short of troops and guns, but the basic emphasis on countering known German tactics was a sound approach.

Whether attacking or defending, many Soviet officers tended to maneuver their units like rigid blocks, making direct frontal assaults against the strongest German concentrations. This was poor tactics at any time, but it was especially foolhardy when the Red Army was so shorthanded and underequipped. The December 1941 Soviet counter-offensive at Moscow suffered from such frontal attacks, exasperating Zhukov. On 9 December, he issued a directive that forbade frontal assaults and ordered commanders to seek open flanks in order to penetrate into the German rear areas. Such tactics were entirely appropriate under the conditions of December (see chapter 6) but would not necessarily have worked against the Germans during their triumphant advance of June through October.

FORCE GENERATION

The abolition of mechanized corps retroactively corrected a glaring error in German intelligence estimates about the Red Army. Prior to the invasion, the Germans had a fairly accurate assessment of the total strength of the active Red Army, but they had almost no knowledge of the new mechanized corps and antitank brigades. German intelligence analysts apparently believed that the Red Army was still at the 1939 stage, when large mechanized units had been abandoned in favor of an infantry support role. Prior to 22 June, the Germans had identified only three of the 16 mechanized corps in the forward military districts.[13] The massed appearance of these mechanized units in the field against the First Panzer Group at the end of June was almost as great a surprise as the first encounters with KV-1 and T-34 tanks.

Yet the greatest German intelligence error lay in underestimating the Soviet ability to reconstitute shattered units and create new forces from scratch. Given the German expectation of a swift victory, their neglect of this Soviet ability is perhaps understandable. In practice, however, the Red Army's ability to create new divisions as fast as the Germans smashed existing ones was a principal cause of the German failure in 1941.

For much of the 1920s and 1930s, the Red Army had emphasized the idea of cadre and mobilization forces, formations that had very few active duty soldiers in peacetime but would gain reservists and volunteers to become full-fledged combat elements in wartime. As war approached in the late 1930s, the Red Army tended to neglect this concept, gradually mobilizing most of its existing units to full-time, active-duty status. Still, prewar Soviet theory estimated that the army would have to be completely replaced every four to eight months during heavy combat. To satisfy this need, the 1938 Universal Military Service Law extended the reserve service obligation to age 50 and created a network of schools to train those reservists. By the time of the German invasion, the Soviet Union had a pool of 14 million men with at least basic military training.[14] The existence of this pool of trained reservists gave the Red Army a depth and resiliency that was largely invisible to German and other observers.

From the moment the war began, the War Commissariat began a process that produced new rifle armies in groups or "waves" over a period of months (see Map 4; also Table 5.1). The General Staff was too busy dealing with current operations, and so on 23 July force generation was delegated to Commissariat headquarters and the military districts. The districts outside the actual war zone established a system for cloning existing active-duty units to provide the cadres that were filled up with reservists. A total of 5,300,000 reservists were called to the colors by the end of June, with successive mobilizations later. Thirteen new field armies appeared in July, 14 in August, 1 in September, and 4 in October. Yet this mobilization system, in conjunction with active duty units that moved from the eastern military districts to the west, retained enough strength to provide 8 more armies to defend Moscow in November and December, and another 10 new armies in the spring of 1942.

By 1 December 1941, the Soviet mobilization system had deployed 97 existing divisions to the west while creating 194 new divisions and 84 separate brigades from the mobilization base. Ten of these new divisions were "People's Volunteers," militant urban workers who, in some cases, lacked the physical stamina and military training necessary to be effective soldiers. Whereas prewar German estimates had postulated an enemy of approximately 300 divisions, by December the Soviets had fielded twice that number. This allowed the Red Army to lose more than 100 divisions in battle and continue the struggle.[15]

Of course, the prewar and mobilization divisions were not interchangeable. For all their shortcomings, the divisions lost in the first weeks of battle were far better trained and equipped than their successors. The later units lacked almost everything except rifles and political officers. Perhaps more important, they had little time to train as units, to practice procedures so that soldiers and subordinate units knew their roles in combat. The continued poor performance of Soviet divisions in fall and winter 1941 must be weighed against the speed with which they were created and the total inexperience of their commanders and troops. This performance, however, contributed to the German impression of an inferior enemy that did not realize it had already been defeated.

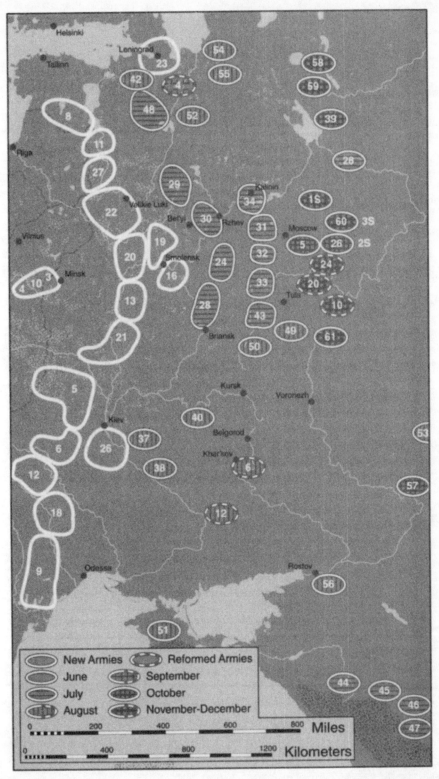

4. *Soviet Dispositions on 31 July 1941 and Reinforcements to 31 December 1942*

Table 5-1. Wartime Mobilization, 1941

Date	Units	Where Deployed
July	24th, 28th, 29th, 30th, 31st, 32d, 33d, 34th, & 43d Armies	Rzhev-Viaz'ma region
	44th Army (June)	Transcaucasus
	45th Army	Transcaucasus
	46th Army	Transcaucasus
	47th Army	Transcaucasus
	48th Army	Novgorod
August	37th Army	Kiev
	38th Army	Kiev
	40th Army	Konotop
	42d Army	Leningrad
	49th Army	Moscow
	50th Army	Briansk
	51st Army	Crimea
	52d Army	Leningrad
	53d Army	Central Asia
	54th Army	Leningrad
	55th Army	Leningrad
	56th Army	Rostov
	6th Army (second formation)	Khar'kov
	12th Army (second formation)	Pavlograd
September	4th (second formation)	*Stavka* reserve Volkov in November
October	5th Army	Mozhaisk
	26th Army (2d Shock in November)	Mozhaisk
	57th Army	Stalingrad
	39th Army	Moscow
November-December	1st Shock Army	Moscow
	24th Army (second formation)	Moscow
	10th Army (second formation)	Riazan'
	58th Army	Siberia
	59th Army	Leningrad
	60th Army (3d Shock on December 25)	Moscow
	61st Army	Moscow
	20th Army (second formation)	Moscow

INDUSTRIAL RELOCATION

The equipment and ammunition shortages of 1941 were exacerbated by the massive redeployment of Soviet heavy industry to avoid capture. Prior to the German invasion, the vast majority of Soviet manufacturing capacity was located in the western part of the country, particularly such major industrial areas as Leningrad and the eastern Ukraine. As early as 24 June, the State Committee for Defense created a Council for Evacuation to relocate these plants eastward to the Urals and Siberia. The task of coordinating this massive undertaking fell on N. A. Voznesensky, head of the Soviet industrial planning agency, GOSPLAN. Voznesensky was one of the few senior civilians who dared to speak bluntly to Stalin; on 4 July, he won approval for the first war economic plan. The actual evacuation was controlled by the council's deputy chairman, the future premier A. N. Kosygin. Voznesensky and Kosygin had to do more than simply move factories and workers. In the centrally directed Soviet economy, nothing would happen without careful advance planning to ensure that these factories would mesh with existing plants and raw material supplies in the new locations. Workers had to be housed and fed in remote towns whose size tripled overnight. Electric plants had to keep operating until the last possible moment to facilitate dismantling in the old locations, then be moved and reassembled at the new sites. All this had to be done while the industry was shifting gears to accommodate wartime demand and the periodic loss of skilled laborers to the army.[16]

The most pressing problem was to evacuate the factories, especially in the lower Dnepr River and Donbas regions of the Ukraine. Here the stubborn delaying tactics of the Southwestern Front paid dividends, not only by diverting German troop strength away from Moscow but also by giving the Council for Evacuation precious time to disassemble machinery.

German reconnaissance aircraft were puzzled by the long lines of railroad cars massed in the region. Eight thousand railcars were used to move just one major metallurgy complex from Zaporozh'e in the Donbas to Magnitogorsk in the Urals. The movement had to be accomplished at great speed and despite periodic German air raids on the factories and rail lines.

In the Leningrad area, the German advance was so rapid that only 92 plants were relocated before the city was surrounded. Plant relocations did not begin in this region until 5 October, but by the end of the year a former Leningrad tank factory was producing KV-1s at a new site in the Urals. More than 500 firms and 210,000 workers left the Moscow area in October and November alone.

All this machinery arrived in remote locations on a confused, staggered schedule and with only a portion of the skilled work force. By the time the trains arrived, bitter winter weather and permafrost made it almost impossible to build foundations for any type of structure. Somehow the machinery was unloaded and reassembled inside hastily constructed, unheated wooden buildings. Work continued even in the sub-zero night, using electric lights strung in trees and supplemented by bonfires.

In total, 1,523 factories, including 1,360 related to armaments, were transferred to the Volga River, Siberia, and Central Asia between July and November, 1941. Almost 1.5 million railcars were involved.[17] Even allowing for the hyperbole so common to Soviet accounts, this massive relocation and reorganization of heavy industry was an incredible accomplishment of endurance and organization.

Because of the relocation, Soviet production took almost a year to reach its full potential. The desperate battles of 1941 had to be fought largely with existing stocks of weapons and ammunition, supplemented by new tanks and guns that often went into battle before they could be painted.

SCORCHED EARTH

Despite their best efforts, the Council for Evacuation was unable to relocate everything of value. In the case of the Donbas mines, which produced 60 percent of the USSR's coal supply, evacuation was impossible. In such cases, the Soviet regime not only had to survive without facilities and resources but it had to ensure that the invaders could not convert those facilities and resources to their own use. The painfully harvested fruits of Stalin's Five-Year Plans had to be destroyed or disabled in place.

Much of the Soviet self-destruction focused on transportation and electrical power. Railroad locomotives and locomotive repair shops that could not be moved were frequently sabotaged, a fact that proved important in the winter weather, when German-built locomotives lacked sufficient insulation to maintain steam pressure. The Dnepr River hydroelectric dam was partially breached by withdrawing Soviet troops, and workers removed or destroyed key components of hydroturbines and steam generators throughout the region. .

In the countryside the extent of destruction of buildings and crops varied considerably from region to region. On the whole, Russia proper had more time to prepare for such destruction than did the western portions of Belorussia and the Ukraine.

Moscow's success in evacuating or destroying so much of its hard-won industrial development shocked German economic planners, who had counted on using Soviet resources to meet both Hitler's production goals and their own domestic consumer demands. Soviet raw materials such as chromium, nickel, and petroleum were vital to continued German war production, and captured Soviet factories had promised an easy solution to overcrowding and labor shortages in Germany.

Moreover, the successful evacuation of the Soviet railroads forced the Germans to commit 2,500 locomotives and 200,000 railcars to support the troops in the East. This, in turn, meant that the Germans had to convert large portions of the captured rail network to their own, narrower gauge, instead of using the existing, broader Russian gauge.[18] Thus the Soviet evacuation effort not only preserved industrial potential for future campaigns but posed a continuing and unexpected drain on the German economy.

Still despite all efforts, a considerable portion of the industrial plant and the harvest fell into German hands. Hitler defined his objectives for 1941 in terms of seizing additional economic resources, and the German advance sought to satisfy those objectives.

CHAPTER 6

To Moscow

OVEREXTENSION

By the end of July 1941, the German invaders were becoming aware of the true scope of their enterprise. The enormous success of their initial advance had caused them to outrun their fragile logistical structure, and on 30 July, OKH declared a virtual standstill so that Army Group Center could rest and refit. Second Panzer Group's embattled bridgehead over the Desna River at El'na was 720 kilometers from the nearest German railhead. Poor roads made it difficult for wheeled vehicles, let alone foot infantry, to keep pace with the dwindling number of tanks in the spearheads. The infantry was running short on boots, and staff officers began to plan for large quantities of winter clothing. By 2 August, the three army groups had suffered 179,500 casualties in six weeks, but had received only 47,000 replacements.[1]

At the same time, Adolf Hitler resisted requests to issue newly produced tanks and major repair assemblies, trying to reserve them for both new and reconstituted panzer units after the campaign season ended. On 14 July, for example, he ordered increased production of submarines and new tanks, reducing the production priority of the army in the field.[2] The extent of Hitler's micromanagement was illustrated by a conference at Army Group Center headquarters on 4 August, when a group of senior commanders had to plead with the dictator to release a mere 350 replacement engines for Mark III tanks.[3]

The one thing the Wehrmacht was not short of was targets. General Franz Halder, who had thought the war won in early July, realized his mistake by August 11:

> The whole situation makes it increasingly plain that we have underestimated the Russian colossus. . . . [Soviet] divisions are not armed and equipped according to our standards, and their tactical leadership is often poor. But there they are, and if we smash a dozen of them, the Russians simply put up another dozen. . . . they are near their own resources, while we are moving farther and farther away from ours. And so our troops, sprawled over an immense front line, without any depth, are subjected to the incessant attacks of the enemy.[4]

Not all German leaders saw the situation so clearly and pessimistically, but many of them sought clearer guidance as to how to bring the war to a quick conclusion. Even Hitler grumbled that, had he known that Heinz Guderian's prewar figures for Soviet tank strength were so accurate, he might not have started the war.[5] The solution that the dictator and many of his senior commanders chose was to emphasize surrounding and destroying Soviet units that had been bypassed previously, apparently to prevent cadres from escaping to fight another day. Younger commanders like Heinz Guderian and Erich von Manstein opposed this policy because it slowed their exploitation and allowed the enemy to reconstruct its defenses after each breakthrough.

KIEV AND BEYOND

Hitler began to seek targets that were still within reach before winter came and that would convince himself and the world that Germany was in fact victorious. He was particularly anxious to seize Soviet industry and crop lands, as well as to push the defenders beyond bomber range of the precious Rumanian oil fields. He therefore continued to insist that taking Moscow was far less important than securing the industry of Leningrad and the industrial and agricultural heartland of the Ukraine, where German Army Group South and First Panzer Group had made spectacular progress after the border battles. Throughout July and August, German forces had driven Southwestern and Southern *Front* forces deep into the Ukraine, encircling most of three armies (6th, 12th, and 18th) near Uman', besieging Odessa, and reaching the outskirts of Kiev and the southern Dnepr by 30 August.

In Fuehrer Directive 33, dated 19 July, Hitler had ordered the bulk of panzer forces removed from Army Group Center during the next phase of the campaign in order to support successful attacks in the north and south. This decision produced a prolonged period of disagreement within the German command. Even those who were willing to delay a direct advance on Moscow were concerned that Hitler's plan would place still more strain on the armored spearheads, denying them the rest and repairs they required to regain their combat effectiveness.

The arguments raged throughout August, while Army Group Center improved its positions south of the Desna River, and the Soviets launched heavy counterattacks against the El'na salient near Smolensk and the Staraia Russa area in the north.[6] The latter attacks caused Hitler to overreact on 16 August, siphoning off a panzer corps to reinforce the area. This brought the weakened Third Panzer Group to a temporary halt. In a new Fuehrer Directive dated 21 August, the dictator specified that the objective for the year was not Moscow but control of the Donets Basin, the Crimea, and the area around Leningrad. The next day, Hitler berated the commander-in-chief, Field Marshal Walter von Brauchitsch, blaming him for the frequent changes in objective! General Halder proposed that both he and von Brauchitsch resign, but the field marshal replied that Hitler would not accept the resignations. Guderian, in turn, felt Hitler's wrath in early September because he was trying to protect, and even widen, the El'na salient on the left bank of the Desna instead of focusing to the south. Guderian felt this was necessary because his progress to the south left his left flank increasingly vulnerable to counterattack.[7]

Hitler was correct, of course, that the Ukraine made a tempting target for operational as well as economic reasons. Because of the rapid advance of Army Group Center and the relatively stubborn opposition met by Army Group South, the Soviet Southwestern Front's defense of Kiev had become a long, triangular projection westward, anchored by the tenacious and skillful defense of M. I. Potapov's 5th Army south of the Pripiat' Marshes. By turning southward from Smolensk, Guderian's Second Panzer Group could slice through the exposed northern flank of the Southwestern Front, link up with Colonel General Ewald von Kleist's First Panzer Group attacking north from Kremenchug on the Dnepr, and complete a huge encirclement of the Kiev region. On 5 August, when G. K. Zhukov pointed out this danger and suggested withdrawal, he was replaced as chief of staff by B. M. Shaposhnikov and sent to Leningrad. Stalin was convinced that the Germans would concentrate on Moscow and Leningrad. The Soviet defenders were even more vulnerable because the newly formed Briansk Front, immediately opposite Second Panzer Group, was in the process of assuming control of the forces at the critical point of Guderian's new attack to the south and planning its own counterstroke against Guderian. Lieutenant General A. I. Eremenko, the unfortunate commander of the Briansk Front, attacked on 2 September into the teeth of Guderian's panzers in an attempt to cut off the German advance. Since the *Stavka* had insisted Eremenko attack in two different directions (toward Roslavl' and Novozybkov) instead of concentrating his limited forces, the counterstroke failed immediately.[8]

By 11 September, the cordon around Southwestern Front was closing from both north and south. Marshal S. M. Budenny and his military council member, N. S. Khrushchev, told Stalin that Kiev must be evacuated. The reply from Moscow was to replace Budenny with S. K. Timoshenko. On 14 September, the chief of staff of the Southwestern Front, Major General V. I. Tupikov, tried in vain to convince Shaposhnikov of the danger. Fall rains turned the Russian roads into canals of mud, reducing

Luftwaffe support still further, and the leading regiment of Guderian's 3d Panzer Division was down to an effective strength of 10 tanks. Nevertheless, on September 16, Second and First Panzer Groups linked up near Lokhvitsa. As the spearheads closed, Timoshenko and Khrushchev, as joint heads of the Southwestern Direction, authorized Southwestern Front to withdraw. General M. P. Kirponos, the *front* commander, was understandably reluctant to do so without confirmation from Moscow, which did not arrive until almost midnight on 17 September.[9]

The encirclement was by no means airtight, and for several days Soviet air and ground attacks pressed the thinly spread German forward units. Significant numbers of Soviet troops escaped, including Budenny, Timoshenko, and Khrushchev. Kirponos and his chief of staff, Tupikov, paid the ultimate price for their obedience during an attempted breakout. The official German figure of 665,000 prisoners in the Kiev encirclement came close to portraying accurately the catastrophic Soviet losses in the operation. Four Soviet field armies (5th, 37th, 26th, and 21st), consisting of 43 divisions, 452,720 men, and 3,867 guns and mortars, had virtually ceased to exist. The Southwestern Front, like the Western Front before it, had to be recreated from scratch from the 15,000 men who escaped encirclement.[10]

As Second Panzer Group retraced its steps north to prepare for a renewed advance on Moscow, Army Group South exploited the Kiev victory to the south and east. German forces entered the industrial basin of the Donbas River in late September 1941, and occupied the entire region by 17 October. Outrunning its logistical and infantry support from Sixth and Seventeenth Armies, First Panzer Group raced for the Don River and the Caucasus beyond. On 21 November, the SS Panzer Division *Leibstandarte Adolf Hitler* entered the key transportation center of Rostov on the Don, but it was so worn down that it withdrew in the face of a Soviet counterattack a week later.[11] Meanwhile Germany's Rumanian allies captured Odessa on 16 October after a bitter and embarrassing struggle (with German assistance) and pushed the defenders out of the Crimean Peninsula. Only the fortified port of Sevastopol' remained in Soviet hands.

Army Group North also advanced rapidly, parried the Soviet counterthrust at Staraia Russa, but fell short of taking Leningrad. The Soviet leadership never expected a threat to this city from the west and had no defenses in that direction. As many as 500,000 men and women labored on field fortifications around the city while the invaders rolled through the Baltic countries during July and August. Twenty thousand Soviet troops held the port of Tallin, Estonia, until 26 August, after which the Red Navy evacuated many of them despite massive German air attacks. At the end of August, largely because of the failure of the Staraia Russa counterstroke,

Stalin dissolved the Northwestern Direction and placed both the North-western Front and the newly created Leningrad Front directly under *Stavka* control. The overextended Eighteenth German Army finally came to a halt on 26 September but only after it had reached Lake Ladoga and virtually surrounded Leningrad.[12]

VIAZ'MA AND BRIANSK

The main struggle had returned to the central sector. Even before the Kiev pocket was closed, Fuehrer Directive 36, dated 6 September, belatedly focused on Moscow for the next phase of operations. To this end, the headquarters and most of the divisions of Fourth Panzer Group redeployed from Army Group North to Army Group Center in late September. This concentrated most of the remaining German mechanized forces on a 400 kilometer front, with Third Panzer Group in the north, Fourth in the center, and Second in the south. Field Marshal Fedor von Bock's initial plan was to have Third and Fourth Panzer Groups, under the operational control of German Ninth and Fourth Armies, respectively, link up in a new encirclement around Viaz'ma, thereby tearing a gap in the Western Front and clearing the main highway to Moscow. Second Panzer Group, which had been weakened both by the Kiev operation and by transferring some units to Fourth Panzer Group, would attack to the northeast through the Briansk area toward Tula.

Soviet sources estimated the strength of these three panzer groups, which included 13 panzer divisions and 7 motorized divisions, at 1,700 tanks. This figure seems improbable after three months of hard campaign-ing. Still, two previously uncommitted panzer divisions were available for the fight, and each panzer group received a limited number of replace-ment vehicles. The actual German strength was therefore probably close to 1,000 tanks.[13]

Colonel General I. S. Konev, a Civil War political officer who had distinguished himself in the defense of Smolensk, assumed command of the Western Front on 13 September from Timoshenko, who was, in turn, assigned to command Southwestern Front. Western Front then consisted of 22d, 29th, 30th, 19th, 16th, and 20th Armies defending from Lake Seliger to south of Iartsevo. This appointment set off another round of changes in commanders throughout the *front*, contributing to the climate of confu-sion and uncertainty. The command structure was further complicated by the presence of Marshal Budenny's Reserve Front, which had two field armies (24th and 43d) on the front line along the Desna River south of Konev's forces, and four other armies (31st, 49th, 32d, and 33d) in second echelon near Viaz'ma itself, approximately 35 kilometers to the east.[14] All of these headquarters were short on trained staff officers and long-range radios. The widespread fear of German signal-intercept operations made many commanders avoid radios, relying instead on liaison officers to communicate their desires to higher and lower headquarters. Needless to say, this system was slow and tenuous, and communications broke down rapidly once the battle began.

As early as 20 September, Konev reported the German preparations for an offensive, but *Stavka* did not order a general alert until 27 September. Despite Konev's best efforts to prepare defensive positions, his six field armies were inadequate to defend the 340–kilometer front line in any depth. Each army had five or six rifle divisions on line and only one division in reserve. The divisions in both *fronts* were a mixture of veteran units that were worn down from the Smolensk battle and new, poorly trained and equipped People's Volunteer formations. Only 45 of Konev's 479 tanks were new models, and the *front* had severe shortages in trained officers, modern aircraft, and effective antiaircraft and antitank weapons. The available tanks and other weapons were widely dispersed, and a continuing shortage of motor vehicles gave the defenders far less maneuverability than the attackers.

The mobility differential was immediately evident when operation Taiphun (Typhoon) began on 2 October. The Germans followed a short artillery preparation with a dense smokescreen along the front, and they launched air strikes that put the Western Front headquarters out of action temporarily. Although the Soviet troops held their forward defenses in most locations, Fourth Panzer Group was able to advance along the weakly defended boundary between the Reserve and Briansk Fronts, enveloping the southern flank of 43d Army. Similarly, Third Panzer Group penetrated between the 19th and 30th Armies northwest of Viaz'ma. The two armored spearheads pressed forward, linking up at Viaz'ma on 8 October.

Konev's deputy, Lieutenant General I. V. Boldin, was in charge of the Western Front counterattack, repeating the role he had performed in June. He was no more successful on the second occasion. Boldin's operational group, consisting of three divisions and two tank brigades, counterattacked the flanks of Third Panzer Group on 3–4 October, and attempted to cover the withdrawal of other Western Front units on 6 October. The *Stavka* had belatedly authorized this withdrawal once the German breakthroughs were apparent, but the Reserve Front lost communications with the headquarters of 24th and 43d Armies, and Konev's Western Front headquarters soon lost contact with Boldin. In the ensuing desperate struggle, most of the 19th, 20th, 24th, and 32d Armies, as well as much of Boldin's operational group, were encircled west of Viaz'ma. The surviving elements of the Western and Reserve Fronts fell back to the next planned defensive line near Mozhaisk and Kaluga. Lieutenant General M. F. Lukin, commander of the 19th Army, assumed command of the encircled forces. German Ninth and Fourth Armies had great difficulty in containing this pocket in the face of repeated Soviet efforts to escape. On the night of 12 to 13 October, at least two rifle divisions broke out to the east through a swampy sector where German armor could not maneuver. Thereafter Lukin ordered his heavy weapons and vehicles destroyed, and much of the encircled force escaped in small groups.[15]

Meanwhile to the south, Second Panzer Group had jumped off on 30 September, penetrating Major General A. M. Gorodniansky's weak 13th Army of the Briansk Front by 2 October and pushing on to Orel on the following day.[16] Stalin telephoned Eremenko to demand an immediate counterattack, but the Briansk Front had few tanks and no reserves. In a later telephone call, Marshal Shaposhnikov insisted on a rigid defense of every position, denying Eremenko the chance to delay the attackers through flexible maneuvering. The German breakthrough was so sudden that streetcars were still running in Orel when 4th Panzer Division rolled in.[17] The bypassed 13th and 50th Armies, together with the headquarters of the Briansk Front, were pushed into two large pockets by German Second Army.[18] *Front* headquarters lost radio contact with the *Stavka*, which had to relay all messages through other units.

At first, *Stavka*'s responses to these new disasters were too slow to parry the German spearheads. All available Soviet bombers concentrated against the Orel breakthrough. Their bombing altitude remained too high for accuracy, although they did shatter the windows of one building around Guderian's ears.

The Germans were finally slowed by a combination of adverse weather and determined counterattacks. The first snow fell in Army Group Center's sector on the night of 6–7 October. It soon melted but was followed by the rainy *rasputiza* (literally time without roads), a period of mud that strikes Russia each spring and fall as the seasons change. German mechanized units used up motor fuel at three times the rate they had planned. The endless mud of unpaved roads deprived the invaders of their mobility until the ground froze solid for the winter.

Even before poor weather arrived, however, a series of Soviet counterblows along the entire front helped stabilize the situation. Perhaps the most effective of these blows fell on Guderian's 4th Panzer Division as it approached Mtsensk on 6 October. Here two Soviet officers who later gained fame as superb battlefield commanders cooperated to ambush the Germans. Major General D. D. Leliushenko's 1st Guards Rifle Corps had rushed to the scene to block the advance of Second Panzer Group.

Leliushenko's troops included two tank brigades, the 4th and 11th, and two airborne brigades, the 10th and 201st of 5th Airborne Corps, flown in to a nearby airfield. Colonel M. E. Katukov's 4th Tank Brigade, equipped with newly produced T-34s, displayed a tactical ability that the invaders had not encountered before. Katukov concealed his armor in the woods while the German advance guard rolled by. Leliushenko's patchwork collection of infantry and airborne troops blocked 4th Panzer from the front, after which Katukov ambushed the Germans from the flanks. The undergunned, underarmored German Mark IV's attempted to break out of the ambush by maneuvering around Katukov but were quickly halted by short counterattacks. By the end of the day, most of 4th Panzer Division's armor had been reduced to smoking hulks. This shock to Second Panzer Group, which had just been redesignated Second Panzer Army, was so great that a special investigation was conducted. Even Guderian grudgingly acknowledged that his opponents were learning.[19]

But it was a near-run race. Following his usual habit, Stalin sent Zhukov from Leningrad to the threatened sector, making him commander of the Western Front on 10 October. Zhukov had to plead with Stalin to keep his former rival Konev as his deputy in order to maintain continuity and morale in the headquarters. Zhukov found almost no surviving units to defend the road to Moscow. Lukin's vigorous struggle in the Viaz'ma pocket, together with Leliushenko's counterattacks, gained just enough time to rebuild a tenuous defense. Even then, Zhukov had to fall back a few kilometers on 18 October because German armored spearheads had taken Kalinin in the north and Kaluga in the south, outflanking his new line.

In Moscow the initial reaction to the disaster was to deny that any breakthrough had occurred and to search for scapegoats. Once the enormity of the danger sank in, Stalin came close to panic. On 13 October he ordered the evacuation of the bulk of Communist Party, *Stavka*, and civil government offices from Moscow to Kuibyshev, leaving only skeleton staffs behind. The news of this evacuation, in combination with repeated German air raids and a variety of wild rumors about the Viaz'ma-Briansk battles, produced a near-panic in Moscow on 16 to 17 October. Much of the population tried to flee, mobbing the available trains for fear of imminent occupation. Only the announcement that Stalin himself remained in the city stilled the panic.[20]

TO THE GATES

By late October, the Wehrmacht and the Red Army resembled two punch-drunk boxers, staying precariously on their feet but rapidly losing the power to hurt each other. Like prizefighters with swollen eyes, they were unable to see their opponents with sufficient clarity to judge their relative endurance.

In retrospect, the German forces had gone as far as possible for 1941 and needed to go into winter quarters. At the time, however, the *Stavka* had to face the possibility that, once the first hard frost restored mobility, the invaders would be able to capture or at least encircle Leningrad, Moscow, Stalingrad, and Rostov. Even if the Soviet regime could survive such a blow politically, the loss of manpower, transportation hubs, and manufacturing capacity might well prove fatal militarily. This was especially true at a time when the evacuated factories were still being reassembled in the Urals. Stalin chose to assemble his next "wave" of armies (Western Front's 16th, 5th, 33d, 43d, 49th, and 50th, some severely shaken in earlier battles) in new defensive positions covering the approaches to Moscow from Gzhatsk through Kaluga and manning the Mozhaisk defense line. In a remarkable imitation of Hitler's micromanagement, the Soviet dictator doled out handfuls of tanks and heavy weapons to shore up each new gap in his forward defenses. At the same time, Stalin and the *Stavka* had to provide two divisions to K. A. Meretskov's 7th Separate Army in the north, where a limited counterattack in early November prevented the Germans and Finns from linking up with each other around Lake Ladoga. The main rail and road lines to Leningrad remained cut, but the Soviets were able to move some supplies across the frozen lake into the city.

For virtually all German commanders, the situation was equally precarious. Only one third of all motor vehicles were still operational, and divisions were at one-third to one-half strength. A further advance to the east might succeed on the tactical level but only at a cost of greater strains on logistics. The scarce railroad trains that brought up fuel and ammunition for a renewed offensive would not be available to carry warm clothing and construction materials, both of which were vital for winter survival regardless of how successful the offensive might be. For all these reasons, on 4 November Field Marshal Gerd von Rundstedt asked that his Army Group South be allowed to halt immediately and rebuild for an offensive in 1942. Other field commanders expressed similar concerns. On 13 November, the principal staff officers of OKH met with the chiefs of staff of the three army groups to discuss how far the army should continue to advance. The conference was held at Orsha, halfway between Minsk and Smolensk. The Orsha conference convinced General Halder that the army was even weaker than he had feared, and that the most it could accomplish in 1941 was to encircle Leningrad and threaten Moscow.[21]

Even Hitler was becoming reconciled to a longer struggle and no longer spoke of destroying the Soviet government or capturing major cities immediately. His comments to this effect were partly rationalizations, but he apparently had a genuine reluctance to become involved in urban fighting after the costly capture of Warsaw in 1939. As early as 30 June, when victory still seemed inevitable, the dictator had warned against allowing panzer forces to enter Moscow without massive infantry support. Considering his later experience at Stalingrad, this reluctance proved to be well founded.[22]

With German Eighteenth Army halted south of Leningrad and First Panzer Group closing in on Rostov in the far south, the obvious site for a final German effort was a double envelopment of Moscow and the Western Front. To that end Third and Fourth Panzer Groups continued their advance toward Klin and the Volga-Moscow Canal to envelope Moscow from the north, while Second Panzer Army thrust from the southwest toward Tula and Kashira to unite with its sister groups east of Moscow.

In early November, Western Front intelligence analysts identified preparations for this encirclement, and Zhukov badgered Stalin into approving a whole series of spoiling attacks on advancing German forces, while other *front* forces manned the prepared defenses covering the approaches to Moscow.[23] One such attack, by Group Belov against Guderian's right flank, caught the German 112th Infantry Division with no antitank weapons that were effective against the attacking T-34s. The result was a panicked retreat by most of the division on 17 November, an event almost unprecedented in the German Army.[24] The day before, however, 44th Mongolian Cavalry Division was committed southwest of Klin in a mounted counterattack across an open, snow-covered field. Two thousand cavalrymen and their horses were cut down by artillery and machine guns of German 106th Infantry Division, which suffered no casualties.[25] Horses proved very useful for getting troops to a battlefield, especially in winter, but those horses were obviously too vulnerable to maneuver in a pitched battle.

While Zhukov's spoiling attacks continued, the ground had frozen hard, and von Bock's Army Group Center resumed the offensive on 15 November. Soviet Western Front forces, now reinforced by 30th Army on the *front's* northern flank, numbered 240,000 men supported by 1,254 guns and mortars, 502 tanks, and 600 to 700 combat aircraft. Zhukov's defenses were anchored on the well-prepared Mozhaisk line defending Moscow, and *front* forces extended to Kalinin in the north and Tula in the south.[26]

In the north, where General Hoth's redesignated Third Panzer Army posed the most immediate threat to the Russian capital, a desperate fight

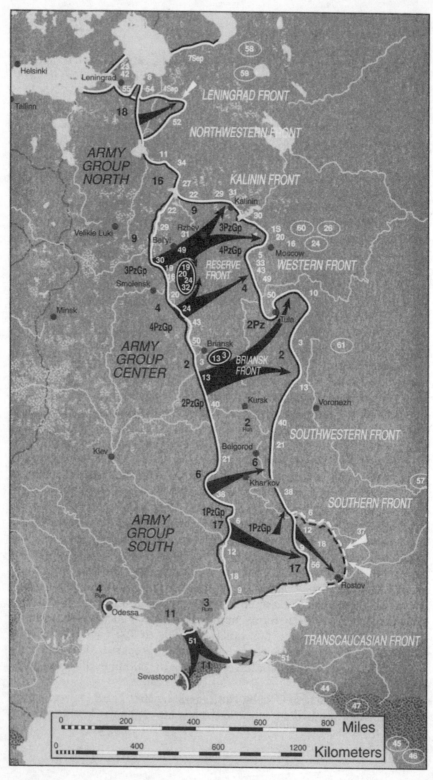

5. *Summer–Fall Campaign (2), 1 October–December 1941*

developed for control of the highway running from Kalinin through Klin
to Moscow. The initial German assault split apart Rokossovsky's 16th Army
from 30th Army, now commanded by D. D. Leliushenko. Zhukov assigned
Rokossovsky's deputy commander, Major General F. D. Zakharov, to cover
the gap near Klin with two rifle divisions and two rifle brigades. The
German armor struggled slowly forward against a fierce resistance in a
see-saw battle that decimated both sides. By late November, both Soviet
and German regiments had been reduced to the size of companies, with
only 150 to 200 riflemen left. Third Panzer Army finally took Klin on 24
November. By 28 November, 7th Panzer Division of this army had seized a
bridgehead across the last major obstacle, the Moscow-Volga Canal, and
stood less than 35 kilometers from the Kremlin. Immediately northwest of
Moscow, Fourth Panzer Group's 2d Panzer Division was even closer, little
more than 20 kilometers from Moscow. German officers said they could
see the spires of the city through their field glasses.[27]

Despite categorical orders to hold in place, Rokossovsky's 16th Army
had been forced back step by step. In an effort to stem the tide, the *Stavka*
began to commit its strategic reserves, including 1st Shock Army and 20th
Army, to hold the Moscow-Volga Canal. Many of these reserves were well-
trained units, but they had to counterattack almost as soon as they disem-
barked from the trains that had brought them forward. By late November,
Zhukov's dwindling mobile forces consisted of 3 tank divisions, 3 motorized rifle divisions, 12 cavalry divisions, and 14 separate tank brigades.
These units were often understrength, however, and included numerous
obsolete light tanks.[28]

In the south, Second Panzer Army resumed the offensive on 18 November, after recovering from the brief panic caused by the Soviet attack of the
previous day. In late October, Guderian had concentrated most of his
remaining tanks into one brigade, commanded by Colonel Eberbach of
the weakened 4th Panzer Division. By mid-November, this brigade had
only 50 tanks left, but it was the spearhead for XXIV Panzer Corps and, in
effect, for the entire army. Eberbach forced his way forward slowly in an
attempt to encircle Tula from the east as a stepping-stone to Moscow.
Lieutenant General I. V. Boldin's 50th Army, tenaciously defending the
outskirts of Tula, launched counterattack after counterattack against
Guderian's front and flank. With temperatures well below freezing and
troops running out of fuel, ammunition, and functioning vehicles, the
German advance slowly shuddered to a halt. Guderian repeatedly asked
that the offensive be canceled, but no one in OKH had the authority to take
such an action without Hitler's consent.[29]

Dogged Soviet defenses did as much to stop the Germans as did bad
weather and poor supply lines. The defending units were still largely

inexperienced troops, but there were more of those troops in better defensive positions than ever before. In contrast to the thin defenses at Viaz'ma, most rifle armies now had two or more divisions in second echelon, plus in some cases a cavalry reserve. The laborers of Moscow gave these armies two belts of fully constructed trenches instead of the hasty foxholes of October. As a result, the typical rifle army had a narrower frontage to defend and could establish a series of defenses to a depth of up to 50 kilometers—three times the typical defensive depth in October. Antitank units, infantry, engineers, and artillery were concentrated along the major avenues the Germans had to use. Thirteen of Western Front's 20 antitank artillery regiments were allocated to the two most threatened field armies, the 16th in the north and the 49th in the south. From Zhukov down to the division commanders, the leaders of the Western Front were now skilled and experienced officers who were much better prepared to counter German tactics.[30]

Two examples of this growing Soviet skill proved to be symbolic of the future. With Tula almost encircled and Second Panzer Army still pushing slowly north in late November, Zhukov again turned to Major General P. A. Belov, commander of 2d Cavalry Corps, to "restore the situation at any cost." From the very small reserves available, Stalin and Zhukov gave Belov half a tank division (112th), two separate tank battalions (35th and 127th), some antiaircraft gunners from Moscow, a combat engineer regiment, one of the new "Katiusha" multiple-rocket launcher units, and the instructors and students from several military schools. On 26 November, the composite force was redesignated as the 1st Guards Cavalry Corps and ordered to attack Guderian's spearhead 17th Panzer Division near Kashira. Considering the desperate equipment shortages of the time, this corps represented one of the first Soviet efforts to revive the prewar doctrine of a "cavalry-mechanized group" for deep penetrations. The German advance guards were so scattered that Belov was able to infiltrate his squadrons forward virtually undetected. On 27 November he counterattacked, drove 17th Panzer Division back, and relieved the pressure on Tula. Thus began the odyssey of the 1st Guards Cavalry Corps, which would continue its long exploitation and operate in the German rear areas for the next five months.[31]

The second example of Soviet effectiveness came during the final German effort, when Fourth German Army attacked due east along the Minsk-Moscow highway on 1 December. This attack had only limited armored support and ran directly into a carefully planned Soviet antitank defensive region. This systematic defense by 1st Guards Motorized Rifle Division at Naro-Fominsk became a legend of tenacity. At the same time, local counterattacks by Lieutenant General M. G. Efremov's 33d Army hit the German thrust in the flanks, effectively ending the German offensive on 5 December.[32]

DECEMBER COUNTEROFFENSIVE

Throughout November temperatures and snowfall had been relatively mild by Russian standards. In early December, the snow and cold finally arrived with a vengeance.[33] German troops were strung out along the few roads, and the Luftwaffe was operating from improvised forward airfields. Both vehicle and aircraft engines had to be heated for hours before attempting to start them. By contrast, the Red Air Force had heated hangers at permanent airfields. The Wehrmacht could do no more, and the initiative passed to the Soviets. The *Stavka* initiated what ultimately became its winter campaign (see Map 6).

The Red Army did not have an abundance of forces to launch a counteroffensive. Soviet historians have claimed that, as of 1 December, there were 1,100,000 Soviet troops facing 1,708,000 Germans in German Army Group Center, with similar disproportions in equipment, such as 7,652 Soviet guns to 13,500 German pieces and 774 Soviet tanks to 1,170 German tanks. These figures vastly overestimate effective German strength, but they correctly assess Red Army strength. Many Soviet units were mere skeletons. The 108th Tank Division, for example, was down to 15 out of 217 authorized tanks, and many rifle divisions had less than 3,000 men.[34]

Still, the Germans were overextended and poorly equipped for winter, while the Soviets were temporarily concentrated at a few critical points. For example, on the Western Front's right wing attacking north of Moscow the Soviets were able to achieve a 2:1 superiority over the Germans in personnel and lesser superiorities in artillery and mortars. The Germans maintained armored superiority.[35] Moreover, German intelligence estimated that Stalin had no more reserves and that it would be an additional three months before the Red Army could raise new forces. The shock of the Soviet counterattacks was therefore all the greater.

The Soviet winter campaign began on 5 December 1941. Driven by necessity, the *Stavka* first sought to blunt and repel the German armored pincers threatening Moscow. When the first series of counterattacks by 1st Shock and other armies near Moscow achieved success, *Stavka* ambitions soared. Within weeks the initial, limited counterattacks were replaced with far more extensive offensive missions for *fronts* and armies from Leningrad to the Black Sea. By early January, an overall concept had emerged that governed subsequent Soviet operations throughout the winter. Because of its hasty formulation and because of the often clumsy

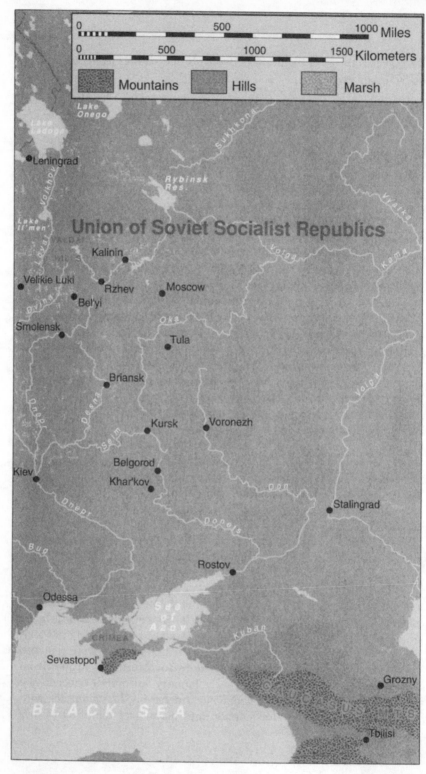

6. *Winter Campaign, December 1941–April 1942*

execution of the concept, the spectacular early gains did not produce the desired strategic results. In particular, the Soviet campaign failed to destroy Army Group Center. The offensive did, however, prove immensely sobering for the German High Command, and, for the first time, raised doubts among some German commanders that the war could indeed be won.

The first goal of the Soviet offensive was to eliminate the threatening pincers north and south of Moscow. In the north, the counterattack began at 0300 hours on Friday, 5 December, when the temperature was 15 degrees below zero and the snow was more than a meter deep. The 29th and 31st Armies of Konev's newly formed Kalinin Front attacked from the northern side of the bulge. The following day, 30th and 1st Shock Armies struck from positions north and south of Dmitrov on the Volga-Moscow Canal.[36] By noon of 7 December, advanced Soviet units were overrunning the headquarters of LVI Panzer Corps outside Klin. Thereafter Zhukov sent three additional armies (20th, 16th, and 5th) into the attack against the southern side of the Klin bulge, seeking to encircle all of Third Panzer Army as well as the XXXXVI Panzer Corps of Fourth Panzer Group. In the 5th Army, Lieutenant General L. A. Govorov concentrated a "shock group" of three rifle divisions (19th, 329th, and 326th) and several tank brigades to attack on 14 December on a narrow front toward Russa. Into the gap charged Major General L. M. Dovator's 2d Guards Cavalry Corps. Hard on the heels of Dovator marched a mobile tank group consisting of 20th Tank Brigade and 136th Separate Tank Battalion.

Although Dovator himself was killed in action on 20 December, these and similar shock group tactics used by other armies slowly unhinged German defenses. The Germans frantically moved the few available forces back and forth along lateral routes to shore up threatened sectors, while other units tried to withdraw from the trap.[37]

In the south, a similar pincer movement was attempted against Guderian's Second Panzer Army. Belov's Cavalry-Mechanized Group immediately cut off the lead German elements near the tip of the Venev bulge, while an attack from Boldin's 50th Army at Tula overran one battalion of the elite *Grossdeutschland* Regiment. From the first day of the Soviet counterattack, Guderian began withdrawing back to the line of the Don River, southeast of Tula, because his line of communications was threatened by Belov. Soviet ski battalions harassed the German withdrawal in the snow, but the Soviet main forces were too weak and immobile to encircle the bulge completely before the Germans escaped. Renewed attacks on 11 December got nowhere because 50th Army had been severely weakened in manpower and equipment after the earlier Briansk encirclement and the battles around Tula. The Soviet attacks in the north were also inconclusive, although several German rearguard divisions were cut up in both pincers. The only major victory was the encirclement and destruction of German XXXIV Army Corps near Elets, on Guderian's southern flank.[38]

These Soviet thrusts reinforced the ongoing crisis in German command circles, bringing Hitler's long-standing distrust of his senior commanders into the open. The first act began in the south on 29 November, when SS Division *Leibstandarte Adolf Hitler* withdrew from Rostov under Soviet pressure. By the time the dictator attempted to reverse this decision, the leading elements of First Panzer Army had begun a general withdrawal back to a more defensible line along the Mius River. The Army Group South Commander, Gerd von Rundstedt, insisted that this withdrawal was essential and requested that he be relieved unless he was allowed to continue. Hitler took him at his word on 1 December, only to be forced the next day to approve the withdrawal that von Rundstedt had demanded.

By 16 December, the Soviet counteroffensive at Moscow had forced the Army Group Center Commander, von Bock, to make a similar request for authority to withdraw and adjust positions as necessary. Late that night, Field Marshal Walter von Brauchitsch, chief of OKH, and General Halder, chief of the General Staff, explained the situation to Hitler, who insisted that a general withdrawal was out of the question. On 18 December, von Bock surrendered his command to Field Marshal von Kluge, ostensibly because of his genuine ill health. Hitler forbade any further major withdrawals, ordering Army Group Center to use "fanatical resistance" to stem the tide until reinforcements could arrive. The next day a disgusted Hitler accepted von Brauchitsch's resignation and personally assumed command of the army. He told Halder that the army should emulate the positive, enthusiastic approach of the Luftwaffe, and he forbade any preparation or discussion of "rear positions" in the event of a Soviet breakthrough.[39]

Heinz Guderian was the next victim. Like many field commanders before December 1941 and thereafter, he was convinced that higher headquarters were out of touch with the real gravity of the situation. Throughout December he had used Hitler's personal adjutant and other acquaintances as back-door channels to convey his concerns to Hitler and the OKH. On 14 December, one of von Brauchitsch's last acts as commander of the Army had been to place Second Army under the control of Second Panzer Army and to authorize Guderian to withdraw so long as he held Orel. Ordered to stand fast, Guderian flew back to Rastenburg on 20 December to explain his desperate situation to Hitler. Although the general's account of this conversation naturally is biased, he undoubtedly insisted his forces lacked clothing, equipment, and shelter, and needed to withdraw to more defensible lines. On Christmas Day, after a final pointless argument with his new army group commander, von Kluge, Guderian in turn found himself relieved.[40]

WIDENING THE OFFENSIVE

By 1 January 1942, Soviet forces had retaken Kalinin in the North and Kaluga in the South and were besieging a series of German strongholds, some of which had already been bypassed and surrounded. Demiansk (in Army Group North's sector), Rzhev, Mozhaisk, Maloiaroslavets, Iukhnov, and a number of other communications centers were crowded with a mixture of German combat and support troops trying to survive both the weather and the Soviet attacks. At this point, Hitler issued his famous order to stand fast. The success of this order in 1942 encouraged him to hold every inch of ground irrationally for the remainder of the war. What Hitler never recognized was that the Soviet counteroffensive of 1941–1942 might well have destroyed Army Group Center had not Stalin tried to do too much too fast.

In January 1942 I. V. Stalin was incredibly overambitious and optimistic. The contrast between the desperation of November and the success of December had encouraged him so much that he attempted to expand his initial counterattacks into a general offensive to encircle all of Army Group Center and a sizeable portion of Army Group North. Stalin was convinced that the Germans were on their last legs, and he attempted to rush into an exploitation phase without concentrating his forces and eliminating bypassed units. On 7 January, Stalin ordered a general offensive along the entire front, concentrated primarily against Army Group Center but also targeting German forces at Leningrad, Staraia Russa, Orel, Khar'kov, and the Crimea.[41] Zhukov and other commanders opposed the general offensive on the grounds that it would dissipate available forces over too wide a frontage. Stalin's initial success depended on a handful of tank brigades, cavalry divisions, and ski battalions, all of which were losing strength rapidly. As the Soviet troops struggled westward, the supporting Red Air Force had to give up its permanent, heated airfields, moving to forward air strips that were as inhospitable as those occupied by the Luftwaffe. By biting off more than his forces could chew, Stalin failed to eliminate the encircled German forces in front of Moscow and made only limited gains elsewhere.

In the North, the attempt to cut off German Eighteenth Army around Leningrad never really got off the ground. South of Leningrad, Stalin intimidated Meretskov, Volkhov Front commander, (recently released from NKVD custody), into a premature attack. Meretskov's troops were dispersed, untrained, and poorly supplied. The head of the Soviet Main

Artillery Administration had to fly in personally with an airplane full of artillery gun sights because Meretskov's newly produced guns had none. By the end of December, 2d Shock Army, the key force in the ensuing Liuban' operation, had assembled only one division. The army commander, Lieutenant General G. G. Sokolov, was an incompetent NKVD commissar and former deputy to L. Beria, head of the NKVD. Meretskov had Sokolov relieved for cause shortly after the Soviet attack commenced.

Although 52d Army penetrated the front, and 2d Shock Army successfully advanced 70 kilometers into the German rear, German counterattacks soon isolated and encircled the unfortunate force.[42] In March, Lieutenant General A. A. Vlasov, sent from Moscow to become Meretskov's deputy after Vlasov's splendid military performance in the Moscow counteroffensive, was sent into the encirclement to take command. Throughout months of arduous combat in frightening conditions, 2d Shock Army could neither be relieved nor could it break out. Finally, in late June, a final German operation to reduce the pocket forced Vlasov to surrender. His later cooperation with German authorities and attempts to raise a German "Russian Army" made him a traitor in Soviet eyes and virtually erased both mention of him and this incident in the history of 2d Shock Army from Soviet military accounts.[43]

In the Moscow region, Stalin ordered the Kalinin and Western Fronts to encircle German forces by attacks on Viaz'ma from the north, east, and south. Kalinin Front forces (22d, 39th, 29th, 31st, and 30th Armies, and 11th Cavalry Corps), commanded by Colonel General Konev, were to advance through Rzhev and Sychevka to the Viaz'ma region, while the left wing of Zhukov's Western Front (43d, 49th, and 50th Armies, and Cavalry Group Belov) destroyed the German Iukhnov group and advanced from the southwest to secure Viaz'ma and link up with Kalinin Front spearheads. Meanwhile, Western Front's right wing (1st Shock, 16th, and 20th Armies) was to penetrate German defenses near Volokolamsk and Gzhatsk, and 5th and 33d Armies would strike directly through Mozhaisk to Viaz'ma. The two cavalry forces of Belov (1st Guards Cavalry Corps and reinforcing tank brigades) and Colonel S. V. Sokolov (11th Cavalry Corps, reinforced) were to play critical roles by leading the exploitation into the German rear and linking up in the Viaz'ma area. Zhukov's aim was to destroy the four defending armies of Army Group Center (Ninth, Fourth, and Third and Fourth Panzer). The threat to the Germans was real, indeed; a gaping hole existed in German defenses south of Kaluga. Within days after the offensive commenced, Belov's cavalry group raced through this hole into the Germans' rear and toward Viaz'ma.[44]

To supplement this already imposing offensive effort, 3d and 4th Shock Armies, on the left flank of Colonel General P. A. Kurochkin's Northwestern Front, were ordered to strike from the forests near Ostashkov toward Toropets and Smolensk, while Colonel General Ia. T. Cherevichenko's Briansk Front launched attacks toward Orel and Briansk. Unfortunately for the Soviets, Zhukov was correct. Stalin's forces lacked both the strength and the skill to carry out this ambitious shallow and deep envelopment of Army Group Center.[45]

Terrain was especially important in this battle. There were only two paved major highways in this area, one running from Smolensk through Viaz'ma to Moscow and the other running diagonally southwest from Moscow through Maloiaroslavets and Iukhnov. Forces such as Major General M. G. Efremov's 33d Army that moved on or parallel to these main roads were much more mobile than the armies on their flanks, which tended to fall behind in the offensive. Once they succeeded in penetrating, Belov's group and other large Soviet formations survived in the German rear area for months because the terrain was so swampy and impassible that the Germans were unable to flush them out until the ground dried out in late spring.

The Kalinin and Western Fronts began the wider offensive with a phased series of attacks from 7 through 9 January. In the north, Lieutenant General I. I. Maslennikov's 39th Army had sufficient strength to penetrate German defenses and begin an advance into the rear with its mobile group, Sokolov's 11th Cavalry Corps, far in advance. This cavalry corps almost reached the Smolensk-Moscow highway in late January, but German Ninth Army, in an audacious February counterattack, closed off the penetration behind them and 39th Army, encircling Major General V. I. Shvetsov's accompanying 29th Army in the process. With only two light cavalry divisions, a motorized rifle division, and a few ski battalions, 11th Cavalry Corps was too weak to cut the German lines of communications.

In the center, the Soviets were able to retake Mozhaisk and Medyn, but thereafter their forces were so weak and the weather so bad that the subsequent advance toward Gzhatsk took place at a snail's pace. Only Efremov's 33d Army was able to penetrate into the German rear, ultimately reaching the suburbs of Viaz'ma, where half of its divisions were also cut off and isolated by a German counterattack.[46]

Meanwhile to the north, Kurochkin's Northwestern Front smashed German defenses in the Valdai Hills and Lake Seliger sector and swept southwestward along two separate axes to the outskirts of Staraia Russa and Demidov, leaving encircled or semi-encircled German pockets in their wake at Demiansk, Kholm', and Belyi.[47] To the south, for months Briansk Front forces pounded away in vain at German forces defending forward of Orel.[48]

In the far south, the Soviets conducted two operations which they hoped to exploit further in the spring. South of Khar'kov, on 18 January, the combined forces of Lieutenant General F. Ia. Kostenko's Southwestern Front and Lieutenant General R. Ia. Malinovsky's Southern Front struck hard at the junction of Army Group South's Sixth and Seventeenth Armies in an attempt to cross the Northern Donets River and envelop Khar'kov from the south. The initial surprise assault by Major General A. M. Gorodniansky's 6th and Lieutenant General D. I. Riabyshev's 57th Army, with 1st, 5th, and 6th Cavalry Corps, exploited to a depth of up to 100 kilometers. The staying power of Soviet infantry and cavalry was limited, however; by 31 January, von Bock's army group had been able to contain the offensive by patching together a cordon of small infantry and armored task forces around what came to be known as the Barvenkovo bridgehead.[49]

Somewhat earlier, on 30 December, the combined forces of the Black Sea Fleet and two armies of the Transcaucasus Front had commenced an ambitious amphibious operation to seize a foothold on the Kerch Peninsula on the Crimea. Their goal was to relieve the Sevastopol' garrison, then under siege by von Manstein's German Eleventh Army and accompanying Rumanian forces. The initial Soviet landing was made by Major General A. N. Pervushin's 44th Army and Lieutenant General V. N. L'vov's 51st Army, supported by the fleet and by ineffective airborne diversionary raids. The Soviets succeeded in routing the defending Rumanian divisions and securing both Kerch and Feodosiia. Von Manstein reacted rapidly, bottling the Soviets up at the western exit from the peninsula and preventing the relief of Sevastopol'. After a siege of over eight months, Sevastopol' ultimately fell on 4 July 1942.[50]

With the front aflame for a distance of over 800 kilometers, the struggle reduced to individual unit heroics, complex off-road maneuvers, and simple battles of attrition on both sides. The Soviets often held the impenetrable countryside, while the Germans clung fast to the cities, villages, and key arteries. Try as they might, neither side was able to budge the other until nature gave the more mobile Germans the advantage in June 1942. Nowhere was this frustrating process more clear than in the Viaz'ma region.

PARACHUTES IN THE SNOW

Given the paucity of mobile armored forces, Stalin threw into the struggle virtually all of his specialized mobile troops, including tank brigades (attached to cavalry corps or serving as the nucleus of army mobile groups), cavalry corps, ski battalions, and, most important, his elite airborne forces. Sheer necessity required these fragile forces to attempt missions that hitherto had been performed by heavy mechanized forces.

In early January, Stalin began committing to combat those portions of his once proud five-corps airborne force that had survived the first few months of war (essentially 4th and 5th Airborne Corps and portions of other reconstituted corps). These forces were to facilitate the advance of *front* forces, assist Soviet forces that had already penetrated into the German rear, and interdict, in concert with numerous diversionary teams, German logistical and communications lines. Ultimately, their mission changed to helping encircled Soviet forces survive and regain the safety of Soviet lines.

The first airborne drops, conducted in multiregimental strength, assisted the advance of 33d and 43d Armies. On 3–4 January, two parachute insertions interdicted the roads just west of Medyn; these units linked up with the advancing ground troops in a few days. On 18 January, 250th Airborne Regiment dropped into the swampy area of the Ugra River bend. From this relatively inaccessible base of operations, it advanced southwest and, on 30 January, helped Belov's 1st Guards Cavalry Corps cross the Iukhnov highway despite the system of mobile patrols and fortified villages that the Germans had established to control the road. In order to accomplish this crossing, however, Belov had to commit one of his two rifle divisions and two ski battalions to create the penetration. He then passed his cavalry through the resulting gap to make contact with the airborne regiment. The defenders closed the gap behind him, separating 1st Guards Cavalry Corps from its attached infantry and most of its artillery.

Thus by late January, the Soviets had achieved several penetrations but had been unable to totally destroy major German formations. In an effort to regain his momentum and capture Viaz'ma, Zhukov planned a much more significant parachute operation, committing the 10,000 men of 4th Airborne Corps in a series of night drops west of that city.[51] However, Soviet logistical weakness plagued this operation from its inception. In order to deploy from Moscow to forward airfields near Kaluga, the 4th Airborne Corps had to conduct a winter river crossing because the key bridge over the Oka River had not been restored. A shortage of transport aircraft meant that the corps could be dropped only over a series of days, damaging any hopes for surprise. Moreover, the elite parachutists were among the very few units that had been issued white winter camouflage garments, and so their appearance near the Kaluga airfields immediately suggested the possibility of an airborne operation. Once the landings began on the night of 27 January, the Germans were able to identify and bomb the airfields involved, which the Luftwaffe had occupied until a few weeks before.

Between 27 January and 1 February, Lieutenant Colonel A. A. Onu-friev's 8th Airborne Brigade landed in a scattered pattern southwest of Viaz'ma. Some of these landings were deliberately intended as small diversions, but the main drops were plagued by bad weather and poor navigation, with much of the equipment, supplies, and radios being lost in the deep snow. Ultimately, only 1,300 of the 2,100 men in this brigade rallied to the brigade commander. The result was, at best, a distraction rather than a major threat to the Germans, and the landings were canceled before the remaining two brigades of 4th Airborne Corps were dropped.

Meanwhile, 1st Guards and 11th Cavalry Corps attempted to envelop Viaz'ma from the southwest and north. For a few hours on 27 January and for more extended periods later, 1st Guards Cavalry Corps and 8th Airborne Brigade. fought see-saw battles for control of segments of the Smolensk-Moscow highway, but these attempts to cut the critical artery ultimately failed. Viaz'ma and its surrounding roads were protected by the surviving elements of 5th and 11th Panzer Divisions, a force that was still formidable to the airborne and cavalry raiders who lacking armor and artillery. Neither Belov's 1st Guards Cavalry Corps and 8th Airborne Brigade nor Efremov's four encircled divisions of 33d Army had enough mass to displace the Germans.

With these two forces and 8th Airborne Brigade in danger of piecemeal defeat, and with the overall Soviet seizure of Viaz'ma in jeopardy, in mid-February Zhukov again attempted to use 4th Airborne Corps to break the stalemate. This time a landing zone was selected along the Ugra River in the same swampy terrain that 250th Airborne Regiment had found so useful in discouraging German rear area protection operations. On the night of 17–18 February, 4th Airborne Corps began another series of parachute drops, again hampered by shortages of transport aircraft and fighter cover. Of the 7,400 parachutists who took off that week, no more than 70 percent ever reached their assembly points. The corps com-mander, Major General V. A. Glazunov, and much of his staff were killed when a German night fighter shot down their airplane. The chief of staff assumed command, attempting to seize the high ground along the Iukhnov highway to facilitate an attack across the highway by Boldin's 50th Army. The result was again stalemate. Despite repeated efforts from February through May, 4th Airborne Corps lacked the vehicles and heavy weapons to accomplish its mission. On the other hand, the Germans were unable to break into the swampy Ugra area to eliminate this force.[52]

The frustrations of 4th Airborne Corps and of Belov's 1st Guards Cavalry Corps were symptomatic of the problems that plagued the entire Soviet offensive. Despite a remarkable performance, the Red Army simply lacked the strength, vehicle mobility, fire support, logistical train, and communications necessary to destroy Army Group Center. Nevertheless, Stalin remained unshakably optimistic and continued to believe that victory was within his grasp until the Soviet Moscow offensive expired in April 1942. Elsewhere along the front, Stalin expended airborne forces near Demiansk, Rzhev, and in the Crimea, with little effect.

If Stalin drew the wrong conclusions from the battles around Moscow, Hitler's conclusions were equally false. The German forces had survived not because of the "stand fast" order but because the Soviets had attempted more than they could accomplish. Similarly, the Luftwaffe's ability to resupply bypassed encircled German strongholds at Kholm', Demiansk, and south of Viaz'ma gave Hitler an exaggerated confidence in the possibilities of aerial resupply. Both of these misconceptions came home to roost a year later at Stalingrad.

CHAPTER 7

Rasputitsa, Spring 1942

Although the winter campaign was not formally terminated until 20 April 1942, and Soviet troops remained behind German lines in the Viaz'ma and other regions until June 1942, all chances for the Moscow counteroffensive to achieve its ambitious objectives had evaporated by early March. The Soviets mercilessly pounded German troops encircled in the Demiansk pocket and in Kholm', while paratroopers and ski brigades waged an intense struggle to collapse the Demiansk pocket from within. In the Viaz'ma region, General P. A. Belov's cavalry and airborne troops sought valiantly to escape isolation in the German rear. Soviet-initiated military operations slowed during the next several months and finally stopped as the *Stavka* began preparing for renewed struggle in the summer.

The spring thaw and *rasputitsa* arrived in the Ukraine in early March and appeared in the Moscow area about two weeks later, derailing German plans to encircle and destroy several Soviet armies in a salient between Army Group North and Army Group Center. The prolonged struggle to relieve German Sixteenth and Ninth Army forces encircled at Demiansk and Kholm' ended in a virtual draw during April, with the relieving force arriving just as the Soviets broke into the encirclement. It is therefore appropriate to pause in this narrative to consider Soviet and German institutional responses to the experience of 1941.

THE WIDER WAR

Throughout the summer and fall of 1941, Great Britain and the United States had watched the progress of Operation Barbarossa, fearing Soviet collapse. Even if the United States had become a formal belligerent, neither country had the forces available to provide an effective diversion by invading western Europe. The average Soviet citizen, and indeed most of the Soviet government, exaggerated British strength and American industrial mobilization while minimizing the difficulties of an amphibious operation. As early as July, the Moscow government encouraged public calls for a British "second front" in the West. Stalin, who until 22 June had believed that Hitler would never risk a two-front war, was impatient for this risk to become a reality. Thus from the very beginning of the Soviet-German conflict, Soviet public opinion suspected that the Western powers were shirking their responsibility and allowing the Wehrmacht and Red Army to bleed each other to death. London and Washington did promise extensive economic aid, but the difficulties of wartime transportation meant that little of this aid arrived during the first year of the struggle in the East.[1]

On 7 December 1941, while Hitler was purging his generals and G. I. Zhukov was trying to destroy Army Group Center, the Japanese attacked the United States in Hawaii and the Philippines. Washington responded by declaring war on Tokyo the next day, but American participation in the European struggle remained limited. Hard pressed in the Pacific, the United States was unprepared politically and militarily for a two-front, global war.

Four days after Pearl Harbor, Adolf Hitler solved the American dilemma. In a speech to the Reichstag, Hitler defiantly declared war on the United States, even though his defensive alliance with Tokyo did not require such action. Undoubtedly, Hitler regarded this declaration as a mere formality after months of U.S. Navy participation in convoys and other antisubmarine actions in the North Atlantic. He apparently hoped that the Pacific War would distract the United States, reducing its contribution to the struggle with Germany. Certainly Hitler underestimated the potential for American industrial and military mobilization, a surprising mistake for a man who had presided over a similar mobilization in Germany during the 1930s. Still, this declaration proved to be as fatal for Germany as the Barbarossa invasion itself. Within six months, Germany had gone from undisputed mastery of the European continent to a desperate struggle with the two greatest powers on earth. The short-term Axis successes of 1941–1942 were eventually dwarfed by the Soviet and American attacks that Hitler had invited.

RESURGENCE OF SOVIET DOCTRINE

The process of Soviet adjustment to the challenges of war continued during the winter and spring of 1941–1942. Throughout 1941, most Soviet commanders had attempted to apply the prewar concept of the deep operation without having sufficient forces to achieve the necessary concentration at a critical point. In December 1941, Zhukov ordered the creation within the Western Front of shock groups to concentrate the few available full-strength units at specific weak points in the German defenses. Thus, for example, 10th Army focused its efforts on penetrating German defenses south of Moscow, and, in turn, 1st Guards Cavalry Corps leapfrogged through the breach created by 10th Army to exploit on a relatively narrow front. This technique, plus fresh troops from the Soviet eastern military districts, allowed the Moscow counteroffensive to achieve initial success. By January, however, the attackers were spread out and lacked the mobility to move faster than their German opponents during the exploitation. The promising Soviet counteroffensive drove the Germans from the immediate Moscow region but did not achieve the strategic goals set for it by the *Stavka*.

Although Stalin never admitted his failure to mass forces, the Red Army institutionalized such concentrations for future operations. *Stavka* Directive No. 03, dated 10 January 1942, repeated Zhukov's *front* order of the previous month. All *front* and army commanders were required to use shock groups for offensive action, focusing their forces on a narrow frontage to achieve overwhelming superiority of strength against a single German unit. Ideally, a *front*-level attack would now have a width of only 30 kilometers, while a rifle army would concentrate on only 15 kilometers. The equivalent frontages in December had been 400 and 80 kilometers, respectively. Thus began the slow process of creating overwhelming concentrations of forces to achieve initial penetrations at a few specific points. In conjunction with sophisticated deception plans, this Soviet technique later caused German officers to believe that they were hopelessly outnumbered along the entire front.[2]

In the same document, the *Stavka* also addressed the use of artillery. All future attacks were to be preceded by an artillery offensive. This meant not only concentrating up to 80 guns or mortars per kilometer of front but using those guns in three successive phases or missions. First, all available guns would concentrate on the prepared defenses along the enemy front line. Second, once the infantry and armor began moving forward to attack, the artillery would concentrate on remaining centers of enemy resistance to support the penetration. Finally, when the initial penetration had been achieved, the artillery would shift to deeper targets to support the exploitation of that penetration. The same directive also ordered the Red Air Force to use available ground-support aircraft for either preparation or accompanying fighter-bomber support of the penetration.[3]

Using artillery in this manner was little more than common sense, a conventional solution to the problems of the offensive. The very fact that the *Stavka* had to issue such a directive indicates the abysmal ignorance of some junior commanders at the time. Still, the artillery directive resulted in a significant improvement in the effective concentration and use of artillery. During 1941, an average kilometer of Soviet front line troops, even in the offensive, was supported by only 7 to 12 gun and mortar tubes. By the summer of 1942, this average had increased to between 45 and 65 tubes per kilometer. This was still far less than the densities achieved later in the war, but it represented another step in the rebirth of Soviet tactical principles and skills.

In addition to endorsing the concept of massing forces in depth for offensive breakthroughs and exploitation, Soviet commanders embraced the idea of density and depth in defensive systems. The successful defense of Moscow and Leningrad, in which dense, integrated trench systems were first used, set a precedent in the neglected field of defensive tactics. Antitank defenses, whereby minefields and antitank guns were designed to support each other, were finally established along the most likely avenues of enemy attack. In practice, of course, most commanders lacked the forces necessary to establish such defenses until 1943, but the concept and the first few tentative experiments were in place by the spring of 1942.

RESURGENCE OF SOVIET MECHANIZED FORCES

At the time, however, Stalin was not thinking about the defensive. The brief but heady taste of victory from December 1941 to January 1942 encouraged the Soviet dictator to believe that his opponents were vulnerable if the Red Army could mass sufficient mechanized forces to launch a renewed offensive in the summer of 1942.

New mechanized forces required new equipment. Despite the enormous dislocation involved in relocating its industry, the Soviet Union was already beginning to out-produce German factories. By a phenomenal effort, the factories in the Urals and the Transcaucasus produced 4,500 tanks, 3,000 aircraft, 14,000 guns, and over 50,000 mortars before active operations resumed in May 1942.

Using this sudden wealth, especially the tanks, was the task of Colonel General Ia. N. Fedorenko, a permanent member of the *Stavka* and chief of the Armored Forces Administration. During the desperate defensive battles of 1941, the only new mechanized forces created in the Red Army had been small tank brigades that lacked accompanying infantry and often fought in an infantry-support role. During the lull of early 1942, however, Fedorenko sought to return to prewar concepts and organization. In order to match the German panzer forces, Fedorenko resurrected the idea of independent, combined-armed mechanized units. Beginning in March 1942, he formed tank and, later, mechanized corps that were actually equivalent to German divisions. The first four such tank corps consisted of two tank brigades, one truck-mounted rifle brigade, and very little else, with a total strength of 5,603 men and 100 tanks (20 KV, 40 T-34, and 40 T-60). Almost immediately, however, Fedorenko decided to add a third tank brigade, plus various combat support elements necessary for sustained combined-arms operations. By July 1942, a typical tank corps included three tank brigades of 53 tanks each (32 medium and 21 light), one motorized rifle brigade, a motorcycle reconnaissance battalion, a mortar battalion, a multiple-rocket launcher (guards mortar) battalion, an antiaircraft battalion, a sapper (combat engineer) company, and, somewhat later, a transportation company and two mobile repair bases. The total authorized strength of this organization was 7,800 men, 98 T-34 medium tanks, and 70 other, lighter tanks.[4] Ultimately, 28 such tank corps were created in 1942.[5]

In September 1942, Fedorenko elaborated on this concept by forming larger mechanized corps. Based on the heavy losses to infantry during the tank corps' summer battles, he gave the mechanized corps three mechanized brigades, each with one tank regiment, one or two tank brigades, and up to two additional tank regiments. Each mechanized brigade's tank regiment included 39 tanks. These maneuver brigades were supported by antiaircraft, antitank, multiple-rocket launcher, and armored car battalions, as well as communications, engineer (sapper), medical, transportation, and maintenance elements. The result was a force of 13,559 men, 100 T-34s, and up to 104 other tanks.[6] A 1942-style mechanized corps was fully equivalent to a panzer division but should not be confused with the much larger mechanized corps of 1940–1941. This new formation used so many scarce resources that only eight mechanized corps were formed during 1942.

Both tank corps and mechanized corps were ideally designed to act as the mobile group of a rifle army, making small-scale, limited penetrations and encirclements of up to 100 kilometers in depth. In order to create major disruptions and encirclements, however, the Red Army needed something larger, a true combined-arms mechanized force equivalent to the panzer corps and armies.

Such an organization represented not just an imitation of the Germans but, more important, a return to the prewar concept of the deep operation. On 25 May 1942, the Commissariat directed that some of the newly created tank corps would be united into two tank armies (3d and 5th). Two additional tank armies (1st and 4th) were formed in July 1942, but these were thrown into battle on the approaches to Stalingrad before their organization was complete, and both were severely damaged and quickly reformed into rifle armies. The actual structure of these tank armies varied widely because they were experimental at a time when the Red Army still had severe shortages of basic equipment, such as trucks. These shortages necessitated that cavalry and rifle infantry divisions be combined with the more mobile tank corps. Insofar as any pattern existed, a 1942 tank army included two or three tank corps, one cavalry corps, and two to six rifle divisions, with some supporting units. Their average strength was 35,000 men, 350 to 500 tanks, and 150 to 200 larger towed artillery pieces.[7]

The debut of these new tank corps and tank armies during May 1942 proved to be a disaster, as discussed in chapter 8. Again, however, the Red Army learned from its combat experience, creating more effective organizations and tactics by the end of 1942. During 1943, Fedorenko elaborated upon the mechanized force structure, forming new tank armies with virtually uniform organization that spearheaded Soviet offensives for the rest of the war.

During spring 1942, the Red Army devoted its available resources to rebuilding the mobile forces and a few privileged Guards divisions.[8] The average rifle division, however, gained only some additional heavy weapons and the return of a few hundred veterans who had recovered from their wounds. When mobile operations began again, the Red Army was still a mixture of understrength veteran units and new, untried formations.

REBUILDING THE WEHRMACHT

The Barbarossa campaign had proved almost as destructive for the German Army and Air Force as for their Red counterparts. The German forces had been seriously overextended even before they fell prey to the Russian winter and the Moscow counteroffensive.

Army Group Center had suffered the most. By January, thinly clad, shell-shocked, and disoriented troops tended to panic at the mere sound of approaching Soviet tanks. Frost, malnutrition, exposure, and battle produced both physical and mental casualties, and the losses in men and matériel far exceeded replacements. At the end of January 1942, Army Group Center was 187,000 troops short of its authorized strength, and it suffered an additional net loss of 40,000 in February. The retreat from Moscow had meant abandoning large amounts of equipment that might otherwise have been repaired or salvaged. On 31 January, Army Group Center's shortages totaled 4,262 antitank guns, 5,890 mortars, and 3,361 larger artillery pieces.[9]

Germany had neither the manpower nor the production capacity to make good on these losses. In December 1941, an additional 282,300 conscripts entered the army, but they all needed training and two thirds had come from the armaments industry. German factories experienced great difficulty in making up for the lost manpower. Italian and French workers were reluctant to work in Germany for fear of RAF night bombing raids. Russian forced laborers were supposed to replace agricultural workers who were needed in the factories, but due to the general transportation shortage and the calculated abuse that the prisoners had suffered at German hands, they were largely unavailable. The weakened survivors who arrived in Germany fell prey to a typhus epidemic.[10]

This labor shortage, combined with fuel problems, raw material deficiencies, and the continued competition between the armed services for available production, almost brought German production to a standstill during December 1941 to January 1942. On 10 January, Hitler issued a new set of production priorities, subordinating his grand plans for new mechanized and expeditionary forces to the need to replace equipment for the field armies. This order marked his belated recognition that Germany was engaged in a long war. On 21 March, Hitler officially subordinated the entire economy to war requirements.

Dr. Fritz Todt, the competent but self-effacing minister for armaments and munitions, died in an airplane crash on 8 February. He was succeeded by Albert Speer, Hitler's favorite architect and a man of some experience in the problems of production. With Hitler's personal backing, Speer achieved significant increases in efficiency and productivity, but he did so without centralizing and rationalizing German industry. Instead, Speer set up a series of coordinating committees, in which the long-time industrialists of the Reich cooperated to manage critical materials and increase production. Marshal Erhard Milch, the long-suffering state secretary who did most of Hermann Goering's work at the Air Ministry, worked closely with Speer in these endeavors. Milch used recycling and other methods to compensate for shortages in raw materials. In 1942, for example, German industry produced 3,780 more aircraft than in the previous year, while using 15,000 fewer tons of aluminum.[11]

These reforms took time, however, and in fact the Wehrmacht was never fully reequipped after the disastrous battles of Moscow. Army Group South, which was designated to conduct the main German attack in 1942, brought its units up to 85 percent of their authorized equipment only by forced transfers from the other two army groups. During November to December 1941, OKH had gathered several thousand trucks from Germany and the occupied territories in the West, but three quarters of these vehicles broke down before they reached the Russian theater. The losses in vehicles and horses forced Army Groups Center and North to begin the 1942 campaign with severely curtailed mobility, especially when operating on largely unpaved roads. Without horses, the available artillery and supply columns were also significantly handicapped.

As with the Red Army, elite German units received enough men and matériel to bring them back to strength. The remnants of the *Grossdeutschland* Infantry Regiment, which at one time was reduced to only 33 riflemen, were withdrawn to the rear to rest and refit. By the end of May, the *Grossdeutschland* had expanded into a lavishly equipped motorized division, with two motorized infantry regiments, an artillery regiment, and battalions of tanks, assault guns, and motorcyclists. The average panzer or motorized division did not fare as well but still regained much of its combat power. Waffen SS units continued to expand and acquire more armor. In general, First and Fourth Panzer Armies had regained a measure of their former strength by the time active operations resumed that summer. For the typical infantry division, however, the winter of 1941–1942 was only the first stop in a long, painful loss of combat power.

The German Army had lost more than soldiers and vehicles; it had suffered a severe blow to its morale. Most of the surviving veterans recognized that they were committed to an open-ended, bitter struggle in an alien land. Desertion and surrender were impossible, since either might lead to unspeakable torture at the hands of a seemingly inhuman foe. The front line soldiers increasingly sought assurances that they were fighting in a just and necessary cause. To provide such assurances, their officers turned to the official Nazi propaganda line of racial and ideological struggle. On 15 July 1942, OKW regularized this process by ordering the assignment of an education or indoctrination officer to all intelligence staffs. As they became accustomed to talking in ideological terms, the German junior officers and soldiers were also more inclined to commit atrocities against the Slavic *Untermenschen*. Paradoxically, the Soviet-German struggle led the Soviets to de-emphasize ideology in favor of nationalism, while it prompted the German Army to embrace a Soviet-styled system of political officers and indoctrination.[12]

SPRING PLANS

With the coming of the spring thaw, both sides planned for the summer campaign. There was no doubt that Germany would renew its offensive, and the Soviet Union could not afford to conduct a full-scale counteroffensive to forestall the Germans. However, Joseph Stalin again misread Germany's intentions and his own strength, in part because of an elaborate and effective German deception plan, code-named "Operation Kremlin," which portrayed Germany's intent to strike on the Moscow axis.[13] He was convinced that Moscow remained the principal German objective and believed that the bypassed German hedgehogs in the Rzhev and Viaz'ma regions would serve as the starting points for such an advance. Most of the Red Army's strategic reserves, supervised by General G. K. Zhukov, were therefore held in the Moscow region.

Instead, Hitler decided to concentrate in the south, seeking to control the economic resources of the Volga River region and the Caucasus oil fields. German planners expected that the Soviets would again accept decisive battle to defend these regions. This, in turn, would give the Wehrmacht another opportunity to destroy the Red Army. Initially, however, the industrial city of Stalingrad was only one of a number of objectives that might force the Soviets to stand and fight. Only later did the city acquire a symbolic value for both sides, diverting German efforts away from the main drive to the Caucasus.

In an attempt to break up the anticipated German offensive, Stalin decided on a series of local, limited operations in late spring. General Zhukov and other commanders again objected to such plans, rightly fearing that it would dissipate their troop strength without decisive results. The dictator, however, remained incurably optimistic about the relative strength and resilience of Soviet versus German troops.

In mid-March 1942, Marshal S. K. Timoshenko and the staff of the Southwestern Direction, including N. S. Khrushchev and the chief of staff, Colonel General I. Kh. Bagramian, proposed two offensives against German Army Group South to spoil German preparations for the Moscow thrust, using Southwestern Front forces and Soviet forces in the Crimea. In the first instance, Timoshenko planned a pincer movement against German positions around Khar'kov, with the Southwestern Front's right wing attacking from bridgeheads across the Northern Donets River northeast of Khar'kov and the Front's left wing attacking Khar'kov from the larger Barvenkovo bridgehead across the Northern Donets, which the Soviets had secured during the winter offensive. Southern Front would support the advance. These pincers would encircle most of German Fourth Panzer Army and Sixth Army, then push westward to the Dnepr River.

At first Stalin considered using Briansk Front to reinforce the offensive, but, after reflection, he decided to withhold the Briansk Front to help deal with the anticipated German offensive on Moscow. As a result, the *Stavka* restricted Timoshenko's effort to a single thrust by the Southwestern and Southern Fronts. Meanwhile, Lieutenant General F. I. Golikov's Briansk Front prepared a local offensive farther north, completely disconnected from Timoshenko's effort.[14] This was the origin of the second battle for Khar'kov, the first trial of the new Soviet armored units, as described in chapter 8.

Stalin planned a second thrust against German forces in the Crimea to relieve the beleaguered Soviet garrison at Sevastopol'. This offensive would emanate from positions on the Kerch Peninsula, which Soviet forces had seized in the audacious winter amphibious operation.

In the north, the *Stavka* launched two local counterattacks to protect the Murmansk railroad, the lifeline for shipping Allied equipment to the rest of the front. Finnish and German troops had failed to cut this railroad during 1941, due in part to Hitler's order on 10 October halting the attacks because he believed the Soviets were on the verge of collapse. Once the Finns had recovered their pre-1940 territories, they were reluctant to continue the offensive. As winter lingered on in the Arctic, the Soviet Karelian Front achieved some success against isolated German units. Because of the difficulties of terrain, weather, and logistics, the forces involved on both sides were far smaller than those in the epic struggles to the south.

In the far north, southwest of Murmansk, Soviet 26th Army forces attacked German XIX Mountain Corps on 28 April 1942. Two ski brigades and the 10th Guards Rifle Division struck the German 6th Mountain Division, while a simultaneous landing by 12th Naval Infantry Brigade attacked the other German flank. The attacking forces suffered heavily because they were not coordinated and concentrated, but the Germans were too weak in the region to exploit their defensive success. Farther south, opposite central Finland, Soviet 14th Army forces attacked the German-Finnish III Corps. Beginning on 23 April, 14th Army sent another ski brigade and a guards rifle division in a vast arc, turning the northern flank of the defending Germans and threatening to cut off their supply line. Again, Soviet forces were too weak and overextended to complete the job. On 5 to 7 May, they were encircled and virtually destroyed. The spring thaw then brought immobility to the region.[15]

CHAPTER 8

Operation Blau: The German Drive on Stalingrad

PLANNING FOR OPERATION BLAU

From the inception of Operation Barbarossa, German planners had envisaged a follow-up campaign down the eastern side of the Black Sea to the Caucasus Mountains.[1] (See Map 7.) Originally, this operation was to begin in the fall of 1941 as the first step in Hitler's grand scheme to envelop Asia Minor and the Middle East. His ultimate objectives were the Suez Canal and the oil-rich region of Iran and Iraq. In November 1941 the German dictator made some concessions towards the reality of the situation. He instructed General Franz Halder to confine the projected operation to Soviet territory, rather than continuing onward into Iran and Turkey. Even this "limited" operation, intended to seize control of the Soviet oil fields in the Caucasus, would require German troops to advance over difficult terrain for a further 800 kilometers beyond the farthest German spearhead at Rostov on the Don River. In anticipation of this, Hitler decided to form a special light infantry division and to withdraw the available mountain troops from combat and refit them for a new push.

In February 1942, the Operations Division of the Army High Command (OKH) issued a series of preliminary instructions for the 1942 campaign, whose principal objective was the seizure of the Caucasus. To this end, as described in chapter 7, Army Group South received priority for replacement troops and equipment. Fourth Panzer Army joined First Panzer Army in the south, bringing with it a number of refurbished divisions from Army Group Center.

In addition, 20 German and 21 other Axis divisions were moved from other theaters to the southern region. These Axis units, including 6 Italian, 10 Hungarian, and 5 understrength Rumanian divisions, generally had fewer weapons and less reliable equipment than their depleted German counterparts. Quite apart from the traditional German contempt for the courage of their allies, these troops in many instances had training and doctrine that was incompatible with those of their dominant partner. Only one Italian division was considered to be equivalent to an average German formation. Naturally enough, German staff officers relegated these allied forces to secondary roles—mopping up and securing the flanks

108

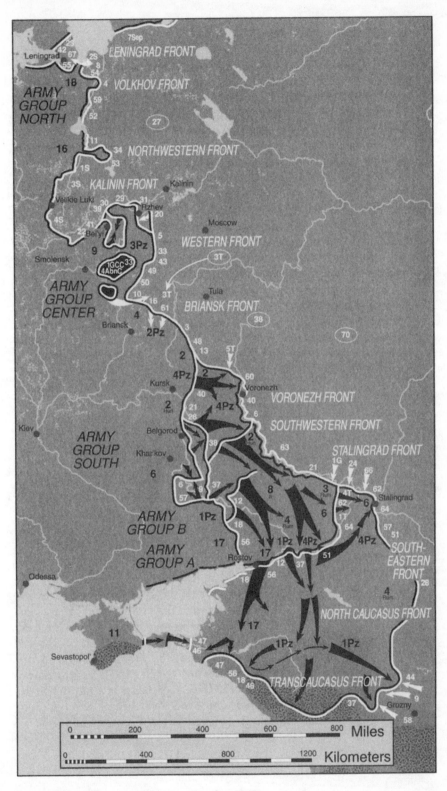

7. *Summer-Fall Campaign, May–October 1942*

behind the advancing German spearheads. The fact that OKH based its plans on such slender reeds illustrates the growing inadequacy of German forces to cover the vast distances of European Russia. Ultimately, the presence of these units and the immense scope of the planned offensive itself proved to be the Achilles' heel of the German plan.

German intelligence sources detected a Soviet troop concentration southeast of Khar'kov, apparently aimed at recapturing the Ukraine. Although the Germans failed to recognize the magnitude of these preparations, they correctly predicted that such an attack would probably begin in early May, after the spring *rasputitza*. OKH therefore planned to absorb the coming Soviet offensive before inaugurating its own drive to the southeast. In the interim, a German deception plan (Operation Kremlin) was implemented to convince the Soviets that the 1942 German offensive would be aimed at Moscow, with Army Group South limited to a feint toward Rostov. Unaware of the renaissance of the Soviet arms industry, German planners also focused on U.S. and British Lend-Lease supplies as a key ingredient for Red Army success in 1942. The advance to the Caucasus would eventually eliminate any possibility of Allied aid reaching the Soviet Union from that direction, but the northern route remained open. On 14 March 1942, therefore, OKW ordered the Luftwaffe and the navy to concentrate their efforts in Scandinavia in an effort to interdict Allied convoys bringing equipment to Murmansk.

In Fuehrer Directive No. 41, dated 5 April 1942, Hitler put his own stamp on the OKH plan, which was renamed Operation Blau (Blue). The principal objective for 1942 remained the Caucasus region, with a secondary goal of capturing Leningrad.[2]

Prior to the main offensive, German forces would conduct a series of limited attacks on their own to consolidate various portions of the front. The most important of these preliminary operations would be to capture Sevastopol' and clear the Kerch Peninsula. The main offensive would then proceed in three phases. First, Army Group South would penetrate the Soviet defenses south of Kursk, conducting local encirclements to prevent the escape of any Soviet units. Next, Army Group South, redesignated Army Group B, would advance eastward into the bend in the Don River while establishing a strong flank defense towards the north. Again, a large encirclement was planned. Meanwhile, the newly created Army Group A, consisting of von Kleist's First Panzer Army, General Richard Ruoff's Seventeenth Army, and (under Ruoff's direction) the Third Rumanian Army, would press forward on the southern wing, crossing the Don near Rostov and then turning to link up with the other spearheads in a large encirclement in the region of Stalingrad. Once this encirclement was achieved, Army Group A would continue its exploitation to the southern oil region.

Although the great industrial city of Stalingrad was a significant objective in the plan, German commanders initially regarded it as a way station en route to the Caucasus oil fields. Only later did the city mesmerize the attention of both sides. With perfect hindsight, German commanders like Erich von Manstein later blamed Hitler for seeking two divergent objectives—Stalingrad and the Caucasus—thereby creating a confused command structure. Certainly the dictator's attempt to supervise the campaign personally was impractical. Still, the creation of two army group headquarters was almost inevitable, given the vast distances and troops involved. As the campaign progressed, Army Group B acquired more and more satellite troops to protect its long left flank along the Don River, to the point where the number of such subordinate armies exceeded the Army Group staff's span of effective control. Some German planners therefore sought to create a third headquarters, Army Group Don, to control that front, freeing the Army Group B staff to focus on the advance in the Stalingrad region. By the fall, Operation Blau was fighting in three different directions and lacked an overall headquarters to direct the campaign.[3] The resulting order of battle of opposing forces is shown in Table 8.1.

All this was in the future in April 1942. After the nightmare of winter warfare, the Wehrmacht began to regain its confidence along with new reinforcements. Although their forces were now weaker than those of 1941, most German commanders were still confident that they could finish off the Red Army in 1942.

SECOND KHAR'KOV

The ill-conceived Soviet spoiling attack that began in the Khar'kov region on 12 May played into German hands, offering up some of the most capable Soviet units for destruction even before Operation Blau began. In the long litany of Soviet trial and error, the Second Battle of Khar'kov was certainly among the most expensive learning experiences.[4]

The *Stavka* had picked a likely area for a limited offensive. Just south of Khar'kov, the Red Army held a large bulge westward, the Izium bridgehead over the Northern Donets River, which it had seized in heavy fighting during the Barvenkovo-Lozovaia operation the previous winter. To the northeast of the city, the Soviets held yet another small bridgehead across the river. This meant that Khar'kov, a key German railhead and logistical area, was somewhat vulnerable to encirclement.

The Southwestern Front's plan, issued on 10 April 1942, called for a double envelopment by simultaneous attacks from the northeast and

Table 8-1. Order of Battle, July 1942

Germany	Soviet Union
Army of Lapland (became Twentieth Mountain Army) (Gen. Eduard Dietl) Finnish Army	Karelian Front (Lt. Gen. V. A. Frolov) 14th, 19th, 26th, 32d, 7th Sep. Armies
Army Group North (Gen. George v. Kuechler) Sixteenth Army and Eighteenth Army (later Eleventh Army from Crimea)	Leningrad Front (Col. Gen. L. A. Govorov) 8th, 23d, 42d, 55th Armies Coastal Operational Group
Army Group Center (Fld. Mar. Guenther v. Kluge) Fourth and Ninth Army Second and Third Panzer Armies	Volkhov Front (Col. Gen. K. A. Meretskov) 4th, 52d, 54th, 59th Armies
Army Group B (Fld. Mar. Fedor v. Boch, succeeded by Gen. Maximilian v. Weichs) Second and Sixth Armies, Fourth Panzer Army, and Third Hungarian Army	Northwestern Front (Col. Gen. P. A. Kurochkin) 1st Shock, 11th, 34th, 53d Armies
Eighth Italian Army (later, Third and Fourth Rumanian Armies)	Kalinin Front (Col. Gen. I. S. Konev) 3d Shock, 4th Shock, 22d, 29th, 30th, 39th Armies
Army Group A (Fld. Mar. Wilhelm List) Seventeenth Army First Panzer Army	Western Front (Col. Gen. G. K. Zhukov) 5th, 10th, 16th, 20th, 31st, 33d, 43d, 49th, 50th, 61st Armies
	Briansk Front (Lt. Gen. F. I. Golokov) 3d, 13th, 48th Armies 5th Tank Army (+ 5 tank corps)
	Voronezh Front (formed 7 July 1942) (Col. Gen. N. F. Vatutin) 6th, 40th, 60th Armies
	Southwestern Front (became Stalingrad Front, 12 July) (Mar. S. K. Timoshenko) 1st and 4th Tank Armies (four armies added later)
	Southern Front (inactivated 28 July— forces to North Caucasus Front) (Lt. Gen. R. Ia. Malinovsky)
	North Caucasus Front (Mar. S. M. Budenny) 12th, 18th, 24th, 37th, 51st, 56th, 57th Armies

Table 8-1 (*Continued*). Significant alterations in the July order of battle were caused by the destructiveness of combat and Soviet transformation of existing and reserve armies. Renumbering of formations developed as follows:

Old Army Designation	New Army Designation	Effective Date
1st Reserve	64th	10 July 42
2d Reserve	63d	May 43
3d Reserve	60th	10 July 42
4th Reserve	38th	Aug. 42
5th Reserve	63d	10 July 42
6th Reserve	6th	June 42
7th Reserve	62d	10 July 42
8th Reserve	66th	Aug. 42
9th Reserve	24th	Aug. 42
10th Reserve	5th Shock	Dec. 42
38th	1st Tank	(July 42)
28th	4th Tank	(July 42); 65th (Oct. 42)
58th	3d Tank	(May 42)
	5th Tank	(May 42)
	27th	(May 42)
	53d	(Apr. 42)
	70th	(Oct. 42)
63d	1st Guards	(Aug. 42); 24th (Oct. 42)
	2d Guards	(Aug. 42)
1st Guards	3d Guards	(Dec. 42)

Note: Formation date is given in parentheses.

southwest sides of the city.[5] To the northeast, the first objective was to penetrate elaborate German defenses containing the Soviet bridgehead on the eastern bank of the Northern Donets. To this end, Lieutenant General D. I. Riabyshev's 28th Army and Lieutenant General V. N. Gordov's 21st Army concentrated six rifle divisions and four tank brigades in a narrow, 15-kilometer sector facing German XVII Army Corps. Neighboring units, notably Lieutenant General K. S. Moskalenko's 38th Army to the south of 28th Army, would conduct supporting attacks. Once the forward German defenses were breached, Major General V. D. Kriuchenkin's 3d Guards Cavalry Corps, consisting of three cavalry divisions and a motorized rifle brigade, would pass through the resulting gap and push into the German rear area to encircle Khar'kov from the north.

The southern arm of the encircling pincers comprised Lieutenant General A. M. Gorodniansky's 6th Army and an ad hoc, army-sized group named for its commander, Major General L. V. Bobkin. Both were in the bridgehead bulging to the west. The 6th Army had eight rifle divisions, four tank brigades, and numerous additional artillery units to penetrate thinly spread German VIII Army Corps. Again, once the penetration had begun, mobile forces would pass through the attacking infantry to exploit the situation. Two of the newly organized mobile formations, Major General G. I. Kuz'min's 21st and Major General E. G. Pushkin's 23d Tank Corps, would punch northward to link up with 28th Army's 3d Guards Cavalry Corps. To protect the left flank of this advance, Group Bobkin was to make a supporting attack, allowing Major General A. A. Noskov's 6th Cavalry Corps to pass through the German lines. This cavalry corps was intended to form the outer layer of the Khar'kov encirclement, halting German counterattacks.

Unfortunately, Stalin, the *Stavka*, and Marshal S. K. Timoshenko were all operating under the assumption that their German opponents were still the understrength, immobilized skeletons of the previous winter. Convinced that the main German effort would occur in the Moscow region, the Soviets seriously misjudged both the strength and the mobility of their rejuvenated opponents in the south. Soviet reconnaissance had not detected the movement of new German formations into the Khar'kov region and, therefore, underestimated the strength of the enemy defense. Southwestern Front expected to find only 12 German infantry divisions and 1 panzer division in the region, whereas the actual strength of the two German corps included 16 infantry divisions, 2 refurbished panzer divisions, and 3 smaller infantry battle groups. In addition, the Southwestern Front paid little attention to the Seventeenth Army, which was in a position to attack 6th Army and Group Bobkin from the south. The Southern Front, opposite Seventeenth Army, provided no intelligence to its neighbor.

The Red Army's inexperience in offensive operations was repeatedly demonstrated during April as it struggled to prepare for the planned offensive. The spring *rasputitza* hampered not only the movement of units but also the construction of supply roads and forward airfields. As there was no overall plan for repositioning units into their attack positions, endless delays and mistakes occurred. Only 17 of the 32 non-divisional artillery regiments assigned to support the offensive were in position to begin the attack on 12 May. The 3d Guards Cavalry Corps, the designated mobile exploitation force for the northern attack, did not gather all its forces in the designated assembly area until 15 May, three days *after* the offensive had begun. Meanwhile, the high levels of activity in the region during April attracted the attention of German aerial reconnaissance units, and the Luftwaffe constantly interdicted river crossings and other chokepoints. For all these reasons, the Southwestern Front was unable to assemble adequate supplies to support the attack. Only about one third of the ammunition planned for the initial artillery barrage was on hand.

As a result, the main attack by 21st and 28th Armies achieved only limited success on 12 May, and even this gain was soon jeopardized by German counterattacks. General Friedrich Paulus, the commander of the German Sixth Army, concentrated his 3d and 23d Panzer Divisions and several infantry regiments on the southern flank of the joint thrust by the 28th Army and 38th Army, counterattacking vigorously on the afternoon of 13 May. At the same time, the Luftwaffe's Fourth Air Fleet massed its aircraft and gained local air superiority in this area. Once he recognized the danger, Hitler redeployed most of the air assets supporting von Manstein's offensive in the Crimea.

In response, Southwestern Front commander, Marshal Timoshenko, moved several rifle divisions and separate tank brigades to the threatened flank and on 14 May stripped airpower away from 6th Army's southern attack in a vain effort to counter the German counterattack. Even though aerial reconnaissance gave them advance notice of Paulus's counterattack, the local Soviet commanders failed to establish antitank defenses on the threatened flank. Meanwhile, the opportunity to exploit the initial breakthrough in the north passed; 3d Guards Cavalry Corps was not yet assembled and Timoshenko hesitated to commit them.

The southern arm of the Soviet offensive had initial success but soon found itself in even greater peril from German counterattacks. On 12 May, carefully focused attacks by two rifle divisions ruptured the weak German 454th Security Division, allowing Noskov's 6th Cavalry Corps to pass through the gap and advance up to 15 kilometers on the first day. The following day, this corps fought off local counterattacks and doubled its advance. This success came in the absence of any Soviet air support. Lieutenant General R. Ia. Malinovsky's Southern Front had been ordered to lend its aircraft to this phase of the offensive, but had never coordinated the action. Moreover, as noted earlier, the German air threat in the north attracted all available Red aircraft to the 28th Army sector.

On 15 May, the Southwestern Direction confidently reported to the *Stavka* that the offensive had forestalled a German offensive in the area. Indeed, at one point the Army Group South commander, Fedor von Bock, had considered switching several divisions to fill the breech south of Khar'kov. However, the original Soviet decision to restrict the offensive to a narrow area around Khar'kov allowed German Sixth Army to borrow troops from other sectors to stem the tide. At the same time, the Southern Front remained completely passive, allowing Ruoff's Seventeenth Army to continue its own preparations for an offensive.

This offensive, code-named Fredericus, had originally been scheduled to begin on 18 May as a two-pronged attack that would cut off the

Izium bulge in which Soviet 6th Army and Army Group Bobkin were concentrated. Hitler had retained personal control over most of the refurbished mechanized formations in the area, but von Bock persuaded him to release them, beginning Fredericus a day early in order to take pressure off Khar'kov.[6]

Once the German counterstroke began on 17 May, every kilometer that the Soviets advanced to the west was another step into the trap. Timoshenko, Stalin, and the *Stavka* remained incurably optimistic about their strength relative to that of the Germans. Not until 20 May, when Seventeenth Army had almost pinched off the Izium bulge, did they recognize the need to break out. The 21st and 23d Tank Corps had indeed been redirected to the southeast on 19 May but were unable to halt the Germans.

By 22 May the encirclement was complete, with 6th Army, Group Bobkin, and two Southern Front armies (9th and 57th) surrounded. A few managed to fight their way out, but the Red Army lost the equivalent of three rifle armies and a tank army, together with a host of senior commanders and staffs.[7]

The Second Battle of Khar'kov was an expensive lesson, and the Red Army drew many conclusions that it was able to apply six months later. Among the problems identified were the need for better reconnaissance, coordination between *front* headquarters, movement plans prior to battle, and the use of engineers.

The Khar'kov disaster also demonstrated to Soviet planners that larger armored organizations would not ensure success until senior commanders learned how to employ those organizations properly. One problem that was identified but not resolved was the delicate question of when to commit mobile formations for exploitation and pursuit. Timoshenko had hesitated too long to commit 3d Guards Cavalry Corps in the north and the two tank corps in the south. In the future, however, Soviet commanders had to avoid going to the other extreme by allowing such formations to become involved in the initial penetration battle.

The Soviet defeat at Khar'kov was magnified by a similar disaster in the Crimea. There, in a sordid tale of military ineptitude, Crimean Front forces under the personal influence of Commissar L. Z. Mekhlis, a crony of Stalin, attempted to launch an offensive to clear German forces from the Crimea. The 27 February offensive was aborted by early April. In May, von Manstein's Eleventh Army struck the inept Soviet defenders and, in a nine-day operation (8 to 19 May), drove Soviet 44st, 47th, and 51st Armies from the Kerch Peninsula into the sea. Soviet losses were so catastrophic that Stalin rebuked his loyal henchman and never again appointed him to a significant military position.[8]

TO THE DON RIVER

Despite the inauspicious beginning of the Soviet spring–summer campaign, the Second Battle of Khar'kov did disrupt German preparations for the summer offensive. Not only were the German units around Khar'kov unable to complete their refitting but the timetable of preparations underwent significant changes. On 1 June, Hitler flew to Army Group South headquarters in Poltova. Based on General Halder's suggestions, he agreed to delay the main offensive until 28 June. In the interim, von Bock's forces continued to exploit their success east of Khar'kov, attempting to eliminate as many Soviet units as possible. Meanwhile, General von Manstein completed his brilliant operations in the Crimea by redirecting his forces to reduce the fortress of Sevastopol'. Hitler allowed Wolfram von Richthofen's VIII Air Corps, an elite force of fighters and bombers, to sustain this attack far beyond the three days originally allocated. The Soviet troops doggedly defended individual fortifications but were eventually overcome. Between 7 June and 4 July, von Manstein methodically reduced the fortress, using air and artillery bombardment to avoid the casualties of house-to-house fighting. Hitler recognized the tactical brilliance of this performance by promoting von Manstein to field marshal, but once the battle was over, the troops were rapidly dispersed, rather than remaining in the south as a strategic reserve.[9]

During these preliminary battles, the *Stavka* belatedly recognized that at least some part of the German offensive would occur in the south. The Red Air Force attempted a number of massed raids on German assembly areas in the south but was still too weak to achieve local air superiority. In addition to 10 rifle armies forming in reserve, Soviet divisions were withdrawn from the central region to provide greater strategic depth (see Map 8). However, many of these reserves remained in the Moscow area, rather than redeploying to the south. As late as 5 July, the *Stavka* still believed that the new offensive was only a prelude to an advance on Moscow, with the attackers wheeling northward once they reached Voronezh.[10]

On 19 June, the operations officer of the 23d Panzer Division crash-landed behind Soviet lines, giving Soviet intelligence analysts a complete corps order for the coming offensive. Stalin suspected this order to be a deception and refused to act on it. Despite this compromise of their plans, the German attack began as scheduled on 28 June. Fourth Panzer Army and Second Army easily penetrated the forward Soviet defenses east of Kursk, striking at the junction between the Briansk and Southwestern Fronts. Two days later Sixth Army struck Soviet defenses southeast of Belgorod. Major General A. I. Liziukov's 5th Tank Army attempted a counterattack from 5 to 8 July, but Soviet inexperience in large-scale

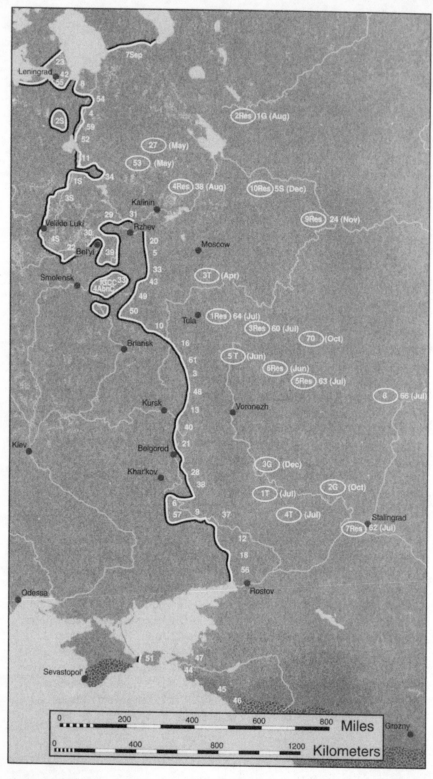

8. *Soviet Dispositions on 30 April 1942 and Reinforcements to 31 December 1942*

offensive operations was again reflected in a piecemeal, hesitant commitment of forces. Fourth Panzer Army's 9th Panzer Division destroyed two Soviet tank brigades and continued to move on Voronezh. A later *Stavka* plan for a counteroffensive east of Voronezh was overtaken by the speed of the German advance.[11]

By 7 July, Fourth Panzer Army had linked up with Sixth Army at Voronezh on the upper Don River. As planned, on 9 July von Bock's Army Group South was redesignated Army Group B, and Field Marshal List's Army Group A began its own offensive from the Artemovsk region on the German southern flank.

One reason for the easy German victory was that, until the fall of Voronezh, the *Stavka* continued to regard Moscow as the primary target and sought to forestall the offensive which, according to German deception operations, was to be launched by Army Group Center. On 5 July, Zhukov's Western Front launched three armies (16th, 61st, and 3d Tank) in a spoiling attack against Second Panzer Army around Bolkhov, north of Orel. Second Panzer Army was barely able to parry this attack, which again suffered from poor coordination between higher headquarters and a failure to effectively coordinate armored and infantry operations.[12]

On 13 July, after it had become clear that large masses of Soviet prisoners were not being taken, Hitler relieved a victorious von Bock of his command following an argument concerning how best to encircle the retreating Southwestern Front. In his stead, Hitler appointed Colonel General Maximilian von Weichs as Army Group B commander.[13] Henceforth, Hitler attempted to direct the two army groups in person. On 16 July, he moved the operational elements of OKW and OKH to field locations code-named *Wehrwolf* near Vinnitsa, in the western Ukraine.

Despite such remote control, the German offensive continued its initial successes. By 13 July, the breakthrough was complete, and Hitler directed that Army Group B pivot to the south and east to encircle Rostov. To accomplish this he resubordinated Fourth Panzer Army and an infantry corps from Army Group B to Army Group A to spearhead the German advance along the south bank of the Don River and relegated the remaining elements of Army Group B to flank and rear security.

The great distances in the Southern Theater placed a severe strain on German logistics, and by mid-July, the spearhead divisions of Fourth Panzer Army were already running short of fuel. First Panzer Army, in its supporting role, was at first better supplied with fuel, but its limited strength faded more each day. Because of the Khar'kov-Izium battles, the mechanized units of this army had begun the offensive at an average strength of only 40 percent; by 16 July, they had been reduced to 30 percent, with only one tank battalion remaining in each panzer division.

Ten days later, the eight mobile divisions of Army Group A averaged only 54 tanks each.[14]

More significantly, the German advance failed to duplicate the massive prisoner hauls of the previous year. Stalin and Timoshenko had learned from their mistakes, and on 6 July, the *Stavka* wisely directed the South-western and Southern Fronts to conduct a strategic retreat, rather than to stand and fight. Some formations were trapped, particularly around Millerovo (9th and 38th Armies) and north of Rostov (elements of 12th and 18th Armies). On 20 July, Hitler virtually halted his advance at Rostov in order to seal the encirclement. Moreover, some of the newly organized and poorly equipped Soviet troops surrendered too easily. On the whole, however, most of the defending armies escaped the initial German thrusts. During the first three weeks of fighting, for example, Army Group A took only 54,000 prisoners.[15]

Soviet commanders were nevertheless disturbed by the speed and depth of the German offensive. The first thrust by Army Group South had cut the direct rail links from Moscow to the south, forcing any strategic reserves to take a time-consuming detour into Central Asia in order to arrive in the southern region. The extensive field fortifications that had been constructed by Soviet troops and civilian labor proved useless be-cause of shortages of skilled engineers and of barrier materials. During the withdrawals of July, the Southwestern Front lost control over many of its subordinate units. By 23 July, the leading German units had reached the Don River, and Rostov was defended only by fanatical NKVD troops. Coming on top of the Khar'kov and Crimean disasters, the repeated retreats of July seemed an ominous repetition of the failures of 1941.

Hitler unintentionally came to Stalin's rescue by dividing the German efforts. After Rostov fell on 23 July, Hitler abruptly focused on the indus-trial and symbolic value of Stalingrad. Fuehrer Directive 45, issued that same day, transferred XXIV Panzer Corps from Fourth Panzer Army to Sixth Army in order to reinforce the latter's advance toward Stalingrad. This advance also took first priority for air support and for the increas-ingly scarce supplies of gasoline. In retrospect, German commanders marked this as the beginning of the Stalingrad debacle. Their offensive henceforth operated on two diverging axes, moving east towards Sta-lingrad and south toward the Caucasus.[16]

Until the railroad network could be restored, German field com-manders were hamstrung by shortages of petroleum and transport. In August, when Army Group A captured the small Maikop oil field, it discovered that the defenders had systematically destroyed all the oil wells and refineries in the area. As they moved farther and farther away from their railheads, the German forces were increasingly worn down at the same time that they had to spread out to cover huge territories. Just as in 1941, German tactical successes did not add up to decisive victory, and each new advance led nowhere. There were no obvious strategic goals east of the Don River, and so attention naturally focused on Stalingrad.

During the Rostov encirclement, even Sixth Army had been virtually immobilized for 10 days due to lack of supplies. This respite allowed the *Stavka* to reestablish a rudimentary defense in the Don bend.[17] The civilian populace of the region was mobilized to construct four defensive belts around Stalingrad. On 12 July, Marshal Timoshenko assumed command of all elements on the approaches to the city, combining the remaining forces of Southwestern Front (21st Army and 8th Air Army) with the newly renumbered 62d, 63d, and 64th Armies from the strategic reserve into a new Stalingrad Front. Five days later, remnants of Southern Front's 28th, 38th, and 57th Armies were absorbed into the new front, and on 22 July, Lieutenant General V. N. Gordov replaced Timoshenko in this critical command position. The next day, Sixth Army encountered the main defenses of 62d and 64th Rifle Armies near the Chir River, 80 miles west of the city. On 25 and 27 July, respectively, the half-formed 1st Tank and 4th Tank Armies conducted a number of disjointed local counterattacks that threatened the XIV Panzer Corps, which was still waiting to refuel.[18] At the same time, the Soviets opened the dams of the Manich River, flooding First Panzer Army's crossing site over the lower Don. The result was the temporary isolation of German forward units in the North Caucasus axis.

Despite this temporary success, the defenders had only a patchwork defense west of Stalingrad and none farther south opposite Army Group A. In late July, the two tank armies were virtually destroyed in confused battles with the Germans.[19] On 29 July, German units blew up the last railroad links from central Russia to the Caucasus region. The near-panic of this period is illustrated by the famous *Stavka* Order No. 227, issued on 28 July 1942. This order is often referred to by its title, *Ni Shagu Nazad!* (Not a step back!) In it, Stalin cited the economic and manpower losses of the previous year, explaining why further retreat was impossible. The order mandated that any commander or political officer who retreated would be assigned to a punishment battalion.[20]

Army Group B paused in early August to accumulate supplies and to move allied troops to its northern flank along the Don River. Both of these actions were hampered by the fact that the entire Stalingrad operation was based on a single, low-capacity railroad line. As it was not possible until September to transport the Third Rumanian Army by rail to the northern flank, Sixth Army had to devote more German divisions to this task. Nor did the Red Army remain passively on the defensive. From 20 to 28 August, a counterstroke by Stalingrad Front's 63d and 21st Armies easily crossed the Don River near Serifimovich, forcing Eighth Italian Army to fall back. At the same time, a counterattack by 1st Guards Army secured another bridgehead across the Don near Kremenskaia. German forces diverted from Stalingrad failed to eliminate these bridgeheads. These and two other bridgeheads opposing Second Hungarian Army to the northeast of the Italians would cause the Germans major difficulties in the future. Meanwhile Western and Northwestern Fronts conducted a series of limited offensives that tied down German reserves and precluded any serious attempt to capture Leningrad in 1942.

On 28 August, the Transcaucasus Front finally halted the leading elements of Army Group A along the crests of the Caucasus and short of Ordzhonikidze. A strong set of field fortifications and local air superiority enabled the Soviet defenders to prevent the Germans from capturing the large Grozny oil fields. Despite the propaganda value when a few German mountain troops planted their flag on the highest point in the Caucasus Mountains, Mount Elbrus, the southern thrust was virtually exhausted by mid-September.

All remaining German resources were focused to the east. Sixth Army resumed its advance on 23 August, crossing the Don River and advancing to the Volga just north of Stalingrad. The same day, the Luftwaffe launched its first massive firebomb raid on the city itself. During the last days of August, Sixth Army moved steadily forward into the suburbs of the city, setting the stage for battle.

STALINGRAD

In 1942, Stalingrad was a vast industrial city that sprawled in a narrow, 15-mile ribbon along the Volga River. Its population of 600,000 was clustered around three huge factory complexes: the Red October Steel Works, the Stalingrad Tractor Factory, and the Barrikady Ordnance Factory. Although numerous Soviet headquarters were involved, the tactical defense of the city rested with Lieutenant General V. I. Chuikov's 62d Army, which began the battle with eight divisions. [21]

To capture this urban complex, Sixth Army and Fourth Panzer Army had a total of 25 understrength divisions. On 16 September, General Paulus, commander of Sixth Army, received operational control over the infantry elements of Fourth Panzer Army, but even this addition proved inadequate.

The Soviet defenders exhibited incredible endurance, struggling onward despite heavy casualties and enormous deprivations. Early in the battle, Chuikov realized that he had to neutralize German superiority in airpower and artillery. He directed his troops to "hug" the Germans, that is, to remain so closely engaged that the German commanders could not use airstrikes without endangering their own men. For weeks on end, small combat groups of Red Army infantrymen and combat engineers were so close to their opponents that often only a single street or even a single wall separated them. Deadly battles of search and ambush were fought out at ranges measured in meters. Even with this tactic, however, the defenders were slowly worn down and forced back. By October, the Soviet defenses had been split into four shallow bridgeheads, with the front lines only 600 feet from the riverfront. The 187th Rifle Division moved into a riverfront factory with orders to hold it at all costs. Within three days, 90 percent of the division was dead or missing, a gruesome achievement for which it was redesignated as a Guards unit.[22]

Using boats and barges to ferry troops across the Volga at night, the Stalingrad Front fed a steady stream of replacement units and individuals into the meatgrinder of urban fighting. Once again, the *Stavka* policy of maintaining large operational and strategic reserves allowed the Soviets to accept incredible casualties and absorb the German offensive capability. Thinly spread German forces, especially in infantry regiments, suffered a steady erosion, but that erosion was achieved by the Soviet Union at enormous human cost. As late as 26 October, General Paulus confidently expected to capture the entire city by 10 November. Hitler agreed on 2 November that the combat engineer battalions of divisions not involved in the fighting would be redirected to the city to help root out the tenacious defenders.[23] Both sides bled heavily for a few dozen ruined city blocks, while the Red Army prepared to counterattack.

CONCLUSIONS

The Soviet Union and its armed forces suffered catastrophic defeats during the 18 months known as the First Period of War. Surprised when it should not have been, neither the state nor its military establishment was ready for war. Although numerically large on paper, the Red Army's training and maintenance were low; its leadership at mid and higher levels was weak, timid, or simply inept, and at the national level it was criminally deficient. As a result, during the first six months of the war, two thirds of the Red Army's initial mobilized strength (3,137,673 men) perished or fell into captivity, along with a sizable portion of its command cadre. Another 1,336,147 were wounded. By the end of 1942, the ghastly casualty total had risen to over 11 million.

The very scale of their success in June to July 1941 hindered the German advance. German panzer columns easily pierced the deepest

Soviet defensive echelons, preempting initial Soviet attempts at counter-attack based on their prewar plans. This preemption, especially along the Dnepr River in July 1941, encouraged an unbridled German optimism that propelled the invaders onward into positions that stretched their logistics to the breaking point and wore out the vaunted panzers. Yet on they went, reaching Leningrad, Rostov, and the outskirts of Moscow by late November and December. Hitler's strategic plan involved objectives that reached beyond European comprehension or practical achievement, but even the German Army's partial success surpassed exponentially the earlier advances in Poland and France.

The superb German fighting machine was defeated by more than distance. The German rapier, designed to end conflict cleanly and efficiently, was dulled by repeated and often clumsy blows from a simple, dull, but very large Soviet bludgeon. That bludgeon took the form of successive waves of newly mobilized armies, each taking its toll of the invaders before shattering and being replaced by the next wave. Its mobilization capability saved the Soviet Union from destruction in 1941 and again in 1942. While the German command worried about keeping a handful of panzer divisions operational, the *Stavka* raised and fielded tens of reserve armies. These armies were neither well equipped nor well trained. Often the most one could say of them was that they were there, they fought, they bled, and they inflicted damage on their foes. These armies, numbering as many as 96, ultimately proved that quantity possesses a virtue of its own. By necessity, those Soviet units that survived were well educated in the art of war.

The Soviet survival in the face of innumerable disasters was miraculous. First and foremost, this survival underscored the capacity of the Soviet population and armed forces for suffering. It was as if the old medical practice of bleeding the patient to restore health was the remedy accepted by the Soviet government. And bleed it did. Whether by design or by chance, the bleeding produced results. By late 1942, those who survived had learned to fight and often fought well. Their sacrifice bought Stalin the time necessary for industrial mobilization, which, with Allied support, provided the survivors with abundant implements to wage war.

On the German side, Operation Barbarossa, with its ill-defined, fantastic objectives, failed. Blame for that failure rested not only on Adolf Hitler but also those military commanders who enlisted in his new crusade, despite the obvious lessons of Charles XII and Napoleon. Barbarossa failed because German military planners applied the templates of military success in western Europe to the geography of eastern Europe, forgetting that Russia is anchored in Asia.

The Blitzkrieg, which had made a rapier of the German Army, was already failing at the gates of Moscow in 1941. It was further discredited at Stalingrad in 1942, and would be buried at Kursk in 1943. The surviving Soviet commanders at all levels often became as proficient at the art of killing as their German tutors. Henceforth, German forces would have to fight the Soviets on new terms, increasingly dictated by the Soviets themselves.

SECOND PERIOD OF WAR
NOVEMBER 1942–DECEMBER 1943

CHAPTER 9

Operation Uranus: The Destruction of Sixth Army

SOVIET PLANNING

Stalingrad marked a turning point not only in the actual conduct of the war but also in the *Stavka's* planning system. While Stalin and many field commanders were gravely concerned with German advances in the South, *Stavka* strategic planners remained remarkably consistent from July 1942 through February 1943. Although the Germans parried various limited Soviet counterattacks during July and August 1942, *Stavka* strategic planners never lost sight of their goal, which was to resume large-scale offensive operations and destroy at least one German army group. The long series of strategic and operational failures—produced in part by Stalin's reliance on his own military intuition and that of numerous political cronies instead of the sound advice of his military experts, such as G. K. Zhukov and A. M. Vasilevsky—finally persuaded Stalin to trust his professional military subordinates and grant them a larger role in planning and conducting major operations. Stalin, however, remained the ultimate authority. He determined the political aims of operations and often shaped the ultimate form of operations after listening to and acting on the recommendations of his senior commanders.[1]

In June 1942, B. M. Shaposhnikov's fragile health had given way under the enormous strain, and he had been replaced as chief of the General Staff. His successor, A. M. Vasilevsky, remained chief of staff, deputy defense commissar, and sometime field representative of the *Stavka* until February 1945, when he assumed command of 3d Belorussian Front, followed in July by command of the Far Eastern Theater. Far less temperamental than Zhukov, Vasilevsky exercised a calm, rational influence on the dictator. Vasilevsky surrounded himself with superbly competent General Staff officers, appointing Colonel General A. I. Antonov as his first deputy and chief of the Operational Directorate in December 1942. To replace the cumbersome Strategic Direction headquarters, Stalin and Vasilevsky began using *Stavka* representatives to coordinate and supervise the conduct of major operations. These senior officers, who included Zhukov, N. N. Voronov, Timoshenko, and others, provided the critical link between operating *fronts* and the General Staff.

They were the vehicle for carrying out *Stavka* decisions effectively and in timely fashion.[2]

Throughout the darkest hours of the defense of Stalingrad, Vasilevsky kept a small group of staff officers, headed by N. I. Bokov, working on plans for a strategic counteroffensive, designed to be the first phase of an ambitious winter campaign that would embrace the entire central and southern regions of the front (see Map 9). On 13 September, Bokov briefed Stalin on the concept of cutting off the German spearhead at Stalingrad by attacking the weak Rumanian forces on its flanks. By mid-October, Stalin was sufficiently confident to focus on this proposal, which became the basis for two major operations planned by the *Stavka* to occur in November 1942.[3] The first, Operation Uranus, was designed to destroy Axis forces in the Stalingrad region. It was to be followed by Operation Saturn, designed to destroy all Axis forces in the southern Soviet Union (Army Groups B and A). At the same time, the Western and Kalinin Fronts, coordinated by Zhukov, would conduct Operation Mars against German Army Group Center to collapse the Rzhev salient, distract German reinforcements from the south, and do as much damage as possible to that army group.

The plan for Uranus was a classic of encirclement. Colonel General N. F. Vatutin, the 41-year-old commander of the Southwestern Front, played a significant role in planning Uranus, although a dispute still rages over who, in fact, was responsible. Vatutin's appointment to *front* command was based largely on his prior *front* staff service and on his close association with Vasilevsky.[4] The shape and form of the ensuing offensive reflected the audacious nature of Vatutin.

In general, Operation Uranus involved the redeployment and use of large mobile formations to penetrate Axis defenses north and south of Stalingrad and subsequently to encircle and destroy German and Axis forces in the region. It was no coincidence that the initial Soviet targets were the threadbare satellite armies deployed on German Sixth Army's flanks. During early November, Lieutenant General P. L. Romanenko's newly refitted 5th Tank Army secretly redeployed from the Briansk Front sector to positions northwest of Stalingrad in the Don River Serafimovich bridgehead held by the Southwestern Front. Vatutin planned to employ his 5th Tank and 21st Armies and the 65th Army of Rokossovsky's Don Front to achieve a shallow encirclement of the overextended Third Rumanian Army. At the same time, 5th Tank Army's 1st and 26th Tank Corps and 21st Army's 4th Tank and 3d Guards Cavalry Corps would wheel southeast to encircle the German defenders at Stalingrad, while 5th Tank Army's 8th Cavalry Corps provided a thin outer encirclement to delay German relief columns. On the German southern flank, A. I. Eremenko, commander of the Stalingrad Front, would launch 51st and 57th Armies, spearheaded by

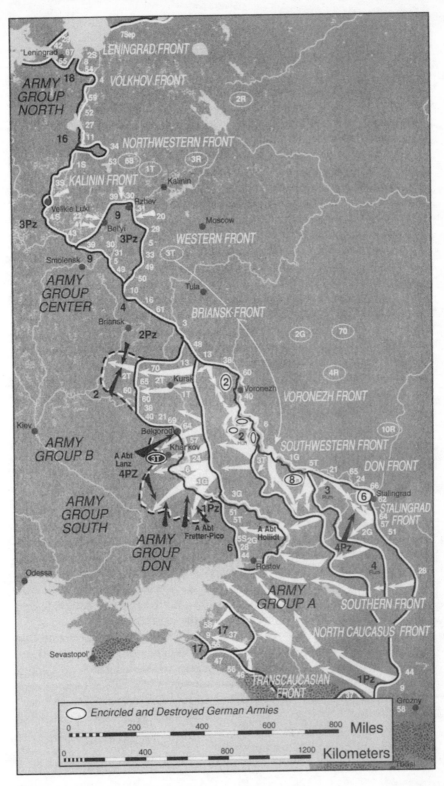

9. *Winter Campaign, November 1942–March 1943*

13th Tank and 4th Mechanized Corps, to push through the Fourth Rumanian Army and link up with 5th Tank Army near Kalach on the Don. The 4th Cavalry Corps would cover Stalingrad Front's left flank. Because 5th Tank Army had to cover 120 kilometers, as opposed to the 90 kilometers expected of the 4th Mechanized Corps, the Southwestern Front would begin its attack one day before the Stalingrad Front.[5]

This plan had inevitable weaknesses, of which the most obvious was the weak outer encirclement of cavalry forces that would have to parry the initial German relief efforts. More significantly, Soviet tank and mechanized forces still suffered from a lack of maintenance, motor transportation, and general logistical support. Once committed to the exploitation, tanks and other vehicles broke down at an alarming rate.

The Red Air Force also intended to use new equipment and new doctrine to wrest local air superiority from the Luftwaffe. In April 1942, Colonel General A. A. Novikov had become Air Force Commander, a post he held for the remainder of the war. Novikov assigned 10 regiments of the latest-model Yak-9 and La-5 aircraft to 8th Air Army at Stalingrad. Recognizing the limited experience of his new pilots, he instituted a strict system of ground control and experimented on the Don Front with the first Soviet system of radar-directed fighter interception. Novikov's chief of staff, F. Falaleev, instructed all air commanders to focus their assets to support the main ground operations, rather than trying to be strong everywhere.[6]

GERMAN PERCEPTIONS AND FAILURES
AT STALINGRAD

From Hitler on down, German commanders were aware of the weakness of their flanks at Stalingrad but generally failed to anticipate a Soviet offensive on the massive scale conceived by the *Stavka*. On 15 August, the *Fremde Heere Ost* Division of OKH had estimated, with considerable accuracy, that the Red Army still had 73 rifle divisions, 86 tank brigades, and a host of other reserve units available for commitment to battle. By 6 November, the same office inexplicably asserted that the Soviets lacked sufficient forces for a major offensive in the south.[7]

One reason for this German error was the Soviet disinformation that no major offensive was planned in the Stalingrad region. Throughout late summer and fall, a series of Soviet offensive actions against Army Groups Center and North and the continued presence of strategic reserves near Moscow contributed to this fiction.[8] In mid-October, the *Stavka* intentionally used unencrypted radios to transmit a long directive on defensive preparations for the coming winter, hoping that German monitors would intercept it. These and other measures were so effective that, as late as 12 November, OKH intelligence suggested that the troop concentrations opposite Third Rumanian Army were only intended for a shallow attack to sever the railroad leading to Stalingrad.[9]

Faced with such comforting estimates, it is no wonder that Hitler and his subordinates underestimated the threat. His solution was to use the newly formed, lightly equipped Luftwaffe "field divisions" to relieve a few veteran panzer units, especially 22d Panzer Division, that were stationed behind the allied armies while they received replacement troops and equipment. These small reserves were no match for the 660 tanks of the four Soviet spearhead corps. Overall, the ratio of Soviet to German forces in the Stalingrad region was significant, especially in light of the large proportion of Rumanian forces that absorbed the real shock of the Soviet blow. While official Soviet sources have long argued that strength ratios were little more than 1:1 in manpower, 1.4:1 in artillery, and 1.3:1 in armor in the Soviet's favor, the actual ratios were closer to 2:1 in all combat categories. In main penetration sectors, Soviet superiority was absolute. In addition to numerical superiority, the Soviets also benefited from surprise and were able to mass huge forces on the weak German flanks.[10] (See Table 9.1.)

The Stalingrad counteroffensive occurred in three phases. First, between 19 and 30 November, the Soviets penetrated Axis defenses and encircled German and Rumanian forces in Stalingrad. Next, between 1 December 1942 and 9 January 1943, they attempted to exploit and develop this success but were hampered by German efforts to relieve the beleaguered Stalingrad force. Finally, between 10 January and 18 March 1943, the *Stavka* supervised the liquidation of the Stalingrad pocket (Operation Ring *[Kol'tso]*) while attempting to expand their success to the entire central and southern regions of the front. This larger effort was stymied by their own errors and by skillful German counterblows.

Initial successes exceeded Soviet expectations (see Map 10). On 19 November, the Southwestern Front began the offensive, with supporting attacks by the neighboring Don Front. The Rumanian defenders had no effective antitank guns and were easily crushed. The 26th and 1st Tank Corps of Romanenko's 5th Tank Army passed through the attacking rifle divisions to enter the battle by noon on the first day. In coordination with Lieutenant General I. M. Chistiakov's 21st Army, 5th Tank Army captured the bulk of three Rumanian divisions (27,000 prisoners) and continued its exploitation. The two tank corps and Major General A. G. Kravchenko's 4th Tank Corps from 21st Army advanced as much as 70 kilometers each day, bypassing any centers of resistance. On 22 November, 26th Tank Corps, commanded by Major General A. G. Rodin, approached Kalach

Table 9-1. Soviet Strength at the Beginning of the Stalingrad Counteroffensive

Front	Personnel	Tanks	Artillery	Aircraft
Southwestern	398,100	410	4,348	447
Don	307,500	161	4,177	202
Stalingrad	429,200	323	5,016	221
Volga Flotilla	8,700			
Total	1,143,500	894	13,451	1,115

Source: G. F. Krivosheev, *Grif sekretnosti sniat: Poteri vooruzhennykh sil SSSR v voinakh, boevykh deistriiakh, i vornnykh konfliktakh* (Moscow: Voenizdat, 1993) 181–182, and K. K. Rokossovsky, ed., *Velikaia pobeda na Volga* (Moscow: Voenizdat, 1965), 254–258.

on the Don, whose bridges were essential to both attackers and defenders. In order to capture the Kalach bridges before the Germans could destroy them, Rodin organized a small forward detachment of five T-34 tanks and two motorized infantry companies under Lieutenant Colonel G. N. Filippov. Filippov brazenly formed this detachment into a closely packed column and drove into Kalach at night with all vehicle headlights blazing.[11] The German sentries assumed that this was a German column and allowed it to enter the town and capture key terrain near the principal bridge, which it held until relieved by the rest of the tank corps. On the afternoon of 23 November, 26th Tank Corps linked up with Major General V. T. Vol'sky's 4th Mechanized Corps at Sovetskoe southeast of Kalach, completing the encirclement.[12] By 30 November, Soviet forces had established an inner encirclement around 22 German divisions totaling 330,000 men, including Sixth Army, Rumanian remnants, and one corps of Fourth Panzer Army. This German force far exceeded Soviet expectations and required seven rifle armies and much command and staff attention to eliminate.

Most German accounts contend that General Friederick Paulus, Sixth Army commander, could have broken out of this encirclement if he had acted promptly. Quite apart from the problem of disobeying Hitler's wishes, this argument assumes a logistical strength that Paulus did not possess. The entire siege of Stalingrad had been conducted on a shoestring, and his forces lacked the fuel, ammunition, and transportation to break out unassisted. In addition, the *Stavka* possessed powerful reserves that could block relief of or breakout by the Stalingrad garrison.[13]

In this extremity, Field Marshal Erich von Manstein was appointed commander of the newly created Army Group Don, with orders to rescue Sixth Army. Hitler still refused to contemplate withdrawing from Stalingrad, however; he wanted von Manstein to drive a corridor through the encirclement to resupply the beleaguered forces. Moreover, Hermann Goering impulsively promised Hitler that his Luftwaffe could supply 600 tons

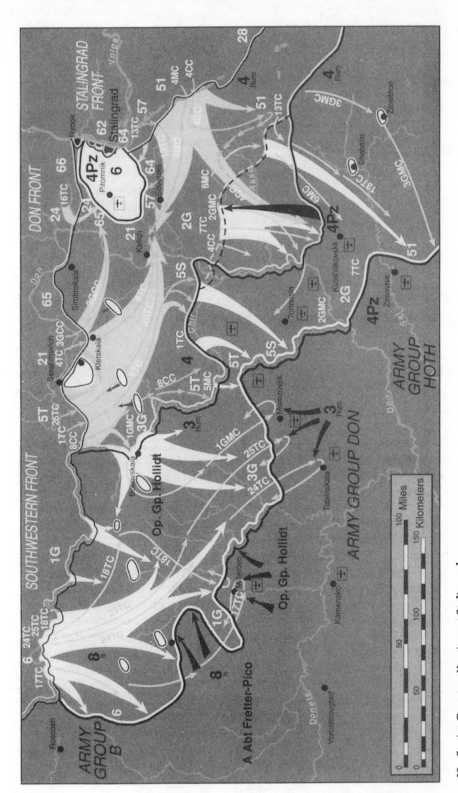

10. *Soviet Counteroffensives at Stalingrad*

per day to Stalingrad, an impossible figure that would have required 375 JU-52 sorties per day. Given the poor weather and airfields in the region, such a goal would have required close to 1,000 JU-52s, far beyond what the Luftwaffe could provide. The Germans did concentrate all available transports, disrupting their training program by dispatching half-trained crews in aircraft that lacked radios and navigation instruments. Despite all these efforts, the daily shipments reached 300 tons on only one occasion.

These slow, unarmed aircraft flew into the first systematic Soviet air defense system of the war. General P. S. Stepanov, the Red Air Force coordinator of the battle, established concentric rings of antiaircraft guns and ground-controlled fighter interceptors. In addition, Stepanov used specially trained night fighters and elite *okhotniki* (free hunters) to seek targets of opportunity. The result was a slaughter. Soviet historians claim to have destroyed 676 JU-52s during the siege of Stalingrad, and even the Luftwaffe acknowledged 266 aircraft lost. Small wonder that, just as in the Soviet armored forces, the Red Air Force commanders at Stalingrad rose to the top of their profession later in the war.[14]

MARS

In the north, the *Stavka* planned another major offensive against Army Group Center in the Rzhev salient, which still threatened the Soviet defenses of Moscow. Planned and supervised by Zhukov, Operation Mars called for massive assaults by Army General M. A. Purkaev's Kalinin Front and Colonel General I. S. Konev's Western Fronts against the eastern and western flanks of the Rzhev salient. The objective was to destroy German Ninth Army, eliminate the salient, and, subsequently, threaten Smolensk.[15] (See Map 11.) This offensive also included supporting attacks by the Kalinin Front's 39th Army against the "nose" of the salient and by 3d Shock Army against Velikie Luki.

Although later explained away as a diversionary operation designed to benefit operations in the south, the scale, scope, and ferocity of the Mars offensive indicate that it was a major attempt to defeat Army Group Center and may initially have been more important than Operation Uranus. General G. K. Zhukov personally planned and directed Operation Mars, and newly revealed Soviet order of battle data indicate that Mars was to be the first stage of an even larger operation. Just as Operation Uranus at Stalingrad was expanded and exploited by Operation Saturn, Operation Mars also envisioned conduct of an expanded second stage, which was to commence in early December after Mars had succeeded in encircling German Ninth Army in the Rzhev-Sychevka region. The second stage,

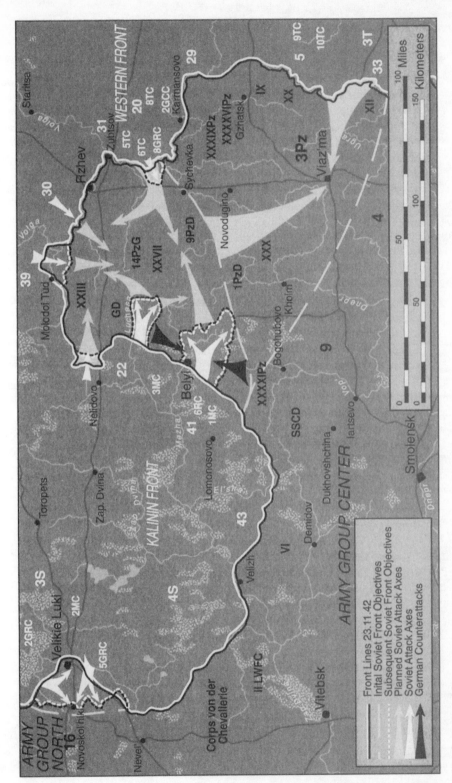

11. *Operation Mars*

perhaps code-named Operation Jupiter or Neptune, was to involve large forces attacking westward toward Viaz'ma to link up with the victorious Soviet Rzhev force and destroy the bulk of Army Group Center. The Viaz'ma thrust was to be conducted by the Western Front's center and included the heavily reinforced 5th and 33d Armies, backed up by two tank corps (9th and 10th) and, perhaps, General Rybalko's refitted and expanded 3d Tank Army from *Stavka* reserve. In the end, the German defeat of Operation Mars aborted the ambitious Soviet strategic offensive against Army Group Center, frustrated Zhukov's plan, and prompted Soviet historians to cover up this powerful, but disastrous, companion piece to the Stalingrad offensive.[16]

The operation began on 25 November, once initial success at Stalingrad had been assured. Purkaev's 22d and 41st Armies struck hard at German defenses north and south of Belyi and the same day Konev's 20th and 31st Armies attacked northeast of Sychevka. Almost simultaneously, 39th Army launched supporting attacks west of Rzhev, and 3d Shock Army, supported by the 215 tanks of Major General I. P. Korchagin's 2d Mechanized Corps, attacked German positions east of Velikie Luki.[17] Major General G. F. Tarasov's 41st Army burst through German defenses both north and south of Belyi. North of that town, Major General M. E. Katukov's 3d Mechanized Corps, equipped with about 200 tanks, immediately rushed forward along the Luchesa River to exploit the success and link up with 41st Army's mobile units east of Belyi. Meanwhile, south of Belyi, Major General S. I. Povetkin's elite 6th "Stalin" Rifle Corps began the exploitation, followed soon by Major General M. D. Solomatin's 1st Mechanized Corps, which had been reinforced to a strength of over 300 tanks (including 50 KV heavy tanks) by the attachment of two extra mechanized brigades. Solomatin's corps made spectacular progress as it advanced to link up with Katukov's armor to encircle Belyi and to meet Konev's lead elements at the base of the Rzhev salient.

Konev's two armies, however, were unable to match Purkaev's success. The 20th and 31st Armies, directed by Zhukov and supported by 6th and 8th Tank Corps and by Major General V. V. Kriukov's 2d Guards Cavalry Corps, repeatedly assaulted the German positions southeast of Rzhev. All of the attacks were repulsed after heavy fighting and appalling Soviet losses. Konev's only success was the insertion of Kriukov's 20th Cavalry Division into the German rear. This division was immediately cut off and spent almost a month in the German rear until a raid by Katukov's mechanized corps rescued the remnants in early January.

Unlike Stalingrad, where few German reserves were available to halt the Soviet attack, at Rzhev the Germans initially were able to commit their 1st and 9th Panzer Divisions, *Grossdeutschland* Division, and 14th Panzer

Grenadier Division, and later sent 12th, 19th, and 20th Panzer Divisions to seal off the Soviet penetrations near Belyi. By mid-December, the Soviet offensive had faltered. In the west, German counterattacks contained 3d Mechanized Corps' thrust in the Luchesa Valley north of Belyi and surrounded 6th Rifle Corps and 1st Mechanized Corps south of the town. Zhukov's attempts on 11 and 13 December to resume the offensive south of Rzhev failed with heavy losses, and in further heavy fighting the two corps south of Belyi were largely destroyed.[18] This costly failure was only partially offset when Colonel General K. N. Galitsky's 3d Shock Army destroyed a German force in Velikie Luki and held off German efforts to relieve that town.

Clearly, Operation Mars failed to meet Soviet expectations. Zhukov's "greatest failure" in the Mars Operation was soon eclipsed, however, by the success of Uranus in the south, where the *Stavka* now focused its attention.

SATURN AND LITTLE SATURN

Once Operation Uranus had succeeded, the *Stavka* commenced planning for the second phase of the campaign in the south. Operation Saturn involved the use of Southwestern Front's left wing and Lieutenant General R. Ia. Malinovsky's powerful 2d Guards Army to penetrate Italian defenses along the middle Don and advance deep to seize Rostov.

At the same time, the Germans sought means by which to relieve their Stalingrad force. In order to break into the Stalingrad encirclement, von Manstein began to assemble two forces. At the confluence of the Chir and Don Rivers, XXXXVIII Panzer Corps received a variety of divisions shipped from elsewhere in the east, while the LVII Panzer Corps formed up near Kotel'nikovskii. Quite naturally, the German and Soviet plans unfolded simultaneously and affected each another. First, the Soviets had to divert 2d Guards Army from Operation Saturn to deal with the task of reducing the Stalingrad encirclement (but without altering the form of Operation Saturn). Then, when von Manstein's LVII Panzer Corps began its advance on Stalingrad from Kotel'nikovskii, 2d Guards Army was shifted to that axis and Operation Saturn was modified into Little Saturn, a shallower envelopment of Italian Eighth Army and Army Detachment Hollidt defending along the south banks of the Don and Chir Rivers.

Soviet action began on 7 December, when 5th Tank Army's 1st Tank Corps, commanded by Major General V. V. Butkov, began spoiling attacks across the Chir to disrupt XXXXVIII and LVII Panzer Corps relief plans.

Then on 10 December, 5th Tank Army's 5th Mechanized Corps, led by Major General M. V. Volkov, joined the attack further west.[19] Although 11th Panzer Division performed herculean feats to parry these attacks, the Chir front barely held. By 10 December, XXXXVIII Panzer Corps had been sufficiently distracted, and LVII Corps' 17th Panzer Division had moved to back it up, thus negating the Chir-Stalingrad relief thrust and severely weakening the Kotel'nikovskii thrust, which nevertheless began on 12 December.

While LVII Panzer Corps pressed Soviet 51st Army northward from Kotel'nikovskii, Southwestern Front, supported by Voronezh Front's 6th Army, launched operation Little Saturn on 16 December against Eighth Italian and Third Rumanian Armies of Army Detachment Hollidt along the Don and Chir northwest of Stalingrad. An unprecedented collection of Soviet mobile corps virtually destroyed the Italian forces. Once these mobile corps had penetrated deep into the German rear, three of them— 24th and 25th Tank Corps and 1st Guards Mechanized Corps—drove straight for German Stalingrad resupply airfields at Tatsinskaia and Morozovsk. Major General V. M. Badanov's 24th Corps was ordered to seize the key airfield and logistical complex of Tatsinskaia. He accomplished his mission but at great cost. The 24th Tank Corps, already reduced to less than 40 percent of its initial strength (200 tanks) and beyond the range of any resupply column, penetrated to Tatsinskaia on Christmas Eve, destroying 56 German transport aircraft and the airfield itself.

Badanov held his position for four days and then escaped a German trap with only the remnants of his force. Late in the operation, at Stalin's personal urging, Badanov was given temporary control over the remnants of the three corps. By this time, however, the three corps had been reduced to less than 20 tanks each and thus were too weak to conduct any further concerted action.[20] This raid did, however, adversely affect German capabilities to resupply their encircled Stalingrad garrison and forced von Manstein to use XXXXVIII Panzer Corps in a defensive role, rather than to relieve Stalingrad. Not coincidentally, the experience led the *Stavka* to order the formation of new tank armies whose multiple corps could successfully conduct joint operations to great depths.

On 12 December, the remaining German relief had begun a vain effort to link up with Sixth Army. The German LVII Panzer Corps' advance was constantly hampered by Hitler's reluctance to concentrate operational reserves on this crucial attack. Despite such obstacles, the panzer corps struggled forward 50 kilometers in 12 days. Then on 24 December, Malinovsky's massive 2d Guards Army counterattacked, driving the Germans back as much as 100 kilometers. For once, the Soviet mobile corps were used with great skill, especially in a flank attack by Major General

P. A. Rotmistrov's 7th Tank Corps. For all practical purposes, the German effort to relieve Stalingrad had failed.

OPERATION RING AND THE DONETS BASIN

At this point, the *Stavka* focused its attention on two equally important and mutually related tasks: reducing the Stalingrad pocket in Operation Ring; and expanding the Winter Campaign to its fullest extent. Colonel General N. N. Voronev, the *Stavka* representative in charge of executing Operation Ring, used a steady artillery bombardment to wear down the German defenses. Sixth Army was so short on supplies that the defenders were soon reduced to living on horsemeat and huddling in the snow. On 24 January, the last major German airfield in the pocket, Pitomnik, was captured. Two days later, the Soviets attacked on a narrow frontage and split the German pocket in half from east to west. By 2 February, the entire force had been liquidated, despite Hitler's last-minute promotion of Paulus to field marshal.

Germany had lost more than its reputation of invincibility at Stalingrad. Because of Hitler's insistence on standing fast and the difficulties of escaping through a wide Soviet encirclement under extreme weather conditions, few Germans were able to escape from the pocket. Only a few thousand seriously wounded soldiers were flown out on empty transport aircraft. This contrasted markedly with the Soviet encirclements during previous battles, when the defenders often exfiltrated enough commanders and key personnel to rebuild their units and fight again. Sixth Army was completely gone, suffering 147,000 dead and 91,000 prisoners of war at a Soviet cost of nearly one half million casualties.[21] (See Table 9-2.)

The encirclement and destruction of German forces at Stalingrad had tied down a large number of Soviet troops for two months, and this materially affected the fate of the Soviet Winter Campaign. As a result, Stalin ended 1942 as he had ended 1941, overoptimistically attempting to conduct a strategic offensive on a shoestring and becoming overextended in the process. West of Stalingrad, the Southwestern and Southern Fronts, spearheaded by 1st, 3d, and 2d Guards and 51st Armies, with attached cavalry and tank corps, continued to press Army Group Don back toward Voroshilovgrad and Rostov in the hope of destroying that army group and cutting off Army Group A, then withdrawing from the Caucasus region.

Von Manstein was hamstrung by Hitler's refusal to release strategic reserves and by the need to protect the rear of Army Group A. The German dictator wanted to keep that army group in the Kuban region south of the Don, even if it were only in a bridgehead along the Sea of Azov, in the hope

Table 9-2. Soviet Casualties at Stalingrad, 19 November–2 February

Front	Unreturned	Sanitary	Total
Southwestern	64,649	148,043	212,692
Don	46,365	123,560	169,925
Stalingrad	43,552	58,078	101,630
Voronezh (6th Army)	304	1,184	1,488
Total	154,870	330,865	485,735

Source: G. F. Krivosheev, *Grif sekretnosti sniat: Poteri vooruzhennykh sil SSSR v voinakh, boevykh deistriiakh, i voennykh konfliktakh* (Moscow: Voenizdat, 1993) 181–182.

of again threatening the Caucasus oil fields later in 1943. Army Group A had already gone into winter quarters when the November counteroffensive began and was very slow to redeploy its forces in the face of the new threat. Von Manstein therefore had to hold Rostov, the key to all the railroad lines and supplies for Army Group A. To accomplish this, two ad hoc German-Axis formations, Army Detachments Fretter-Pico and Hollidt, tried to defend the Chir River line. Both detachments had wide-open flanks. On the northern flank, 1st Guards, 3d Guards, 5th Tank, and 5th Shock Armies pressed in, while in the south, 2d Guards, 51st and 28th Armies continued toward Rostov with the counteroffensive, which had begun on 24 December. By 3 January, both German detachments were forced to begin withdrawing to the Donets River despite Hitler's demands that they stand fast. Meanwhile 51st Army's 3d Guards Mechanized Corps, the renamed 4th Mechanized Corps, now commanded by Major General V. T. Vol'sky, thrust straight down the Don River valley toward Rostov. It was stopped only by the premature commitment of a new "wonder weapon," the first half-trained battalion of German Mark VI Tiger tanks. A short, savage engagement at Zimovniki on 7 January left 18 T-34s and 20 Tigers out of action.[22]

Both sides were hampered by a typical Russian winter. On 24 January, a brief thaw produced puddles on the roads, which became a sheet of ice when the temperature dropped to $-15°$ Fahrenheit on 26 January. The next day, a three-day snowstorm began.

Hitler now took action to resolve the precarious situation in the Donets basin. Von Manstein had repeatedly urged him to move First Panzer Army north, but the actual decision was far less bold. On 27 January 1943, Hitler decided to move the army and corps headquarters of First Panzer Army north through Rostov, but he sent only one panzer, one infantry, and two security divisions along. The remaining divisions of First Panzer Army were temporarily left with Seventeenth Army, which went into a defensive bridgehead. Eventually all these forces were evacuated to the Crimea, but for the moment they were unavailable to von Manstein.

WIDENING THE BREACH

Military historians have long credited von Manstein with staving off disaster in the winter of 1943. Between January and March, he managed to overcome both Hitler's obstinate opposition to a maneuver defense and a Red Army flushed with the victory of Stalingrad. He achieved a stunning setback on the advancing Soviets that restored stability to the southern wing of the Eastern Front at a time when collapse was imminent. Despite von Manstein's exertions, however, the Germans and their allies suffered staggering losses in the Winter Campaign.

Von Manstein's victories in the Donets Basin (or Donbas) and at the Third Battle of Khar'kov were far more significant than even this tribute suggests. Unknown to the Germans, Soviet strategic aims had expanded far beyond the simple defeat of German forces in southern Russia; the *Stavka* sought to collapse enemy defenses along virtually the entire Eastern Front.

In December 1942, the Soviet High Command had already formulated Plan Saturn to smash large elements of Army Group B, seize Rostov, and isolate or destroy Army Group A. Although this plan was later modified into Little Saturn, the *Stavka* continued to undertake operations that were beyond its resources. Soviet miscalculation of the defensive strength of Sixth Army, as well as a series of other Soviet misjudgments, were preconditions to von Manstein's ultimate victories in February and March.

Building upon the success of Little Saturn, the *Stavka* continued the process in January 1943, gradually expanding the offensive to include Army Group Center as well as Army Groups Don and A. This new series of offensives began with attacks aimed at the Hungarian and German forces defending along the middle Don and at the German-Rumanian forces trying desperately to hold Rostov for Army Group A. Between 13 and 27 January, Voronezh Front's 40th, 6th, and 3d Tank Armies conducted the Ostrogozhsk-Rossosh operation, severely damaging Second Hungarian Army and paving the way for further efforts.[23] On 24 January, the Briansk Front's 13th Army joined the Voronezh Front's 38th, 60th, and 40th Armies and attacked Second German Army, defending the Voronezh salient along the upper Don River. Despite snows so deep that only tracked vehicles could operate, in a matter of days the mobile corps attached to Soviet 13th and 40th Armies encircled two of the three corps in Second German Army.[24] Meanwhile, in Operations Gallop and Star, Voronezh Front's 40th, 69th, and 3d Tank Armies and Southwestern Front's 6th, 1st Guards, and 3d Guards Armies, spearheaded by Mobile Group Popov, burst through the ad hoc German formations that had replaced Germany's allies northwest of Rostov. Von Manstein found himself redeploying larger and larger elements of First and Fourth Panzer Armies to protect his lengthening northern flank.[25]

In mid-February, the greatest threat came from Soviet tank forces spearheading the Southwestern Front offensive, including four under-strength tank corps formed into a mobile group under the command of Lieutenant General M. M. Popov as well as the full-strength 25th and 1st Guards Tank Corps in the Southwestern Front's reserve. Popov's Mobile Group, the forerunner of a modern tank army, crossed the Donets River in early February and pressed forward into the German rear, reaching Krasnoarmeiskaia by 12 February. Three days later, Vatutin committed his two fresh tank corps on a drive through Pavlograd to Zaporozhe on the Dnepr River, an obvious node that controlled the last major road and rail lines to Rostov. Zaporozhe was also the headquarters of Army Group Don (renamed Army Group South), Fourth German Air Fleet, and a number of other major formations.

Despite this threat, Hitler was determined to conduct a counteroffensive. He assembled the SS Panzer Divisions *Das Reich* and *Leibstandarte Adolf Hitler* under a new SS corps headquarters, and ordered them to hold Khar'kov against advancing Voronezh Front forces, while simultaneously counterattacking against the Southwestern Front. The new SS headquarters lacked the experience to perform either mission and retreated on 14 February at the same time that First Panzer Army retreated from the Donets to the Mius River. Instead of punishing the SS for disobedience, Hitler relieved General Hubert Lanz, the army officer who had tried to make the SS Panzer Corps obey orders.

By this time, von Manstein was verging on open insubordination, to the point of suggesting that he should be placed in command of the entire Eastern Front. Knowing that Group Popov had been temporarily checked at Krasnoarmeiskaia, but unaware of the rapid advance of fresh armored forces on Zaporozhe, Hitler flew there on the afternoon of 17 February to berate von Manstein.[26]

Fortunately for Hitler and Army Group South, von Manstein was in the process of shifting Fourth Panzer Army headquarters to that area to assume control of SS Panzer Corps (now joined by SS Panzer Division *Totenkopf*) and other threadbare panzer divisions for a counteroffensive against Soviet forces, which themselves were reaching the end of their logistical tether. Hitler finally released seven understrength panzer and motorized divisions to von Manstein. The Fourth Air Fleet, under von Richtofen, had also regrouped and improved its maintenance status, producing an average of 1,000 sorties per day after 20 February, as compared to 350 sorties per day in January. For the last time in Russia, the Luftwaffe was able to provide clear air superiority for a major German counterthrust.

At the time, however, Stalin and his subordinates continued to believe that they were on the verge of a great victory. German defenses throughout southern Russia appeared to be crumbling, and the *Stavka* sought to expand that victory to include Army Group Center. Once Stalingrad fell on 2 February, Stalin and Zhukov immediately redirected the forces used in the encirclement to a new location farther north. Rokossovsky's Don Front headquarters and two of his rifle armies (65th and 21st), together with the newly formed 2d Tank and 70th Rifle Armies, received orders to move to the Voronezh-Livny area and form a new Central Front. The veteran 16th Air Army and 2d Guards Cavalry Corps were also redeployed to this area. Three other Don Front armies (24th, 64th, and 66th) refitted in the Stalingrad area and awaited orders to join either Rokossovsky's or Vatutin's *fronts*.

The overall concept for this culminating stage of the Soviet Winter Campaign envisaged three successive operations against Army Group Center. First, beginning on 12 February 1943, the combined forces of the Western and Briansk Fronts were to encircle and destroy German units in the Orel salient. Then, between 17 and 25 February, the two *fronts*, joined by the new Central Front, were to clear the Briansk region of German forces and secure bridgeheads across the Desna River. During the final phase, between 25 February and mid-March, the Kalinin and Western Fronts would join in to seize Smolensk and, in concert with their sister fronts to the south, destroy Army Group Center in the Rzhev-Viaz'ma salient. The entire offensive was timed to coincide with the anticipated successes of the Voronezh and Southwestern Fronts, so that by mid-March the strategic offensive would carry Soviet forces westward to the Dnepr River.[27]

To plan such an operation was one thing; to carry it out was another. Rokossovsky's shock force received only six days to redeploy and an additional five days to prepare for an offensive in an entirely new region. Although 2d Tank Army and 2d Guards Cavalry Corps were already concentrated in the Livny region, 70th Army's forces had to move over 200 kilometers on Russian winter roads, and 21st and 65th Armies had to complete arduous rail and road movements from Stalingrad. Heavy spring snows hampered movement, the spring thaw was due any day, and the roads from the assembly areas to the front were already in poor condition. Only one single-track rail line was available from Stalingrad northward, and movement schedules became a fiction.

Rokossovsky objected to the stringent time schedule imposed by the *Stavka* but dutifully attempted to achieve the impossible. Ultimately, he was unable to attack until 25 February and, even then, had to march elements of 2d Tank and 65th Armies directly from the railheads to their assault positions.

Rokossovsky began his offensive on 25 February with Rodin's 2d Tank Army and Lieutenant General P. I. Batov's 65th Army in the vanguard of his assault.[28] Lieutenant General G. F. Tarasov's 70th Army, an elite force made up of NKVD border guards from the Trans-Baikal and Far Eastern regions, and Chistiakov's 21st Army were to join the attack as soon as they arrived but before they were fully concentrated. Both armies were still on the march through the muddy, congested roads. Meanwhile, on 22 February, as Briansk Front's 13th and 48th Armies pounded the weakened right flank of Second Panzer Army, Lieutenant General I. Kh. Bagramian's 16th Army of the Western Front struck Second Panzer's other flank north of Zhidzhra. Rain and a skillful German defense hindered Bagramian's advance, and by 24 February, he had made only insignificant gains, a situation that subsequent attacks could not remedy.[29]

The Central Front made greater progress. With 13th Army covering his right flank, Batov's 65th Army advanced deep into the German rear area against only light resistance. Rodin's 2d Tank Army and a Cavalry-Rifle Group (the latter commanded by Major General Kriukov and consisting of 2d Guards Cavalry Corps and cooperating rifle and ski units) exploited rapidly westward through Sevsk toward Novgorod-Severskii.[30] By 1 March 1943, Rokossovsky had achieved considerable success, enveloping the flanks of Second Panzer Army to the north and Second Army to the south. By this time, 70th Army's divisions had filtered forward and joined battle on Batov's right flank to threaten a further advance on Orel and Briansk deep in the German rear.

German resistance stiffened as their forces conducted a skillful withdrawal and new units from other front sectors were brought into combat on the shoulders of Rokossovsky's penetration. At this juncture, Rokossovsky needed the additional strength of 21st, 62d, and 64th Armies, but they were still en route and unavailable. By 7 March, Kriukov's Cavalry-Rifle Group reached the outskirts of Novgorod-Severskii, marking the deepest Soviet advance during the winter campaign. The tide, however, was already shifting in favor of the Germans. Unreinforced, Rokossovsky's advance ground to a halt in the face of increasing resistance southwest of Orel. His attempts to restore momentum by shifting Rodin's tank army from the Briansk to the Orel axis only weakened his left flank and center, which were soon counterattacked by a multidivision force assembled by German Second Army. As Rokossovsky's offensive faltered, catastrophe in the south sounded the death knell for his ambitious offensive.

The entire plan for attacking Army Group Center was predicated on the assumption of continued offensive success further south, an assumption that collapsed during late February. By this time, the increasingly threadbare mobile forces of the Southwestern Front were operating well beyond their logistical umbilicals and were advancing into a trap set by von Manstein.

What followed is known by the Germans as the Donetz Campaign and by the Russians as the Donbas and Khar'kov operations. Both were classics of mobile warfare.[31] Beginning on 20 February, Fourth Panzer Army's XXXX Panzer Corps (7th and 11th Panzer Divisions and SS Motorized Division *Viking*) surrounded and destroyed the remnants of Group Popov in what became a running fight from Krasnoarmeiskaia to the Northern Donets River. On 23 February, General Eberhard von Mackensen's First Panzer Army was able to join the panzer corps in a thrust to the northeast. The day before, SS Panzer Corps (SS Panzer Divisions *Das Reich* and *Totenkopf*) and XXXXVIII Panzer Corps (6th and 17th Panzer Divisions) struck the flanks of Southwestern Front's exploiting 6th Army and 1st Guards Army, cutting the supply lines of 25th Tank Corps, which was then approaching Zaporozh'e, and virtually encircling the entire force. Deprived of fuel, the crews of 25th Tank Corps abandoned their equipment and joined the swelling mob of fugitives trying to escape to the north. As so often before, however, German forces were too weak to seal off the encircled Soviet forces and captured only 9,000 prisoners.[32]

Von Manstein followed up with an advance on Khar'kov. Between 1 and 5 March 1943, in a vicious battle south of the city, Fourth Panzer Army mauled Lieutenant General P. S. Rybalko's 3d Tank Army, which had been dispatched to assist beleaguered Southwestern Front forces and had continued its advance to Khar'kov and beyond. The SS Panzer Corps commander, Lieutenant General Paul Hauser, ignored a direct order, as well as common sense, and entangled both SS Panzer Division *Das Reich* and *Leibstandarte* in three days of house-to-house fighting before capturing Khar'kov on 14 March.

The Donets River campaign effectively halted the Soviet Stalingrad offensive in the south, and by early March the *Stavka* had to divert 62d and 64th Armies, en route from Stalingrad to Rokossovsky, to restore the front north of Khar'kov. Even then, the Soviet High Command sought to continue the offensive against Army Group Center. On 7 March, Rokossovsky received orders to scale down his offensive but to continue to attack northward toward Orel. His 21st Army was to join his attack within days. The same day, however, the Second German Army concentrated its 4th Panzer Division and several Hungarian infantry units in a counterattack against Rokossovsky's western flank. Kriukov's 2d Guards Cavalry Corps was spread too thinly to contain this threat. This counterattack, in conjunction with von Manstein's renewed advance north of Khar'kov on 17 March, forced the Red Army to halt its Winter Campaign and finally assume the defensive. The legacy of Rokossovsky's failed offensive was the Kursk bulge, a large Soviet salient that became the natural focus of both German and Soviet plans for the summer of 1943.[33]

CHAPTER 10

Rasputitsa and Operational Pause, Spring 1943

By late March 1943, mud and rain had again brought mobile operations to a halt in Russia. The two sides rebuilt their forces and planned for a third summer of war. This pause is another appropriate occasion to place the struggle in its larger context of grand strategy, changing tactics and organization, and concepts for the next campaign.

THE WIDER WAR

From the first moments of the 1941 invasion, the Soviet Union had borne the brunt of Germany's military power, absorbing the force of at least 75 percent of all German land and air units. In the course of 1942 and early 1943, however, Great Britain and the United States made a small but growing contribution to the struggle against Hitler. This contribution was never large enough to satisfy Stalin and his hard-pressed generals, who suspected their allies of waiting on the sidelines while the Germans and Soviets bled each other to death. Nevertheless, those allies helped in ways rarely acknowledged by Soviet leaders or historians.

Throughout the 1942 campaign, Hitler worried constantly about the threat of an Allied invasion in Western Europe. Week after week, he announced new plans to pull elite mechanized units out of Russia and redeploy them to the West. Sometimes, as in the case of the *Grossdeutschland* Motorized Infantry Division, his advisers were able to dissuade him, but he was prey to constant anxiety. In this respect, the British-Canadian raid at Dieppe, France, on 18 to 19 August 1942, was a tactical failure but a significant strategic success. Hitler immediately shifted more reserves to France. A few weeks later, he shipped the 22d Infantry Division from the Crimea to Crete, where he feared an Allied landing. In May 1943, he sent the 1st Panzer Division to mountainous Greece.[1] For the rest of the war, the threat of an Allied invasion tied down a small but growing number of divisions, often mechanized units, in the West. Some of these were depleted units that had been withdrawn from Russia to rest and refit, but their absence was far more significant to the German Army than a similar deficit would have been to the larger Red Army.

November 1942 proved to be a severe strain for the German war machine. At the Second Battle of Alamein (23 October to 4 November), the British Eighth Army shattered Panzer Army Afrika. Immediately afterward, a combined British-American force invaded French North Africa. Instead of cutting his losses in the Mediterranean, Hitler responded predictably by sending all available reserves, included several elite parachute units, to Tunisia. Compared to the titanic struggles in Russia, the German forces involved in North Africa were quite small, generally equivalent to less than six divisions. However, coming on top of the losses in the East, the North African campaign had a disproportionate effect on German strategic reserves. At the end of October, German forces in the East were already short a total of 300,000 replacements after the heavy fighting of August and September.[2] Given the sudden priority on troops and weapons for North Africa, German commanders found it impossible to assemble any strategic reserves or even to keep the infantry units in Stalingrad up to strength.

Perhaps the greatest Allied contribution to the Soviet cause from 1942 to 1943 was in the air. Four hundred Luftwaffe aircraft redeployed from the East to the Mediterranean between November and December 1942 in response to the threat in North Africa. In fact, German losses in the Mediterranean between November 1942 and May 1943 totaled 2,422 aircraft—40.5 percent of the entire Luftwaffe strength.[3] Hardest hit was the Luftwaffe's transport arm. In addition to the vain effort to resupply Stalingrad, the transport pilots were called upon twice for major surges of supplies and reinforcements to North Africa—once in November 1942, after the initial Allied invasion, and again in May 1943, when the remaining German forces were destroyed in Tunisia. This latter effort alone cost 177 Ju-52s and 6 of the scarce Me-323 "Giant" transports. Taken together, these three major airlifts in six months destroyed the Luftwaffe transport force, depriving it not only of aircraft but also of irreplaceable instructor pilots. Without these transports, future parachute and aerial resupply operations were impossible.

The strategic bombing offensive over Western Europe was equally costly to the Luftwaffe. Much has been written about the appalling losses suffered by the U.S. Army's Eighth Air Force in daylight bombing raids in 1943. What is often overlooked is the heavy loss rate among its opponents, the Luftwaffe's fighter interceptors. From March 1943 onward, German fighter losses in the West consistently exceeded those in the East. Even in July 1943, at the height of the Kursk Offensive, 335 German fighters fell over Germany but only 201 over Russia.[4] Goering's and Hitler's determination to defend the Reich caused them to concentrate more and more fighter squadrons and antiaircraft batteries in Germany at the expense of the

Eastern Front. This concentration on home air defense and the accompanying high losses among fighter aircraft were major causes of the loss of German air supremacy in the East. Whether they realized it or not, the Red Air Force and Red Army owed at least some of their success during 1943–1945 to the sustained bravery of R.A.F. Bomber Command and the U.S. Eighth Air Force.

1942–1943 was also the period in which significant amounts of Lend-Lease aid began to reach the Soviet Union. The standard Soviet estimate of Lend-Lease is that it represented only 4 percent of Soviet production, but in reality it was far greater. The United States and Great Britain willingly provided vast quantities of aluminum, manganese, coal, and other materials to replace the supplies captured by the Germans in 1941, thereby allowing Soviet manufacturing to recover much more rapidly than might otherwise have been the case. In addition to raw materials, the Allies shipped 34 million uniforms, 14.5 million pairs of boots, 4.2 million tons of food, and 11,800 railroad locomotives and cars. The Americans balked at a few unusual Soviet requests, of course. In 1943, the Soviet Purchasing Committee in the United States had the effrontery to ask for eight tons of uranium oxide, an obvious bid for fissionable material to support the fledgling Soviet nuclear program! Overall, however, the Allies poured materials into the Soviet Union between 1942 and 1945, prompting one recent historian to remark, "The Allies bought the German defeat with Russian blood and paid in Spam."[5]

Lend-Lease trucks were particularly important to the Red Army, which was notoriously deficient in such equipment. By the end of the war, two out of every three Red Army trucks were foreign-built, including 409,000 cargo trucks and 47,000 Willys Jeeps. It is no coincidence that even today "studabaker" and "villies" are familiar words to Russian war veterans. Lend-Lease trucks solved one of the Red Army's greatest deficiencies: the inability to resupply and sustain mobile forces once they had broken through into German rear areas. Without the trucks, each Soviet offensive during 1943–1945 would have come to a halt after a shallower penetration, allowing the Germans time to reconstruct their defenses and force the Red Army to conduct yet another deliberate assault.

Other Lend-Lease equipment, particularly combat vehicles and aircraft, proved less successful, increasing Soviet suspicions that they were being given junk. Soviet commanders complained bitterly about Western-furnished weapons whose design flaws often had nothing to do with Allied politics. The British Valentine and Matilda tanks, for example, had turrets so small that no gun larger than 40 mm would fit, making those tanks almost useless against the heavier, newer German tanks. By contrast, the Soviet T-34 and the U.S. M4 Sherman tanks had turrets sufficiently large to accommodate bigger main guns later in the war. The Sherman, however, disappointed the Soviets because its narrow treads made it much less mobile on mud than its German and Soviet counterparts, and it consumed greater quantities of fuel. In fact, the U.S. Army Ordnance planners had standardized this width to ensure that Shermans would fit onto ocean transports and across existing U.S. bridging equipment, two considerations that meant nothing to the Soviets.

Similarly, the Red Air Force valued Western transport aircraft but considered the Lend-Lease combat planes to be inferior. Based on their experience in 1941, the Soviets wanted close air support, ground attack aircraft, and low-altitude fighters. Unfortunately, the British and American airpower advocates had neglected these functions in favor of fighter interceptors and long-range bombers. The superb A-20 light bomber performed well in the Soviet inventory, but the same could not always be said for fighters. In the interests of speed, the Soviet Purchasing Committee had to accept existing, obsolescent aircraft that were already in production, including the P-39 Aircobra, the P-40 Warhawk, and early model British Hurricane fighters. The Soviet Union complicated the situation further by refusing to allow Allied mechanics and instructor-pilots to train their Soviet counterparts on the aircraft. Still, Soviet air aces such as A. I. Pokryshkin and G. A. Rechalov used P-39s to achieve numerous victories. In spring 1943, these aircraft were instrumental in enabling the Red Air Force to achieve air superiority over the Kuban bridgehead held by German Seventeenth Army east of the Sea of Azov.[6]

STRETCHED THIN

Despite von Manstein's notable victories in the Donbas and at Khar'kov, the German Army in the East faced a grim future in spring 1943. Quite apart from the loss of the entire Sixth Army and four satellite armies, attrition had once again reduced that force to a shadow of its 1941 strength. On 1 April 1943, the German Army's strength in the East stood at 2,732,000 men in 147 infantry and 22 panzer divisions, 1,336 tanks, and 6,360 guns. By contrast, the Red Army had 5,792,000 soldiers organized into more than 500 division equivalents and supported by more than 6,000 tanks and 20,000 artillery pieces.[7]

This imbalance was particularly evident in ordinary infantry divisions. Even before Operation Blau, 69 of the 75 divisions in Army Groups North and Center had been reduced from the standard complement of nine infantry battalions with four-gun artillery batteries, to six battalions with three-gun batteries.[8] After the 1942 campaign, this reduction became almost universal. Some divisions retained three regimental headquarters with only two battalions each, while others reduced the proportion of support to infantry troops by having only two regiments of three battalions. In either case, the resulting division lacked the manpower to defend broad frontages and still retain some reserve for counterattacks. The continuing reductions in available horse and motor vehicles made this division far less mobile than its 1941 predecessor; artillery batteries were sometimes overrun because their crews could not move the guns, and local reconnaissance and counterattack forces were often mounted on bicycles.

During 1942, many infantry divisions had received new 75 mm antitank guns that were much more effective against Soviet armor, but there was a general shortage of ammunition for these guns.[9] The situation was even worse in the case of the various *ersatz* units, such as security divisions or Luftwaffe field divisions, which had even fewer troops and heavy weapons than normal infantry divisions. The 22 Luftwaffe divisions were particularly vulnerable, because few of the leaders in those units had extensive experience in ground combat and logistics. Each newly formed unit had to pay its own terrible price to acquire the experience that conventional German units had in their institutional memories. German Army officers, constantly aware of the personnel shortages in their own units, were appalled at the thought of 170,000 above-average Luftwaffe troops wasted in their own formations instead of bringing existing army units back up to strength.[10] Throughout the war, the Luftwaffe and Waffen SS continued to recruit volunteers into their own separate units to the detriment of conventional army formations.

To complicate matters further, Hitler attempted to eradicate the German defensive doctrine that had proved so successful in both World Wars. During the summer of 1942, the weakened infantry units of Army Groups North and Center had been forced to conduct several local withdrawals under the continuing pressure of Soviet attacks. To halt this tendency, on 8 September 1942, Hitler issued a Fuehrer Defense Order, his most detailed statement on the matter.

This order was a rambling mixture of theory and detailed practice, but it included three major points.[11] First, Hitler explicitly rejected the famous elastic defense, harking back instead to the rigid (and extremely costly) German defensive battles in France during 1916. Unfortunately, that concept assumed that the defender had not only ample infantry manpower but also large supplies of barbed wire, antitank mines, and other materials for constructing field fortifications. Second, Hitler suggested that defending units should be moved laterally in the path of the Soviet attacks to increase strength. This assumed that the German defenders could accurately identify Soviet troop concentrations and predict the sites of future attacks, an assumption that was repeatedly disproved by superior Soviet deception plans. Moreover, given Hitler's insistence that the defenders stand fast, concentrating forces in this manner simply put more troops at risk from massive Soviet artillery barrages. Once the Soviet penetration occurred, the defending commander would have even fewer troops to fill the resulting gaps. Finally, Hitler announced his intention to manage the defensive battles personally, requiring all commanders in the East to provide him with extremely detailed maps of their positions and assessments of their supplies and capabilities. This requirement struck yet another blow at one of the hallmarks of German tactical success—the independence of subordinate leaders in choosing the means to accomplish their assigned missions.

This Defense Order was another indication of Hitler's frustration about his inability to resolve the war in the East. He expressed this frustration by continuing the long-standing trend toward micromanagement, eliminating professional soldiers who disagreed with him. On 9 September 1942, Hitler ended a series of disagreements with Field Marshal Wilhelm List by relieving him and assuming personal command of Army Group A, leaving List's chief of staff to relay orders. Two weeks later, Hitler also relieved Colonel General Franz Halder as chief of OKH and came close to firing General Alfred Jodl, because the latter had supported List's arguments. Halder's young successor as chief of the General Staff was General Kurt Zeitzler. Zeitzler was by no means a passive tool of the dictator; on five occasions over the next two years, he formally offered his resignation on matters of principle. Yet Zeitzler lacked the prestige and authority of his predecessors; Hitler even deprived him of control over the careers of general staff officers.[12]

While the German Army as a whole and the infantry in particular declined steadily, the armored and mechanized forces experienced an unexpected renaissance in 1943. In February, the confused state of tank production and the poor condition of the panzer divisions prompted Hitler to recall Heinz Guderian from his forced retirement. Wise in the ways of National Socialist bureaucracy, Guderian insisted that he report directly to Hitler as inspector-general of panzer troops. His appointment included independent authority over tank production as well as control of the organization, doctrine, and training of all armored forces, including panzer elements of the Waffen SS and Luftwaffe. In practice, of course, the independent fiefdoms of the Third Reich did not allow Guderian to succeed completely. Nevertheless, during the period 1943–1944, Guderian worked wonders by increasing production, discouraging some of the more ill-conceived design changes, and repeatedly rebuilding the panzer force to fight again.[13]

RETURN OF THE DEEP OPERATION

In 1941, the Red Army had temporarily simplified its force structure and abandoned its elaborate military theories because it lacked the initiative, the weaponry, and the trained leaders to employ that structure and those theories effectively. After Stalingrad, however, the Soviets had accumulated enough of these scarce commodities to begin elaborating on their force structure and updating their tactical concepts. Tested from 1942 to 1943 and perfected between 1944 and 1945, the new Red Army developed rapidly to the point where it could conduct the ideal Deep Operation.

From mid-1941 until early 1943, virtually all Soviet rifle armies consisted of a half-dozen divisions and separate brigades subordinated directly to an army headquarters. In the course of 1943, however, the Defense Commissariat began to re-form rifle corps, each with three to five divisions and supporting specialized units, subordinated to an army headquarters. Rifle brigades were steadily reorganized into full rifle divisions, and worthy rifle divisions were reorganized as guard formations. As production and manpower permitted, the rifle armies, corps, and, finally, divisions gradually received attached units of the various specialized arms, such as armor, engineers, antiaircraft guns, and mortars. These attachments were particularly common in guards units and in any rifle corps or army assigned to conduct a deliberate attack on German defenses. From being little more than a collection of infantry and field guns with a few tanks and antitank guns, a typical rifle army grew into a complex structure that could integrate a variety of combat arms and services—in essence, a combined-arms army.[14]

To support the *fronts* and armies, the *Stavka* organized an impressive array of combat support formations, which it assigned to field forces based on operational requirements. The intent was to create a force structure capable of providing requisite support to all types of operations, but especially penetrations, deep exploitations, and attacks against heavily fortified positions in the field or in urban areas. Gun, howitzer, antitank, antiaircraft, self-propelled, and multiple-rocket launcher artillery battalions, regiments, and brigades emerged during 1942 and 1943. Eventually, this artillery was grouped into imposing artillery divisions and corps. The artillery penetration corps of 1943, which contained an immense number of gun tubes and multiple-rocket launchers, were assigned to *fronts* and even individual armies that were to conduct major attacks. This lavish concentration of firepower enabled Soviet commanders to pulverize the most imposing German defenses. Soviet organizational efforts in other support arms followed the same pattern, leading to a proliferation of engineer, railroad, transportation, and logistical formations.

The most significant structural change, however, occurred in the armored forces. During the Battle of Stalingrad and the ensuing Winter Campaign, the tank and mechanized corps organized in 1942 had proven their worth as instruments for limited, tactical exploitation of enemy defenses. For the remainder of the war, high-priority combined-arms armies would control one or two tank or mechanized corps for the purpose of encircling German defenders to a depth of 50 to 200 kilometers behind the front lines.

However, the Red Army needed a larger mechanized formation, analogous to a panzer corps or panzer army, for deeper, operational exploitations up to 500 kilometers. This new organization, the tank army, should not be confused with the ad hoc tank armies of 1942. The 1943 version of the tank army comprised units that shared a common level of mobility and armored protection rather than a mixture of tank, cavalry, and rifle units. The new tank army was built around two tank corps and one mechanized corps, supported by a variety of specialized regiments for motorcycle reconnaissance, multiple-rocket launchers, heavier howitzers, antitank weapons, and antiaircraft guns. By Soviet standards, this structure was lavishly supported by aviation, signals, transportation, and maintenance units.[15]

The design for the new tank army was based on mobile operations in late 1942 and early 1943. V. M. Badanov's Tatsinskaia Raid in December 1942 demonstrated the need for multiple tank corps to operate in tandem, and General M. M. Popov's mobile group operations in February 1943 represented a test of a prototype of such an army. Meanwhile, in January 1943, the Peoples' Commissariat of Defense (GKO) approved the establishment of such a force and the first modern tank armies were born.[16] For the remainder of the war, the five (later six) tank armies were the spearhead of Soviet deep attacks, conducting operational maneuver and seeking operational objectives in the German rear areas. On a map, the Soviet offensive plans often resembled a set of Russian nesting dolls, with encirclements inside of other encirclements. The separate tank and mechanized corps attached to forward combined-arms armies would encircle one or more German corps immediately behind the main German defense lines, while the tank armies bypassed these struggles, straining to penetrate as far as possible into the operational depths and thereby achieve larger encirclements.

Thus the tank and mechanized corps, tank armies and, on occasion, reinforced cavalry corps, or cavalry-mechanized groups, formed mobile groups to support armies and *fronts*, as envisaged by the interwar theorists. Ideally mobile groups would enter the battle only after rifle divisions had penetrated German forward defenses, allowing the mobile corps and tank armies to pass through a narrow gap in those defenses. In practice,

Soviet commanders often misjudged the time to commit their mobile groups, or deliberately sent them into battle to complete the penetration begun by rifle units. In such circumstances, the mobile corps and tank armies were delayed and reduced in strength by the need to finish the initial penetration. Once they had accomplished that task, they were free to seek deeper objectives. When the mobile group was logistically exhausted and could go no farther, it attempted to seize bridgeheads over the next major water obstacle and then halted while the rest of the forces came forward.

An offensive battle involved three separate questions for the Soviet commanders: how to concentrate enough forces and firepower on a narrow front to overcome enemy resistance; how to expand and develop the tactical penetration to the point where the Germans could no longer seal it off; and when to stop the operational exploitation by mobile forces? This last problem involved bringing supplies and troop units forward to support the mobile groups. Rifle armies (redesignated combined-arms armies in early 1943) were to create and widen the penetrations, tank and mechanized corps and tank armies were to exploit those penetrations, and transportation and supply units were the key to sustaining that exploitation.

All of these changes—from the formation of rifle corps to the use of tank armies on deep, independent missions—were part of a gradual decentralization of power in the Red Army. Two years of war had produced a number of skilled staff officers and commanders, and Stalin himself had come to trust his subordinates to an unprecedented degree. On 9 October 1942, at the height of the Stalingrad defense, a decree restored unitary command and reduced military commissars to the rank of deputy commander for political affairs. Increasingly, the dictator relied on a combination of skilled *Stavka* planners in Moscow and ruthless "representatives of the *Stavka*"—of whom G. K. Zhukov was only the most famous—in the field. Paradoxically, as Hitler strove to eliminate all subordinate initiative and flexibility in the German Army, Stalin moved in the opposite direction. In their memoirs, senior German officers blamed Hitler's interference and rigid control for all manner of evils, but few of them recognized that their opponents were developing the very command procedures that had once made the Wehrmacht supreme.[17]

One characteristic that the Red Army and the Wehrmacht shared was a general shortage of personnel. The Soviet Union was mobilized to a far greater degree than Germany, but there were never enough troops to fill completely the ranks of the many new wartime formations. Most of the new tank armies were built around the discarded headquarters of shattered rifle armies. High-priority units, such as mechanized or guards formations, received more replacements and equipment than normal units. Even the tables of organization were different: a guards' rifle division was authorized to have 10,670 soldiers, as compared to the normal 9,435, and more field guns and automatic weapons than a typical rifle division. In practice, however, the typical rifle division, like its German counterpart, was seriously understrength in men and matériel. Consequently, an average Soviet rifle division with 7,000 troops in summer 1943 was down to as few as 2,000 troops in 1945.[18]

THE GERMAN DILEMMA

After two years of constant attrition in the East, the Wehrmacht was no longer capable of conducting a general offensive on a wide front. In their efforts to find some more limited goal for an offensive, the Germans focused on the Kursk salient, where the front lines bent westward, forming a bulge that was 250 kilometers from north to south and 160 kilometers from east to west. This salient appeared to be designed for an encirclement battle; all the Germans had to do was pinch it off by attacking at the northern and southern shoulders, thereby tearing a huge hole in the Soviet defenses. Instead of becoming overextended, as had happened in the previous two summer campaigns, the Germans would actually be able to shorten their defensive lines after such an encirclement. The OKW issued Operational Order No. 5 on 13 March and No. 6 on 16 April 1943 outlining this plan.

The new chief of the General Staff, Kurt Zeitzler, was especially interested in the proposal. Unfortunately, even Guderian could not rebuild panzer units overnight, and the Germans lost valuable time recovering from the Winter Campaign. On 3 May 1943, Zeitzler persuaded Hitler to attend a meeting in Munich to discuss the proposed Kursk offensive, Operation Zitadelle (Citadel). General Walter Model, who as commander of Ninth Army would have to make the principal attack, described the elaborate Soviet defensive preparations identified by aerial photography and argued that the proposed offensive was exactly what the Soviets were preparing to meet. Von Manstein, as commander of Army Group South, also felt that the moment of opportunity had passed, but his counterpart at Army Group Center, Field Marshal Guenther von Kluge, was enthusiastic about the proposal. The ever-optimistic Zeitzler argued that the newly formed units of Mark V (Panther) and Mark VI (Tiger) tanks would give the Germans a decisive technological advantage over their opponents. Guderian and Albert Speer pointed out the technical problems involved in producing these new weapons, especially the Panthers, but they were overruled. Hitler, as so often happened in 1943–1945, was unable to make a decision. In a private conversation with Guderian a week later, Hitler remarked that "whenever I think of the attack [at Kursk] my stomach turns over."[19] Ultimately, Hitler saw no alternative politically and agreed to the plan, with 5 July as the final target date.

THE SOVIET STRATEGY

During the winter offensives of 1941–1942 and 1942–1943, the Red Army had repeatedly attempted to do too much too rapidly. Planning, troop concentrations, fire support, and especially logistics had all suffered from this haste. Von Manstein's brilliant counteroffensive during February to March 1943 finally convinced most senior Soviet officers that they had to set more modest, realistic goals for the future, rather than trying to end the war in a single, climactic offensive.

Zhukov and A. M. Vasilevsky concluded that the 1943 Soviet offensive and ensuing summer campaign, like those of the previous two years, must be preceded by a defensive battle to absorb and reduce German striking power. Still flushed from the destruction of Sixth Army, Stalin was initially inclined to disagree and sought to resume the offensive as soon as the *rasputitza* ended. In a meeting at the Kremlin on 12 April 1943, the commanders made their case for a temporary defensive. Zhukov, Vasilevsky, and General Staff Chief of Operations A. I. Antonov convinced Stalin to stand on the defensive but only as a prelude to a planned offensive campaign. Stalin again vacillated in early May but finally accepted the *Stavka* view.[20]

The *Stavka's* strategic plan for the 1943 summer-fall campaign required the Voronezh and Central Fronts to defend the Kursk bulge, flanked to the north by the Briansk and Western Fronts and to the south by the Southwestern Front. In the rear, Stalin created a large strategic reserve, the Steppe Military District, which would deploy forward when necessary at the Steppe Front. Until May, Soviet planners were uncertain whether the main German thrust would fall against Kursk or south of Khar'kov. As a precaution, therefore, the *Stavka* ordered all six *fronts* to erect strong defenses. Initially, the reserve armies of the Steppe Military District, including 5th Guards Tank Army, concentrated east of Khar'kov, a location from which they could deploy to meet either German thrust.[21]

From the start, this defensive preparation was an integral part of the larger *Stavka* plan for a subsequent ambitious offensive. As soon as the expected German offensive was halted, the Western, Briansk, and Central Fronts would attack the Orel bulge, the German salient immediately north of Kursk. Shortly after the German attack was halted and after necessary regrouping, the Voronezh and Steppe Fronts would attack to the south of Kursk, toward Khar'kov. In the interval between these two strokes, the Southern and Southwestern Fronts would conduct diversionary attacks on the Northern Donets and Mius Rivers. These diversions were intended to draw German reserves away from the point where the main Soviet thrusts would occur.

After the Red Army had seized Orel and Khar'kov, neighboring forces would broaden the offensive further. The ultimate Soviet strategic objective was the Dnepr River line. (By fall, however, the *Stavka* would once again expand its objectives to encompass all of Belorussia and the Ukraine.) In late spring, the *Stavka* also ordered extensive reconnaissance measures to determine German intentions and dispositions, and strict *maskirovka* (deception) steps to conceal the assembly and redeployment of the Steppe Front.

As June turned into July, both sides put the finishing touches on their massive preparations. With all chance of surprise gone, the German forces placed increasing faith in new equipment and in the rebuilt panzer divisions, which had never before failed to achieve an initial penetration and encirclement. It is a measure of Soviet self-confidence that the senior commanders were looking beyond the German attack, beyond its failure, to the first major Soviet summer offensive.

CHAPTER 11

Kursk to the Dnepr

PLANS AND FORCES

Given the peculiar shape of the Kursk salient, the German operational plan was obvious to both sides: two massive, armor-tipped thrusts, aimed at the northern and southern shoulders of the bulge, would seek to meet in the middle, surround all the forces in the pocket, and tear a fatal wound in the Soviet defensive front. Fifty divisions, including 19 panzer and motorized divisions with 2,700 tanks and assault guns, would be supported by over 2,600 aircraft.[1] (See Map 12.)

On the northern shoulder in the region of Field Marshal Guenther von Kluge's Army Group Center, General Walter Model's Ninth Army included the XXXXVII and LI Panzer Corps. These two corps included the 2d, 4th, 8th, 12th, 18th, and 20th Panzer Divisions. The main assault, however, was to be delivered on the southern shoulder by Erich von Manstein's Army Group South. Colonel General Hermann Hoth's Fourth Panzer Army controlled not only the lavishly equipped II SS Panzer Corps of three divisions (SS *Totenkopf*, *Leibstandarte*, and *Das Reich*) but also the XXXXVIII Panzer Corps, with the refurbished 3d and 11th Panzer Divisions and the oversized Panzergrenadier Division *Grossdeutschland*. In addition, an army detachment named for its commander, General Werner Kempf, was to protect Hoth's eastern flank from counterattack, using the three divisions (6th, 7th, and 9th Panzer) of III Panzer Corps and a variety of nondivisional armored units. As spring gave way to summer, all these units had ample opportunity to make up their equipment shortages and weld new replacements into an effective team. The rolling terrain of central Russia echoed with a series of live fire exercises and tank gunnery practices.

German confidence rested on more than just mass and training, however. The belated mobilization of the German war economy produced a number of the new Mark V Panther and Mark VI Tiger tanks, both armed with the deadly 88mm gun. Hitler delayed the start of Operation Zitadelle several times to allow more Panthers and Tigers to be fielded. Yet even the SS divisions had only one company of Tiger tanks each, and the hasty construction and delivery left many design problems to be resolved in the

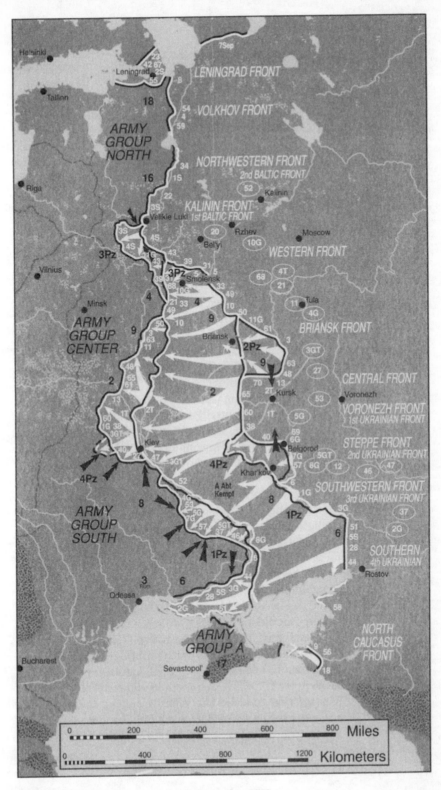

12. *Summer–Fall Campaign, June–December 1943*

field. Mark III and IV tanks were still the most common armored vehicles in the German arsenal, but, thanks to Guderian, some of these received armored skirts that protected their tracks and roadwheels, causing short-range Soviet antitank shells to detonate prematurely.

Much has been written about the design failures of the new German weapons, particularly the Ferdinand or Porsche Tiger, which was armed with an 88mm main gun but no secondary machine gun. This omission made the 90 Porsche Tigers at Kursk extremely vulnerable to close-range attack by Soviet infantrymen. In his memoirs, Guderian says that he was fully aware of this problem but was pressured by Hitler to find some use for the Tigers.[2] The premature commitment of small units of Tigers during the winter battles at Leningrad and Khar'kov had allowed the Soviets to capture and study the new weapons. The obvious conclusion was that the Red Army needed larger, high-velocity antitank weapons to accompany infantry and armored units. This accelerated the natural tendency to produce larger main guns. The SU-152 tank destroyer, a 152mm gun/howitzer mounted on a KV-1 tank chassis, was hurried into production in February and March 1943 to join the existing SU-76 and SU-122 self-propelled guns. At the same time, Soviet designers began to upgrade the workhorse T-34, giving it an 85mm main gun in place of the 76.2mm; however, this change did not occur in time to help the Red tankers at Kursk.[3]

Soviet air and ground reconnaissance observed every detail of the German preparations. As the Central Partisan Headquarters in Moscow developed greater control over the various partisan groups in the field, the Stavka was able to use those forces in conjunction with scout units of the Red Army that infiltrated the German rear areas to both observe and hamper every German movement. Equally important, by mid-1943 the General Staff's Main Intelligence Directorate (GRU) had created an effective hierarchy of staff officer analysts to collect, analyze, and disseminate all available intelligence information. Each front-level intelligence department controlled agents, SPETSNAZ reconnaissance units, and radio-intercept teams, and supervised the collection efforts of subordinate intelligence sections. Air reconnaissance units were attached to every headquarters, from combined-arms army upward. By 12 April, for example, the Voronezh Front had correctly identified all the mobile divisions in the Fourth Panzer Army. Nor did the GRU sit passively with such information. Throughout June and July, specialized engineer "destroyer" brigades within each front conducted a series of raids on bridges, railroads, and other key facilities, thereby complicating German logistics and security.[4]

The long delays in the Germans' preparations allowed their opponents the luxury of constructing an elaborate defensive system. During March and April, the Stavka issued a series of engineer publications on defensive systems that showed increasing sophistication, using every fold in the ground to cover and conceal troops. The core of each Soviet position was its antitank defenses, organized into an elaborate network of antitank strongpoints and regions with minefields packed densely along the German avenues of approach and covered by the interlocking fires of thousands of antitank guns. Each forward company facing the Germans had at least three artillery guns, nine antitank guns, one tank or self-propelled gun, and a platoon of combat engineers within its defensive position. In the most likely areas of German attack, similar defensive positions were arrayed eight deep in front of the attackers. The average number of mines per kilometer of front reached 3,200 by the time the battle began. The opportunity to plan and prepare so thoroughly also meant that the traditional weaknesses of the Red Army, such as artillery fire direction and field communications, were eliminated. Every artillery target, every meter of field telephone wire was checked and rechecked.[5]

On the northern half of the Kursk bulge, Army General K. K. Rokossovsky's Central Front controlled Lieutenant General A. G. Rodin's 2d Tank Army and three combined-arms armies, with Lieutenant General N. P. Pukhov's 13th Army and Lieutenant General I. V. Galanin's 70th Army opposite the main thrust of Model's Ninth German Army (see Map 13). In the south, the young Army General N. F. Vatutin, with N. S. Khrushchev as his political commissar, commanded the Voronezh Front waiting for the main German assault. Here the *Stavka* placed its best combined-arms armies, commanded in many cases by rising stars in the Soviet hierarchy. The first-line defense was divided between four such armies: Lieutenant General N. E. Chibisov's 38th, Lieutenant General K. S. Moskalenko's 40th, Lieutenant General I. M. Chistiakov's 6th Guards, and Lieutenant General M. S. Shumilov's 7th Guards Armies. Behind them stood Lieutenant General M. E. Katukov's 1st Tank Army and Lieutenant General V. D. Kriuchenkin's 69th Army, with a guards rifle corps and two guards tank corps in reserve.[6]

By themselves, these forces should have been sufficient to contain the German attacks. According to declassified Soviet archival materials, the Soviet Central and Voronezh Fronts fielded 1,087,500 soldiers, 13,013 guns and mortars, and 3,275 armored vehicles to oppose the 435,000 soldiers, 9,960 guns and mortars, and 3,155 tanks of German Ninth Army, Fourth Panzer Army, and Army Detachment Kempf.[7] (See Table 11-1.) However, the *Stavka* did not rely upon this force alone to thwart a German breakthrough. It backed up Rokossovsky's and Vatutin's forces with General I. S. Konev's Steppe Front, which numbered 449,133 men, 6,536 guns and mortars, and 1,506 tanks and SP guns. This increased Soviet superiority in the Kursk region to 3:1 in manpower and 1.5:1 in armor.

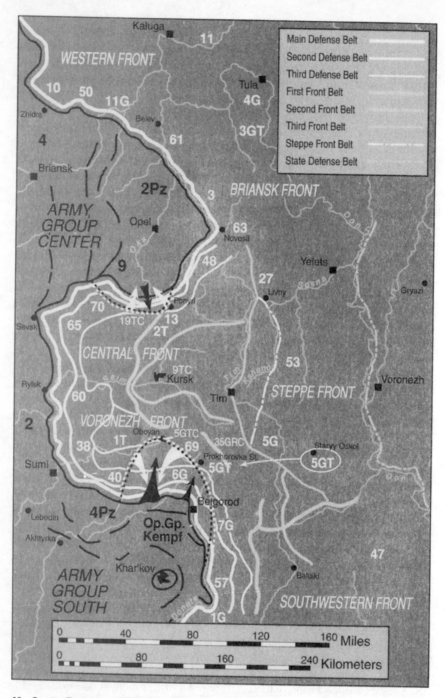

13. *Soviet Defensive Actions in the Battle of Kursk, 5–23 July 1943*

Table 11-1. Correlation of Combat Forces, Battle of Kursk

	Soviet	German	Correlation
Central Front			
Men	667,500	267,000	2.6:1
Tanks	1,745	1,455	1.21:1
Guns/mortars	14,163	6,366	2.22:1
Voronezh Front			
Men	420,000	168,000	2.5:1
Tanks	1,530	1,700	1:1.1
Guns/mortars	10,850	3,600	3:1
Overall			
Men	1,087,500	435,000	2.5:1
Tanks	3,275	3,155	1:1
Guns/mortars	25,013	9,966	2.5:1

Source: V. N. Simbolikov, *Kurskaia bitva, 1943* (Moscow: Voroshilov Academy of the General Staff, 1950).

In 1941 and 1942, Stalin and his generals had repeatedly misinterpreted the Germans' offensive plans and had concentrated their forces in the wrong areas. The obvious threat to the Kursk salient allowed the Soviets for the first time in the war to reduce their defenses on secondary fronts and concentrate them at all potentially critical points. It was this concentration, more than any overall strategic superiority, that allowed the Soviets to outnumber the Germans in the Orel-Kursk region by 2.7 to 1 (2,226,000 to 900,000) in troops, 3.3 to 1 (33,000 to 10,000) in gun tubes, and 2.6 to 1 (4,800 to 1,800) in armored vehicles.[8]

True to their tradition of building strong strategic reserves, the *Stavka* created sizeable reserves across the entire expanse of their front from Moscow to Voronezh. This structure was intended to do more than just provide additional depth to the defenses. It could also reinforce the most threatened sector of the defense and conduct major counteroffensives on its own. In the course of the battle, Konev passed control of four corps and two complete armies to Vatutin. Again, the growing number of experienced Soviet commanders and staff officers meant that Steppe Front could plan for a counteroffensive rather than dealing with the desperate defensive struggles. This enabled the Steppe Front to plan farther ahead than could its German opposite number. In addition, Briansk and Western Fronts to the north of Kursk and Southwestern and Southern Fronts to the south were prepared to conduct a series of counteroffensives once the German onslaught was blunted.

Had they known the full scope of Soviet preparations, even the most confident German commanders would have been daunted. Although they studied the forward Soviet defenses in great detail, those commanders were often misled about forces further to the rear. In the Voronezh Front, for example, dummy troop concentrations were established to mislead the German aerial reconnaissance, while the actual troops of the Steppe Front and other strategic reserves were carefully concealed from view.[9]

CAULDRON

The German attack was finally scheduled for the morning of 5 July 1943. Through defectors and reconnaissance reports, the Soviet commanders were able to predict this attack to the minute. One half hour before the German artillery was scheduled to begin firing, the Red artillery launched its own counterpreparation against every area where the attackers were likely to assemble. A Soviet effort to bomb the forward German airfields was less successful, but the German attack schedule was certainly disrupted and delayed. On the northern side of the salient, German Ninth Army attacked 13th and 70th Armies on a frontage of 50 kilometers but, in seven days of fierce fighting, was able to penetrate only 8 to 12 kilometers into the massive Soviet defenses. Beginning on 6 July, Rokossovsky launched a series of counterattacks with 2d Tank Army and other reserves, culminating in bloody sea-saw battles at Ponyri Station and further west. By 12 July, his forces had halted the Germans in their tracks. After that day, Ninth Army made no further advances, and, in fact, began to withdraw on 14 July.

In the south, Fourth Panzer Army had slightly better success. Here the Germans used their new Tiger and other heavy tanks as a wedge or shield behind which the older medium tanks and the few available infantry personnel carriers could advance. Hoth's XXXXVIII and II SS Panzer Corps eventually penetrated into the third Soviet defensive belt, a depth of 35 kilometers, but were stopped by Katukov's 1st Tank Army.[10] In the south, as in the north, the Germans were never able to achieve a significant operational penetration and were, therefore, unable to encircle and disrupt their enemy's rear areas.

The battle reached its critical point between 11 and 12 July, when Hoth turned his panzer spearhead northeast to envelop 1st Tank Army's defense. About 400 tanks of II SS Panzer Corps succeeded in penetrating to Prokhorovka Station, an obscure railroad junction in the heart of the Voronezh Front's defenses. Vatutin then recommended, and G. F. Zhukov as representative of the *Stavka* approved, launching a general counterattack of five armies, including two from the Steppe Front. Over twelve hundred tanks on both sides were engaged in this struggle, but the psychological and tactical key to the issue was possession of Prokhorovka. Lieutenant General P. A. Rotmistrov, the commander of 5th Guards Tank Army, received two extra tank corps to reinforce his attack at Prokhorovka itself. The Red counterattack was pressed home in spite of two significant German advantages. Stuka dive-bombers outfitted with new automatic cannon had already proved highly effective in penetrating the thin armor on the tops of T-34 tanks. Moreover, the few surviving German Tigers and Panthers, with their 88mm guns and thick frontal armor, were able to engage the T-34s at much longer ranges than the attacking Soviet tankers could counter. Despite these German advantages, 5th Guards Tank Army's 18th and 29th Tank Corps conducted an almost suicidal charge across open, rolling terrain in order to close to a range where all tank guns were equally effective.[11] In the process, Rotmistrov lost over 400 of his 800 tanks, but the Germans lost 320 tanks and self-propelled guns as well. The panzer spearheads, worn down by a week of struggle against elaborate antitank defenses, were no match for the fresh reserves of the Soviet tank forces.

By the end of 12 July, the Prokhorovka area was a graveyard of burned out Soviet and German tanks. Hoth still hoped to continue the attack to exploit the more successful German advance by III Panzer Corps on its secondary axis east of Belgorod. At this juncture, however, Hitler ordered von Manstein to begin withdrawing II SS Panzer Corps from battle so that it could be moved west to deal with the deteriorating Axis situation in Sicily. Von Manstein vigorously objected, but nonetheless complied, and all German hopes for a renewed offensive, however unrealistic they may have been, evaporated. On 18 July, Fourth Panzer Army and its flank guard, Army Detachment Kempf, began a fighting withdrawal to their initial positions. The Soviets' engineer and antitank preparations, concentrated forces in depth, superb intelligence, and the mobility of their new tank armies had given the Blitzkrieg its worst defeat. It was the first time a German strategic offensive had been halted before it could break through enemy defenses into the strategic depths beyond.

OREL AND BELGOROD-KHAR'KOV

The German commanders had no choice but to retreat. On 12 July, the Red Army began its own carefully planned strategic offensive, which began with Operation Kutuzov against the Orel salient, immediately to the north of the Kursk bulge. With most of Ninth German Army still locked in struggle on the northern shoulder of the Kursk salient, this attack by the Western, Briansk, and, ultimately, Central Front forces caught the Germans off balance.

Colonel General V. D. Sokolovsky's Western Front initiated the main attack on 12 July, with 11th Guards Army, supported by Briansk Front's 61st Army, on its left flank. A day later, the Briansk Front made its main attack using 3d and 63d Armies, each attacking on a narrow, nine-kilometer front to punch a hole through the German defenses. This hole permitted passage for Lieutenant General P. S. Rybalko's 3d Guards Tank Army on 14 July. Meanwhile, Soviet 1st and 5th Tank Corps exploited the success of 11th Guards Army. Because of the significant depth of the German defense around Orel, the Red Army ignored its own doctrine in order to achieve a requisite density of attackers.[12] Each attacking division focused five or six infantry battalions, 160 to 200 guns, and up to 18 infantry support tanks against a single kilometer of the German defensive line. After an artillery preparation of two-and-one-half hours, the guns shifted to a creeping barrage, a concentration of shells that moved slowly forward so that the attacking infantry could advance behind it. The German defenses were so tenacious that the Soviets still had to commit their tank corps to complete the penetration and break into the German rear. Operation Kutuzov was a perfect example of the newly sophisticated Soviet way of war. On 5 August, after weeks of heavy combat, 3d Guards Tank Army entered Orel, and by 18 August, the Briansk Front had reached the approaches to the city for which it was named, completely eliminating the German salient in the region.

From the German viewpoint, worse was to follow. The Western and Briansk Fronts had not been involved in the initial struggle for Kursk and were, therefore, able to begin their offensives at full strength. The German commanders were surprised, however, by the ability of the same Soviet forces that had fought them to a standstill at Kursk to shift over to the offensive in August, only two weeks after the German withdrawal. Von Manstein had been so confident of the inability of the Soviets to mount a new offensive of their own south of Kursk that he had dispatched most of his armored reserves (II SS, XXIV, and XXXXVIII Panzer Corps) southward to deal with Soviet offensives across the Dnepr and Mius Rivers into the Donbas region. These offensives succeeded in their intention, which was to draw German reserves away from the most critical Khar'kov axis, where the principal Soviet offensive effort had been planned.[13]

The new offensive toward Khar'kov, code-named Rumiantsev, was to be launched by Voronezh and Steppe Fronts from the southern shoulder of the Kursk salient. However, to attract German reserves, a notional tank army and combined-arms army were simulated massing on the western side of the bulge. An elaborate series of radio signals and false troop movements supported this deception. *Stavka* representative Zhukov, together with *front* commanders Vatutin and Konev, planned for 5th and 6th

Guards Army—two elements that had borne the brunt of the German offensive—and 53d Army to attack on a sector totaling only 30 kilometers. This enormous concentration of infantry and artillery was necessary to penetrate the five successive German defensive lines between Kursk and Khar'kov. Then, 1st Tank Army and 5th Guards Tank Army, supported by two additional mobile corps, would act as the *front*'s mobile groups, developing the success by encircling Khar'kov from the north and west. To the west of this main penetration, 27th and 40th Armies, supported by four separate tank corps, would make a secondary attack; to the east and southeast, 69th and 7th Guards Armies, followed later by Southwestern Front's 57th Army, would also join the attack.[14]

The initial attacks by the three armies on 3 August symbolized the growing sophistication of Soviet offensive practice. Each attacking rifle division was reinforced with so much artillery that it had specialized, multibattalion artillery groups to support the attacking infantry regiments. Other artillery units provided long-range artillery fire at German reserve positions while keeping a specialized antitank group on hand to halt any counterattack. Still, just as at Orel, the German defenses proved so tenacious that the leading brigades of the two tank armies had to enter the fray to help complete the penetration. Late in the day on 5 August, the third day of the Rumiantsev offensive, the forward tank elements were free to exploit deep into the German rear area. The same evening, the city of Belgorod fell, and Katukov's and Rotmistrov's tank armies reached a depth of over 60 kilometers behind the initial German lines. During the next few days, the combined-arms armies on both sides of the main attack sector began to press forward against the Germans from the north and east in an ever-widening ripple, each army joining in as its neighbor achieved a breakthrough.

At this point, the German mobile reserves, hastily moving south from the heavy combat in the Orel region and north from the Donbas, where the earlier Soviet diversionary offensives had drawn them, attempted their usual task of counterattacking to break up the Soviet offensive, but the magic was gone. *Grossdeutschland* Division detrained and entered combat immediately, before its forces were fully assembled. The most the division could achieve on 6-7 August was to delay 40th Army in its secondary attack to the west of the main offensive. Under cover of such local counterattacks, von Manstein assembled four infantry and seven panzer or motorized divisions. Former divisions of II SS Panzer Corps—now under the control of III Panzer Corps, since its parent corps had been summoned westward to deal with the crisis in Sicily—attempted to use the same maneuver schemes that they had employed when capturing Khar'kov five months earlier. This time, however, it was the Germans rather than the Soviets who were worn down and overextended. On 11 August, the 1st Tank Army's leading corps clashed with the SS at the key road junction of Bogodukhov, 30 kilometers northwest of Khar'kov. Initially, the German forces halted the Soviets and severely mauled the leading three brigades of 1st Tank Army. The next day, however, 5th Guards Tank Army sent reinforcements, and the Germans were fought to a draw between 13 and 17 August. For the first time, a major German counterattack had failed to destroy a Soviet exploitation force. The two tank armies remained in possession of the ground, thereby ensuring seizure of the city of Khar'kov by Konev's rifle forces on 28 August. The Rumiantsev offensive, including the clash around Bogodukhov, is usually referred to as the Belgorod-Khar'kov operation by the Soviets and the Fourth Battle of Khar'kov by the Germans. It marked the end of the Battle of Kursk, the last major German offensive in Russia, and the beginning of the Soviet summer-fall campaign.[15]

WIDENING THE GAP

For the third time in the war, in early August Stalin and the *Stavka* ordered a general offensive to build upon their successes at Orel and Belgorod. As it had been in the late winter, their objective was the Dnepr River line from Smolensk to the Black Sea. In one of his rare periods of realistic policymaking, Hitler also recognized the need to withdraw to the Dnepr in order to restore the continuous front of Army Group South. The Germans had done nothing to fortify this river, although it was a major obstacle in itself. Indeed, the Bug, Dnepr, and Don Rivers all have higher banks on their western sides, making them good defensive positions for the Germans facing east.

As the Germans fell back in the south, Moscow launched a series of *front* and multi-*front* attacks as part of Stalin's general offensive. Against Army Group Center, where the Germans had been preparing defensive positions for as long as 18 months, these well-planned attacks often experienced great difficulty. On 7 August 1943, for example, Army General V. D. Sokolovsky's Western Front, supported by Colonel General A. I. Eremenko's Kalinin Front, attempted a concentric attack to retake Smolensk from German Fourth and Ninth Armies (Operation Suvorov). However, German defenses were strong, the attackers were less coordinated than those who took part in the Kursk operation, and German aerial reconnaissance detected the Soviet main effort despite hasty attempts at deception. When the scarce German troop resources were relocated to contain the first Soviet attack, the *Stavka* representative coordinating the attack, General

N. N. Voronov, recognized that surprise had been lost. A renewed offensive beginning on 7 September finally captured Smolensk by the end of the month but at a heavy cost. Although it had only limited success, the Smolensk offensive did succeed in drawing 16 German divisions northward from the Khar'kov region.[16]

Although the *Stavka* ordered a series of such offensives in the north and center, these attacks were less coordinated and took place against heavy defenses and over less favorable terrain than found in the Kursk region. As a result, the greatest Soviet successes of 1943 remained in the south. To the south of Smolensk and Briansk, Rokossovsky's Central Front also experienced difficulties in advancing against German Second Army after the Orel bulge was reduced in August. Rokossovsky had five combined-arms armies, 2d Tank Army, and two independent mobile formations, 9th Tank and 7th Guards Mechanized Corps. All of these forces were severely worn down by the heavy fighting around Kursk and Orel, yet, even in adversity, they displayed superb staffwork and remarkable flexibility in adjusting to changing circumstances.

The initial attack on 26 August bogged down rapidly because German stay-behind agents had identified the focus of the main Soviet attack, allowing Second Army to regroup its forces. In four days of fighting, Central Front advanced only 25 kilometers. Rokossovsky recognized his problem as early as 27 August and transferred 9th Tank Corps and 13th Army 100 kilometers to the south at night, using strict noise and light discipline. The Germans lost track of these formations. Rokossovsky renewed his attack against the southern flank of Second Army while the bulk of German reserves were still in the North. By 22 September, Central Front's 13th, 60th, and 61st Armies, supported by the two mobile corps, were closing on the Dnepr River north of Kiev.[17]

Meanwhile, on September 1, Army General M. M. Popov's Briansk Front commenced operations against its namesake city. After skillful maneuvering by Colonel General I. V. Boldin's 50th Army against Ninth Army's left flank, Briansk fell to the Soviets on 17 September. Thereafter, Popov's forces caught up with Rokossovsky's advance and reached the banks of the Dnepr and Sozh Rivers north of Gomel' on 3 October.[18]

Rounding out this first wave of offensives, General R. Ia. Malinovsky's Southwestern Front and General F. I. Tolbukhin's Southern Front struck into the Donbas on 16 and 18 August, respectively, this time with more than a diversionary intent. Although they lacked large mechanized reserves, German Army Group South's First Panzer and Sixth Armies avoided encirclement and fought a skillful month-long withdrawal to the Panther defensive line running from Zaporozh'e on the Dnepr to the Black Sea.[19]

PURSUIT

Throughout September, the two opposing armies raced to the Dnepr, with the Germans scorching the earth in the path of the Red Army. Vatutin, commander of the Voronezh Front, urged his troops forward with the exhortation, "They are burning the bread, we must attack."[20]

At the time, and in retrospect, the Germans believed that the pursuing Soviet forces were huge. In fact, the Soviets were weak from the Kursk battles and strung out along the dusty roads, a situation complicated by the systematic German destruction of central Russia. Resupply was difficult and refitting was impossible, but the weakened mobile forces continued the pursuit. The 5th Guards Tank Army, for example, had only 50 of its 500 tanks left after the Belgorod-Khar'kov operation. Rotmistrov concentrated these remaining tanks into three detachments and moved phantom radio nets around to simulate the rest of his tank army and deceive the German signals intelligence teams.[21]

Between 19 and 23 September 1943, Vatutin's lead tank and rifle elements reached the Dnepr north and south of Kiev. Despite a lack of bridging equipment, 40 bridgeheads were improvised between 19 and 26 September, primarily south of Kiev. One bridgehead in particular seemed promising: during the pursuit, two tank corps of Rybalko's 3d Guards Tank Army, reinforced by a separate cavalry corps, had been reassigned to form the mobile spearhead of the Voronezh Front. The infantry elements of these three corps seized a bridgehead at Velikii Bukrin, just below Kiev, but they needed reinforcement to continue the offensive. In anticipation of such a development, in early September the *Stavka* had directed that several airborne units receive refresher parachute training. After a year and a half as ground infantry troops, the 1st, 3d, and 5th Airborne Brigades were reorganized as a provisional airborne corps and given to Vatutin's *front* to use in the exploitation. Two of these brigades were scheduled to jump near Velikii Bukrin on the night of 24–25 September.[22]

Unfortunately for the Soviets, the headlong pursuit to the Dnepr had outrun the ability of the GRU to provide timely intelligence about German defensive dispositions. Unbeknownst to Vatutin, five German divisions— two panzer, two infantry, and one motorized—were approaching the drop zone selected for the airborne assault, and lead elements of 19th Panzer Division were already in the drop zone. The result was a shambles, with highly-trained parachutists scattered over the drop zone and decimated by the unexpected defense. This failure soured Stalin on large-scale airborne operations for the rest of his life.

Stalin's frustration over the course of events near Velikii Bukrin was more than compensated for by successes along other offensive axes. On 15

October, while the race to the Dnepr was under way, Rokossovsky's Central Front punched through German Dnepr River defenses south of Gomel' and occupied favorable positions for a subsequent advance into southern Belorussia. Further south, General F. I. Tolbukhin's Southern Front smashed through Army Group South's Panther line defenses on 13 October and raced to the Dnepr, ultimately isolating German Seventeenth Army in the Crimea.[23]

From late September through mid-November, both sides settled down to a new stalemate along the Dnepr. Although Soviet forces had seized significant bridgeheads near Velikii Bukrin (Voronezh Front) and south of Kremenchug (Steppe Front), the Germans tightly contained both bridgeheads and retained a bridgehead of their own on the east bank, opposite Nikopol'. However, one Soviet rifle division had achieved a smaller bridgehead in the bogs near the small village of Liutezh north of Kiev, an area so impassable that the overextended Germans had not placed major forces to contain it. The Voronezh Front, renamed 1st Ukrainian Front in early November, attempted to exploit this omission.[24] To do so required violating all the normal rules of vehicle movement in swampy terrain. Initially, Vatutin dispatched Lieutenant General A. G. Kravchenko's 5th Guards Tank Corps to reinforce the Liutezh bridgehead. Kravchenko was instructed to move his corps laterally across several rivers and then link up with the small infantry bridgehead. They got there by the dangerous expedient of sealing up their T-34s as much as possible and charging through the streams at full speed. The corps commander laconically reported that he had managed to get "most" of his vehicles across in this manner, but undoubtedly numerous tanks and crews sank in the muddy streams. Then, at the end of October, Vatutin secretly moved all of Rybalko's 3d Guards Tank Army into the bridgehead, together with significant infantry and artillery reinforcements. On 3 November 1st Ukrainian Front's reinforced 38th Army and Rybalko's tank army burst from the bridgehead and overwhelmed the surprised German defenders. By 6 November, Vatutin's troops had taken Kiev, and soon his *front* had formed an imposing strategic foothold across the Dnepr on Ukrainian soil.[25]

Vatutin's forces exploited their success at Kiev relentlessly. Rybalko's 3d Guards Tank Army raced forward through Fastov toward Kazatin, deep in the German rear, followed closely by K. S. Moskalenko's 38th Army, while 1st Guards Cavalry Corps and 60th Army sped westward to seize Zhitomir and threaten Korosten'. Von Manstein reacted quickly, trying to repeat his February victory south of Khar'kov, when he destroyed the better part of three Soviet armies. He redeployed XXXXVIII and XXIV Panzer Corps from the Velikii Bukrin region to destroy the Soviet armored spearheads and drive the enemy back into the Dnepr. Circumstances had changed, however, and the antiarmor capability of Soviet infantry units, backed up by their own tank forces, exacted a terrible toll on the counterattacking Germans. On 10 November, XXXXVIII Panzer Corps halted 3d Guards Tank Army's advance near Fastov. As they had done at Bogodukhov, three months before, the panzers lopped off and destroyed Rybalko's forward brigades, but von Manstein could not retake Fastov.

Frustrated, von Manstein turned XXXXVIII Panzer Corps westward in an attempt to locate and turn Vatutin's right flank. Again he achieved initial but fleeting success. Zhitomir was reportedly defended by drunken troopers of 1st Guards Cavalry Corps, who had found and exploited Fourth Panzer Army's liquor stores. These forces were routed, but again redeploying Soviet infantry, armor, and antitank units halted the Germans near Brusilov. Twice more, in late November and in early December, von Manstein maneuvered his XXXXVIII Panzer Corps skillfully against Vatutin's right flank. Each time the German attack faltered after initial success. Finally, on 19 December, von Manstein made what turned out to be his last attempt to eradicate the dangerous bridgehead. In fierce fighting along the Korosten'-Kiev rail line, von Manstein encircled and destroyed what he believed to be four Soviet corps. In fact, the Germans had attacked the deception force that had been established to mask the assembly of a formidable Soviet strike force further south in the Brusilov region. As von Manstein contemplated his supposed successes near Korosten', his armored forces again ground to a halt after negligible gains. The next day, Christmas 1943, all his optimism evaporated as the Soviets launched a massive surprise assault near Brusilov, ripping a gaping hole through the German forces and signaling the beginning of the next Soviet winter campaign.

Further south, General I. S. Konev's 2d Ukrainian Front, with Lieutenant General P. A. Rotmistrov's 5th Guards Tank Army in the lead, continued to expand the bridgehead of Krivoi Rog, further rupturing the Dnepr defensive line. Just as winter arrived in November and December, a series of counterattacks by German SS and panzer units barely succeeded in containing this bridgehead. On numerous occasions, Soviet attempts to eliminate the German Nikopol' bridgehead failed. These attempts distracted German commanders from the dangerous situations further north along the Dnepr.

Although attention is usually focused on the more dramatic and successful Battle for the Dnepr in the south, an equally important, though less successful, Soviet offensive developed opposite the German Army Group Center. Capitalizing on the fall of Smolensk, in late September the *Stavka* ordered the beginning of the liberation of Belorussia. In early October, General A. I. Eremenko's Kalinin Front seized the critical city of Nevel' by a coup de main, severing Army Group Center's communications with

Army Group North and threatening Vitebsk from the north. Soon thereafter, Rokossovsky's Belorussian Front launched the Gomel'-Rechitsa operation into southern Belorussia, while Sokolovsky's Western Front repeatedly pounded German defenses at Orsha and Mogilev, east of Vitebsk. Initial success led the *Stavka* to order the Baltic, Western, and Belorussian Fronts to launch concentric blows in early November, with the goal of seizing Minsk and all of eastern Belorussia. This ambitious offensive faltered by mid-November in the face of strong and skillful German resistance and deteriorating weather conditions.[26]

With the situation in Belorussia stabilized and Soviet forces supposedly contained in their Dnepr bridgeheads, the Germans halted operations for the winter, confident that a lull in fighting would ensue. The Soviets, however, did not accommodate them.

CONCLUSION

The "Second Period of War" from November 1942 through December 1943 was pivotal in many ways. On a strategic level, the Germans began this period believing that they were within a few hundred yards of victory at Stalingrad and ended it with no illusions about the ultimate outcome of the struggle. After Kursk, Germany could not even pretend to hold the strategic initiative in the East. Moreover, a vast area of central Russia had returned to Soviet control, although this area was so devastated that it would require a decade to recover from the German occupation.

Organizationally, the Wehrmacht was clearly in decline by late 1943. In addition to the death of Sixth Army and several allied armies, the German panzer force and air transport force had been shattered repeatedly. Hundreds of ordinary infantry divisions were reduced to two thirds of their original strength, with declining mobility and inadequate anti-tank defenses. Even the belated industrial mobilization of Germany, fueled by slave labor and directed by the organizational genius of men like Speer and Guderian, could do little beyond patching together the existing units. Indeed, after Kursk a vicious cycle set in. Each new setback forced the Germans to commit their newly recruited replacement troops and their refurbished panzer units to battle more rapidly and with less training. Poorly trained troops suffered abnormally high casualties before they learned the harsh realities of combat. These casualties, in turn, meant that commanders had to call on the next wave of replacements at an even earlier stage in their training.[27]

This grim German situation did not arise solely because of Hitler's errors nor even because of the often-exaggerated numerical superiority of the Soviet armed forces. Perhaps the principal cause of the reversal in the East was the revolution in Soviet command, staff, and operational and tactical techniques. By mid-1943, Stalin had come to trust his commanders and staff officers as professional leaders, and they had justified this trust by learning the painful lessons of mechanized warfare. Indeed, an entire section of the General Staff was devoted to the study and dissemination of "War Experience," based on exhaustive post-mortem analysis of each battle, operation, and campaign. These lessons were grafted onto the existing, prewar concepts of the Red Army, producing a new series of regulations and procedures.

During the summer and fall of 1943, the Soviet commanders experimented with a variety of strategic and operational concepts and techniques. In particular, they worked out most, but not all, of the difficulties of integrating the different arms and services into a true combined-arms operation. At Kursk, Soviet commanders and planners demonstrated their sophisticated understanding of intelligence, deception, and antitank defense. Similar improvements were evident in the careful orchestration of artillery, engineers, infantry, and armor to penetrate German defenses by focusing overwhelming forces on extremely narrow fronts. In the counterstroke at Prokhorovka and in the Kutuzov, Rumiantsev, and Suvorov operations, the Red Army also tested the tank armies and separate tank and mechanized corps that were henceforth the hallmark of Soviet deep operations. With experienced commanders, competent staff officers, and improved logistics based on American trucks, these armored formations demonstrated their ability to match the best efforts of the German panzer force.

Many problems remained to be solved, particularly the correct timing and procedure for introducing these tank units into battle during or after the initial penetration attacks. In addition, ways had to be found to reduce the often catastrophic number of casualties suffered by the Red Army even in its successful offensive operations, lest victory be snatched from the Soviets' grasp by an army and nation bled white.[28] Yet the future outline of Soviet offensive capability was clear, and realistic German commanders began to recognize that they faced an entirely new and far more competent Red Army.

THIRD PERIOD OF WAR
JANUARY 1944–MAY 1945

"Under the banner of Lenin, forward to victory!"
(poster by A. P. Voloshin, 1941)

"The Motherland calls!" (poster by I. M. Toidze, 1941)

Chiefs of the Red Army (clockwise): General Staff Marshals of the Soviet Union B. M. Shkaposhnikov and A. M. Vasilevsky, and General of the Army A. I. Antonov

Marshal of the Soviet Union G. K. Zhukov, Stavka *representative, Western and 1st Belorussian Front commander*

General of the Army N. F. Vatutin, Voronezh and 1st Ukrainian Front commander

Marshal of the Soviet Union I. S. Konev (right) and his chief of staff Lieutenant General M. V. Zakharov planning the Korsun'-Shevchenkovskii operation, January 1943

Marshal of the Soviet Union R. Ia. Malinovsky, 2d Ukrainian Front commander

Marshal of the Soviet Union K. K. Rokossovsky, 3d Belorussian Front commander

General of the Army I. Kh. Bagramian, 1st Baltic Front commander, 1944

General of the Army I. D. Cherniakhovsky, 3d Belorussian Front commander, 1944

Lieutenant General P. A. Rotmistrov (center), 5th Guards Tank Army commander, and his staff

Surviving Soviet front commanders at war's end. From left to right first row: *I. S. Konev, A. M. Vasilevsky, G. K. Zhukov, K. K. Rokossovsky, and K. A. Meretskov;* second row: *Eremenko, and I. Kh. Bagramian*

Colonel M. T. Leonov, commander of the Voronezh Front's 112th Tank Brigade, and his brigade staff conduct tabletop training for a forthcoming operation in the Kursk region, 1943

Soviet "Shturmovik" aircraft in action, 1943

Red Army "Katiusha" multiple rocket launchers firing during battle of Kursk, 1943

Soviet T-34 tanks in the attack

Soviet infantry assault

Soviet infantry assault

Soviet tanks and infantry assault a village

Soviet tank column enters a city

Soviet tank and infantry assault

Soviet tank assault with infantry on board tanks

Soviet forces crossing the Dnepr, November 1943

Soviet attack on a German column, Belgorod-Khar'kov operation, August 1943

A defeated German soldier, Kursk 1943

German prisoners of war in the streets of Moscow, July 1944

"Glory to the Red Army!" (poster by L. F. Golovanov, 1946)

Third Winter of the War

FORCE STRUCTURE AND DOCTRINE

The campaigns of late 1943 through May 1945 were almost continuous, punctuated by brief pauses while the Soviet war machine gathered itself for another major offensive. This period, known to Soviet scholars as the Third Period of War, witnessed the final maturity of both armed forces. It is therefore appropriate to examine the relative strengths of the two antagonists before resuming the operational history of the war.

After Kursk, the strength and combat effectiveness of the German armies in the East entered a period of almost constant decline. Periodic influxes of new conscripts and equipment, especially for the mechanized units and the Waffen SS, gave the defenders the means to conduct local counterattacks and counterstrokes. Yet these attacks were steadily less effective, both due to the growing sophistication of the Soviet troops and the steady decay in the level of German training and effectiveness.

The German infantry formations were even more emaciated than their mechanized counterparts. The six-battalion division became standard, a division that was largely helpless if a Soviet mobile group attacked in its sector. In December 1943, after much argument, Heinz Guderian won his case to have an older model of Czech tank chassis reconfigured as a self-propelled tank destroyer. Unfortunately for the German infantrymen, there were never enough tank destroyers or even large-caliber towed guns to equip more than one third of each division's antitank units.[1] The steady withdrawal of the Luftwaffe to defend the Reich, in conjunction with the steady growth of the Red Air Force, made the German troops equally vulnerable to air attacks. Light antiaircraft batteries eventually appeared in panzer and motorized divisions, but the average infantry formation had little effective air defense.

By contrast, the Third Period of War marked the full development of Soviet force structure, equipment, and operational and tactical concepts. Before considering this development, however, it should be recognized that the Soviets, like the Germans, suffered from severe manpower shortages. The staggering civilian and military casualties of the war, the large factories needed to maintain weapons production, and the demands of rebuilding a shattered economy in land reclaimed from the Germans all strained the supposedly inexhaustible supply of Soviet manpower. The manpower needed to build new specialized units could come only by reducing the number of replacements provided to existing front-line units. Moreover, with the Soviets almost continuously on the offensive, they inevitably suffered heavier casualties at the tactical level than the German defenders. As a rule of thumb, during the Third Period of the War the Soviet combat units directly involved in an offensive suffered 22 to 25 percent casualties in order to accomplish their objectives.[2]

By 1944, the Red Army faced a manpower crisis that was, in its own way, as serious as that confronting the Wehrmacht. Many rifle divisions had an effective strength of 2,000 or less. The number of artillery pieces in such divisions dwindled in favor of nondivisional penetration artillery units that could be concentrated at critical points. Tank and guards formations had a higher priority for replacements than the rifle divisions, but they suffered such heavy casualties that they, too, were frequently understrength. Among the hardest-hit units were the rifle and submachine gun companies that rode on the back of T-34s as accompanying infantry during exploitation and pursuit operations. For this reason, beginning in late 1942, the Soviets had begun creating numerous fortified regions (*ukreplennye raiony*)—and later, field fortified regions—which were "economy of force" formations made up of high firepower but low manpower. These regions consisted of artillery and machine-gun battalions designated to occupy large sectors of the front, thereby releasing other, more mobile combat forces for concentration along critical attack axes.

The resulting disparity between the authorized and actual sizes of many Soviet units goes far to explain the seemingly amazing performance of some German counterattacks. The ability of a full-strength Waffen SS division to halt a Soviet "corps" or "army" probably resulted more from the numerical weakness of the Soviet units than from the supposed tactical superiority of the German attackers.

In the First Period of War, the Red Army had frittered away an enormous numerical advantage because it lacked the skill to deploy and maneuver its forces. During the Second Period, neither side had an overwhelming strategic advantage in numbers, but the Soviets had slowly developed the maneuver and deception skills necessary to create a favorable correlation of forces at the critical point. During the Third Period, the Soviets had both the numbers and the skill to destroy the German forces, but the manpower crisis necessitated a continued emphasis on sophisticated maneuver attacks. Massive frontal assaults occurred but more infrequently, and they were usually examples of failure on the part of Red Army commanders.

Structurally, the Red Army continued the trend toward creation of fully combined-arms organizations for both rifle and mobile forces. Infantry (combined arms) and guards armies generally consisted of three to four corps each plus an impressive array of artillery, antitank, mortar, "guards mortar" (*katiusha* multiple-rocket launchers), and antiaircraft units. Guards armies and the specially designated shock armies tended to have higher proportions of artillery and of infantry-support tanks.[3]

The real innovations were the manner in which these forces were tailored and employed. At every level, units designated to make the main attack were reinforced with additional artillery, engineer, and tank troops. The 1944 *Field Regulations of the Red Army*, or *Ustav*, formalized procedures for a host of techniques that had developed during 1943, including the artillery offensive and the air offensive to provide continuous support to the attacking ground forces. More important, however, the *Ustav* stressed the importance of maneuver, surprise, and initiative, three hallmarks of interwar German and Soviet theory:

> Maneuver is one of the most important conditions for achieving success. Maneuver consists of the organized movement of troops for the purpose of creating the most favorable grouping and in placing this grouping in the most favorable position for striking the enemy a crushing blow to gain time and space. Maneuver should be simple in conception and be carried out secretly, rapidly, and in such a way as to surprise the enemy. . . .
>
> The readiness to take responsibility upon oneself for a daring decision and to carry it to the end in a persistent manner is the basis of the action of all commanders in battle. Bold and intelligent daring should always characterize the commander and his subordinates. Reproach is deserved not by the one who in his zeal to destroy the enemy does not reach his goal, but by the one who, fearing responsibility, remains inactive and does not employ at the proper moment all of his forces and means for winning victory.[4]

The doctrinal publications of most modern armies express similar sentiments, but the Red Army paid far more than lip service to these ideas. While it is true that failure was still dealt with harshly, the Red officer corps, particularly in mobile formations and units, was encouraged and expected to take risks and make decisions as needed.

Because the Third Period of War consisted of an almost unbroken series of Soviet offensives, it is worth examining the procedures used for such operations.[5] Once Stalin approved a *Stavka* recommendation to attack in a certain region, the first step was to concentrate overwhelming local superiority without giving warning to the German defenders. As the war progressed, Germany lost most of the sympathizers and stay-behind agents who might have provided information about such troop concentrations. Only German aerial reconnaissance and signal-intercept units provided any information about the Soviet rear areas, and these units were vulnerable to the growing Soviet skill in operations security and deception. Although German intelligence analysts frequently had a good picture of the front-line Soviet units opposite them, they were consistently deceived about the location and strength of second-echelon rifle forces and especially of the mobile units. Time after time, the Red Army was able to mass its forces undetected while distracting the defenders with the fantasy of an offensive elsewhere along the front.

Each level of Soviet forces, from the rifle regiment to the *front* headquarters, had its own specialists in reconnaissance work. The undermanned German defenses were often a sieve of individual and unit infiltrators. Reconnaissance and diversionary SPETNAZ [*voiska spetsial'nogo naznacheniia*] teams identified key targets and destroyed bridges and other vulnerable sites. The traditional German tactic of holding forward positions with as few troops as possible played into the hands of Soviet reconnaissance. By 1944, it was not uncommon for the Red reconnaissance troops to conduct a reconnaissance-in-force [*razvedka boem*], capturing the first line of German defensive positions up to 24 hours before the actual offensive began.

If a formal artillery preparation seemed necessary, Soviet gunners provided not only massive weights of exploding metal but also sophisticated firing schedules designed to catch the defenders off guard. For example, the Germans often remained in deep bunkers until the enemy artillery fire slackened, then rushed outside to take up positions before the Red infantry and armor arrived. Recognizing this, Soviet artillery preparations often included a period of massive artillery fire, a few minutes without firing, and then renewed shelling to catch the defenders in the open after they left their bunkers.

The actual offensive normally began with infantry forces supported by engineers and tanks or self-propelled guns. If German armor was in the area, heavy self-propelled guns would take up overwatching positions behind the first line of attackers, waiting to ambush the German tanks when they appeared. Artillery and air support moved forward along with the attackers, who tried to brush past the German front-line defenses and reach the rear as rapidly as possible.

On occasion, the German defenses proved too strong for a rapid penetration. At this point, the best Soviet commanders, like N. N. Voronov at Smolensk in September 1943, were perfectly willing to shift their plans and renew the attack at a weaker point in the German lines. This flex-ibility was made possible by the pattern of attacking at multiple points while holding significant forces back from the initial assault. If one spear-head failed, the second-echelon rifle forces, as well as the mechanized exploitation formations, could then be switched to exploit success some-where else.

Once a breakthrough appeared imminent, senior commanders fo-cused on the most effective time to introduce mobile forces onto the battlefield. On the one hand, mechanized forces committed too early might become bogged down in the penetration battle; on the other hand, forces committed too late might encounter German counterattacks or reorganized defenses. In the key breakthrough areas, each attacking combined-arms army commander had one or more mobile units, each equivalent in size to a reinforced panzer division. These separate mecha-nized corps, tank corps, and cavalry corps had relatively long-range tactical or short-range operational objectives, seeking to capture a key river crossing or encircle a German division or corps.

The true stars of the Soviet offensive were the tank armies and cavalry-mechanized groups (usually made up of a tank or mechanized corps paired with a cavalry corps), controlled by *front* commanders or even, in the case of a major offensive, by the *Stavka* representative coordinating two or more *fronts*. The tank armies and cavalry-mechanized groups (the latter operating over more difficult terrain) had much deeper, operational objectives, often hundreds of kilometers in the German rear. In some cases, the tank armies encircled entire German field armies. As the war progressed, it became axiomatic that where Soviet mobile forces suc-ceeded, the offensive succeeded; where they failed, the offensive failed. As if to ratify the importance of tank armies, a sixth such organization was created on 20 January 1944 by combining two separate mobile corps under the veteran "tankist" Lieutenant General A. G. Kravchenko.[6]

Yet even the tank armies did not move as compact masses. During the exploitation and pursuit, every Soviet commander, from reinforced rifle division up to tank army, dispatched a forward detachment ahead of his main body. Such detachments tended to grow in size and in the scope of their missions as the war progressed. Each separate mobile corps would be led by a reinforced brigade of 800 to 1,200 troops, and, in turn, each tank army would be preceded by a separate tank brigade or one of its three corps of 2,000 to 5,000.[7] During an exploitation, forward detach-ments might precede the main body of their parent units by 20 to 50 kilometers, depending on the size of the units involved and the strength of the German defenses. In all cases, the forward detachment commanders were expected to use extraordinary initiative and skill, bypassing centers of German resistance in order to continue the advance. If, by chance, a forward detachment became pinned down by the Germans, the parent unit would maneuver to counterattack or, more commonly, bypass the German defenders and continue the advance.

Just as the German encirclements of 1941 and 1942 had often failed to prevent the escape of the surrounded units, so the Soviets experienced difficulty in sealing off the Germans they were able to encircle. However, the encircled Germans often were unable to obtain permission from higher headquarters to escape or were too far from their own lines to escape successfully. With a few notable exceptions, the Soviet encirclements of 1944–1945 usually ended with the capture of most or all of the bypassed Germans. Ultimately the Red Army solved the difficult problem that had so often thwarted the Wehrmacht—holding an encirclement closed with one set of units while continuing to pursue with a separate group of mobile forces.

CLEARING THE RIGHT BANK OF THE UKRAINE

According to official German and Soviet figures, in late 1943 the Germans fielded 2,468,500 troops (and 706,000 satellite troops) in the East, including 26 panzer divisions, 151 other divisions, 2,304 tanks and self-propelled guns, 8,037 guns and mortars, and 3,000 aircraft. The Red Army boasted 6,394,500 men, including 35 tank and mechanized corps, more than 480 other division-sized formations, 5,800 tanks, 101,400 artillery pieces and mortars, and 13,400 aircraft of all types.[8] These Soviet forces were grouped into 60 combined-arms armies, 5 shock armies, and 5 (soon to be 6) tank armies.

To make their numerical advantage overwhelming at the critical points, the Soviet leaders used concentration and deception. In early December 1943, the *Stavka* issued its operational plans for the third winter campaign, designed to clear German forces from the approaches to Leningrad in the north, from Belorussia in the center, and from the Crimea and the Ukraine in the south (see Map 14). Although the 1st, 2d, 3d, and 4th Ukrainian Fronts were involved in the southern portions of this offensive, their attacks were scheduled in a staggered pattern from late December 1943 through April 1944. This series of initially successive and then simultaneous offensives permitted the *Stavka* to switch key artillery and mechanized resources from one *front* to another while concealing for some time the true scope of the planned offensive.

Winter in the Ukraine was usually far less severe than the winters in Russia proper, where the principal fighting had occurred in the previous

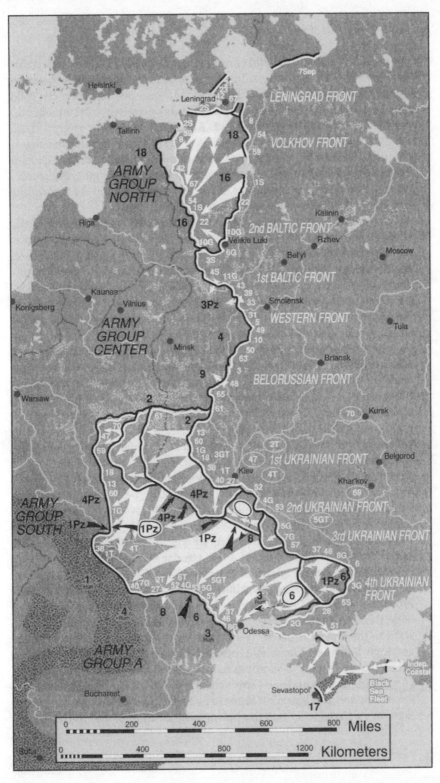

14. *Winter Campaign, December 1943–April 1944*

two years. The relatively mild climate in the south made for unpredictable weather and terrain trafficability; both sides found themselves thwarted by sudden thaws throughout the season. In general, however, the mild climate allowed the Red Army to continue its operations without a break, much to the dismay of its opponent. Meanwhile, partisan groups—both those directed by Moscow and those seeking Ukrainian independence— made the German rear areas increasingly chaotic and insecure. In a series of savage struggles with the Germans and with various other guerrilla organizations, the separatist Ukrainian Insurgent Army (*Ukrainska Povstanska armiia* or UPA) came out on top by early 1944.

The first phase of the Soviet offensive to free the right bank of the Ukraine lasted from December 1943 through late February 1944. It consisted of five major operations, each conducted by one or two *fronts*. Erich von Manstein, the commander of Army Group South, switched his available reserves from point to point to meet these thrusts, but he was preoccupied with the possibility that Army Groups South and A might become pinned against the Carpathian Mountains or Black Sea and separated from the rest of the German defenders.[9]

The first two operations, conducted by N. F. Vatutin's 1st and I. S. Konev's 2d Ukrainian Fronts, were virtually a continuation of the earlier operations to expand the bridgeheads across the Dnepr River. On 25 December 1943, after repeated counterstrokes by von Manstein's XXXXVIII Panzer Corps to expunge the Kiev bridgehead had failed, Vatutin's secretly reinforced *front* struck from the bridgehead toward Zhitomir in the Zhitomir-Berdichev operation. Only after extreme exertions were the Germans able to halt the exploiting Soviet 1st Tank and 3d Guards Tank Armies just short of their objectives. Meanwhile, Konev's 2d Ukrainian Front wheeled westward from its earlier objective, Krivoi Rog, and, spearheaded by 5th Guards Tank Army, seized Kirovograd. The result was a large salient occupied by two German corps along the Dnepr River in the Korsun'-Shevchenkovskii region, where, ironically, Soviet forces had seized their first bridgehead across the river at Velikii Bukrin.[10]

After these Soviet offensives had worn the Germans down, Zhukov coordinated Vatutin's 1st Ukrainian Front with Konev's 2d Ukrainian Front in the Korsun'-Shevchenkovskii operation.[11] Southeast of Kiev, a huge German salient around Korsun'-Shevchenkovskii jutted northeastward to the Dnepr River at the boundary between German First Panzer and Eighth Armies. The salient represented the last segment of the "Dnepr Line" that remained in German hands, and Hitler would not authorize von Manstein to withdraw. This salient, with 1st Ukrainian Front to its northwest and 2d Ukrainian Front to its southeast, was an obvious candidate for encirclement, but the timing and location of the Soviet attack eluded German intelligence. Konev used the headquarters communications of 5th Guards Tank Army and a limited local attack on his southern flank in a partly successful deception effort, while shifting the bulk of his forces 100 kilometers to the north, southeast of the town of Korsun'-Shevchenkovskii. At dawn on 24 January, Konev's shock group of 4th Guards and 53d Armies attacked behind a massive artillery barrage, penetrating up to five kilometers into the German positions. The next morning, Rotmistrov's 5th Guards Tank Army, followed by 5th Guards Cavalry Corps, passed through the attackers and struck due west.

Even more surprising to the Germans was the sudden appearance—literally out of the snow—of the newly created 6th Tank Army on the other, northwestern face of the German bulge. Here, Vatutin attacked two days after Konev but found it difficult to penetrate the German defenses. General A. G. Kravchenko's 6th Tank Army had a newly created headquarters and understrength maneuver corps, but by 3 February, it had linked up with 5th Guards Tank Army, forming a thin outer encirclement around the German XI and XXXXII Corps. The Red 27th, 52d, and 4th Guards Armies held the inner encirclement around the two German corps, which included at least five understrength infantry divisions and the 5th SS Panzer Grenadier Division *Viking*.

Despite orders to hold onto the Dnepr at all costs, the commander of the XXXXII Corps, General Werner Stemmermann, had anticipated this disaster by constructing supplementary defenses and stockpiling some supplies in the area that became the Cherkassy pocket. Konev hammered away relentlessly at the pocket, capturing the western portion around Korsun' on 10 February, but Stemmermann continued a stubborn defense. Other German officers, including the senior commanders of the SS Division, were evacuated by the transport aircraft that were able to enter the pocket. Between 9 and 14 February 1944, the Luftwaffe claimed that it brought up to 185 tons per day into the pocket, but renewed winter weather put a halt to this resupply.

By 8 February, von Manstein had assembled the 1st, 16th, and 17th Panzer Divisions and SS Panzer Division *Leibstandarte Adolf Hitler* to launch a counterstroke that made some progress against the understrength 6th Tank Army. Stalin reinforced Vatutin and Konev and demanded renewed efforts, with Konev controlling the inner encirclement forces and the 2d Air Army in a determined effort to liquidate the defenders before relief could arrive. Using volunteer pilots in a snowstorm, Konev dropped incendiaries on the towns that sheltered the remaining German forces. By the morning of 17 February, Stemmermann had used up his available supplies, destroyed his heavy weapons, and directed the survivors to escape to the west. In the process, they ran the gauntlet of 27th and 4th

Guards Armies. Stemmermann's troops were still several kilometers short of friendly lines when dawn arrived, bringing with it Soviet tanks and Cossack cavalry who massacred the fleeing Germans.

Although German accounts claim that 30,000 troops escaped, the Soviet version is far more credible: by their accounting, 55,000 Germans were killed or wounded, and another 18,000 became prisoners. Any units that may have escaped had lost all equipment and had to be reorganized in Poland. A jubilant Stalin promoted Konev to marshal of the Soviet Union and made Rotmistrov the first marshal of tank troops.[12] The brilliant young Colonel General N. F. Vatutin might have received similar recognition, but on February 29, while completing plans for yet another operation, he was fatally wounded in an ambush by Ukrainian separatists. He did not die until 15 April, but G. K. Zhukov immediately assumed his command of 1st Ukrainian Front and set about executing Vatutin's new plan.

While German attention was riveted to the Korsun'-Shevchenkovskii salient, Soviet forces struck against both flanks of Army Group South, taking advantage of the fact that panzer operational reserves had been summoned to the sounds of the guns at Korsun'. On the 1st Ukrainian Front's right flank, Vatutin threw his 13th and 60th Armies, supported by 1st and 6th Guards Cavalry Corps, against von Manstein's overextended left flank south of the Pripiat' Marshes. Between 27 January and 11 February, an audacious cavalry advance through inhospitable swampy terrain unhinged German defenses and seized Rovno and Lutsk, favorable positions from which to conduct future operations into Army Group South's rear.[13]

Further south, Army General R. Ia. Malinovsky's 3d Ukrainian Front and Army General F. I. Tolbukhin's 4th Ukrainian Front launched concentric blows against German defenses anchored opposite the great bend of the Dnepr River. Attacking on 30 January, Soviet forces collapsed the irksome Nikopol' bridgehead on the Dnepr's south bank, seized the salient in the great bend, and captured the city of Krivoi Rog.

The initial five blows on the right bank of the Ukraine had, by the end of February, cleared German defenders from the entire Dnepr River line. Deprived of their river defenses, von Manstein's forces were now vulnerable to complete defeat in detail in the vast interior plains of Ukraine.

FREEING THE UKRAINE

Despite continued slow progress against Army Groups North and Center, the Soviet offensive in the South continued virtually without a halt, even through the spring thaw. During the second phase of this offensive, from early March through mid-May 1944, five additional Soviet offensives completed the process of clearing the Ukraine and the Crimea.[14] In preparation for this, the *Stavka* reshuffled its forces and committed all six tank armies in the south. The main effort remained with Vatutin's (later Zhukov's) and Konev's *fronts*, each of which had 36 rifle divisions and 3 tank armies. Their goal was to split the entire German front, separating Army Groups Center and South, and destroy Army Group South by pinning it against the Black Sea or Carpathian Mountains.

The *Stavka* sought to capitalize on German perceptions that the Soviet main effort would be toward Vinnitsa, Army Group South's headquarters in the central sector of the Army Group, where First Panzer Army stood on the defense. Instead, the Soviets shifted their main effort northwestward into the Rovno-Dubno region against German Fourth Panzer Army. Here 1st Ukrainian Front's right flank had achieved considerable success in the minor Rovno-Lutsk operation, at a time when German attentions were devoted exclusively to the crisis at Korsun'-Shevchenkovskii. The *Stavka* "castled" three tank armies to the right together with the bulk of Vatutin's *front*. (It was during this period of complex regrouping that Vatutin was mortally wounded while traveling between headquarters.) Von Manstein's intelligence organs finally detected the shift and hastily moved First Panzer Army westward into the threatened Proskurov sector, but it was too late to deflect the Soviets' initial blow.

On 4 March, 1st Ukrainian Front, now commanded personally by Zhukov, launched its powerful drive to the southwest from the Shepetovka and Dubno region, toward Chernovtsy near the Rumanian border.[15] Zhukov committed his regrouped 3d Guards and 4th Tank Armies and tore a gaping hole in German defenses. On 7 March, the two tank armies approached Proskurov, where they were halted by redeploying German III and XXXXVIII Panzer Corps. Soon thereafter, however, 1st Tank Army joined the action, and on 21 March, together with 4th Tank Army, it again ripped through German defenses and into the German operational rear. Katukov's 1st Tank Army advanced remorselessly, even at night, with headlights and sirens on to disorient the defenders. It reached the Dnestr River and crossed without pausing on 24 March, then cut the rail line behind First Panzer Army. By 27 March, Lieutenant General D. D. Lelivshenko's 4th Tank Army and Lieutenant General K. S. Moskalenko's 38th Army had completed a loose encirclement around 21 poorly equipped divisions, all that remained of First Panzer Army.

On 25 March, von Manstein convinced an angry Hitler that First Panzer Army must be given permission to break out. This concession was all the more unusual because OKW had recently issued Fuehrer Order No.

51, which required the defense of all major cities. A 15-kilometer gap remained in the encirclement, which 4th Tank Army, reduced to a mere 60 tanks, was unable to fill. Zhukov concentrated his available forces to the south of the encirclement, where he anticipated a breakout attempt into Rumania. Instead, the remnants of First Panzer Army were able to escape to the west in early April, aided by a counterattack launched by II SS Panzer Corps. Still, by 17 April, the forward detachments of 1st Tank Army had reached the Carpathian Mountains, effectively cutting off von Manstein's renamed Army Group North Ukraine from forces to the south. For its feats, on 25 April, Katukov's tank army received the Guards designation.[16]

Konev's 2d Ukrainian Front commenced the Uman'-Botoshany operation on 5 March, one day after Zhukov's *front* had struck and after German operational reserves had moved westward out of the Uman' sector.[17] Along with the usual massive artillery and infantry preparation, Konev took the risky step of committing Lieutenant General S. I. Bogdanov's 2d Tank and Lieutenant General P. A. Rotmistrov's 5th Guards Tank Armies from the very beginning of the attack. They were soon followed by elements of Lieutenant General A. G. Kravchenko's 6th Tank Army. Fortunately for the attackers, the German defenses proved so brittle that Konev's gamble paid off, and the tank forces plunged forward, supported by Colonel General K. A. Koroteev's 52d Army. By 10 March, they had captured the major rail junction and supply depot of Uman' in the western Ukraine, where hundreds of German tanks and thousands of tons of supplies were immobilized by the spring mud. The same day, Konev's leading forces captured Vinnitsa, until recently the site of von Manstein's army group headquarters.[18]

Ignoring the bypassed and immobilized German forces, the mobile groups raced westward to seize the rivers of the western Ukraine. By 11 March, forward detachments of S. I. Bogdanov's 2d Tank Army and A. G. Kravchenko's 6th Tank Army held bridgeheads across the lower Bug River. Within two days, 2d Ukrainian Front had improvised crossings on an 80-kilometer front. By the afternoon of 17 March, 29th Tank Corps of 5th Guards Tank Army had reached the Dnestr River near Soroki and immediately pushed rifle forces across. By 21 March, an entire mechanized corps was across the river, and First Panzer Army in the north was effectively separated from Eighth Army in the south.

While the six tank armies set the pace in 1st and 2d Ukrainian Fronts, the other two *fronts* were far from idle. R. I. Malinovsky's 3d Ukrainian Front launched its own offensive along the Black Sea Coast on 6 March 1944 (the Bereznegovataia-Snigirevka operation).[19] Lieutenant General I. A. Pliev, a veteran cavalry commander since the start of the war, commanded a cavalry-mechanized group consisting of 4th Guards Cavalry Corps and 4th Mechanized Corps. Pliev reached the southern reaches of the Bug River on 22 March and thrust onward with the ultimate objective of the Danube on the Soviet frontier. Operating in the region that had made it famous during the Civil War, Soviet horse cavalry once again proved its value in terrain that would not support heavy mechanized vehicles. Although almost encircled by the Soviet advance, German Sixth Army painstakingly extricated itself and fought a delaying action westward across the southern Ukraine. By late March, 3d Ukrainian Front commenced its final spring offensive to secure Odessa, and in early April it closed into positions alongside 2d Ukrainian Front along the Dnestr River and the Rumanian border.[20]

The next blow in the south was the recapture of the Crimea, launched by Colonel General F. I. Tolbukhin's 4th Ukrainian Front on 8 April.[21] The 2d Guards and 51st Armies, supported by 19th Tank Corps and (on the Kerch Peninsula) by the Separate Coastal Army, all attacked the German-Rumanian Seventeenth Army and, by 16 April, drove the Axis force back into Sevastopol'. Hitler insisted on defending the Crimea, which he regarded as a convenient base for bomber attacks against the Rumanian oil fields. The German defense was tenacious but did not endure as long as that of the Red Army two years earlier. Between 6 and 10 May, while the city was under assault, a half-hearted attempt was made to evacuate the remaining defenders by sea. Somewhat less than 40,000 men of Seventeenth Army's original force of 150,000 made it out of the Crimea.[22]

By May 1944, the Red Army had freed virtually all Soviet territory in the south and, in the process, shattered large portions of First Panzer, Sixth, Eighth, and Seventeenth Armies. The strategic attention of Hitler and the German High Command was riveted on the southern region. The presence of all six Soviet tank armies in that region led them to conclude that it would be the focus of the Soviet summer offensive. This preoccupation goes far to explain the Germans' surprise when the next great offensive was aimed at Army Group Center.

The victories of winter–spring 1944 had significant political as well as military consequences. In late March, Marshal Ion Antonescu of Rumania flew to Berlin to appeal for the evacuation of Rumanian troops in the Crimea. He had already lost the region of present-day Bessarabia and Moldova, which Rumania had annexed, and now faced defeat in the Crimea, where Rumanian arms had shone so brilliantly in 1942. He persuaded Hitler to concentrate the remaining Rumanian forces under a new Army Group South Ukraine, which was geographically isolated from the rest of the German line. But Rumania was clearly on the edge of annihilation, and Antonescu had already extended diplomatic feelers to

Moscow and London. Meanwhile, on 19 March, German troops had occupied Hungary to prevent its defection. Only the Bulgarian government clung desperately to Germany.[23]

LENINGRAD AND THE CENTRAL SECTOR
OF THE FRONT

Soviet efforts in the Leningrad region were finally rewarded with success in 1944. The birthplace of the Bolshevik Revolution had been under siege for more than two years and initially had to resort to the use of a tenuous ice road over Lake Ladoga for resupply. In 1943, the Soviets were able to open a narrow corridor to the city, but the corridor was easily interdicted by German artillery fire. German long-range artillery had shelled the city intermittently throughout the siege, although in 1943 a centralized counter-battery organization in Leningrad had begun to coordinate the location and destruction of these German batteries.

By January 1944, the German High Command was distracted by the growing threat in the south, and Army Group North had focused on a growing threat in Belorussia. Instead, General L. A. Govarov's Leningrad Front and General K. A. Meretskov's Volkhov Front joined forces in the Novgorod-Luga offensive operation to clear the Germans from the immediate approaches to Leningrad.[24] The combined effort finally pushed the Germans back from the immediate approaches of Leningrad.

Fortunately for the Soviets, the Finns were never as eager to capture Leningrad as were their German allies. At the start of the war, Finnish troops had reoccupied the Mannerheim Line and other territory seized by Stalin in 1940. Thereafter, however, they had shown little interest in pressing forward against Leningrad. This neglect, plus the withdrawal of German reserve forces to fight farther south, made the German Eighteenth Army extremely vulnerable by late 1943.

To avoid a simple frontal assault, the *Stavka* insisted that 2d Shock Army be moved by sea into the Oranienbaum bridgehead, a narrow strip of land west of Leningrad that had never been occupied by the Germans. This now became the springboard for a pincer attack against Eighteenth Army. Throughout November, as the ice gradually closed in on the Gulf of Finland, 2d Shock Army slowly infiltrated into this bridgehead on night convoys of barges and small craft, escorted by minesweepers and patrol boats. The cover story was that the Russians were evacuating the bridgehead, but by January, there were 5 rifle divisions, 600 guns, and various tank and assault-gun units. On 14 January 1944, 2d Shock Army began its slow breakout from the bridgehead, despite mists and intermittent snow. A day later, after mines had been cleared and the German attention was focused on Oranienbaum, the rest of Govorov's Leningrad Front joined in the attack, as did Meretskov's Volkhov Front farther south around Novgorod.

Yet the Soviet advance during the Novgorod-Luga operation was slow and fumbling, a far cry from the brilliant successes in the south. Many of the senior commanders had spent the war in and around Leningrad and had not had an opportunity to develop the offensive experience of their comrades elsewhere. Instead, Govorov fumed at his subordinates for their linear, frontal tactics and for scattering their forces and depending too much on unsupported infantry. Armor, artillery, and reconnaissance units were often idle. The bungling tactics of 1941 reappeared one more time.[25] In addition, the Germans had constructed major defensive works that were overcome only by the desperate courage of Soviet infantry and sappers. Still, by 20 February, the Soviets had penetrated the German lines and forced their withdrawal. By 26 February, Leningrad was officially declared free, and the naval and land artillery fired off a victory salute.

Even then, the pursuit was so poorly coordinated that Eighteenth Army was able to elude the planned encirclement. In February, the *Stavka* dissolved the Volkhov Front, concentrating forces under Govorov's Leningrad Front and General M. M. Popov's 2d Baltic Front. The Germans were repeatedly able to break contact and withdraw, bringing down the severe censure of the State Defense Committee on the hapless Popov and his political council member, N. A. Bulganin. Even such pressure could not overcome the logistical and tactical problems of advancing in the northern winter, and the northern offensive fell short of its goals. At the end of February 1944, the Germans fell back west of Luga and Lake Il'men' to the new *Panther Stellung* [line] running from Lake Peipus to Vitebsk, but for the moment Estonia and Latvia remained beyond the reach of the Soviet troops.[26] With Leningrad safe and Army Group North in retreat, the Finnish government began to look for an exit from the war. Helsinki joined Bucharest in sending out diplomatic feelers to the allies.

Meanwhile, to the south opposite German Army Group Center, 1st Baltic Front, now commanded by Army General I. Kh. Bagramian, Sokolovsky's Western Front, and Rokossovsky's Belorussian Front continued hammering away at German positions around Vitebsk, and east Orsha and Rogachev. While Bagramian conducted the month-long Gorodok operation against the northern approaches to Vitebsk, between 29 December 1943 and 29 March 1944, the Western and Belorussian Fronts launched at least seven distinct offensives, costing them over 200,000 casualties, but were unable to make further significant advances into Belorussia.[27]

In four months the Soviet offensive machine had freed Leningrad, the Ukraine, and the Crimea and made inroads into Belorussia. Two of Hitler's most effective operational leaders, Erich von Manstein and Ewald von Kleist, lost their commands. In the process, 16 German divisions, comprising at least 50,000 troops, were wiped off the map through encirclement and attrition, another 60 German divisions were reduced to skeletal strength. Whereas the late winter and spring of 1942 and 1943 had been periods of rest and refitting for the Germans, the corresponding period of 1944 was one of unremitting struggle for survival. The German panzer and Waffen SS divisions rushed from place to place, shoring up the tottering defenses. As a result, Army Group Center, the one area of relative stability during this period, had become a huge salient to the east, denuded of most of its reserves. With German political and strategic attention focused on the Balkans, Stalin and the *Stavka* prepared to deal, once and for all, with Army Group Center.

CHAPTER 13

Operation Bagration: The Death of Army Group Center

STRATEGIC PLANNING

In March 1944, the State Defense Committee (GKO) and the Soviet General Staff began an exhaustive staff analysis of the entire front, examining each area to find opportunities for the next round of offensive action. In doing so, the planners had to select a course of action that would accomplish the most in both military and political terms. The Western Allies had finally promised an amphibious landing in France to commence in May; future Soviet operations needed to take this into account, to project the most likely outcome of the war in terms of which Ally would conquer which portions of the continent.

The most obvious option for the main summer offensive, and the one the German commanders expected, would be to continue in the south, advancing into southern Poland and the Balkans and thereby driving several Axis satellites out of the war. Yet, this option would overextend the Red forces, committing them to the difficult terrain of the Balkans while leaving large portions of the Soviet Union unredeemed.

A second option was to launch a massive thrust from the Ukraine northwestward through Poland to the Baltic Sea. During three previous general offensives, however, even Stalin had learned that such a grandiose plan was beyond Soviet capabilities, especially in the realms of command, control, and logistics. The Wehrmacht was still far too strong to succumb to a single attack; the previous Soviet offensives had validated painfully the prewar concept of successive offensives.

A third possibility was to focus the main effort in the north, with the objective of defeating Finland and completing the reconquest of the Baltic states. It was past time to eliminate the Finnish threat to both Leningrad and the Murmansk supply line, but, by itself, such an offensive would occupy only a fraction of available resources. Continuing the advance westward into the Baltics risked a prolonged frontal battle against strong German defenses, which, even if successful, led to a strategic dead end against the Baltic coast.

Finally, the Red Army could attack Army Group Center, its old nemesis, which was concentrated in the "Belorussian balcony" that jutted eastward north of the Pripiat' Marshes. If successful, such an attack would decimate the few German field armies that were still relatively intact and cut off Army Group North from its lines of supply and retreat. A Belorussian offensive would also complete the liberation of Soviet territory and place the Red Army in Poland, poised along the most direct route to Berlin. Moreover, success in Belorussia might condition subsequent Soviet success along other strategic axes.[1]

In retrospect, the decision to make the main effort in Belorussia appears almost self-evident. In fact, this offensive, which Stalin himself named Operation Bagration after a hero of 1812, was only the centerpiece of five different planned offensives in the summer of 1944. Knowledge of the true scope of the plan was restricted to a handful of men—Stalin, G. K. Zhukov, A. M. Vasilevsky, and his deputy, A. I. Antonov. Moreover, for logistical and operational reasons, these five offensives were staggered, beginning in the north and working successively to the south. The five offensives, with their ultimate starting dates, involved the following geographic locales: Karelian Isthmus/Finland, 10 June 1944; Belorussia (code-named Bagration), 22 June 1944; L'vov-Sandomierz, 13 July 1944; Lublin-Brest, 18 July 1944; and Iassy-Kishinev, 20 August 1944. For similar reasons, even within the Belorussian operation, the actual attacks generally began at the northern flank and rippled southward (see Map 15).

Even before the final strategic plan was devised, the *Stavka* restructured its field organization and reshuffled commanders. The huge Western Front was divided into two more manageable commands (the 2d and 3d Belorussian Fronts), and other *fronts* were redesignated and their areas of operations shifted. By April there were eight Soviet *fronts* north of the Pripiat' Marshes, including (from north to south) the Karelian and Leningrad Fronts, the 3d, 2d, and 1st Baltic Fronts, and the 3d, 2d, and 1st Belorussian Fronts. Immediately south of the Pripiat' marshes, 1st Ukrainian Front, which, along with the left wing of the 1st Belorussian Front, held a salient reaching far to the westward, would also be involved in the main offensives. By mid-May, I. S. Marshal Konev had assumed command of 1st Ukrainian Front from Zhukov, who had taken charge upon the death of Vatutin. Meanwhile two field army commanders who had distinguished themselves in the Crimea were promoted to *front* command. At 38 years of age, Colonel General I. D. Cherniakhovsky became the youngest man to command a *front*, although he had already commanded a tank corps in 1942 and 60th Army at Kursk. Despite his Jewish origin (a factor that often aroused Stalin's prejudices and suspicions), Cherniakhovsky's brilliant record had won him the recommendation of both Zhukov and Vasilevsky. He assumed command of 3d Belorussian Front west of Smolensk, built around the headquarters of the former Western Front.

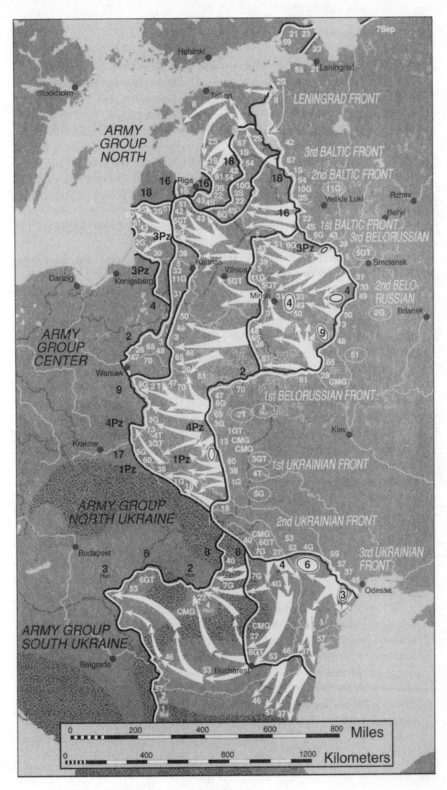

15. *Summer–Fall Campaign, June–October 1944*

Colonel General I. E. Petrov was also promoted to command 2d Belorussian Front in the Mogilev area. Unfortunately for Petrov, the pernicious influence of L. Z. Mekhlis was still alive in the Red Army. Mekhlis convinced Stalin that Petrov was sick and incompetent, getting him replaced by Colonel General G. F. Zakharov, another victorious commander of the Crimean operation. Eventually, Petrov was given command of 4th Ukrainian Front, created later in 1944 in the south.[2] As for the other *fronts*, the veteran K. K. Rokossovsky commanded the oversized 1st Belorussian Front, which held the extended line from Kovel', south of the Pripiat' Marshes to the Rogachev-Zhlobin region, while the newly promoted Marshal I. Kh. Bagramian commanded 1st Baltic Front on the northern flank of the proposed Bagration operation.

Superimposed above these *front* commanders were *Stavka* representatives, who by this stage in the war sometimes had their own independent staffs. Marshal Vasilevsky, chief of the General Staff and coordinator of 1st Baltic (Bagramian) and 3d Belorussian (Cherniakhovsky) Fronts on the northern side, brought along a small element of the General Staff. Zhukov, the deputy commander-in-chief, was assigned to coordinate 1st (Rokossovsky) and 2d (Zakharov) Belorussian Fronts in the center and south.[3]

This elaborate command structure did not mean that the field leaders were simply executing *Stavka* orders. On the contrary, repeated debates occurred as to how to crush Army Group Center. The basic problem was that, even at this late stage in the war, the Red Army forces opposite Army Group Center were still too weak to achieve a crushing, overall numerical superiority. When the *Stavka* first began to plan the battle, it found that there were 42 German divisions, totaling 850,000 men, opposite the approximately one million men in the 77 divisions and 5 mobile corps of 1st Baltic and the 1st, 2d, and 3d Belorussian Fronts. The search for sufficient numerical advantage eventually led to the reinforcement of Soviet forces opposite Army Group Center by 5 combined-arms armies, 2 tank armies, 1 air army, 1 Polish field army, and 11 mobile corps—a total of over 400,000 men—and to a greater emphasis on destroying the forward German forces as rapidly as possible.[4]

To resolve such matters, Stalin summoned most of the commanders facing German Army Group Center forces to a planning conference in Moscow on 22-23 May. In addition to Antonov, Zhukov, and Vasilevsky, the conference included Rokossovsky, Bagramian, A. A. Novikov (Red Air Force commander), A. V. Khrulov (head of Rear Services), and the Military Councils of 1st Baltic, 1st Belorussian, and 3d Belorussian Fronts. The 2d Belorussian Front was omitted because it was not originally assigned a major offensive role.

The General Staff planners presented their preliminary concept, which centered on encircling and destroying much of Army Group Center in a huge pocket east of Minsk. Simultaneously with this deep pincer operation, Bagramian and Cherniakhovsky planned to encircle German forces in Vitebsk, and Rokossovsky intended to conduct a tactical double envelopment, using two tank corps to surround the forward German forces around Bobruisk, just north of the Pripiat' Marshes. Stalin, who was always suspicious of complicated maneuver schemes, was violently opposed to the Bobruisk plan, but Rokossovsky stood his ground and eventually won his point.[5]

The conference arrived at the final outline for Bagration, at least north of the Pripiat' Marshes. The offensive would begin with two tactical encirclements conducted by army-level mobile groups to eliminate the German anchor positions on the northern and southern flanks of the "balcony" (see Map 16). The 1st Baltic and 3d Belorussian Fronts would cooperate to encircle Vitebsk, northwest of Smolensk, while 1st Belorussian Front would encircle Bobruisk. At the same time, 5th Guards Tank Army and a cavalry-mechanized group, cooperating with 3d Belorussian Front in the North and a collection of mobile corps and cavalry-mechanized group from 1st Belorussian Front in the south, would conduct the deep encirclement of Minsk. 1st Baltic Front would protect the northern flank by attacking due westward along the banks of the Western Dvina River through Polotsk in the direction of East Prussia, while the left flank of 1st Belorussian Front, south of the Pripiat' Marshes, would subsequently launch 2d Tank Army in a deep thrust westward from the Kovel' region toward the Vistula River. The date for the offensive was tentatively set for 15–20 June 1944.

Ten days after the conference, Stalin summoned Konev to explain how 1st Ukrainian Front could broaden the scope of Bagration. Because the majority of tank armies were still concentrated in the south, Konev had an enormous mass of mechanized forces at his disposal. He proposed a double thrust, which was to become the L'vov-Sandomierz operation. On his northern flank, Konev would concentrate 14 rifle divisions, 1st Guards Tank Army, and a cavalry-mechanized group in a 10-kilometer penetration sector west of Lutsk and attack to encircle German forces at L'vov from the north. Farther south, in his center sector, Konev envisioned a simultaneous attack by 15 rifle divisions, 1 cavalry corps, and 3d Guards and 4th Tank Armies on a slightly wider penetration frontage.

Konev's intent was to encircle and destroy the German forces and reserves east of L'vov and then launch 3d Guards and 4th Tank Armies northwestward toward the Vistula River in the vicinity of Sandomierz, southern Poland. Konev also planned a complex deception to convince the

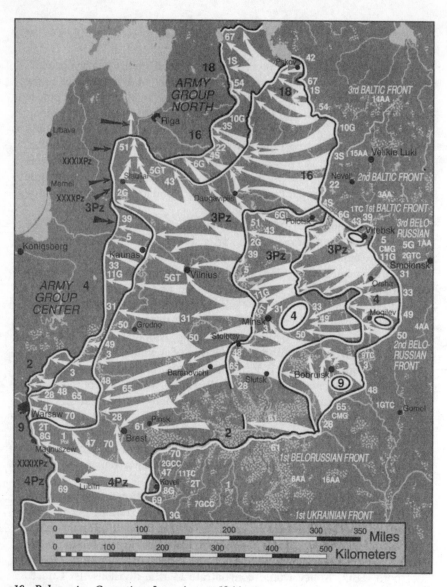

16. *Belorussian Operation, June–August 1944*

Germans that his attack (which they expected) would emanate from the
Stanislaw sector just north of the foothills of the Carpathian Mountains.
Again, as with Rokossovsky's proposal, Stalin resisted such a complicated
plan, particularly the encirclement of L'vov. He finally permitted Konev to
proceed but with the clear warning that the marshal would suffer the
consequences of failure.[6] Konev's assault would take place after the fall of
Minsk but before the attack by 1st Belorussian Front's left wing from the
Kovel' region.

PRELUDE

The *Stavka* issued the basic directive for Bagration on 31 May 1944. Unlike
previous general offensive plans, this scheme limited the *fronts* to attain-
able goals, with initial *front* objectives west of Minsk not more than 150
kilometers from their starting positions. Indeed, the enormous success of
this offensive caught Soviet commanders off guard, and they had to adjust
their plans during the operation to encompass even deeper objectives.

All this planning involved massive logistical concentrations as well as
the secret strategic movement of numerous forces laterally across the front,
including 6th Guards and 11th Guards Armies from 2d to 1st Baltic Front's
sector, 5th Guards Tank and 8th Guards Armies from Moldavia to Belorussia, 28th Army and a cavalry-mechanized group from the Ukraine to
southern Belorussia, and 2d Tank Army from the Rumanian border to the
Kovel' region. During May and June 1944, Chief of Rear Services Khrulov
constantly was bombarded by the preemptory demands of Stalin, Zhukov,
and Vasilevsky to hasten the massive rail movements. Everything had to be
done under strict security measures in order to sustain the deception that
the main offensives would be against the German southern wing.[7] Ultimately, it proved impossible to meet the original schedule. Almost by
accident, the starting date for Bagration slipped to 22 June, the third
anniversary of the German invasion.

By 20 June, the four *fronts* involved in Bagration itself, minus the left
wing of 1st Belorussian *Front*, included 14 combined-arms armies, 1 tank
army, 4 air armies, 118 rifle divisions and two rifle brigades (most organized into 40 rifle corps), 7 fortified regions, 2 cavalry corps (with
6 cavalry divisions), 8 mechanized or tank corps (4 of which were separate corps) and scores of supporting artillery formations. The total
combat force involved was 1,254,300 men, including 4,070 tanks and self-
propelled guns, 24,363 artillery pieces, and close to 5,327 combat aircraft.
Another 1,007 aircraft were involved in long-range aviation missions.
The 1st Belorussian *Front's* left wing included another 416,000 men,

1,748 tanks and self-propelled guns, 8,335 guns and mortars, and 1,456 aircraft organized into 5 combined-arms armies, 1 tank army, 1 air army, 36 rifle divisions (in 11 rifle corps), 2 cavalry corps, and 4 tank and mechanized corps.[8]

While preparations for the main offensive continued apace, Generals L. A. Govorov (Leningrad Front) and K. A. Meretskov (Karelian Front) lifted the curtain for the summer campaign by striking against Finland. Since the front had stabilized around Leningrad in late 1941, when the German advance on the city had been thwarted, Finnish forces remained inactive after reoccupying the territories the Soviets had seized from them in 1940. Although pleased by Finnish military passivity, the ever-cautious Stalin maintained significant forces in Karelia and further north lest the Finns should have a change of heart and again actively join the struggle. By mid-1944, Stalin decided to end the conflict with Finland, retake his lost territories, and free the valuable forces for use elsewhere.

The Karelian operations, the first phase of the summer campaign, were designed to drive Finland from the war, divert attention from Soviet offensive preparations further south, and embarrass the Germans by driving one of their allies from the war. The *Stavka* ordered the Leningrad and Karelian Fronts to secure the Karelo-Finnish isthmus and the expanse of Karelia north and northwest of Leningrad. Govorov's *front*, supported by the Baltic Fleet, was ordered to attack on 10 June to secure Vyborg (Viipuri) within 10 days, and Meretskov's *front* was to strike north of Lake Ladoga beginning on 21 June.

The Soviet commanders well recalled the difficulties they had experienced penetrating the Mannerheim Line in 1939 and 1940. To avoid replicating the earlier four-month struggle, planning was careful, and the Soviets built up a sizable force superiority prior to the offensive.[9] Govorov's offensive unfolded virtually as planned. By 21 June, the left flank of his 21st Army had secured Vyborg despite intense and sordid negotiations between the Finns and Germans over the possible dispatch of German assistance. Govorov then reinforced his forward forces at Vyborg with units of 59th Army, which were transported by ship to the Finnish city. The same day, Meretskov's 7th Separate Army commenced operations into central Karelia from its positions along the Svir River. The combined Soviet operations north and south of Lake Ladoga ultimately forced the Finns to sue for peace in September, and although token German assistance finally did arrive, the die was already cast for the Finns.[10] Soon events elsewhere rendered the Karelian operations a distinct sideshow to the main military effort taking place to the south in Belorussia. For their efforts against the Finns, both Govorov and Meretskov were promoted to the rank of marshal of the Soviet Union.

The Finnish campaign had the added bonus of keeping German attention focused away from Army Group Center. In fact, an organized strategic deception campaign portrayed major Soviet offensives on the northern and southern flanks, with only limited attacks on Army Group Center expected later in the summer. The 3d Baltic Front in the north and 2d and 3d Ukrainian Fronts on the Rumanian border portrayed notional troop concentrations and conducted active operations well into May. So successful were these measures that, up to the day of the Soviet attack in Belorussia, German intelligence believed that 2d Tank and 5th Guards Tank Armies and 5th and 8th Guards Armies were opposite Army Group South Ukraine.[11]

The Soviet *maskirovka* [deception] plan played directly to the German's preoccupation with their allies on the northern and southern flanks. Colonel Reinhard Gehlen, the famous head of the intelligence office known as Foreign Armies East [*Fremde Heere Ost*], continued throughout May and June to predict major Soviet attacks in the north and south. At the same time, German strategic attention was distracted by Anglo-American operations in Italy and preparations for operations in France, and the Luftwaffe continued to place air defense of the Reich above the tactical needs of the Eastern Front.

German intelligence officers at every level had a fairly accurate picture of the forward-deployed Soviet infantry and artillery but little information concerning operational and strategic forces located in the rear. The continued decline in German air strength in the East and draconian Soviet *maskirovka* discipline made aerial reconnaissance consistently ineffective. Ground reconnaissance and the few remaining agents were increasingly less able to move about in the Soviet rear areas. Moreover, Soviet radio silence along large portions of the front made signals intelligence impossible. Overall, German intelligence officers failed to note the arrival of three combined-arms armies, a tank army, and several mobile corps opposite the Army Group. Moreover, the delay in launching Bagration made it difficult for even the most astute analyst to determine the correct starting date.[12]

At corps level and below, many German commanders and their intelligence officers anticipated some form of attack, but their concerns appeared exaggerated to higher headquarters, who turned a deaf ear. For example, a week before the start of Bagration, a battalion commander in the German 12th Infantry Division described the threat to General Martinek, commander of XXXIX Panzer Corps, who was on an inspection tour. Martinek agreed completely but replied by citing the proverb, "Whom God would destroy, he first strikes blind."[13] Higher German headquarters did not fully recognize the offensive threat of Bagration until June 25, three days after it had started.

Given this blindness, Army Group Center was little more than a hollow shell by the time the Soviets attacked. In late May, Hitler categorically forbade the withdrawal of any portion of the Army Group behind the Dnepr or Berezina River lines. Preoccupied with the possibility of a Soviet offensive farther south, OKH transferred control of LVI Panzer Corps to Army Group North Ukraine, thereby depriving Field Marshal Ernst Busch, the Army Group Center commander, of one of his few counterattack elements. Only 20th Panzer Division remained in reserve west of Bobruisk, and it was controlled by OKH rather than the Army Group.

A typical German infantry division of six battalions had a 32-kilometer-wide sector to defend. Wide gaps between the forward battalions were covered only by listening posts and periodic patrols. In most instances the German commanders supplemented their forward network of obstacles, trenches, and bunkers by constructing a secondary defense line a few hundred meters to the rear, and the division established a sketchy secondary line of defense four-to-six kilometers behind the front. Virtually no defenses were prepared farther to the rear, and reserve or counterattack forces at every level of command were woefully inadequate to the task ahead of them. Thus, the traditional German defensive doctrine, which allowed local withdrawals to facilitate immediate counterattacks, could not be applied. Instead, significant forces remained tied down in the rear, conducting antipartisan campaigns that weakened but did not destroy the Soviet guerrilla network.

ATTACK

German and Soviet accounts differ as to the actual starting date for the Bagration offensive, in part because of the staggered nature of the Soviet attack. On the night of 19–20 June 1944, the surviving partisans launched a wave of attacks against railroad junctions, bridges, and other key transportation points throughout Army Group Center's rear area. Although the local German defenses thwarted many of these attacks, more than a thousand transportation nodes were put out of action, making German retreat, resupply, and lateral troop movements impossible.[14]

Beginning on the night of 21–22 June, massive bombing attacks struck the German rear areas, while the Soviet reconnaissance battalions began to move into sparsely held forward German positions, peeling back the German defenses one layer at a time. The main attacks were actually launched on 23 June, in many cases without resort to lengthy artillery preparations, thanks to the reconnaissance elements' success. These attacks consisted of carefully organized mixed task forces made up of tanks, self-propelled guns, and infantry, supported by dedicated artillery and air support. The entire offensive was led by engineer tanks, with plows attached to clear lanes through minefields. At night, searchlights and flares robbed the Germans of their night vision and helped guide the continuing Soviet advance.[15]

The 50mm antitank guns that equipped most German regimental antitank companies were largely ineffective against the frontal armor of T-34 and heavier tanks. Instead, the German infantrymen used antitank mines, explosive charges, Panzerfausts, and similar short-range weapons to exact a price from the attacking forces. Most Soviet commanders simply bypassed the isolated centers of German resistance and continued their advance into the rear.[16]

In the Vitebsk sector, late on 24 June, small mobile task forces of Lieutenant General A. P. Beloborodov's 43d Army swept aside the remnants of the thoroughly demoralized German Corps Group E and seized crossings over the Western Dvina River west of the city. By midday on 25 June, they had linked up with the armored forward detachments of Lieutenant General I. I. Liudnikov's 39th Army, cutting off German LIII Army Corps' withdrawal routes from the city. Virtually without a pause, Lieutenant General I. M. Chistiakov's 6th Guards Army, supported by Lieutenant General V. V. Butkov's 1st Tank Corps, wheeled westward and began pursuing the remnants of Third Panzer Army toward Polotsk.

To the south, Rokossovsky began his assault on 24 June, as his lead divisions emerged miraculously from the swamps to engage the surprised Germans. Painstaking advance engineer work enabled his units to build wooden causeways and ramps through the swamps along the eastern side of the Ptich River without German detection.[17] Once the German defenses had been overwhelmed by lead infantry units, Rokossovsky unleashed his armored forces straight down the swamp-bound roads through the German defenses and into the German rear area. By midday on 25 June, Lieutenant General M. F. Panov's 1st Guards Tank Corps had penetrated over 40 kilometers forward to the southern approaches to Bobruisk while Lieutenant General I. A. Pliev's Cavalry-Mechanized Group followed behind, preparing to swing westward toward Slutsk. The 20th Panzer Division, unable to determine whether the main attack was coming from Rogachev in the east or from south of Bobruisk, wasted two days marching and countermarching in response to confused orders. Ending its agony, on 26 June, Lieutenant General B. S. Bakharov's 9th Tank Corps broke free from German defenses west of Rogachev and raced to seize crossings over the Berezina River south of Bobruisk just as 1st Guards Tank Corps did likewise on the west bank of the river.

The lightning drive of the Soviet armor, followed by a torrent of troops from 65th, 48th, and 3d Armies, caught German XXXV Corps and part of XXXXI Panzer Corps, together with 20th Panzer Division, in a cauldron of fire in and southeast of Bobruisk. While attempting to run the gauntlet to freedom, the fugitives were pounded unmercifully by Soviet air power at the crowded road junction at Titovka.[18] Only the most stoic and lucky were able to survive the carnage and break out northwest of the city. In a sense they were assisted by the fact that Soviet commanders were already urging their forces onward to the west and toward Minsk.

In the secondary Soviet attack opposite Orsha and Mogilev, the German experience was initially less harrowing. Lieutenant General I. T. Grishin's 49th Army mounted a small-scale penetration on 24 June against the junction of German XXXIX Panzer and XII Corps.[19] The paucity of his armor forced Grishin to use a separate tank brigade with infantry mounted on the tanks as the nucleus of his mobile exploitation force. News of mounting disaster prompted the German Fourth Army to begin a slow withdrawal back to Mogilev on the Dnepr. By 27 June, Grishin's forces were across the river north and south of the city, and the now desperate defenders contemplated further retreat to Minsk, which itself was being threatened with capture. On Hitler's orders, however, Mogilev was also to be held to the last man. Some obeyed those orders, but many did not. Those who escaped headed westward to the sound of the guns and to an experience as harrowing as the battles for Vitebsk and Bobruisk. While avoiding immediate defeat in tactical and operational encirclement at Mogilev and along the Dnepr, they fell victim to a much larger strategic encirclement at Minsk.

Wherever these encirclements occurred, Hitler consistently declared the towns to be fortresses that must be defended to the last man. In many cases, these towns consisted of wooden buildings with no cellars, making effective defense impossible. By this stage of the war, experienced German commanders at regimental and lower levels learned to avoid any town that might conceivably be declared a fortress. If they happened to be caught in such an indefensible site, they would use any opportunity to fight their way out. On 27 June, for example, the 12th Infantry Division, together with thousands of support troops and hundreds of wounded soldiers, became encircled at Mogilev. Two battalion task forces from the division broke out on their own. They experienced an almost miraculous escape across the Berezina River and were able to reach German lines along the Neman River, southwest of Minsk.[20]

By 27 June, major gaps had opened in the north between Third Panzer and Fourth Armies and in the south between Fourth Army and the stricken Ninth Army. The two tank corps of Rotmistrov's 5th Guards Tank Army, plus Lieutenant General V. T. Obukhov's separate 3d Guards Mechanized Corps, advanced through the first gap, with their brigades moving on parallel roads in order to seek any possible crossing sites on the Berezina River. Pliev's Cavalry-Mechanized Group raced into the southern gap across the Ptich River and on to Slutsk, which it occupied midday on 29 June.

OKH had belatedly reacted to these threats, and a limited number of mechanized units arrived by rail and road. 5th Panzer Division detrained at Borisov and, together with a collection of lightly armed rear area security units, attempted to close the gap between Third Panzer and Fourth Armies. The best they could achieve, however, was to ambush Soviet corps' forward detachments by hiding in woods or villages and opening fire at close range. Such tactics only delayed the advance for a few hours until the Red commanders located alternate routes and bypassed the defenders.[21] Rotmistrov and other tank commanders, however, were to learn that armored fighting in Belorussia was vastly different and more costly in terms of tanks than it had been in the steppes of the Ukraine.[22]

FALL OF MINSK

On 2 July 1944, only a handful of understrength German regiments were in and around Minsk. The recapture of this city was a classic example of Soviet forward detachments and tank corps exploiting a breakthrough. In essence, the entire German defense was simply preempted by the rapid movement of small forward detachments passing through the town. On the northern side of Minsk, 5th Guards Tank Army's 29th Tank Corps bypassed the town, seeking out any German counterattack forces to the west while seizing a crossing over the Svisloch River. Meanwhile 3d Guards Tank Corps moved into the northwestern corner of the city on 3 July, and Colonel O. A. Losik's 4th Guards Tank Brigade of Major General A. S. Burdeinyi's 2d Guards Tank Corps cleared the northeastern side.[23] The city was effectively secured in one morning, with the Soviets seizing key locations before the German defense was organized. On the afternoon of 3 July, forward elements of 1st Guards Tank Corps arrived from the south, completing the occupation of the town. Immediately behind them were the rifle elements of 3d Army (from the southeast) and 31st Army (from the northeast). Thus, at the same time as the city was seized by mechanized forces, rifle units arrived to establish the inner encirclement around bypassed German Fourth Army forces still defending east of Minsk. The entire process was accomplished virtually without a pause in the exploitation.[24]

Farther south, remnants of the German Bobruisk force continued desperate attempts to escape after the two Soviet tank corps completed their envelopment. German sources admit that this latter encirclement included two corps, comprising about 70,000 men, of German Ninth Army. As was done in the case of 5th Panzer Division in the north, OKH dispatched 12th Panzer Division with orders to restore the situation. Dutifully responding to the call, the division began detraining in the Osipovichi area, 50 kilometers from Bobruisk, on 27 June. The chief of staff of Ninth Army welcomed the division commander with the ironic comment, "Good to see you! Ninth Army no longer exists!"[25] This remark was true in all but name, although a determined counterattack on 30 June by a combat group of 12th Panzer Division rescued up to 10,000 unarmed German troops escaping from the Bobruisk area. The remaining 60,000, however, were subjected to massive Red air strikes and eventually capitulated. German Sixth Air Fleet, which had begun the battle with only 45 fighters in the area, was so hampered by lack of fuel and aircraft that it could do nothing against the massive Soviet air superiority.

Worse was to come for the defenders. On 27 June, Hitler issued Operations Order No. 8, another stand-fast directive that ordered the reconstruction of a front with troops that were already surrounded. German commanders continued to request permission to withdraw or maneuver and were consistently refused until it was too late. Ultimately, LIII Army Corps capitulated at Vitebsk, and a massive encirclement east of Minsk accounted for most of Fourth Army.[26]

While 2d Belorussian Front's 33d, 49th, and 50th Armies engaged in the gruesome task of eradicating the encircled Fourth Army, Cherniakhovsky's and Rokossovsky's *fronts* drove westward without a halt to maintain the momentum of the advance. They seized the key towns of Molodechno and Baranovichi, which dominated the narrow movement corridors traversing the swampy and heavily wooded regions of central Belorussia. Further development of the offensive toward Vilnius and Bialystok required Soviet seizure of the key towns before the Germans could erect new defenses around them.

By 3 July, while 5th Guards Tank Army reassembled west of Minsk, Obukhov's Cavalry-Mechanized Group (3d Guards Mechanized and 3d Guards Cavalry Corps) began the fight for Molodechno against German 5th Panzer Division and the remnants of XXXIX Panzer Corps, and further south, Pliev's Cavalry-Mechanized Group fought along the approaches to Baranovichi. Additional German reinforcements in the form of 7th Panzer Division in the north and 4th Panzer Division in the south stiffened German resistance. On 5 July, however, Rotmistrov's 5th Guards Tank Army joined the advance on Vilnius. By 8 July, 3d Belorussian Front, together with Cavalry-Mechanized Group, 5th Army, and 11th Guards Army, had encircled German defenders in Vilnius and begun a complex fight to reduce the garrison, block German relief attempts, and, simultaneously, continue the advance to the banks of the Neman River. Heavy fighting raged in Vilnius until 13 July as Rotmistrov's tanks supported costly block-by-block street combat in the city.[27]

That day brought another example of German heroics as a small combat group of newly arrived German 6th Panzer Division penetrated 30 kilometers through Soviet lines and rescued a small portion of the garrison. At the same time, however, Soviet forces reached the Neman River southwest of the city. Meanwhile, to the north, Bagramian's 1st Baltic Front had secured Polotsk and, joined in the offensive by the neighboring 2d Baltic Front, raced northwestward along both banks of the Western Dvina River. Additional Soviet reinforcements in the form of 2d Guards and 51st Armies, newly arrived from the Ukraine and Crimea, added momentum to Bagramian's thrust and threatened to route the already weakened northern flank of Army Group Center.[28] The fighting along this axis now focused on a Soviet drive toward Kaunus, Riga, and the shores of the Baltic Sea, a drive which threatened to sever communications between German Army Groups Center and North.

The fall of Vilnius was accompanied by Germans' loss of Lida and Baranovichi, key communications nodes to the south. The Soviet 50th and 49th Armies rejoined their parent *fronts* after reducing the Minsk pocket, and the 2d and 1st Belorussian Fronts focused, respectively, on the seizure of Grodno and Bialystok, even deeper in the German rear. Within a week, the advance through southern Belorussia expanded into an even larger battle for the approaches to the Polish border and the Vistula and Narew River lines, as 1st Belorussian Front's left wing went into action west of Kovel'.

In the twelve days between 22 June and 4 July, Army Group Center had lost 25 divisions and well over 300,000 men. In the ensuing weeks, it lost more than 100,000 additional men. The Soviet drive finally slowed by the end of the month, as its armored spearheads had become worn down and dulled. Tank losses in combat and the wear and tear of three weeks of mobile battle forced most tank formations to stand down to repair and refit. Losses had been particularly heavy in 5th Guards Tank Army. Rotmistrov was soon removed from command of this army and elevated to chief of Soviet Armored and Mechanized Forces, ostensibly for permitting such heavy losses to occur. Lieutenant General V. T. Vol'sky ultimately took command of Rotmistrov's army.[29]

The slowing of the Soviet advance offered little consolation for the Germans. After the initial series of catastrophic defeats, Field Marshal

Walter Model, commander of Army Group North Ukraine, was also given command of Army Group Center on 29 June so that he could coordinate the redistribution of the few surviving forces and erect new defense lines somewhere to the west. Model had already shifted fresh panzer divisions into Belorussia. Soon, however, he was beset with new problems as his old front from L'vov to Kovel' erupted in flame and destruction and soon merged into one gigantic struggle raging from the Baltic to the Carpathian Mountains.

L'VOV-SANDOMIERZ AND LUBLIN-BREST
OPERATIONS

On 28 June, the *Stavka* had ordered a general advance by all four *fronts*— 1st Baltic and 1st, 2d, and 3d Belorussian. They were joined on 13 July by Konev's 1st Ukrainian Front, which accelerated its plans for the L'vov-Sandomierz offensive south of the Pripiat' Marshes to capitalize on the German disaster in Belorussia.

In accordance with earlier plans, the *Stavka* ordered Konev to destroy elements of German Army Group North Ukraine in the L'vov and Rava-Russkaia regions by delivering two simultaneous blows northeast and east of L'vov.[30] In the north, Colonel General M. E. Katukov's 1st Guards Tank Army, secretly redeployed from the south, and Lieutenant General V. K. Baranov's Cavalry-Mechanized Group (1st Guards Cavalry Corps and 25th Tank Corps) were to strike southwestward along the Styr River from the Lutsk region toward Rava-Russkaia and the western approaches to L'vov. Simultaneously, Colonel General P. S. Rybalko's 3d Guards Tank Army and Colonel General D. D. Leliushenko's 4th Tank Army, and a second cavalry-mechanized group commanded by Lieutenant General S. V. Sokolov, would exploit a penetration begun by Soviet 38th and 60th Combined-Arms Armies directly on L'vov from the east. To deceive the Germans, Konev carefully orchestrated a feint to the south in the Stanislaw region. By virtue of a massive secret regrouping of forces, Konev was able to create a significant numerical superiority over the German defenders.[31]

Konev's offensive began in the northern sector on 13 July, when 3d Guards and 13th Army reconnaissance units found German forward positions unmanned. Immediately, forward battalions and main forces joined the advance and, by day's end, penetrated up to 15 kilometers into the German defenses. Within days, Sokolov's cavalry-mechanized group followed by Katukov's tank army plunged into the yawning gap in the German defenses. Katukov employed his customary forward detachment,

1st Guards Tank Brigade, to deceive the Germans as to where his army would enter combat, and hence was able to deal effectively with German operational reserves, 16th and 17th Panzer Divisions, which he initially brushed aside to the north.[32] The 16th Panzer Division was later able to disengage, conduct a long flank march to the west, and reach the L'vov area in time to participate in the city's defense.

While Katukov led the march deep into German defenses in the north, Konev's combined-arms armies on the direct approaches to L'vov were unable to open the planned corridors for Rybalko's and Leliushenko's armor. The 38th Army's attack faltered in the German tactical defenses, and 60th Army opened only a small hole through German defenses east of the village of Koltov. Quickly responding to the changed circumstances, Konev ordered both Rybalko and Leliushenko to thrust their armies successively through the narrow corridor on 60th Army's front, accompanied by 31st and 4th Guards Tank Corps, whose missions were to hold open the shoulders of the penetration. Meanwhile, Sokolov's cavalry-mechanized group was to swing northward along the path of 1st Guards Tank Army and help lead the race to the Vistula.

Beginning early on 14 July, the more than 1,000 tanks and self-propelled guns of Konev's mobile force thrust into the Koltov corridor. Despite desperate counterattacks by the German 8th and 1st Panzer Divisions to close it, the armored armada traversed the gauntlet of fire successfully.[33] On 18 July, lead elements of 3d Guards Tank Army linked up northeast of L'vov with forward brigades of Sokolov's Cavalry-Mechanized Group, trapping German XIII Corps in the Brody pocket. Subsequently, while rifle forces reduced the pocket and 60th Army, supported by Lieutenant General P. P. Poluboiarov's 4th Guards Tank Corps, held off German relief attempts by 1st and 8th Panzer Divisions, 3d Guards and 4th Tank Armies attempted to envelop L'vov from the north and south. Heavy fighting raged on the approaches to the city as the German XXXVI Army Corps and III Panzer Corps fended off the Soviet tank armies' attacks.

In the end it was the rapid advance of 1st Guards Tank Army and Sokolov's Cavalry-Mechanized Group toward the Vistula River deep in the German rear that unhinged the German defense of L'vov. On 23 July, Katukov's army approached Peremyshl', severing German communications with L'vov, and Konev ordered Rybalko to swing his army westward to join Katukov astride German communications lines. On 7 July, when the lead elements of Sokolov's cavalry and tank force were but 20 kilometers from the Vistula, the Germans abandoned L'vov. Konev immediately ordered both Katukov and Rybalko to turn their armies toward the Vistula, while German armor struggled to redeploy from the L'vov region to meet the new threat. While Leliushenko's 4th Tank Army and Baranov's Cavalry-Mechanized Group fended off German counterattacks from the south, the 1st and 3d Guards Tank Armies raced northwest toward the river. On 29 and 30 July, forward detachments of Katukov's army, along with vehicular mounted elements of Lieutenant General N. P. Pukhov's 13th Army, seized a series of small bridgeheads across the Vistula River south of Sandomierz. Within days they were joined by the remainder of their armies and by Rybalko's 3d Guards Tank Army.

A long and arduous struggle ensued for possession of the bridgehead.[34] For over a month, German reserves redeployed from Hungary and units from the L'vov region, organized into LIX, III, and XXXXVIII Panzer Corps, hammered vainly at Soviet positions in and around the bridgehead. Further south, German XXIV Panzer Corps struck at the Soviet south flank east of the Vistula. The heavy fighting only proved the prevalent German adage that a Soviet bridgehead, once occupied, could not be destroyed.

The challenge to Field Marshal Walter Model's skill was only beginning. No sooner had Minsk fallen and the Soviet attack commenced along the L'vov axis than he had to contend with an equally severe threat on the Kovel'-Lublin axis. There, on 18 July, the left wing of Rokossovsky's 1st Belorussian Front joined the fray.[35] After feinting on 9–10 July to draw German attention away from Soviet offensive preparations at L'vov and after Konev's initial success in the south, Rokossovsky's armies went into action.

On 18 July, Lieutenant General N. I. Gusev's 47th Army and Colonel General V. I. Chuikov's 8th Guards Army tore into German defenses, and by 21 July they had reached the Western Bug River. The next day, Lieutenant General S. I. Bogdanov's 2d Tank Army began its exploitation toward Lublin and the Vistula, while 11th Tank and 2d Guards Cavalry Corps led the drive northwest toward Siedlce to cut off the retreat of Army Group Center forces defending around Brest and Bialystok.

Although Bogdanov was wounded on 23 July during the fighting for Lublin and was replaced by Major General A. I. Radzievsky, the rapid advance continued, carrying the lead elements of 8th Guards Army and 2d Tank Army to the shores of the Vistula on 25 July. While Chuikov's army seized a bridgehead near Magnuszew and Lieutenant General V. Ia. Kolpakchi's 69th Army secured one near Pulawy, the *Stavka* ordered Radzievsky to turn his army northward toward Warsaw to help cut off the withdrawal of Army Group Center.[36]

By 28 July, Radzievsky's army, with three corps abreast, engaged German 73d Infantry Division and the Hermann Goering Panzer Division 40 kilometers southeast of Warsaw. A race ensued between Radzievsky, who was seeking to seize the routes into Warsaw from the east, and the

Germans, who were attempting to keep those routes open and maintain possession of Warsaw. The nearest Soviet forces within supporting range of Radzievsky were 47th Army and 11th Tank and 2d Guards Cavalry Corps, then fighting for possession of Siedlce, 50 kilometers to the east. On 29 July, Radzievsky dispatched his 8th Guards and 3d Tank Corps northward in an attempt to swing northeast of Warsaw and turn the German defenders' left flank, while his 16th Tank Corps continued to fight on the southeastern approaches to the city's suburbs.

Although Lieutenant General A. F. Popov's 8th Guards Tank Corps successfully fought to within 20 kilometers east of the city, Major General N. D. Vedeneev's 3d Tank Corps ran into a series of successive panzer counterattacks orchestrated by Model. Beginning on 30 July, the Hermann Goering and 19th Panzer Divisions struck the overextended and weakened tank corps north of Wolomin, 15 kilometers northeast of Warsaw.[37] Although the corps withstood three days of counterattacks, on 2 and 3 August, 4th Panzer Division and SS Panzer Division *Viking* joined the fight. In three days of intense fighting, 3d Tank Corps was severely mauled, and 8th Guards Tank Corps was also sorely pressed. By 5 August 47th Army's forces had arrived in the area, and 2d Tank Army was withdrawn for rest and refitting. The three rifle corps of 47th Army were stretched out on a front of over 80 kilometers, from south of Warsaw to Siedlce, and were unable to renew the drive on Warsaw or to the Narew River. German communications lines eastward to Army Group Center had been damaged but not cut.

On 1 August, the Polish Home Army of General Tadeusz Bor-Komorowski had launched an insurrection in Warsaw.[38] Although the insurgents seized large areas in downtown Warsaw, they failed to secure the four bridges over the Vistula and were unable to hold the eastern suburbs of the city. For two months, the Polish Home Army struggled and ultimately perished in Warsaw but received little material help from the Soviets. Instead, 1st Belorussian Front focused on defending the Magnuszew bridgehead against heavy counterattacks in mid-August, and on driving forward across the Bug River to seize crossings over the Narew River. In each case, the intent was to gain starting points to facilitate future operations rather than to help the Polish insurgents in the short run.

Soviet 47th Army remained the only major force opposite Warsaw until 20 August, when it was joined by Lieutenant General Z. M. Berling's 1st Polish Army. Soviet forces finally forced the Bug River on 3 September, closed up to the Narew River the following day, and fought their way into a bridgehead across the Narew on 6 September. On 13 September, lead elements of 47th Army entered Praga in Warsaw's eastern suburbs. Three days later, elements of two Polish divisions launched an assault across the river but made little progress and were evacuated back across the Vistula on 23 September.[39]

The Soviets have long maintained their sincerity in attempting to assist the Polish uprising. Indeed, German resistance in the region was probably sufficient to halt any Soviet attack, at least until mid-September. Thereafter, a Soviet advance on Warsaw would have involved a major reorientation of military efforts from Magnuszew in the south—or, more realistically, from the Bug and Narew Rivers axis in the north—in order to muster sufficient force to break into Warsaw. Even if they had reached Warsaw, the city would have been a costly place to clear of Germans and an unsuitable location from which to launch a new offensive.

Regardless of the military reasons for the Red Army's failure to take Warsaw, it was undoubtedly true that, for political reasons, Stalin was in no hurry to aid Bor-Komorowski. The Polish insurgents owed allegiance to the British- and American-backed exile government in London, and it was politically convenient to have the Germans and Poles kill each other off. The limited Soviet-Polish efforts to reach Warsaw on 10 September and again on 16-17 September only encouraged the rebels to fight on. Until mid-September, Stalin refused permission for the U.S. Army Air Force to use Soviet airfields in their planned efforts to parachute supplies to the insurgents. By the time the first such mission was flown, the area of Warsaw remaining in Polish hands was too small for parachute drops. After two months of heroic resistance, the Poles capitulated on 2 October.[40] Three more months would pass before the Soviets accumulated enough force to break out of their Vistula bridgeheads.

CONCLUSIONS

Operation Bagration, together with the L'vov-Sandomierz and Lublin-Brest operations, had propelled the Red Army across the Neman River to the border of East Prussia and across the Vistula and Narew Rivers in northern and central Poland. Except for the German counterattacks at Warsaw and in Lithuania, it was logistical overextension, rather than German strength, that had halted the exploitation. The destruction of more than 30 German divisions and the carnage wrought in a host of surviving divisions, accompanied by a Soviet mechanized advance in excess of 300 kilometers, had decimated Army Group Center, the strongest German army group, severely shaken Army Group South Ukraine, and brought the Red Army to the borders of the Reich.

German manpower losses during the two months were staggering. Army Group Center lost almost 450,000 men and its strength fell from

888,000 to 445,000, despite reinforcement from the flanks. Another 100,000 fell elsewhere. Hitler, however, was encouraged, since the front was now shortened. On 7 July, he ordered the formation of 15 new panzer grenadier divisions and 10 panzer brigades. Formed around the staffs of decimated divisions, the new forces soaked up all replacements earmarked for the Eastern Front for July and August 1944 and absorbed 45,000 troops released from hospitals.[41] Yet, despite the Germans' need to direct new divisions and equipment eastward, throughout June and July the Wehrmacht was still able to contain the Allied bridgehead in Normandy.

The strategic success of Bagration did not come without cost for the Soviets. Of the 2,331,000 troops engaged in the Belorussian and Lublin-Brest operations, 178,507 were killed or missing and 587,308 were wounded. In addition, 2,957 tanks and self-propelled guns, as well as 2,447 guns and mortars were lost in combat or for logistical reasons. Soviet casualties in the L'vov-Sandomierz operation totaled 65,001 killed or missing and 224,295 wounded, and meant the loss of another 1,269 tanks and self-propelled guns and 1,832 guns and mortars.[42]

Despite these losses, Soviet manpower strength on the Eastern Front continued to rise from 6,394,500 troops (with another 727,000 in hospitals) on 12 March 1944 to almost 6,500,000 troops in late fall, while overall German strength ranged from 2,460,000 (plus 550,000 of its allies) on 1 June, to 1,996,000 (plus 774,000 allies) on 1 August; 2,042,000 (plus 271,000 allies) on 1 September; and 2,030,000 (190,000 allies) on 1 November. Even more telling, Soviet armored strength rose from 7,753 tanks and self-propelled guns on 1 June 1944 to 8,300 on 1 January 1945, while German armor strength rose from 2,608 on 1 June to 3,658 on 1 August, and 3,700 on 1 November. From 1 June 1944 to 1 January 1945, Soviet artillery strength increased from over 100,000 guns and mortars to 114,600, while German artillery strength went from 7,080 on 1 June to 5,703 on 1 August, and down to 5,700 on 1 November.[43] While Albert Speer's German mobilization program kept pace in equipment, Soviet industry more than matched the effort. And Speer could not generate the resources Germany needed most—trained and ready military manpower.

In mid-August 1944, while the Soviet victors rested and refitted along the Vistula River, the *Stavka* turned its attention to achieving similar spectacular offensive successes on the northern and southern flanks.

CHAPTER 14

Clearing the Flanks

The Soviet success against Army Group Center prepared the way for future operations on the strategic flanks, both south and north. By the end of 1944, these operations had ejected the German Army from all Soviet territory and begun the creation of the postwar Soviet domination of eastern and central Europe.

GERMANY ON THE DEFENSE

Quite apart from the disaster in Belorussia and southern Poland, the month of July 1944 was a difficult time for the German High Command. Overwhelming Anglo-American airpower not only dominated the skies over the Reich but made the German defense against the Allies in Normandy untenable. On 17 July, Field Marshal Erwin Rommel was seriously wounded when his car was strafed by a British fighter-bomber. On 25 July, in Operation Cobra, a combination of tactical and strategic bombers blasted a hole through the German defenses west of St. Lo, signaling the beginning of the Allied breakout from the hedgerow country of Normandy. Within days, General George S. Patton's U.S. Third Army began an operational exploitation into Brittany and eastward toward Paris. For one of the few times on the Western Front, the Germans were faced with an armored thrust comparable to the deep operations by Germans in 1941–1942 and the Russians in 1943–1944. That thrust soon produced a nearly catastrophic encirclement of another German army group at Falaise.

On 20 July 1944, the long-simmering plots against Hitler culminated in a botched attempt to assassinate him. Not only did the bomb fail to kill its principal target but the conspirators had made no real preparations to seize control of Germany. In response, Hitler became even more paranoid and arbitrary in his actions.

Among these actions was a decision to replace Kurt Zeitzler as chief of the General Staff. With so many senior officers under suspicion for failure in battle or conspiracy in the rear, it was almost inevitable that Hitler's eye should light on the one commander who had not been actively involved in either—Heinz Guderian. Within hours after the bomb exploded, Guderian found himself head of OKH, trying to reassemble a functioning staff in the ruins of the explosion just as he tried to reestablish a front in the ruins of Army Group Center.[1] In the process, Guderian withdrew five panzer divisions and six German infantry divisions from General Ferdinand Schoerner's Army Group South Ukraine, the mixed German-Rumanian force defending the lower Dnestr River and Rumania with its back to the Carpathian Mountains.

This army group, which had been in tatters after the winter–spring campaign of 1944, had reestablished its structure, discipline, and morale. Organized into two mixed German-Rumanian groups of two field armies each (Groups Wohler and Dumitrescu), Army Group South Ukraine held strong forward positions with the seemingly impenetrable Carpathian Mountains as a fall-back position. Since its once powerful armored force had been sent as fire brigades to other sectors of the front throughout July, it was weak in mobile reserves, having only the 13th Panzer Division, the 10th Panzer Grenadier Division, and the poorly trained Rumanian Panzer Division "Great Rumania." It was also hampered by a tenuous logistical system, in which entire trains would disappear until they were located by air and their Rumanian engineers bribed to bring them to the front. Moreover, Germany's nominal Hungarian allies were more belligerent toward the Slovaks and Rumanians than they were toward the Soviets. As one German staff officer remarked, Army Group South Ukraine had to fight on three different fronts—against the Soviets, against the satellite countries of Hungary, Slovakia, and Rumania, and against the OKW.[2]

For political reasons and to protect the key Rumanian cities of Iassy and Kishinev, the Army Group was required to defend the extensive terrain from the Carpathians to Dubossary on the Dnestr River and a huge bulge along the lower Dnestr River (now Moldova) to the Black Sea. The Soviets had already secured several small bridgeheads over the river. Schoerner repeatedly requested permission to withdraw from this bulge but got nowhere with Hitler and the OKW. Ultimately, OKH quietly authorized him to begin constructing a fall-back position in the Carpathians but to do so in a manner that did not attract Rumanian attention.

Indeed, the satellite armies were the Achilles' heel of this entire defense. Just as in the Crimea and at Stalingrad two years earlier, some Rumanian divisions fought loyally and even valiantly alongside their German counterparts, but others had little interest in prolonging the war, especially given their catastrophic losses at Stalingrad. German commanders accurately predicted that the next major offensive would be against the Army Group and that the main efforts would come against Rumanian forces, but neither the Soviets nor the Germans were prepared for the speed of the Rumanian collapse in August 1944.

IASSY-KISHINEV OPERATION

In essence, the Soviet conquest of the Balkans in the fall of 1944 consisted of one carefully planned penetration operation and deep exploitation—the Iassy-Kishinev operation of 20–29 August 1944—followed by a long pursuit that ended at the gates of Budapest four months later.

In planning this campaign, the *Stavka* was motivated by political as well as terrain considerations. In late July 1944, its attention shifted to the south, seeking to destroy Army Group South Ukraine and introduce Soviet power into the region of Rumania, Bulgaria, and Yugoslavia. At the same time, Hitler's remaining strategic oil reserves in the Ploesti oil fields of Rumania and those of the Hungarian Balaton region were a natural strategic target. Moreover, on practical grounds, the Soviets wanted to avoid the difficulties of fighting in the Carpathian Mountains and to reduce the number of river-crossing operations by operating parallel to and between the Dnestr, Prut, Siret, and other rivers of the Balkans. For all these reasons, the initial strategic thrust of the coming campaign was oriented to the south, rather than over the Carpathian Mountains to the west.

Army Group South Ukraine, with a total strength of approximately 500,000 German troops and 170 tanks and assault guns, and 405,000 Rumanians with modest amounts of supporting armor, was opposed by Army Generals R. Ia. Malinovsky's 2d and F. I. Tolbukhin's 3d Ukrainian Fronts. As was often the case at this stage in the war, German intelligence seriously underestimated the capabilities of these two *fronts*, which totaled 1,314,200 men with 1,874 tanks or assault guns.[3] It must be admitted, however, that some of this strength consisted of untrained and ill-equipped recruits. Just as with their German counterparts, the Red Army commanders often had to use soldiers with little or no training. During the winter–spring campaigns of 1944, the two Ukrainian *fronts* had become seriously depleted and had made up their losses by sweeping all available manpower from the liberated regions of the Ukraine and Bessarabia. Men were pulled out of villages, haystacks, or wherever they could be found, put into uniform, issued weapons, and incorporated into rifle divisions. One rifle division of 5th Shock Army grew from 3,800 to 7,000 men in this manner, but these new recruits were only marginally effective. As a result, Soviet rifle units no longer had the same staying power they had possessed earlier in the war, forcing Soviet commanders to use ever-increasing amounts of concentrated infantry, artillery, and armor support.[4]

The *Stavka* plan for what became the Iassy-Kishinev operation called for a coordinated attack by R. Ia. Malinovsky's and F. I. Tolbukhin's

2d and 3d Ukrainian Fronts, in cooperation with the Black Sea Fleet, to destroy German and Rumanian forces in the Iassy, Kishinev, and Bendery regions and, subsequently, to advance deep into Rumania to seize Bucharest and the Ploesti oilfields.[5] Just as in Belorussia, penetration attacks in two principal sectors would be accompanied by secondary attacks in neighboring sectors, preventing the Germans from shifting their reserves. The 2d Ukrainian Front was to penetrate German-Rumanian defenses northwest of Iassy, then commit Major General V. I. Polozkov's 18th Tank Corps to seize Prut River crossings in the rear of German Sixth Army. After participating in the penetration with their lead brigades, Lieutenant General A. G. Kravchenko's 6th Tank Army and Major General S. I. Gorshkov's Cavalry-Mechanized Group (5th Guards Cavalry Corps and 23d Tank Corps) were to race southward, and seize the Siret River crossings and the key pass known as the Focsani Gap to facilitate a further dash by the tank army to Bucharest.

The 3d Ukrainian Front would launch a similar concentrated attack farther south from a small bridgehead over the Dnestr in the Tiraspol'-Bendery area, and then introduce Major General V. I. Zhdanov's 4th Guards and Major General F. G. Katkov's 7th Mechanized Corps for deep exploitation. The two exploiting corps would then turn north and link up with 18th Tank Corps from 2d Ukrainian Front, encircling the bulk of German forces in the Kishinev area. Instead of passively forming an outer encirclement around the Germans, however, the greater portion of the mobile forces (6th Tank Army and 4th Guards Mechanized Corps) would continue to thrust southward toward Bucharest and the Ploesti oil fields.

To achieve sufficient concentration in the penetration sectors, the field armies of these two *fronts* had been specially configured so that they varied greatly in strength. Some armies with an economy of force or deception mission had as few as five divisions. In each of the two designated penetration sectors, however, Malinovsky and Tolbukhin concentrated two full armies, each with nine rifle divisions, ample artillery units, and supporting armor. This armor included some of the first issues of Joseph Stalin heavy tanks specially designed for infantry support.[6]

Despite such massive concentrations, the Soviet attack did not run smoothly when it began on 20 August 1944. In the southern penetration sector at Bendery, two German infantry divisions held firm for several days. The Bendery bridgehead was so small that Tolbukhin's troops had great difficulty in launching the attack. The 7th Mechanized Corps became entangled with the assaulting infantry on crowded roads, delaying the exploitation for critical hours on 20 and 21 August. In the north, the attack progressed much more rapidly, with 6th Tank Army entering the exploitation phase on the very first day of the battle. Much of this success occurred because the Rumanian defenders put up only token resistance. On 23 August, the Soviet attack prompted a coup against the pro-German government in Bucharest, and two days later the new government declared war on Germany. Under such circumstances, many Rumanian units lost heart. By 24 August, for example, 3d Ukrainian Front's 46th Army had surrounded Third Rumanian Army in eastern Rumania along the shores of the Black Sea. Third Rumanian Army surrendered on the following day, and, within weeks, this army had changed sides, appearing in the Soviet order of battle.[7]

Faced with this unexpected collapse, isolated German units fought delaying actions with their customary skill and courage. The 10th Panzer Grenadier Division, in particular, conducted a long rear-guard action in the vicinity of Iassy, allowing numerous Rumanian and German units to escape the trap. Meanwhile, most of four corps of the German Sixth Army were trapped in a large pocket east and southwest of Kishinev. The overwhelming Soviet air superiority pounded this pocket without mercy during the hot days in late August. The German defenders stubbornly tried to break out, stretching the pocket to the west. They were unwittingly assisted in this by Tolbukhin, who asked the *Stavka* to remove 4th Guards Army, a 2d Ukrainian Front unit that had entered the sector of 3d Ukrainian Front. The method chosen to resolve this issue was to send 4th Guards Army north to cross the Prut River and then retrace its steps on the western bank of the Prut.

By this stage in the operation, 6th Tank Army and the other mobile forces were well to the southwest, and 5th Shock Army, involved in the original attack, had begun entraining for movement north to Poland. These maneuvers, conducted on 27 and 28 August, created a power vacuum near the Kishinev pocket, facilitating the German attempt to break out. The bubble around the surviving elements of Sixth Army moved westward and was not halted until 5 September, when Major General A. O. Akhmanov's 23d Tank Corps was recalled to block them. Within sight of escape at the Siret River, the remnants of Sixth Army were finally brought to bay and destroyed.[8]

By 29 August, Army Group South Ukraine had suffered a fate similar to that of Army Group Center—the destruction of Sixth Army and two Rumanian armies and the utter collapse of the German front in Rumania. The Germans lost control of the Ploesti oilfields and Bucharest by 2 September. German and Rumanian losses exceeded 400,000 men at a cost to the Soviets of about 67,000 casualties.[9] By 1 September, Army Group South, renamed Army Group South Ukraine, had strength returns of only 200,000 men, with 2,000 allied forces.[10] An Axis retreat ensued across the

Carpathians, which did not halt until Soviet forces had penetrated Bulgaria and swung westward into the plains of eastern Hungary.

ADVANCE ON BUDAPEST

The Soviet pursuit continued across the Balkans, placing great demands on Soviet logistical capabilities. Indeed, by this stage in the war, the distance that a Soviet offensive could cover depended more on its logistical support than on the strength of the Axis defenders. Germany had no operational reserves in the Balkans; all its available forces were committed to a vain effort to control the insurgents in Yugoslavia. Like a great swinging door, the leading edge of the Soviet pursuit moved clockwise through the regions.

By the end of September, Tolbukhin's 3d Ukrainian Front had completed its sweep of Bulgaria. Leaving Lieutenant General M. N. Sharokhin's 37th Army to support the Bulgarian government, which now joined the Soviet war effort, Lieutenant General N. A. Gagen's 57th Army advanced into western Bulgaria. Supported by the 2d Bulgarian Army, it prepared for future operations against German Army Group "E" and "F" forces in Yugoslavia. Lieutenant General I. T. Shlemin's 46th Army, having entered Bulgaria, swept back into southern Rumania and, supported by the 4th Bulgarian Army, advanced on Timisoara in concert with 2d Ukrainian Front's left wing.[11]

Meanwhile, Malinovsky reorganized his forces for the advance across the Carpathians into western Hungary. Gorshkov's Cavalry-Mechanized Group, with Lieutenant General F. F. Zhmachenko's 40th Army and Lieutenant General S. G. Trofimenko's 27th Army, cleared the passes through the Carpathians north of Ploesti into Transylvania. At the same time, Kravchenko's tank army (now designated as Guards for its spectacular performance in Rumania) with Lieutenant General I. M. Managarov's 53d Army attempting to keep pace with the rapid pursuit, swept west from Bucharest, crossed the Carpathians, and reached the Hungarian border west of Cluj. Thus by the end of September, Malinovsky's forces had occupied the passes through the mountains on an 800-kilometer front and had pressed the light covering forces of German Eighth Army and Hungarian Second and Third Armies to and, in some cases, across the Hungarian border.

Malinovsky's *front* now consisted of four combined-arms armies (40th, 7th Guards, 27th, and 53d), 6th Guards Tank Army, Gorshkov's cavalry-mechanized group, several separate mobile corps, and two Rumanian armies (1st and 4th) newly incorporated into the Soviet fold. The *Stavka* ordered Malinovsky to destroy German and Hungarian forces in Hungary and drive Hungary from the war in cooperation with Colonel General I. E. Petrov's 4th Ukrainian Front, which had just been reformed in the northern Carpathian region between 1st and 2d Ukrainian Fronts.

To conduct operations in Hungary, the *Stavka* reinforced Malinovsky's *front* with the addition of the 46th Army (and shortly 4th Guards Army, as well) from Tolbukhin's *front* and two mechanized corps (2d Guards and 4th Guards). Malinovsky also gained a second cavalry-mechanized group (2d and 4th Guards Cavalry Corps and 7th Mechanized Corps), commanded by Lieutenant General I. A. Pliev, the great practitioner of cavalry operations in adverse terrain, who had distinguished himself in Belorussia. Since 2d Ukrainian Front was deployed on an exceedingly broad front, its operational densities remained low throughout the Hungarian operations, and logistical sustainment was difficult. Thus Malinovsky was forced to conduct a series of successive army or multiarmy operations, each preceded by a short operational pause and limited regrouping of forces. In particular, he had to husband and shuffle his *front* mobile elements.[12]

Malinovsky's initial plan called for an advance in the center from Oradea-Mare northwest toward Debrecen, while flank armies cleared northern Rumania and advanced into southern Hungary via Szeged. Malinovsky sought to trap all German forces in eastern Hungary in a pincer between his 2d and Petrov's 4th Ukrainian Fronts. In early September, Petrov had begun a thrust into the Carpathian Mountains from the western Ukraine, in concert with 1st Ukrainian Front's left flank, to exploit gains made in the L'vov-Sandomierz operation and assist a partisan uprising in Slovakia. Thereafter, Malinovsky intended to shift his axis of attack westward toward Budapest.

German defenses in Hungary were relatively thin. General Johannes Friessner, commander of the renamed Army Group South, had two German armies and two Hungarian armies available to him for the defense of Hungary. German Eighth Army (Group Wohler) was withdrawing from Transylvania to positions east of Cluj, while a reorganized Sixth Army (Group Fretter-Pico) covered the Oradea-Cluj sector, along with elements of Second Hungarian Army. East of Oradea Third Hungarian Army held a long defensive line westward to Szeged. The only German operational reserves were 23d Panzer Division and the lead elements (1st Panzer Division) of a four-panzer division task force promised by Hitler to reinforce Friessner's hard-pressed army group.[13]

The first phase of this offensive, called the Debrecen operation, began on 6 October against the junction of German Sixth and Eighth Armies.[14] Within three days Group Pliev had advanced 100 kilometers northwest to the Tisza River. When Kravchenko's 6th Guards Tank Army failed to seize Debrecen, Malinovsky quickly moved Pliev's Group eastward to assist the tank army. Together, on 20 October, the combined mobile forces seized Debrecen. Subsequently, Pliev's Group and Gorshkov's Cavalry-Mechanized Group, which had approached Debrecen from the east, sped north and seized Nyiregyhaza on 22 October. At that point, however, Pliev and Gorshkov were struck by a concerted German panzer counterattack by newly arrived III Panzer Corps and Group Wohler's XVII Army Corps, which severed the mobile groups' communications. By 27 October, they were forced to abandon their advanced positions and most of their equipment and withdraw south.

With both German and Soviet forces tied down in heavy combat north of Debrecen, the *Stavka* and Malinovsky capitalized on the German weakness further south by mounting a drive on Budapest from Malinovsky's left flank, north of Szeged.[15] On 29 October, Malinovsky's forces, spearheaded by 2d and 4th Guards Mechanized Corps, penetrated the Hungarian Third Army's defenses and advanced through Kiskoros and Kecslemet to the southern approaches to Budapest. Resistance from the hastily redeployed German III Panzer Corps (Group Breith-1st and 13th Panzer Divisions, and Panzergrenadier Division *Feldhernhalle*), assisted by 23d and 24th Panzer Divisions and by Hungarian forces, brought the Soviet advance to an abrupt halt short of the city on 3 November.

After regrouping Group Pliev and 2d and 4th Guards Mechanized Corps eastward, Malinovsky struck at Szeged, east of Budapest on 10 November. Yet, by 20 November, bad weather and stiffened German resistance had again halted the Soviet drive short of Budapest. Further south, however, on 27 November, Tolbukhin's 3d Ukrainian Front, having completed the liberation of Belgrade, deployed forward to the banks of the Danube River near Sombor and attacked across the river with General N. A. Gagen's 57th Army and Lieutenant General I. V. Galanin's 4th Guards Army. By 3 December, against relatively light resistance, Tolbukhin's two armies reached the shores of Lake Balaton, southwest of Budapest.[16]

Malinovsky struck again on 5 December, this time north and south of Budapest in a two-pronged attack to envelop and seize the city. Kravchenko's 6th Guards Tank Army and Pliev's Cavalry-Mechanized Group advanced to envelop the city from the north via Sahy, and a second force, spearheaded by Lieutenant General K. V. Sviridov's 2d Guards Mechanized Corps, advanced south of Budapest from small bridgeheads over the Danube River seized in late November to secure Szekesferhervar and Esztergom, west of Budapest. Despite a spectacular initial Soviet advance, the Germans shifted their operational reserves, and Budapest neither fell nor was encircled. The Soviet advance south of the city bogged down against the German Margareithe Defense Line between Lake Balaton and the southern outskirts of Budapest. Both 6th Guards Tank Army and Pliev's Cavalry-Mechanized Group penetrated into the hills north of the Danube but failed to encircle the city.

While Malinovsky's new offensive unfolded and ultimately faltered, OKH dispatched new reinforcements to Friessner in the form of 3d and 6th Panzer Divisions and three 60-tank Tiger battalions to restore the situation around Budapest.[17] The question was where to use the armor to greatest effect: in the north against 6th Guards Tank Army or in the south against Tolbukhin's threatening spearhead? A nasty debate ensued between OKH and Friessner, which was further complicated by bad weather that limited the mobility of the new armor. In the end, Friessner deployed the infantry from the panzer divisions in the north and left the unsupported armor to bolster defenses in the south.

The bad weather and German maldeployments played into Malinovsky's and Tolbukhin's hands. On 20 December, they struck massively north and south of Budapest. The 6th Guards Tank Army and Cavalry-Mechanized Group Pliev, supported by Colonel General M. S. Shumilov's 7th Guards Army, penetrated and rolled up German defenses in the north and reached the Danube opposite Esztergom on 27 December. Meanwhile, Tolbukhin's 46th and 4th Guards Armies, supported by 18th Tank, 2d Guards, and 7th Mechanized Corps and by Lieutenant General Gorshkov's 5th Guards Cavalry Corps, penetrated the Margareithe Line and, routing the unsupported German armor, plunged northwestward to Esztergom. By 27 December, forces from the two *fronts* linked up along the Danube, leaving German IX SS Mountain Corps' four divisions and two Hungarian divisions trapped in Budapest. Because of the catastrophe around Budapest, both Friessner and Fretter-Pico were relieved of command. Wohler became commander of Army Group South, and General Hermann Balck, one of the few remaining practitioners of armored warfare, took command of Sixth Army.[19]

Somewhat ironically, within days the lead elements of German IV SS Panzer Corps began arriving in the area. Throughout the remainder of December and into January 1945, the Soviets parried several heavy and partially successful counterattacks by the SS panzer corps to relieve the beleaguered garrison.[20] Although the German thrusts failed, their partial success did plant in Hitler's mind the seeds for what would become the final major German offensive operation of the war—the offensive at Lake Balaton in March 1945.

While Malinovsky and Tolbukhin ravaged German defenses in the Balkans, the Soviets began operations to penetrate the German Carpathian Mountain defenses and reach Slovakia and eastern Hungary. The

1st Ukrainian Front's left flank, 38th Army, commanded by Colonel General K. S. Moskalenko, was the first to strike in early September toward the Dukla Pass in an attempt to link up with Slovak partisans, who were conducting an uprising against German authorities.[21] On 8 September, Moskalenko attacked near Krosno, using his army's three rifle corps to effect a penetration, after which 25th, 4th Guards, and 31st Tank Corps and 1st Guards Cavalry Corps were to exploit and seize the Dukla Pass. General Ludwig Sloboda's 1st Czech Corps and Czech tank and airborne brigades participated in the operation.

Initial Soviet success was short-lived as the Germans dispatched their 1st and 8th Panzer Divisions and other reinforcements to bolster the defenses of Colonel General Gotthard Heinrici, commander of First Panzer Army. Moskalenko's forces penetrated German defenses and committed their mobile forces into the operation, but German counterattacks thwarted further Soviet advance, encircled Lieutenant General V. K. Baranov's 1st Guards Cavalry Corps for several days, and turned back the Soviet threat short of the Dukla Pass.[22] Although the Soviets airlifted the Czech airborne brigade into Slovakia, the partisan uprising expired before the Red Army could reach it.

On 9 September, Petrov's 4th Ukrainian Front joined the attack, advancing with Colonel General A. A. Grechko's 1st Guards Army and Major General I. M. Afonin's 18th Separate Guards Rifle Corps toward Uzhgorod.[23] Again, a successful initial attack degenerated into a slugging match and slowed the Soviets' progress. In almost two months of heavy fighting, First Panzer and Hungarian First Armies gave ground only grudgingly, and by 28 October, Soviet forces had taken Uzhgorod and Mukachevo in Ruthenia but had failed to clear Slovakia of German forces. By this time, Petrov's right flank had joined Malinovsky's forces near Chop on the Tisza River. Further progress by the joined flanks of the two *fronts* remained slow and painstaking throughout the remainder of 1944 and winter of 1945. His defensive efforts earned Heinrici the sobriquet of Germany's finest defensive specialist and, ultimately, on 20 March 1945, the command of German forces along the Oder River.

The campaign against the German southern flank made major strategic gains, drove Rumania from the Axis camp, and added several Rumanian and Bulgarian armies to the Red Army's order of battle. It also struck a major economic blow to the Third Reich by depriving Germany of the valuable Hungarian granary and the oilfields of Rumania and Hungary that were so critical to the German war effort. Militarily, operations in Hungary drew to the region critical German armored reserves, including 1st, 3d, 6th, 23d, and 24th Panzer Divisions, and, finally, the two superbly equipped divisions of IV SS Panzer Corps. The absence of these units from the critical Warsaw-Berlin axis would soon prove disastrous for the German cause.

DRIVE TO THE BALTIC COAST

In late summer and fall 1944, equal disaster befell the German northern flank. During the pursuit phase of the Belorussian operation, the Soviets vigorously exploited the gap between Army Group Center and Army Group North in the Siauliai operation, which commenced on 5 July as an extension of the Belorussian operation. By 31 July 1944, the forward detachments of three 1st Baltic Front armies—Lieutenant General A. P. Beloborodov's 43d, Lieutenant General Ia. G. Kreizer's 51st, and Lieutenant General P. G. Chanchibadze's 2d Guards, spearheaded by Lieutenant General V. T. Obukhov's 3d Guards Mechanized Corps, had pressed through the gap to the Gulf of Riga. Lieutenant General I. M. Chistiakov's 6th Guards Army covered the Latvian capital on their right flank.[24] This thrust and the narrow Soviet corridor to the Baltic that resulted severed communications between Army Groups Center and North.

One of Guderian's first tasks as chief of the General Staff was to eliminate this penetration. After much argument, in mid-August the Germans were able to assemble a few separate tank and self-propelled gun brigades to launch a limited counterattack near Riga. This force chopped off the Soviet spearhead and established an east-west corridor about 30-kilometers wide between the two German army groups.[25]

Further to the south, in Lithuania, XXXX and XXXIX Panzer Corps of Third Panzer Army received a more generous share of Guderian's meager reserves. Three understrength panzer divisions (5th, 14th, and 7th), plus the Panzergrenadier Division *Grossdeutschland*, attacked eastward on 16 August, seeking to seal off the Soviet penetration and retake the key road and rail junction of Siauliai.

But Blitzkrieg had lost its magic. General I. Kh. Bagramian, commanding the 1st Baltic Front, reacted promptly by establishing a standard, deep defensive system directly in the path of the German advance.[26] Most Soviet units were now lavishly supported by a mixture of towed antitank weapons and self-propelled antitank guns, both of which were a match for German armor. Chanchibadze's 2d Guards Army, the Soviet force threatened most directly, deployed its main antitank reserve, 93d Antitank Brigade. Behind this army, Bagramian set up a second defensive belt, using two rifle divisions and several other antitank brigades. In addition, Bagramian committed Lieutenant General V. V. Butkov's 1st Tank Corps, Lieutenant General V. T. Obukhov's 3d Guards Mechanized Corps, and

Lieutenant General M. D. Solomatin's understrength 5th Guards Tank Army (recently returned from operations to seize Kaunus) as counterattack forces. This rapid reaction, in combination with significant Soviet air superiority, halted the German attack by 20 August. Third Panzer Army had reopened a narrow corridor to Army Group North, but at a prohibitive cost.

On 17 September, Army General A. I. Eremenko's 2d and Colonel General I. I. Maslennikov's 3d Baltic Fronts resumed their offensive toward the Baltic and Riga. Lieutenant General I. I. Fediuninsky's 2d Shock Army smashed German defenses at Tartu, and Lieutenant General N. P. Simoniak's 67th and Lieutenant General N. D. Zakhvataev's 1st Shock Armies did likewise north of Valga. These blows, combined with attacks by 2d Baltic Front due east of Riga, brought the entire defensive structure of Army Group North to the brink of collapse. To make matters worse, while Bagramian fended off the German attacks at Siauliai, his 43d and 4th Shock Armies drove past Baldone northwards toward the outer defenses of Riga.

General Ferdinand Schoerner, appointed as new commander of Army Group North on 23 July, learned much from the subsequent German defeat in Rumania. He recognized that his position in Estonia and Latvia was untenable and that the narrow corridor from Army Group Center to Army Group North was a hostage to any serious Soviet attack. Therefore, he orchestrated a general German withdrawal, albeit hard-pressed by Soviet forces, back toward Riga.[28]

By the end of September 1944, Marshal L. A. Govorov's Leningrad Front had cleared German forces from virtually all of Estonia except the Baltic islands. Maslennikov's and Eremenko's 3d and 2d Baltic Fronts were approaching the outskirts of Riga, and Bagramian's 1st Baltic Front had fended off German counterattacks, seized Elgava and Dobele, and threatened Riga from the south. Schoerner's army group, however, had stiffened its resistance outside Riga, bolstered by heavily prepared defenses covering the approaches to the city.

Faced with these realities and anticipating new attempts by the Germans to solidify the links between Army Groups Center and South, the *Stavka* decided to end the issue once and for all by attacking between the two enemy army groups to the sea. To do so required changing the 1st Baltic Front's offensive axis from Riga to the west and southwest. On 24 September, the *Stavka* ordered the Leningrad Front and the Baltic Fleet to complete the liberation of Estonia and to mount an amphibious operation against German forces on the Hiumma and Saaremaa Islands. The 2d and 3d Baltic Fronts were to storm Riga and clear the Baltic coast of Germans. More important, Bagramian's 1st Baltic Front and part of Colonel General I. D.

Cherniakhovsky's 3d Belorussian Front would deliver a powerful blow along the Siauliai-Memel' axis, cut off Army Group North from East Prussia, and facilitate future destruction of all German forces in the Baltic region.[29] To support the assault, Cherniakhovsky was to prepare a simultaneous or subsequent direct attack along the Konigsberg axis into East Prussia.

The reorientation of 1st Baltic Front's operations required an immense regrouping of all 1st and 2d Baltic Front forces. The resultant shock group included 6th Guards, 4th Shock, and 43d and 2d Guards Armies backed up by the *front* mobile group, the refitted 5th Guards Tank Army and second echelon 51st Army. Between 24 September and 4 October, Bagramian secretly moved five armies comprising 50 rifle divisions, 15 tank brigades, and 93 artillery regiments into new attack positions.[30] The Germans detected Soviet attack preparations but were too late to prepare a response.[31]

On 5 October, Bagramian's forces struck, and by evening Vol'sky's 5th Guards Tank Army was exploiting deep into the German rear area.[32] By 9 October, 5th Guard Tank Army's headlong assault had overrun Third Panzer Army headquarters and reached the Baltic coast north and south of Memel', locking German XXVIII Army Corps into the encircled city and isolating another Third Panzer Army corps with the remainder of Army Group North in the Riga area and Courland.

Faced with these unpleasant realities, Schoerner insisted that Army Group North had to withdraw onto a bridgehead in the Courland Peninsula. This withdrawal took place under fire. Breaking contact with a determined Soviet enemy and reestablishing a new, longer defensive line in Courland required great skill and daring. By 23 October 1944, Army Group North had retreated into Courland, salvaging most of its forces and supplies. Hitler insisted that it remain there, so only limited elements were evacuated by sea for use on other fronts.[33]

With Army Group North safely ensconced in Courland and useless to support operations elsewhere, the *Stavka* turned its attention to the remnants of Third Panzer Army now digging in along the borders of East Prussia to defend the German heartland. While 1st Baltic Front approached the Neman River from the north, the *Stavka* authorized Cherniakhovsky's 3d Belorussian Front to strike into Prussia along the Gumbinnen-Konigsberg axis. In the ensuing Gumbinnen operation, Cherniakhovsky planned to penetrate German defenses with 5th and 11th Guards Army and then exploit with 2d Guards Tank Corps and the fresh 28th Army of Lieutenant General A. A. Luchinsky.[34] The 31st and 39th Armies would support the assault on the flanks.

On 16 October, Colonel General N. I. Krylov's 5th Army and Colonel General K. N. Galitsky's 11th Guards Army went into action and drove 11 kilometers into the German defenses. The following day 31st and 39th Armies joined the assault, and Galitsky's army crossed the East Prussian border. German resistance was fierce, and German fortified lines were so formidable that it took four days for Cherniakhovsky's armies to penetrate the tactical defenses. The second defense line along the German border was so strong that Cherniakhovsky committed his tank corps to overcome it. On 20 October, 11th Guards Army and 2d Guards Tank Corps finally ruptured the defense and approached the outskirts of Gumbinnen. On the following day, Cherniakhovsky committed 28th Army to battle, but the entire advance faltered in the Stallupinen defensive region, as heavy German panzer reinforcements arrived to stiffen the defense. Fighting continued until 27 October as the flank Soviet armies closed up with 11th Guards Army's forward positions. At a cost of heavy casualties, the Soviets had advanced 50 to 100 kilometers into East Prussia, and learned from experience what preparations would have to be made in the future to conquer Germany's East Prussian bastion.

THE FAR NORTH

Far to the north, after the Karelian operations against the Finns had regained and expanded the territory lost in 1941, the Soviets bided their time and conducted desultory operations that pressured Marshal Carl Mannerheim's Finnish government and continued bleeding the Finnish Army white. By mid-July, the Soviets had replaced most of their front-line troops with defensive units and fortified regions, and went over to the defense as the priority shifted to offensives farther south. The subsequent collapse of Army Group North's defenses in the Baltic and the impending loss of Riga ultimately forced Helsinki to sign an armistice on 4 September 1944.[35]

Colonel General Lothar Rendulac, commander of the German Twentieth Mountain Army, had anticipated this defection and begun to withdraw his forces into blocking positions in northern Norway and the tip of the Soviet Kola Peninsula, west of Murmansk. Under strong pressure from the Soviets to adhere to the armistice terms, Finnish forces engaged the withdrawing German units on 28 September, but Rendulac was generally able to complete his withdrawal. Simultaneously, the OKW staff persuaded Hitler that the entire region should be evacuated, but this second evacuation had not yet started when the Soviets, on 7 October, launched their last offensive in the north, the Petsamo-Kirkenes operation.[36]

Although the operation did not contribute decisively to ultimate Soviet victory in the war, and it was dwarfed in scale by other operations to the south, it was unusual because of its venue and because it combined land and amphibious operations.

The setting for this operation was unique, with its harsh, lunar terrain and equally harsh weather. The fact that the ground was not frozen in October made cross-country movement even more difficult. Indeed, the outcome of the entire offensive hinged on control and use of the few east-west roads in the area, and large numbers of engineer troops on both sides were dedicated to creating and maintaining such roads.

Marshal Meretskov, the Karelian Front commander, and many of his subordinates were veterans of the Finnish wars and had considerable knowledge of the difficulties of arctic warfare. Most Soviet troops in the area, however, lacked the broader experience that their southern counterparts had acquired in the preceding three years. Characteristic of this stage of the war, the *Stavka* provided Meretskov with a number of new units that were specially configured for operations in the region. The most unusual were the 126th and 127th Light Rifle Corps, light infantry units with 4,334 ski troops and naval infantry each. These units were designed to fulfill the deep penetration and by-pass role ordinarily performed by large mechanized units. Meretskov also assembled 30 engineer battalions, numerous horse- and reindeer-equipped transportation companies, and two battalions of U.S.-supplied amphibious vehicles for river crossings. Under the overall command of the Karelian Front, Lieutenant General V. I. Shcherbakov, a veteran of the Russian Civil War and the 1939 Finnish War, headed the 14th Army, controlling Meretskov's maneuver elements.

Meretskov aimed the main attack at the German 2d Mountain Division on Rendulac's southern flank, with the intent of bypassing and encircling the entire German force. The attack plan included all the elaborate preparations typical of a 1944 Soviet penetration; 2,100 artillery tubes, half of them mortars, were massed for the attack, and 7th Air Army had 750 aircraft to support the offensive. The preparatory artillery fires were scheduled to include 140,000 rounds of conventional artillery and 97 tons of multiple-rocket launcher ammunition. Shcherbakov even had 110 tanks and assault guns, despite the difficult terrain and the total absence of German armor in the region. Overall, 14th Army outnumbered the German XIX Mountain Corps, the main target of the offensive, by 113,200 to 45,000.[37]

Despite these preparations, the initial attack on 7 October was hampered by poor visibility, making air and artillery support difficult. The 131st Rifle Corps quickly achieved a bridgehead over the Titovka River in the German center, but the 99th Rifle Corps, responsible for the main attack against 2d Mountain Division, found that the planned fire support had not suppressed the German defensive fires. By the time the 99th Rifle

Corps had reorganized to continue the attack, the Germans had with-drawn behind the Titovka and blown their bridges. The absence of roads hampered the forward movement of supplies and artillery, so that the Soviet troops rapidly outran their support. Meanwhile, on the night of 9–10 October, small elements of the 63d Naval Infantry Brigade landed at three points along the German left flank. These landings threatened to cut the main highway along the coast.

By the morning of 13 October, the Soviets were poised to attack the northern anchor of the German defenses, the port of Petsamo, from three sides, and the 126th Light Rifle Corps had established a weak blocking position across the only escape road to the west. Rendulac authorized XIX Mountain Corps to withdraw, and the 2d Mountain Division was able to break through the Soviet roadblock on 14 October. Petsamo fell to the Soviets the following day, but the Soviet troops were so exhausted that Shcherbakov had to order a three-day pause.

The rest of the Petsamo-Kirkenes campaign was a race along the northern coast of Norway. Time after time, the light rifle corps or other small Soviet units outran the Germans and established a roadblock, only to be so short of food and ammunition that they were unable to hold their positions. Aerial resupply alleviated some of these problems, but the Germans escaped with the bulk of their forces intact. The Soviet armor was restricted to the coastal road and played a very limited role in the campaign. German rear guard actions, supported by artillery and (as they withdrew into Norway) by aircraft, repeatedly held up the Soviets. Finally on 29 October, with the polar night approaching, Meretskov halted all operations except reconnaissance.

The Petsamo-Kirkenes operation freed the Soviet arctic flank and eventually denied the Germans nickel and iron supplies from several mines in the region. On the negative side, despite all their efforts to anticipate problems, the Soviet commanders had underestimated the difficulties of moving on such terrain. The light infantry forces involved on both sides encountered the inherent physical limitations of exhaustion. It is not surprising, however, that Meretskov and his staff were among those sent to the Far East in summer 1945. There, they applied the lessons of Petsamo-Kirkenes in their plans to defeat the Japanese in the equally harsh terrain of Manchuria.

CONCLUSIONS

Overall, the summer and fall of 1944 were an unmitigated string of disasters for the German forces. The summer offensives alone cost the Axis forces an estimated 465,000 soldiers killed or captured. Between 1 June and 30 November 1944, total German losses on all fronts were 1,457,000, of which 903,000 were lost on the Eastern Front. Equally important for an army with few motor vehicles, outside of the Panzer units, the Germans lost 254,000 horses and other draft animals.[38] By the end of 1944, only Hungary remained allied with Germany. The Germans felt besieged and isolated, with the Red Army lodged in East Prussia in the North, along the Vistula River in Poland, and across the Danube in Hungary, and with Allied armies within striking distance of Germany's western borders.

The Soviet Union also suffered heavily during this period, coming ever closer to the bottom of its once-limitless barrel of manpower. In an effort to compensate for this, Soviet plans used steadily increasing amounts of artillery, armor, and airpower to reduce manpower losses. In the process, moreover, the Soviet commanders had the opportunity to test out their operational theories within a variety of tactical and terrain considerations. These commanders still made occasional mistakes, but they entered 1945 at the top of their form.

By the end of 1944, the Red Army was strategically positioned to conquer the remainder of Poland, Hungary, and Austria in a single operation. The only question that remained was whether this last strategic thrust would propel Soviet forces as far as to Berlin, and, if so, where would the Allied armies complete their operations? Soviet-styled shadow governments had accompanied the Red Army into eastern Europe, and the Yalta Conference, to be held in February 1945, would tacitly legitimize these regimes. Where the contending armies advanced in 1945 would have a decisive influence over the political complexion of postwar Europe. This stark fact underscored the importance of subsequent operations during the race for Berlin and, coincidentally, generated more than a little suspicion in the respective Allied camps.

CHAPTER 15

Battles in the Snow, Winter 1945

THE ARDENNES AND HUNGARY

The first shots that led to the complete Soviet occupation of Poland were actually fired in the Ardennes Forest, 800 kilometers to the west of the Vistula River. On 16 December 1944, Hitler launched a major offensive in the Ardennes region, committing most of his available mechanized forces in an effort to knock the Western Allies out of Europe before the next Soviet blow fell in the East. General Hasso von Manteuffel's Fifth Panzer Army and SS General Sepp Dietrich's Sixth SS Panzer Army, supported on the flanks by two infantry armies, attempted to rush through the region and seize the Meuse River bridges, dividing the Allied front. In weeks of desperate fighting, the German offensive fell short of its goal, halted by a combination of skillful armored maneuvers, stubbornly held road junctions, and, when the skies cleared, overwhelming Allied tactical air power.

In the crisis of the Bulge, the Western governments asked Stalin to take the pressure off them by resuming the offensive. Ultimately, as will be described, Stalin responded by launching his next major offensive eight days ahead of schedule. This episode only reinforced the Soviets' belief that they were carrying the brunt of battle in the war. It is worth noting, however, that the growing concentration of German mechanized forces and logistical support in the West made the Soviet task in the East far easier than it would otherwise have been.

Similarly, continued Soviet operations in Hungary had the desired effect of drawing off German forces from Poland. In late December 1944, Marshal R. Ia. Malinovsky's 2d Ukrainian Front and Marshal F. I. Tolbukhin's 3d Ukrainian Front had renewed their offensive, penetrated the imposing German Margareithe defenses located between Lake Balaton and the southern outskirts of the capital, and encircled three SS divisions, 13th Panzer Division, and numerous Hungarian units in the city itself. The task of capturing the city was no mean task, and initial Soviet attacks into Budapest itself vividly demonstrated that seizure of the city would require considerable time and effort.

To do so Malinovsky created an ad hoc group consisting of three rifle corps of 46th Army (23d, 10th Guards, and 37th Guards) to reduce Buda, and 18th Separate Guards Rifle Corps, 7th Rumanian Corps, and 30th Rifle Corps from 7th Guards Army to seize Pest.[1] This loose organization under dual army command made little progress in the last days of December. The veterans of city fighting at Stalingrad were few and far between in the Red Army of 1944, and the Germans did their usual systematic job of organizing a defense. Moreover, the commitment of large forces to reduce German defenses in the city weakened the Soviet outer encirclement line 40 kilometers west of Buda and provided an opportunity for the Germans to mount a relief effort for their beleaguered garrison.

On Christmas Day, Hitler responded to the southern threat and attempted to exploit the relief opportunity by directing the redeployment of IV SS Panzer Corps from the area north of Warsaw to Hungary.[2] Two full-strength SS panzer divisions (*Totenkopf* and *Viking*) detrained northwest of Budapest and launched a surprise night attack on New Year's Day, hitting the 4th Guards Army of Tolbukhin's *front* on its vulnerable western flank just south of the Danube River. The violent attack, which nearly destroyed the Soviet 18th Tank Corps, finally ground to a halt only 20 kilometers west of Budapest, blocked by redeployed reserves from both 46th and 4th Guards Armies. On 6 January, a *Stavka*-directed counterattack by Colonel General A. G. Kravchenko's 6th Guards Tank Army and Colonel General M. S. Shumilov's 7th Guards Army jumped off north of the Danube in an effort to encircle the attackers but made little headway. A second German attack was launched by III Panzer Corps north of Szekesfehervar on 7 January. Designed to take advantage of IV SS Panzer Corps' success to the north, it was halted by Soviet 4th Guards Army forces with only limited gains. This assault, however, demonstrated that Soviet defenses southwest of Budapest were relatively weak and perhaps could be crumbled by a larger German force.

The German tactical commanders now showed flashes of their old brilliance. After conducting one more lunge towards Budapest from the northwest (from 10–12 January), which again alarmed the Soviets and drew more forces to the region, SS General Herbert Gille suddenly disengaged his IV SS Panzer Corps late on 12 January, redeployed them to the Szekesfehervar area, and launched a renewed attack eastward with III Panzer Corps on 18 January. By good fortune, the Germans struck 135th Rifle Corps on 4th Guards Army's weakened left flank at a time when all its supporting tanks and self-propelled guns had been withdrawn for maintenance and refitting. Within two days, Gille had brushed aside four Soviet corps and reached the Danube River. He then turned northward, striking back toward Budapest from the Soviet rear. By 24 January, the SS panzers were within 25 kilometers of the southern suburbs of Budapest. However, Hitler would not allow the city garrison to break out, insisting that the attackers relieve the siege. This, plus Malinovsky's rapid shifting of large forces (18th and 23d Tank, 1st Guards Mechanized, 5th Guards Cavalry, and 30th and 133d Rifle Corps) into blocking positions south of the city, gradually absorbed the shock of the German attack. After a final German attempt to drive through to the city, German forces began withdrawing to their initial positions on 27 January.[3]

Meanwhile, Soviet troops continued to inch forward into the city of Pest. On 10 January, the *Stavka* urged Malinovsky to establish more centralized control over the three corps involved, and the next day Malinovsky formally appointed Major General I. M. Afonin, commander of 18th Guards Rifle Corps, to head the Budapest Operational Group. Afonin launched an attack to split Pest in two, reaching the Danube River by 14 January. In a world of snow and mist, Soviet assault squads and German defenders fought out a deadly battle, block by block. As the defenders ran short of fuel and ammunition, their tanks and other heavy weapons gradually fell silent. On 12 January, the attackers seized the racetrack that had served as the last emergency landing strip for JU-52 resupply aircraft. By 17 January, the remaining German defenders fell back to the river, only to find that the Soviets had used the sewers to reach the bank ahead of them. At least half of IX SS Mountain Corps ceased to exist. More than 36,000 Germans had died and 63,000 had surrendered by 18 January. The misery of the remaining German defenders would continue west of the river, in Buda.[4]

At this point, the *Stavka* gave Malinovsky's 2d Ukrainian Front the task of clearing the western (Buda) bank of the river, leaving Tolbukhin's 3d Ukrainian Front to defend the outer encirclement against continuing German relief efforts. When Afonin was wounded in close-in fighting on 22 January, Colonel General I. M. Managarov, commander of 53d Army and an experienced urban fighter, succeeded him in command of the assault forces, which now consisted of 75th Rifle Corps and 37th Guards Rifle Corps.

Both sides continued to suffer heavy casualties, with the fighting in Budapest approaching that of Stalingrad in ferocity. The struggle went on until 12 February, when about half of the remaining German garrison of 26,000 men attempted to break out. In bloody, desperate fighting, the force was destroyed, and on the following day Buda fell. Loss of the city, however, would not end Hitler's fixation on operations in Hungary, to the detriment of operations elsewhere.

The Soviet Union could ill afford the losses suffered in the heavy fighting around Budapest, but the Germans could afford their losses even less, especially the drain on armor resources that were so critically needed elsewhere. Moreover, Soviet-German combat in Hungary throughout

December 1944 and January 1945 served a crucial strategic purpose by keeping Hitler's attention riveted to the south rather than focusing on the east. Most damaging to the German cause was Hitler's decision on 16 January to commit Sixth SS Panzer Army (belatedly withdrawn from the Ardennes) in Hungary rather than Poland. This decision was even more incomprehensible since it came after the Red Army renewed its offensive on the Vistula. Bereft of strategic reserves, Germany's remaining eastern armies waited for the inevitable renewal of Soviet attacks in the East along the critical Warsaw-Berlin axis.

PLANNING FOR THE WINTER CAMPAIGN

Planning for this renewed offensive had begun in late October 1944. The victories of the summer and fall had created a much more favorable situation for Soviet offensive action: the overall front had been shortened from 4,450 kilometers to 2,250 kilometers, significant German forces were uselessly locked in Courland, and the Soviet Union clearly held the strategic initiative. Soviet intelligence estimates indicate that, during 1944, 96 German divisions had been captured or destroyed and another 33 so weakened that they were disbanded.[5] New equipment, including the Iosif Stalin heavy tank, the SU-122 and SU-152 self-propelled assault guns, and newer models of multiple-rocket launcher had also improved the technical capabilities of the Red Army. Still, even the seemingly inexhaustible strength of the Soviet Union had its limits, and the planners sought a means for rapid and relatively bloodless victory.

Once again, the *Stavka* evaluated the entire front to determine the location and goals of the coming offensive. In East Prussia, 13 German divisions occupied as many as six successive defensive belts, some dating back to prewar times, to a depth of 120 kilometers. The previous Soviet attempt in October 1944 had clearly indicated that any assault on such heavy fortifications would become a slow, grinding, expensive advance. Indeed, Marshals Zhukov and Rokossovsky had to persuade Stalin not to persist in the fall offensive in this area, where Soviet armies, weakened after a long advance, were suffering heavy casualties with little results.

At the other end of the front, the Soviets might reinforce 2d and 3d Ukrainian Fronts, launching the main advance on Germany from Hungary. Like the Germans before them, however, the Soviet troops in the Balkans were operating on a logistical shoestring over difficult terrain and a limited rail and road network. The Hungarian-Austrian region was more useful as a means to divert German reserves than as a major strategic axis in its own right.

Three hundred kilometers northeast of Budapest, the Soviet line jutted westward across the Vistula River in the area of Sandomierz, where Konev's 1st Ukrainian Front had seized a bridgehead at the end of the 1944 summer offensives. West of this bridgehead lay the industrial regions of Katowice and Silesia, a tempting target for a Soviet state that had lost so much of its own industry in the war. Yet the factories and mines of these regions could easily become a trap, forcing the attackers to root out German defenders while destroying much of what they wanted to seize. As a result, Stalin planned to bypass and encircle Silesia, rather than assault it frontally.

The remaining avenues of advance lay through central Poland. The most obvious axis led from the Vistula River around Warsaw northwestward to the Oder River barrier. The rolling terrain here seemed designed for a rapid mechanized exploitation, although its western reaches were traversed by the German Meseretz Fortified Region. Even against the seven understrength German armies defending from the Baltic to the Carpathians, a successful attack would require long and careful preparation, especially for logistics.

While the Soviet engineers and rear service forces rebuilt the shattered communications lines leading to the Vistula River, operational planners sketched the outline of the coming campaign. On 28–29 October 1944, senior commanders met with Stalin. After considerable wrangling, Stalin agreed to let his forces go on the defensive in preparation for the next attack. In addition, Stalin and Zhukov agreed that the shorter front lines made it possible to control the entire front directly from the *Stavka*, dispensing with the *Stavka* representatives and coordinators who had represented the high command in the field during the previous three years. Instead, the forces for the new offensive would be restructured into a smaller number of extremely powerful *fronts*, and Stalin himself would (nominally) coordinate the battle from Moscow. Stalin gave Zhukov the plum assignment to command 1st Belorussian Front, which was to advance directly on Berlin, with Konev's 1st Ukrainian Front following a parallel course just to the south and Rokossovsky's 2d Belorussian Front advancing westward north of the Vistula River toward Danzig to cover Zhukov's right flank. The usual Soviet security measures were employed to conceal from the Germans the reinforcement of these three *fronts*.

Stalin's decision to assume direct control was obviously intended to enhance his postwar prestige and reduce that of his most prominant wartime marshals, especially Zhukov. In doing so, he relied heavily on General A. I. Antonov, who as operations chief of the General Staff had effectively headed the *Stavka* for the past two years, while chief of staff Marshal A. M. Vasilevsky had acted as a *Stavka* coordinator in the field.

Vasilevsky, in fact, was relegated to the largely nominal role of *Stavka* coordinator for 1st and 2d Baltic Fronts on the northern flank.

As eventually developed, the *Stavka* campaign plan envisaged a two-stage operation (see Map 17). During November and December, as described earlier, the 2d and 3d Ukrainian Fronts continued to advance in Hungary, drawing off German reserves. Then the main offensive, tentatively scheduled to begin between 15 and 20 January 1945, would shatter the German Vistula and East Prussian defenses in two large-scale operations. The lesser of these attacks, conducted by Cherniakhovsky's 3d and Rokossovsky's 2d Belorussian Fronts, had the onerous task of clearing Army Group Center from East Prussia. Cherniakhovsky was to bull his way westward through the German defenses toward Konigsberg (now Kaliningrad), while Rokossovsky would envelop East Prussia from the south and perform the vital task of protecting Zhukov's flank as 1st Belorussian Front made the main attack. To accomplish this, 2d Belorussian Front was reinforced to a total of seven field armies, plus Colonel General V. T. Vol'sky's 5th Guards Tank Army, and several separate mobile corps. Marshal K. A. Vershinin's 4th Air Army would provide air support.

At the same time, Zhukov and Konev would launch the main offensive across Poland against German Army Group A. Zhukov arrayed a total of eight combined-arms armies, two tank armies, two guards cavalry corps, and an air army to launch three major penetration operations. The main attack would come from the Magnuszew bridgehead, a 24-kilometer by 11-kilometer bulge over the Vistula just south of Warsaw, opposite German Ninth Army. Colonel General V. I. Chuikov's 8th Guards Army, the heroes of Stalingrad, in concert with Colonel General P. A. Belov's 61st Army and Lieutenant General N. E. Bezarin's 5th Shock Army, was to make the initial attack here, seeking to advance up to 30 kilometers on the first day. This attack would open the German lines for exploitation by Colonel General M. E. Katukov's 1st Guards Tank Army, Colonel General S. I. Bogdanov's 2d Guards Tank Army, and Lieutenant General V. V. Kriukov's 2d Guards Cavalry Corps.

At the same time, the right flank divisions of 61st Army were to turn north toward Warsaw. This advance was intended to facilitate Zhukov's second penetration, on his extreme northern flank. Here Major General F. I. Perkhorovich's 47th Army, supported by Lieutenant General S. G. Poplavsky's 1st Polish Army, would cooperate with the southern flank of Rokossovsky's 2d Belorussian Front to encircle German forces in the Warsaw area.

In the southern portion of the 1st Belorussian Front, a third attack would debouch out of the smaller Pulawy bridgehead. Colonel General V. Ia. Kolpakchi's 69th and Colonel General V. D. Tsvetaev's 33d Armies, each

17. *Winter Campaign to April 1945*

with a separate tank corps under its control, were assigned to penetrate the German defenses on a 13-kilometer front, then race westward to link up with neighboring forces, thereby creating tactical encirclements on both flanks.

Konev, by contrast, had a simpler plan, concentrating almost entirely on the Sandomierz bridgehead. Colonel General N. P. Pukhov's 13th, Colonel General K. A. Koroteev's 52d, and Colonel General A. S. Zhadov's 5th Guards Armies, with flanking support from Colonel General V. N. Gordov's 3d Guards Army in the north and Colonel General P. A. Kurochkin's 60th Army in the south, were to conduct the penetration operation. Konev could not hope to conceal the site of his attack; instead, he tried to deceive the Germans as to his objectives by creating a concentration of over 400 dummy tanks and self-propelled guns behind 60th Army, with a full network of newly constructed supply routes, to foster the impression that he would advance westward toward Krakow. In fact, Konev planned to commit General P. S. Rybalko's 3d Guards Tank Army and Colonel General D. D. Leliushenko's 4th Tank Army on the very first day of the operation, attacking northwest in cooperation with 1st Belorussian Front. Colonel General A. S. Zhadov's 5th Guards Army was also given control of the 4th Guards and 31st Separate Tank Corps, with orders to seize or bypass Krakow and exploit toward the upper Oder River. Lieutenant General I. T. Korovnikov's 59th Army in second echelon would eventually reduce Krakow itself, while Colonel General D. H. Gusev's 21st Army followed the main Sandomierz attack as a second echelon force, and two separate mobile corps were in *front* reserve.[6]

In both *fronts* extreme concentrations were created to achieve penetration with minimum loss of time and life. In the Magnuszew bridgehead, for example, Zhukov crowded in more than 50 percent of his rifle forces and 70 percent of all artillery and tanks, creating a numerical superiority of 10:1. Virtually all the heavy infantry support tanks and self-propelled guns were attached to the assault battalions of rifle divisions, and the number of artillery guns was as high as 250 per kilometer of the penetration sector. In order to achieve these concentrations at the critical points, of course, the Soviet commanders spread out their few remaining forces, including two fortified regions (119th and 115th), to cover the rest of the front.[7]

The Allied request for assistance during the later stages of the Battle of the Bulge prompted Stalin to accelerate the planned start of the offensive. On 8 January, Antonov ordered Konev to launch his attack on the 12th, eight days prior to his original timetable. This last-minute change placed even greater stress on staff officers and logisticians, so it is not surprising that the Vistula-Oder and East Prussian operations actually developed in a staggered pattern. Konev's 1st Ukrainian Front attacked as directed on 12

January, followed the next day by Cherniakhovsky's 3d Belorussian Front on the extreme northern flank in East Prussia. Not until 14 January did Zhukov's 1st Belorussian and Rokossovsky's 2d Belorussian Front launch their own assaults. Regardless of the cause, the net effect of this staggered start was to further confuse the defenders, keeping German reserves stationary at the flanks while the main assaults were launched in the center.

THE VISTULA-ODER OPERATION

In fact, OKW and the two German army group headquarters had anticipated a repetition of the Bagration offensive, with the main Soviet spearheads striking at the northern and southern flanks in preparation for a huge operational encirclement of the center. For this reason, defensive positions and reserves were concentrated on the flanks, in East Prussia and east of Krakow. The reserves were inadequate to the task in any case. Only 12.5 understrength panzer divisions remained in the two army groups. Guderian's efforts to transfer four additional divisions from the west failed when OKW redirected those units to Hungary.[8]

With the exception of elite units, such as the Hermann Goering Panzer Corps, *Grossdeutschland* Panzer Corps, and some portions of the Waffen SS, by January 1945, virtually every German division was severely understrength in terms of men and equipment. German tank production peaked in December 1944, with 1,854 armored vehicles that month, but much of this production had been squandered in the Ardennes and Hungary. Aircraft production had already peaked in September, and the Luftwaffe was in full retreat, both in the East and the West. Shortages of raw materials made it increasingly difficult to meet the needs of the front. In January, the number of trucks authorized in motorized and mechanized formations was reduced by 25 percent. More important, the loss of Rumania and the frequent bombings of synthetic fuel plants were seriously reducing available fuel. Even on its new, reduced tables of organization, the German Army was 800,000 men understrength.[9]

Guderian, his intelligence officer Reinhard Gehlen, and the field commanders in the East all anticipated the approximate date of the coming offensive, even if Soviet deception measures once again concealed the locations and total strength of the attacks. Even allowing for the self-serving nature of most postwar memoirs, these professional soldiers undoubtedly tried and failed to convince Hitler of the danger in Poland.[10] The most that the German commanders could hope for was to prolong the war, although Hitler, by this time, was expecting a miracle and was most concerned about not losing his own nerve. In fact, his determination to defend every inch of ground once again played into Soviet hands. At Hitler's insistence, the second and main German defensive positions were constructed within a few thousand meters of the forward lines. This faulty positioning made them both vulnerable to devastating initial Soviet artillery bombardment. Similarly, the scant German reserves were concentrated too far forward. For example, the two panzer divisions (16th and 17th) of XXIV Panzer Corps were situated well forward, opposite the Sandomierz bridgehead, rather than farther back where they could maneuver. Fourth Panzer Army had located a pair of panzergrenadier divisions in immediate support farther to the north as a mobile reserve between the two major Soviet bridgeheads. In theory, such forward positioning made sense when the enemy's air power could well disrupt the movement of defensive reserves. In practice, however, these reserves often became decisively engaged from the very start of the Soviet attack. (See Table 15-1 for the order of battle in the Vistula-Oder Operation.)

At 0500 hours on 12 January 1945, Konev's forward battalions attacked after a 15-minute artillery preparation. They occupied the first and, in some instances, the second line of German positions, eliminating key strongpoints in accordance with the 1944 regulations.[11] Then at 1000 hours, a second artillery preparation began. Because the winter mists hampered close air support, this second bombardment went on for 107 minutes. Thirty minutes before the scheduled end of the preparation, Soviet rifle platoons began to advance in gaps carefully left in the barrage. The Germans, believing this to be the main attack, rushed out of their bunkers to occupy their firing positions. The leading Soviet riflemen then lay down, and another 15 minutes of artillery shelling followed, ending with a volley of multiple-rocket launchers. The Soviet infantry and support tanks advanced together, preceded by a rolling barrage.

This elaborate scheme was sufficient for the Soviets to penetrate through the two German defensive lines for a distance of as much as eight kilometers within three hours. By 1400 hours on 12 January, the 3d Guards and 4th Tank Armies, plus the two separate tank corps, passed through the attacking infantry. When the poor weather cleared after noon, 466 aircraft sorties were flown. Frequently, a designated air division was assigned in direct support of a tank army, with forward air controllers on location with the leading tank and mechanized brigade headquarters.[12]

By the end of 12 January, 1st Ukrainian Front had pierced the German defenses on a 35-kilometer-wide frontage, advancing up to 20 kilometers. The three defending infantry divisions of XXXXVIII Panzer Corps (a panzer corps in name only), occupying German forward defenses facing the bridgehead, were literally vaporized by the initial assault and virtually ceased to exist. The 16th and 17th Panzer Divisions of XXIV Panzer Corps

Table 15-1. Order of Battle, Vistula-Oder Operation

German Forces	Soviet Forces
Army Group Center Col. Gen. Hans Reinhardt Third Panzer Army	**3d Belorussian Front** Col. Gen. I. D. Cherniakovsky 39th, 5th, 28th, 2d Gds, 11th Gds, 31st, and 1st Air Armies; 1st Tank and 2d Gds Tank Corps
Fourth Army Second Army	**2d Belorussian Front** MSU K. K. Rokossovsky 50th, 49th, 3d, 48th, 2d Shock, 65th, 70th Armies 5th Gds Tank Army 4th Air Army 8th Gds Tank, 8th Mechanized, and 3d Gds Cavalry Corps
Army Group A Col. Gen. Josef Harpe Ninth Army Fourth Panzer Army	**1st Belorussian Front** MSU G. K. Zhukov 47th, 1st Polish, 61st, 5th Shock, 3d Shock, 8th Gds, 69th, and 33d Armies 1st Gds and 2d Gds Tank Armies 16th Air Army 9th and 11th Tank Corps 2d Gds and 7th Gds Cavalry Corps
Seventeenth Army	**1st Ukrainian Front** MSU I. S. Konev 6th, 3d Guards, 13th, 52th, 5th Gds, 60th, 21st, and 59th Armies 3d Gds and 4th Tank Armies 2d Air Army 4th Gds, 25th, and 31st Tank Corps 7th Gds Mechanized Corps 1st Gds Cavalry Corps
First Panzer Army	**4th Ukrainian Front** Col. Gen. I. E. Petrov 38th, 1st Gds, and 18th Armies 8th Air Army

were overrun in their assembly areas before they had received any orders to counterattack. Thereafter, they commenced a battle around Kielce for their very survival. Soviet forward detachments continued to press forward all night.[13]

By the end of the second day, the penetration was 60 kilometers wide and 40 kilometers deep. The badly shaken and damaged 16th and 17th

Panzer Divisions dug in to defend the road hub at Kielce, between the two main Soviet bridgeheads, but by 18 January, they had been surrounded by 3d Guards Army and 4th Tank Army, and had to break out to the west. The remnants of this panzer corps, with survivors of XXXXVIII Panzer Corps and the relatively intact but enveloped divisions of XXXXII Corps, made their way northwestward, forming a large bubble in a sea of advancing Soviet forces. Repeatedly assaulted by ground and air but bypassed by Soviet main forces as they raced westward, the encircled German bubble shrank and broke up into smaller bubbles as it strove to escape the expanding torrent of Soviet troops. While most of these bubbles were destroyed, the largest one, now reduced to a few thousand men, finally rejoined German lines 10 days later, far to the northwest.[14]

By 18 January, Konev was five days ahead of schedule. Rybalko's tank army had seized Czestochowa, and Lieutenant General P. P. Poluboiarov's 4th Guards Tank Corps, supported by 59th Army, had encircled Krakow. The ancient city fell with surprisingly little resistance on 19 January, as German Seventeenth Army fell back to meet newly arrived German reserves and establish a new front east of upper Silesia. This withdrawal did not save the Seventeenth, for its northern flank was left open after the virtual destruction of the neighboring Fourth Panzer Army. On the evening of 20 January, Konev turned Rybalko's 3d Guards Tank Army 90 degrees southward to envelop this open flank, while 21st Army and 1st Guards Cavalry Corps attacked the Germans frontally. Within hours, Rybalko reoriented his forward detachments along the new direction of attack, forcing the Germans to abandon their defensive bastion around the Katowice industrial region. As Rybalko and elements of 4th Ukrainian Front closed on Silesia in late January, they deliberately left an escape route to the south, pressing the Germans out of the region while avoiding a major struggle.[15]

Meanwhile, at first light on 14 January, Zhukov's 1st Belorussian Front fell upon the German Ninth Army. Soviet reconnaissance units moved forward after a 25-minute artillery preparation. The sheer scale of this "reconnaissance" effort far exceeded the previous German experience of such probes. Following the 1944 Regulations, Zhukov launched 22 reinforced rifle battalions and 25 other rifle companies to eliminate specific strongpoints on a 100-kilometer front. This effort so unhinged the German defenses that a planned artillery preparation of 70 minutes duration was canceled except in the 61st Army sector. Elsewhere, the German first defensive positions were in Soviet hands by 1000 hours on 14 January, and, by the end of the day, the *front* had penetrated 12 kilometers, leaving the badly damaged remnants of two German divisions in their wake. In a master stroke of daring, 5th Shock Army's 26th Guards Rifle Corps seized a heavy bridge over the Pilitsa River before the German engineers could detonate their charges.[16] This allowed the armored vehicles of Bogdanov's 2d Guards Tank Army to move forward much earlier than expected, although they still did not enter the battle. Meanwhile, Zhukov's secondary attack by 69th and 33d Armies advanced up to 22 kilometers on the first day, and their separate tank corps passed through the assault troops and began their exploitation at 1400 hours on 14 January, racing forward toward Radom in the rear of German LVI Panzer Corps.

On 15 January, XXXX Panzer Corps' 19th and 25th Panzer Divisions launched a determined counterattack to back up the decimated German infantry divisions defending at the Magnuszew bridgehead, but Soviet fighter-bombers and antitank gunners broke the attack up quickly. With the assault infantry 15 kilometers into the German positions, Katukov's 1st Guards Tank Army was introduced on schedule through 8th Guards Army, aiming for Lodz, 130 kilometers northwest of Magnuszew. North of Warsaw, 47th Army assaulted across the Vistula River to help encircle the Polish capital with forces of 1st Polish Army, which were following Zhukov's advance out of the Magnuszew bridgehead.

In turn, Bogdanov's 2d Guards Tank Army and 2d Guards Cavalry Corps entered the fray out of the Pilitsa River bridgehead and penetrated up to 80 kilometers to complete the encirclement of German forces in the Warsaw area. By 17 January, this encirclement had been reduced, and 1st Polish Army had occupied its capital.[17]

By the end of 18 January, both 1st Belorussian and 1st Ukrainian Fronts were in full pursuit toward the Oder River, having destroyed the German forward defenses and counterattack forces. The *Grossdeutschland* Panzer Corps, sent by train from East Prussia with orders to "restore the situation," began debarking its divisions at Lodz on 16 January. Panzer Parachute Division Hermann Goering went into action the following day against the spearheads of Soviet 11th Tank Corps and accompanying 8th Guards Army. In the days that followed, advancing troops from Soviet 2d Guards Tank Army intercepted and destroyed follow-on trains of *Grossdeutschland* Corps north of Lodz, while the Corps' Hermann Goering Panzer and Brandenburg Panzergrenadier Divisions and remnants of 19th and 25th Panzer Divisions formed defensive hedgehogs south of Lodz to fend off Soviet attacks and try to rescue fleeing and disorganized infantry units.[18] From 21 to 28 January, this mass of soldiers and fugitives, numbering in the thousands and organized into Groups Nehring and von Sauchen, fought desperately to survive, cut through the advancing Soviets, and regain German lines far to the rear. On 29 January, the pitiful remnants of what had been Ninth Army and Fourth Panzer Army reached German lines along the Oder. The situation was so bad that these survivors were immediately thrown back into combat to shore up sagging German defenses along the Oder, which had already been breached in numerous sectors.[19] Numerous other encircled German groups, less fortunate than Groups Nehring and von Sauchen, were mopped up by follow-on Soviet forces.[20]

While encircled German troops fought for their survival, Soviet tank armies and corps were operating up to 100 kilometers ahead of the rest of 1st Belorussian Front and 35 kilometers in front of 1st Ukrainian Front. Some forward detachments covered up to 70 kilometers in 24 hours, fighting meeting engagements and seizing river crossings to facilitate the advance of their parent units.

The belated German response involved the movement of up to 40 divisions from other sectors of the front. Hitler authorized five divisions and a corps headquarters to evacuate Courland by sea. Enraged by the fall of Warsaw, Hitler had a number of OKH staff officers whom he suspected of deceit arrested on 18 January. He also brought General Ferdinand Schoerner, his favorite defense commander, from Courland to assume command of Army Group A from the hapless Colonel General Joseph Harpe. Schoerner, in turn, relieved General Simili von Luttwitz, commander of Ninth Army, and began to issue optimistic situation reports.[21]

The Soviet pursuit continued. Following close behind the armored forward detachments and the lead tank armies, Chuikov's 8th Guards Army showed almost as much initiative and dash as the tank armies. On 19 January, Chuikov seized the industrial city of Lodz, 130 kilometers northwest of Magnuszew, intact. On 22 January, following the path of Katukov's 1st Guards Tank Army, he surrounded 60,000 Germans in Poznan, another 120 kilometers to the northwest, although a long siege would ensue before the German force would surrender.[22] Meanwhile, on 20 January, elements of Rybalko's 3d Guards Tank Army and Koroteev's 52d Army crossed the German frontier in the process of maneuvering against the Germans in upper Silesia.

By 31 January, lead elements of Bogdanov's 2d Guards Tank Army had reached the Oder River near Kustrin, over 400 kilometers from its starting positions two weeks earlier. The following day, Katukov's 1st Guards Tank Army broke through the Meseretz Fortified Zone and reached the Oder just north of Frankfurt. As if by habit, they immediately dispatched assault parties to secure bridgeheads on the river's far bank. Within days, they were joined by the lead divisions of 5th Shock, 8th Guards, and 69h Armies. Unlike previous bridgeheads, however, these were but 60 kilometers from Berlin.[23]

As always, these spearheads were at the limit of their logistical umbilical, strung out and understrength. The 2d Guards Tank Army had a 160-kilometer-long open right flank, which was subject to counterattack by the newly created Army Group Vistula in Pomerania. This was one of Hitler's most desperate creations, consisting essentially of SS administrative staffs, the hastily assembled Eleventh SS Army, and home guard forces under the command of SS Leader Heinrich Himmler. The second-echelon Soviet combined-arms armies (61st, 47th, and 1st Polish) easily contained Himmler's first hesitant attacks from Pomerania in early February, but further Soviet advance across the Oder toward Berlin was becoming problematical, in particular since the Soviet assault into East Prussia had drawn Rokossovsky's 2d Belorussian Front toward the Baltic Sea and away from Zhukov's right flank, which Rokossovsky was supposed to protect.

THE ASSAULT ON EAST PRUSSIA

The *Stavka* concept for the East Prussian operation required Cherni-akhovsky's 3d and Rokossovsky's 2d Belorussian Fronts to launch coordinated assaults to cut off German forces in East Prussia from those in Poland and pin them against the shores of the Baltic.[24] Then, in subsequent operations, Cherniakhovsky's *front* and Bagramian's 1st Baltic Front would chop up and destroy the encircled German force. After reaching the Vistula River south of Danzig, Rokossovsky's *front*, in coordination with Zhukov's 1st Belorussian Front, would continue its advance along the main axis across the Vistula River and through eastern Pomerania to Stettin on the Oder River.

Cherniakhovsky planned his main attack with four combined-arms armies (39th, 5th, 28th, and 2d Guards) and two tank corps (1st Tank and 2d Guards Tank) directly into the teeth of main German defenses through Insterberg and toward Konigsberg, moving along the boundary of defending German Third Panzer and Fourth Armies. A fifth army (11th Guards) would exploit from second echelon, a single army (31st) would cover the *front's* extended left flank, and Bagramian's 1st Baltic Front would cover the right flank. Rokossovsky planned his main attack with five armies (3d, 48th, 2d Shock, 65th, and 70th) from two bridgeheads over the Narew River through German Fourth Army defenses toward Mlawa and Marienburg. Vol'sky's 5th Guards Tank Army, secretly regrouped from Lithuania only days before the assault, would exploit westward toward Elbing, and the *front's* right flank armies would brush past and isolate German forces in East Prussia. The sizable pre-attack regrouping accorded the Soviets significant force superiority over their foes, but elaborate German prepared defenses reduced this Soviet advantage.[25]

Cherniakhovsky's forces struck German defenses on the Konigsberg axis early on 13 January. The advance quickly turned into a prolonged penetration operation, which limited the utility of the two tank corps serving as army mobile groups. Unwittingly, however, OKH assisted the Soviets when it ordered the principal reserve force in East Prussia, Panzer Parachute Division Hermann Goering (as well as Panzer Corps *Gross-deutschland* to the south), southward to meet the developing threat in central Poland. Deprived of reserves, the German defense sagged danger-ously and then gave way on 18 January as Cherniakhovsky committed his 11th Guards Army and 1st Tank Corps against the vulnerable German left flank. With their defenses unhinged, the Germans began a slow but steady withdrawal toward the outer defenses of the Konigsberg fortress and the Heilsberg Fortified Region.

Further south, Rokossovsky's forces had attacked on 14 January, quickly penetrated German defenses opposite both bridgeheads, and unleashed their operational maneuver units into the German rear. With 8th Mecha-nized Corps, 8th Guards Tank Corps, and 1st Guards Tank Corps already beginning the exploitation, Vol'sky's 5th Guards Tank Army entered the fray on 16 January. The 7th Panzer Division, the only sizable German mobile reserve, was quickly overwhelmed, and, together with German infantry forces, it began a painful and increasingly rapid withdrawal westward.[26] The commitment of the Soviet armored host split the German defenders, driving XXIII and XXVII Corps westward and the remainder of Second and Fourth Armies northward into southern East Prussia. Vol'sky's army and the cooperating mobile corps drove in an immense armored wedge to the outskirts of the Marienburg Fortress, the banks of the Vistula River near Grudziaga, and the shores of the Baltic Sea.

Fanatic German resistance, however, drew Soviet rifle forces into fierce battles against forces conducting a fighting withdrawal into East Prussia. Soon these Soviet forces had to contend with German attempts to break through the Soviet cordon separating the encircled Army Group Center from the main German front lines along the west bank of the Vistula River. So intense was the fighting that Rokossovsky's thrust gravi-tated away from that of Zhukov, leaving the latter's right flank along the Vistula and adjacent to Pomerania somewhat unprotected.

By 2 February, Cherniakhovsky's 3d Belorussian Front had bottled up Third Panzer Army in Konigsberg and the adjacent Samland Peninsula. Having failed in its attempt to break out westward, German Fourth Army was hemmed into a hedgehog defensive position anchored on the Heilsberg Fortified Region. This beleaguered German force, renamed Army Group North on 26 January and reinforced by a German corps from Memel', was essentially immobilized and ripe for future destruction.[27] Unwittingly, how-ever, its very existence and continued resistance disrupted existing Soviet plans and helped forestall an immediate Soviet advance on Berlin.

THE FEBRUARY DILEMMA

In late January, based on the rapid progress of Zhukov's forces, the *Stavka* still planned to continue the advance on Berlin. Reports from both Zhukov and his army commanders, in particular Chuikov, encouraged that intention. Developments during the last few days of January and early February, however, forced the *Stavka* to change its mind. This decision was not immediate; rather it was made over a period of several days, as circumstances mitigating against an immediate advance on Berlin mounted.

By late January, German resistance was stiffening on both flanks of the main Soviet thrust across Poland. In the north, German garrisons bypassed by advancing Soviet forces stubbornly held out in Torun and Schneidemuhl, and Army Group Vistula's Eleventh SS Army began assembling in Pomerania. Although this was never a significant force, Soviet signals intelligence noticed the gaggle of units and the German redeployment of divisions from Courland and East Prussia into Pomerania (including Third Panzer Army headquarters, 4th Panzer Division, and several infantry divisions).[28] German confusion in Pomerania, in fact, probably increased Soviet apprehension. Most important, action in East Prussia had diverted Rokossovsky's thrust northward, and his left flank now fought along the Vistula near Grudziaga out of supporting distance of Zhukov's spearheads, which were operating south of Pomerania.

Zhukov's force had its problems as well. Although Chuikov argued strenuously for a continued advance on Berlin, one of his corps and one of 69th Army's corps were tied down besieging German forces in Poznan. Troop reinforcements from German V SS Mountain Corps were arriving along the Oder River east of Berlin, and German air activity was taking a heavy toll on Soviet aircraft operating on the Berlin axis. In addition, 2d Guards Tank Army, necessary for a rapid thrust to Berlin, itself was fencing with increased German activity on its right flank near Stargard.[29]

Nor was Zhukov's left flank secure. Konev's spearheads had reached and breached the Oder on a broad front from west of Smigiel southward to Ratibor. Although Konev had seized large bridgeheads near Keben and south of Breslau, German resistance was stiffening (bolstered by forces redeployed from Hungary), and Fortress Breslau formed an immense obstacle to Konev's further progress. Any drive on Berlin would require Konev to regroup his forces to his right flank so that they could support Zhukov, and that regrouping could not occur until Breslau had been neutralized and the Keben bridgehead had been enlarged.

Faced with this dilemma, the *Stavka* initially sought to clear its flanks while retaining hopes for continuing the drive on Berlin. Although Soviet open sources have consistently cited 2 February as the date the *Stavka* declared the Vistula-Oder operation at an end, implying that the drive on Berlin was definitively canceled at this time, evidence indicates that this was not the case. Orders issued to Konev concerning his Lower Silesian operation (which commenced on 8 February) clearly anticipated further advance toward Berlin in concert with Zhukov's forces to the north.[30] A few days after Konev's operation had begun, it became clear that his progress would be difficult and Breslau, although encircled, would continue to hold out. At the same time, Soviet intelligence continued detecting German attack preparations in Pomerania. In response, on 10 February, Rokossovsky's forces launched an assault into Pomerania from its bridgehead over the Vistula west of Grudziaga. The *Stavka* had directed Rokossovsky to clear German forces from Pomerania and reach Stettin. This attack also faltered in the face of heavy resistance, and when German attacks, albeit feeble, began against Zhukov's right flank on 16 February in the Stargard region (Army Group Vistula's operation Sonnenwende), it was clear that only a major redeployment of Zhukov's *front* could deal with the new threat and guarantee the success of a future drive on Berlin. The actual Soviet decision to this effect was probably made between 10 and 16 February.[31] In addition to delaying the drive on Berlin, the *Stavka* decision to halt the westward drive fueled subsequent controversy regarding the justification, wisdom, and consequences of the delay.[32]

CLEARING THE FLANKS

Once the *Stavka* made the decision to halt the drive on Berlin, the flank problem took on two aspects. The first related to clearing the flanks immediately adjacent to the projected drive on Berlin, specifically against German forces in Silesia and Pomerania. This would involve the conduct of three operations: the lower Silesian operation (already under way on 8 February); an operation into upper Silesia; and an operation to clear German forces from Pomerania. Second, the Germans could not be permitted to use the Soviet delay to reinforce their Oder front defending Berlin. Preventing such reinforcement required the conduct of operations on the deep flanks, against German forces in the Konigsberg and Samland regions of East Prussia and against German Army Group South in Hungary.

These flank clearing operations took place in two stages: the first occurred in February, immediately after the decision to halt the advance on Berlin, to deal with the most pressing threats to a future advance; and the second, in March, as an immediate prelude to the final Berlin operation.

On 8 February, Konev's 1st Ukrainian Front struck along the Oder River north and south of Breslau.[33] Rybalko's 3d Guards and Leliushenko's

4th Tank Armies attacked from the Keben bridgehead and advanced westward against stiffening German resistance, while 5th Guards Army, supported by 31st and 4th Guards Tank Corps, thrust westward south of Breslau and encircled the German garrison, which nevertheless stubbornly continued to hold out. By 25 February, the Soviet advance had closed up to the Neisse River and joined with Zhukov's right flank at the junction of the Oder and Neisse Rivers.[34]

Meanwhile, on 10 February, Rokossovsky's 2d Belorussian Front attacked northwestward into Pomerania from positions west of Grudziaga. Five days later, the ad hoc Eleventh SS Panzer Army launched a premature, hopelessly piecemeal counteroffensive farther west. This attack struck Soviet 47th and 61st Armies near Stargard, just east of the Oder River. The 1st Belorussian Front easily parried this threat, but the Stargard offensive (Operation Sonnenwende) prompted the *Stavka* to accelerate its plans to reduce German forces in Pomerania. Additional forces, including 19th Army and its attached 3d Guards Tank Corps, arrived from Finland to launch multiple assaults northward, aiming for the coast. Soviet operational security was so effective, and the German preoccupation with Berlin was so great, that the Germans did not detect any preparation until just before the renewed Pomeranian offensive began on 24 February.

Because of the weak German defenses in the area, Zhukov was able to commit his 1st and 2d Guards Tank Armies within hours of the initial assault.[35] Katukov's 1st Guards Tank Army linked up with 2d Belorussian Front forces on 4 March and was then transferred to Rokossovsky's control to continue clearing the coastline to Danzig. The result was a huge gap in the German defenses from the Oder River east to the Danzig region. Most of Army Group North (the new designation that Hitler had given Army Group Center in late January) was trapped in the pocket of East Prussia, where Cherniakhovsky's 3d Belorussian Front continued to press forward toward Konigsberg. The final battle against Army Group North in early April was an extension of the heavy fighting throughout February and March. It took the form of the final reduction of the Konigsberg Fortress (5–9 April) and the remaining German forces on the Samland Peninsula (13–25 April).[36] In the savage fighting at Konigsberg, the Soviets claim to have killed 42,000 Germans and to have captured another 92,000.[37] The Samland operation pushed German forces onto the narrow spit of land between the Frischer Haff and the Baltic, where, on 8 May, 22,000 surviving Germans surrendered.[38]

The bitter battles in the German heartland of East Prussia claimed many casualties, among them the youngest *front* commander of the Red Army. Cherniakhovsky, leading from the front as always, was fatally wounded at Mehlsack, East Prussia, and died on 19 February. This unexpected loss brought Marshal A. M. Vasilevsky back from the brink of obscurity. Stalin had promised Vasilevsky that he would command the follow-on operation against Japanese Manchuria, but, in the interim, he had so little role that he had voluntarily resigned his post as chief of staff so that Antonov might get the formal title for the position that he had effectively held for many months. Cherniakhovsky's death allowed Stalin to give Vasilevsky a real *front* command, while still retaining him as deputy defense commissar and a member of the *Stavka*. Actions like this, and Stalin's similar moves to favor Konev, were obviously intended to limit the prestige of Deputy Supreme Commander Zhukov.[39]

With the immediate flank problems solved, in March the *Stavka* turned its attentions to the deep flanks. Ironically, they did so just as Hitler was returning to his pet preoccupation with events in Hungary. The *Stavka* mandated the conduct of two operations: the left wing of Konev's 1st Ukrainian Front was to clear German forces from the salient anchored on Oppeln along the Oder River in upper Silesia; and Malinovsky's 2d and Tolbukhin's 3d Ukrainian Fronts west and southwest of Budapest were to complete the liberation of Hungary and to seize Vienna, Austria. The twin operations would tie down German forces in those regions, prevent the reinforcement of German defenses along the Oder east of Berlin, and facilitate future operations against the last large bastion of German forces outside the Berlin area, in the Czech region and Slovakia. Both operations were planned to commence on 15 March.

Konev's upper Silesian operation was launched as planned on 15 March, when 21st and 4th Tank Armies thrust southward west of Oppeln.[40] Within days, they linked up near Neustadt with 59th Army and 7th Guards Mechanized and 31st Tank Corps forces, which had attacked westward from the Oder, and encircled a portion of German Seventeenth Army. In heavy subsequent fighting, the encircled force was reduced and Soviet forces closed up to the Slovak border by 31 March.[41] Although the operation placed Soviet forces in a more advantageous position from which to launch new offensives toward Dresden and Prague, it also forced Konev to conduct an extensive and complicated regrouping before his forces could participate in the Berlin operation.

Simultaneously, Malinovsky and Tolbukhin planned to commence their Vienna operation.[42] Tolbukhin's 3d Ukrainian Front was to smash German defenses west of Budapest with Lieutenant General N. D. Zakhvataev's 4th Guards Army and Colonel General V. V. Glagolev's elite 9th Guards Army. Thereafter, Kravchenko's 6th Guards Tank Army would exploit into Austria. On the right, Malinovsky's 46th and 7th Guards Armies were to join the attack north and south of the Danube River, and General P. A. Pliev's 1st Guards Cavalry-Mechanized Group, supported by Malinovsky's center and right flank armies, would advance on Bratislava. Further south, Tolbukhin's 57th Army and the Bulgarian 1st Army would crush Second Panzer Army's defenses south of Lake Balaton and advance into southern Austria.

In the midst of these offensive preparations, Soviet intelligence reported that the Germans were planning to steal the march and conduct a counteroffensive of their own in the Balaton region.[43] The intelligence was correct. While the German defenses crumbled in the East, Hitler did, in fact, plan one more desperate offensive in Hungary, prompted by the IV SS Panzer Corps' previous successes in January. For this purpose he planned to use the last of his major armored reserves, General Sepp Dietrich's Sixth SS Panzer Army, dispatched to Hungary from the Ardennes region in late January. Although the *Stavka* knew of Germany's offensive intentions and had a good picture of the German order of battle, it prohibited Tolbukhin from using forces in his defense that had been earmarked to spearhead the Vienna operation. In essence, the *Stavka* ordered Tolbukhin to conduct a vigorous defense and to continue his preparations for the offensive, just as had been done 18 months before at Kursk. In 1945, however, the *Stavka* entertained no doubts about the viability of the defense.

On 6 March 1945, the German Sixth Army, joined by Sixth SS Panzer Army launched a pincer movement north and south of Lake Balaton.[44] Ten panzer and five infantry divisions, including large numbers of the new heavy King Tiger tanks, and organized into the III Panzer, II SS Panzer, and I Cavalry Corps, struck 3d Ukrainian Front, hoping to cut that *front* in half, reach the Danube, and link up with German Second Panzer Army forces attacking south of Lake Balaton. The ferocity of the German assault north of the lake tore into Tolbukhin's defenses and drove a wedge between the Soviet 26th and 27th Armies. The German success, however, was short-lived. The terrain was a mass of canals and mud, and Tolbukhin had created a deeply echeloned and complex defense system, integrating such novel and nasty techniques as highly electrified, barbed-wire anti-infantry and antitank barriers. Minefields, antitank strongpoints and regions, effective fire control, and hastily repositioned tactical reserves plugged the holes in the defense and took a devastating toll on the attacking Germans. Tolbukhin was sufficiently alarmed by the German progress to request release of some of the reserve armies earmarked for the offensive phase. The *Stavka* categorically denied his request, and the defenses bent but did not break. By 15 March, the German advance had expired after tremendous losses to both sides.[45] Once again, the Soviets could absorb these losses, for their primary offensive force had not been damaged.

Between 14 and 16 March, while heavy fighting raged east of Lake Balaton, four Soviet armies secretly regrouped into attack positions west of the city, adjacent to the left flank and rear of attacking German forces. On 16 March only one day behind schedule, Soviet 46th, 4th Guards, and 9th Guards Armies struck German defenses west of the city, to be followed on 19 March by General A. G. Kravchenko's 6th Guards Tank Army.[47] Within days, all of 2d and 3d Ukrainian Fronts' armies joined the offensive, and German defenses and morale visibly began to crack. The Germans barely escaped being pinned back against the shore of Lake Balaton, and Kravchenko's 6th Guards Tank Army exploited the confusion to burst through the German defenses.

The same bad weather and terrain problems that had hindered the German offensive also slowed the initial Soviet advance and permitted Sixth SS Panzer Army to avoid entrapment against the shores of Lake Balaton. The Soviet advance subsequently accelerated as German morale and the wear and tear of weeks of heavy combat eroded German strength. In cooperation with 4th and 9th Guards Armies, Kravchenko's tank army entered Vienna on 13 April 1945, two days before Soviet guns opened a barrage of unprecedented fury along the Oder River east of Berlin.[47]

CONCLUSION

Soviet operations in late fall and early winter 1944–1945 had slashed away at the German strategic flanks and reached the Baltic coast and the Budapest region. German forces dispatched to meet the crisis on the flanks were barely able to stem the Soviet tide. Then, in less than two months, German defenses in Poland and East Prussia were torn asunder, and Soviet forces advanced up to 700 kilometers to the west, to within 60 kilometers of Berlin. In the process, German Army Groups A and Center were decimated. After the Germans dispatched reinforcements to the Oder front to defend Berlin, in February and March, the Soviets again struck on the flanks, battering Army Group Vistula and consuming Army Group South's (and Germany's) last strategic reserves. By mid-April, Soviet forces had reached the Oder-Neisse River line on a broad front from Stettin in the north to Gorlitz on the Czech border, and further to the outskirts of Graz and the Czech border north of Vienna. As had been the case in 1944, the baggage of these Soviet armies contained the nuclei of governments that would ensure Soviet political dominance over central and eastern Europe for decades to come.

These catastrophic defeats lost Germany much of the industry that had been dispersed in Poland to shield it from Allied bombing. Soviet estimates that Germany lost 60 divisions, 1,300 tanks, and a similar number of aircraft are undoubtedly simplistic, since many small units survived and infiltrated elsewhere. Moreover, although German losses in these operations were high (in excess of 660,000), replacements and transfers from other theaters caused German troop strength in the East to decline from 2,030,000 (with 190,000 allies) to just under 2,000,000 at the end of March. However, 556,000 of these troops were isolated in Courland and East Prussia and were virtually irrelevant to future operations. To make matters worse, the Soviets' 6,461,000 troops could now be concentrated on the most critical axis.[47] For over a third of these forces, the next stop would be Berlin.

CHAPTER 16

End Game

WAITING FOR THE STORM

Most popular Soviet accounts of operations against the German homeland in 1945 are a combination of dry narratives, idealized accounts of individual bravery, and stereotyped condemnations of fascism.[1] Subconsciously, the reader develops an image of the Soviet leadership as cold-blooded and calculating as it closed in for the kill. In fact, everyone from I. V. Stalin down to the lowest soldier was emotionally and mentally preoccupied with seizing Berlin. After more than three years of enormous destruction and horrendous casualties, the Soviet forces were determined to destroy the enemy regime and bring the war to an end. Moreover, having expended so much blood and energy to defeat the German Army in the field, Soviet commanders were in no mood to allow their Western allies to seize the final victory. Quite apart from Stalin's desire to dominate postwar Central Europe and the Allied agreement that the Soviets should seize the city, this emotional preoccupation drove the Red Army forward toward Berlin.

The German defenders were equally determined and desperate. Only the most fanatical adherents of National Socialism retained any hope of ultimate victory, but the brutality of the Red Army in the eastern provinces of the Reich boded ill for the safety of anyone, civilian or soldier, who fell into Soviet hands. Indeed, German accounts of the final Soviet campaigns have given the Red Army a justified reputation for atrocities. The equal, if not greater, horrors perpetrated by the Wehrmacht in Russia—horrors that explain but do not excuse Soviet vengefulness—have been all but forgotten.

Hitler's regime made a final convulsive effort to gather strength for its own defense. Leaving only limited forces to face the British, Americans, Canadians, and French in the West, OKW assembled an estimated 85 divisions and numerous smaller, separate units for the final struggle on the Eastern Front.[2] Of course, many of these organizations were composed of old men, boys, and soldiers whose wounds or physical ailments made them unsuited for active service. *Volkssturm* troops of this kind had only limited training and fighting capacity and had significant shortages in heavy weapons. Moreover, even though Germany could still muster thousands of aircraft and armored vehicles, the Allied air superiority and shortages in fuel limited the effectiveness of these weapons. Still, the defenders were well equipped with small arms and short-range antitank weapons like the *Panzerfaust*. As the Allies closed in on the Reich, the Germans were also able to divert thousands of antiaircraft guns, previously aimed skyward at B-17 and Lancaster bombers, to ground defense.

Perhaps most significant, the vastly shortened front and the wealth of half-trained infantry formed around a core of hardened veterans permitted German commanders to man two and even three successive defensive lines simultaneously. This proved to be a significant advantage. In the battles of 1944, Soviet commanders had acquired the habit of breaking through a thin German defensive line and exploiting so rapidly that, even when Hitler authorized a withdrawal, the enemy was unable to pull his scarce troops back to the next defensive line in time. Now, however, the Red Army lacked the operational depth in which to maneuver. With the large city of Berlin only 60 kilometers to their front and with the forward lines of their Allies only 100 kilometers beyond, the Soviets faced the unwelcome prospect of conducting repeated penetration attacks against successive, fully manned, defensive lines anchored on increasingly urbanized terrain.

Neither side remained passive while the Red Army built up for the inevitable assault on Berlin. In early March, hard on the heels of the Soviet lower Silesian operation, Field Marshal Ferdinand Schoerner, commander of Army Group Center, launched a number of local counterattacks in Silesia, particularly at Lauban, where a multidivision attack on 2–5 March took the city back from Rybalko's surprised 3d Guards Tank Army. However, Schoerner lacked both the time and the force to achieve significant results against Konev's 1st Ukrainian Front. In addition, heightened Soviet activity in Silesia and Hungary prompted Hitler to assess (perhaps wishfully) that the next major Soviet offensive effort would be a drive from the Ostrava and southern Slovakian regions into western Czechoslovakia against Army Group Center. On 15 March, in spite of renewed Soviet activity in these regions, Hitler finally became concerned with the Oder front, and he ordered Ninth Army to smash the Soviet bridgeheads south of Kustrin.[3]

Hitler's sudden concern for the Berlin axis was prompted by the collapse of German defenses in Pomerania and forward of the lower Oder River and by the knowledge that the Courland pocket, which had been under assault since 27 February, could not hold out much longer. His concerns were valid. Throughout March, the three Soviet Belorussian *fronts* hammered away at the remaining German enclaves along the Baltic coast, eventually taking Danzig on 28 March. As a consequence of the disasters in Pomerania and Hitler's desire for a credible defense along the

Oder, Heinz Guderian persuaded Heinrich Himmler to resign his command of Army Group Vistula, to be replaced by Colonel General Gotthard Heinrici, the vaunted defensive specialist and commander of First Panzer Army.

As soon as he arrived at Himmler's headquarters, however, Heinrici found himself thrust into a desperate battle for control of the island fortress of Kustrin at the confluence of the Oder and Warta Rivers. Beginning on 22 March, Colonel General V. I. Chuikov's 8th Guards Army had isolated the fortress in an effort to widen its bridgehead over the Oder. At Hitler's insistence, on 27 March Ninth German Army launched a four-division counterattack from Frankfurt-am-Oder northward toward Kustrin. The 20th and 25th Panzer-Grenadier Divisions, the Fuehrer Escort Division, and the ad hoc Panzer Division *Munchenberg* caught the Soviets by surprise and advanced to the outskirts of Kustrin. General Chuikov found himself bracketed by German artillery that killed an aide and wounded one of his principal staff officers. Yet the attack rapidly lost momentum, and the Germans were decimated in open terrain.[4]

This fresh disaster cost Germany one of its best remaining military leaders. In talks with Hitler, Guderian vigorously defended the commanders involved in the Kustrin attack, General Theodor Busse of Ninth Army and General Heinrici. Hitler was determined to find a scapegoat. As the culmination to months of tension and arguments, Kustrin proved to be the final straw in the stormy relationship between dictator and general. On 28 March, Guderian suddenly found himself relieved for "ill-health." In his place, Colonel General Hans Krebs became the last chief of the German General Staff.[5]

PLANNING FOR BERLIN

The *Stavka* painstakingly prepared for the Berlin operation. It recalled the fate of earlier Russian armies at the gates of Berlin in 1760 and Warsaw in 1920, when Russian hopes had been thwarted by over-optimism and unfortunate circumstances. Then, certain victory had been followed by unanticipated defeat. The Soviets were determined that history would not repeat itself in 1945. The Soviet command estimated the Germans would field against them a force of one million men—the desperate remnants of the German Army—and, deep down, they were unsure of how many Germans in the West would join their comrades along the Oder to face the more dreaded and feared Red Army. Experience had demonstrated that a force of one million men could render credible resistance along a formidable river barrier, even against a force more than twice its size. Thus, the

Soviets embarked on preparing an offensive fitting to the task—an offensive whose conduct would impress the Allies, who were approaching Berlin from the west.

Stavka's strategic aims in the Berlin operation were to destroy German forces defending along the Berlin axis, seize Berlin, and link up with advancing Allied forces on the Elbe River. In early April 1945, American and British forces were driving forward toward the Elbe River, only 100 to 120 kilometers from the German capital, and there were growing Soviet concerns that, despite agreements to the contrary, the Allied armies themselves would advance on the city.[6] This concern, together with the prospect that German troops might gravitate eastward, had the effect of accelerating Soviet attack preparations.

German forces defending the approaches to Berlin included Army Group Vistula (Third Panzer and Ninth Armies), commanded by Heinrici, Fourth Panzer Army of Schoerner's Army Group Center, and the ill-defined Berlin Garrison. Army Group Vistula consisted of 6 corps (25 divisions) and a large number of separate and specialized units and formations; Army Group Center defended the Neisse River-Dresden axis with 2 corps; and the Berlin Garrison consisted of 1 corps (LVI Panzer with 5 to 6 divisions) and over 50 *Volkssturm* battalions. The combined force numbered about 800,000 men.[7]

German defenses along the Berlin axis were deep but only partially occupied by troops. They consisted of the fully occupied Oder-Neisse defense line to a depth of 20 to 40 kilometers, which in turn included three defensive belts, and the Berlin defensive region, which consisted of three ring defensive lines (external, internal, and city). For control purposes, the city was further subdivided into nine sectors. The central sector, which included governmental and administrative organs such as the Reichstag and Imperial Chancellery, was thoroughly prepared for defense. All defensive positions were interconnected by integrated communications systems. The metro (subway) system was used to conceal the movement of forces. In an engineering sense, German defenses were strongest opposite the Kustrin bridgehead and from the bridgehead through the Seelow Heights to the outskirts of Berlin.[8]

Formal *Stavka* planning for the operation commenced on 1 April, the day after Konev's *front* completed operations in Upper Silesia and three days before Rokossovsky's and Zhukov's *fronts* finished operations to clear German forces from Pomerania. That day Zhukov and Konev met in Moscow with Stalin, the *Stavka*, and the General Staff to present their operational concepts. They were joined by Rokossovsky the next day. After thorough review, the *Stavka* approved the proposals and set the tentative attack date at 16 April, leaving a scant two weeks for detailed attack preparations.[9]

Meanwhile, throughout March and early April, Soviet rear services troops assembled the masses of matériel needed for the next push, while Soviet commanders attempted to prepare their troops for a final effort. As the headquarters that had survived at Stalingrad, 8th Guards Army still retained a special knowledge of the problems of urban warfare. Chuikov's staff produced a pamphlet that Zhukov distributed throughout 1st Belorussian Front. Each rifle division formed a special unit to train in city fighting. Little was left to chance, although in German-held territory the Soviets often lacked the detailed intelligence that partisans had previously provided. Soviet forces along the entire front conducted similar detailed preparations.[10]

The plan that finally emerged from intensive *Stavka* efforts involved the delivery of several powerful blows along a broad front by three *fronts*—Rokossovsky's 2d Belorussian in the north, Zhukov's 1st Belorussian in the center, and Konev's 1st Ukrainian to the south—to encircle and dismember the Berlin group and destroy each segment individually. Subsequently, within 12 to 15 days, Soviet forces were to capture Berlin and advance to the Elbe to link up with Allied armies.[11]

Zhukov's *front*, consisting of seven Soviet and one Polish combined-arms armies, two tank armies, and four separate mobile corps, was to make its main attack from the Kustrin bridgehead with four armies (47th, 3d and 4th Shock, and 8th Guards) and one tank corps (9th). On the first day, these armies, supported by 731 infantry-support tanks and self-propelled guns, were to penetrate the strong German tactical defenses on the Seelow Heights and secure the commitment of 1st and 2d Guards Tank Armies to combat. The two tank armies, numbering 1,373 tanks and self-propelled guns, would then advance in tandem through German Ninth Army directly into Berlin, which was expected to fall on the sixth day of battle.[12] Zhukov planned two secondary attacks: one north of Kustrin with two armies (61st and 1st Polish), and one south of Kustrin with two armies (69th and 33d) and a cavalry corps (2d Guards). Zhukov's assault was to begin in darkness and be illuminated by 143 searchlights to light the terrain and disorient the enemy.

On Zhukov's left flank, Konev's *front*, consisting of five Soviet and one Polish combined-arms armies, two tank armies, and four mobile corps, was to launch its main attack with three armies (3d Guards, 13th, and 5th Guards) across the Neisse River toward Cottbus against the remains of Fourth Panzer Army and the southern wing of Ninth Army. Lead forces were to reach the Spree River by the end of the second day and protect the commitment to combat of the 963 tanks and self-propelled guns of 3d and 4th Guards Tank Armies. Once in the operational open, the two tank armies would then exploit toward Brandenburg, Dessau, and the southern limits of Berlin.[13] Konev also planned a secondary attack with portions of two armies (52d and 2d Polish) and two mobile corps (7th Guards Mechanized and Polish 1st Tank) toward Dresden to cover his right flank and prepare for future operations into Czechoslovakia. A reserve army (28th) would reinforce Konev while his advance was in progress. In theory, Konev was to reach the Elbe River and Dresden 12 days into the operation. Konev, however, had the option to swing northward toward Berlin if Zhukov's advance could not keep up. In anticipation of such a development, Stalin rather pointedly failed to define the boundary line between 1st Belorussian Front and 1st Ukrainian Front beyond the initial stage of the operation.

On Zhukov's northern (right) flank, Rokossovsky's *front*, consisting of five combined-arms armies and five separate mobile corps, was to attack two to three days after his fellow *front* commanders. Three armies (65th, 70th, and 49th), with armor support, were to attack in the Stettin-Schwedt sector, destroy German forces around Stettin, prevent Third Panzer Army from reinforcing German forces in Berlin, and advance to occupy northern Brandenburg and link up with British forces along the Elbe.[14]

The Soviet force earmarked to launch the offensive numbered 2.5 million troops (2,062,100 combat, including 155,900 Polish forces), 6,250 tanks and self-propelled guns, 41,600 guns and mortars, and 7,500 combat aircraft. This force ultimately opposed up to one million Germans (766,750 first-line combat by Soviet estimates) supported by 1,519 tanks and assault guns, and 9,303 guns and mortars.[15]

The creation of shock groups necessary to launch the attack was a major challenge for Soviet planners, for it required an extensive regrouping over long distances during an exceedingly short period by all three *fronts*. On 1 April, for example, the bulk of 2d Belorussian Front forces were located in the Danzig region, over 500 kilometers from the Oder front, and Konev's forces were concentrated on 1st Ukrainian Front's center and left flank in Silesia. A total of 29 armies had to reposition themselves—15 of them at a distance of up to 385 kilometers and three between 300 and 530 kilometers—all at a time when the rail network was struggling to build up fuel and ammunition stores sufficient to sustain the operation. All of these movements had to be completed within 15 days, as compared to the 22 to 48 days available to move forces prior to the Belorussian, East Prussian, and Vistula-Oder operations.[16]

Once deployed into forward assembly areas, the operational plan required extensive tactical concentration of forces to conduct a successful penetration of such formidable and deep defenses. To sustain the penetration, all first-echelon combined-arms armies and their constituent rifle corps and divisions arrayed themselves in two echelons. That is, a typical division would attack with two rifle regiments on line and a third behind them, while a corps would attack with three or four divisions on line and one or more divisions in second echelon. The result was extremely narrow penetration frontages: 2.5 to 10 kilometers for an army, and only 35 to 44 kilometers for an entire *front*. A typical kilometer of this penetration sector would average 1.5 to 2.5 rifle divisions, 260 guns, and up to 30 infantry-support tanks or self-propelled guns. In addition, 8th Guards Army, responsible for making one of the main attacks out of the Kustrin bridgehead, had direct control over the 9th Assault Aviation Corps to support river crossings, help the penetration of forward defenses, accompany the armored exploitation forces, and prevent the movement of German reserves.[17]

Extensive specialized support operations took place before the offensive. On six occasions, reconnaissance aircraft prepared aerial photo surveys of Berlin, all approaches to the city, and the defensive belts. On the basis of these surveys, captured documents, and POW interrogations, detailed schemes, diagrams, and maps of the defenses were distributed to all commanders and staffs. The 1st Belorussian Front's engineering forces constructed 25 bridges and 40 ferry crossings over the Oder River. To assist in crossing the Neisse River, 1st Ukrainian Front prepared 2,440 wooden sapper boats, 750 assault bridges, and more than 1,000 wooden bridge segments.[18] All assault forces conducted special training to sharpen their skills in river crossings and in urban, forest, and night fighting. In particular, small combined-arms task forces and combat teams were designated in advance for street fighting in large cities.

Despite these extensive preparations and the amassing of enormous resources, the Soviet timetable, which called for the entire operation to be completed within 15 days, was too optimistic. The terrain was heavily urbanized and industrialized, and crosshatched with villages, rivers, and canals. While some Germans had lost heart, others were prepared to fight with a superhuman desperation. The Berlin Operation would not be a walkover.

Just as had been the case in the Vistula-Oder offensive, the assault on Berlin was made more difficult by a last-minute decision to accelerate the attack. Until early March, the Western Allies were still west of the Rhine River, and Stalin obviously felt that he had ample time to take Berlin. Then, as the Germans crumbled in the West, the possibility that the Western Allies might capture Berlin suddenly seemed very real. On 31 March 1945, General Dwight Eisenhower sent representatives to the *Stavka* to coordinate the junction of the two forces. Based on political guidance from the Yalta Conference, Eisenhower proposed to divide

Germany by linking up with Soviet forces along the general north–south axis of Leipzig–Dresden. Stalin hastily agreed to this proposal, claiming that Berlin no longer had much strategic significance. In reality, however, Eisenhower's advance into central Germany in early April increased Soviet suspicions of Allied intentions and prompted the *Stavka* to advance the timetable for the Berlin offensive.

THE PENETRATION

At 0730 hours on 14 April 1945, after a 15- to 20-minute fire raid, reinforced rifle battalions from 1st Belorussian Front and 1st Ukrainian Front's first-echelon rifle divisions began reconnaissance-in-force actions on main attack axes (see Map 18). In some sectors, first-echelon regiments joined the attack. In two days of combat, some of these forces succeeded in wedging up to five kilometers deep into the German defenses. By this time, however, the German defenders were familiar with this tactic; prisoners confidently told their Soviet captors that the main attack would come two or three days later.

The Soviet air offensive began on the evening of 15–16 April in 1st Belorussian and 1st Ukrainian Fronts' sector when 4th and 16th Air Army began pounding the Germans' first defensive belt positions. As the ground offensive commenced, the four assault aviation corps of 18th Air Army shifted the air attacks to targets in the Germans' second defensive belt.

At 0500 hours on 16 April, the artillery of 1st Belorussian Front complemented the air effort with a furious 30-minute bombardment. This preparation was so excessive that in many areas it created more obstacles than it destroyed, without clearing the second German defensive positions on the Seelow Heights. Dust and smoke filled the predawn air. Zhukov's surprise tactic, which involved 143 searchlights trained on the enemy defenses, only added to the confusion without penetrating the smoke clouds in front of the attackers. The few roads near the Oder River soon became congested, and the shoulders of these roads were too swampy to permit vehicles to advance. The infantry, themselves blinded or disoriented by the searchlights, floundered forward 1.5 to 2 kilometers to the Haupt Canal that ran along the foot of the Seelow Heights. The Soviet troops had great difficulty crossing that barrier. Even where the supporting armor was able to approach the heights, the slopes were too steep for the vehicles to accompany the infantry. By late morning Chuikov's 8th Guards Army had made only limited progress, and Colonel General V. Ia. Kolpakchi's 69th Army to its south was completely stalled.[19]

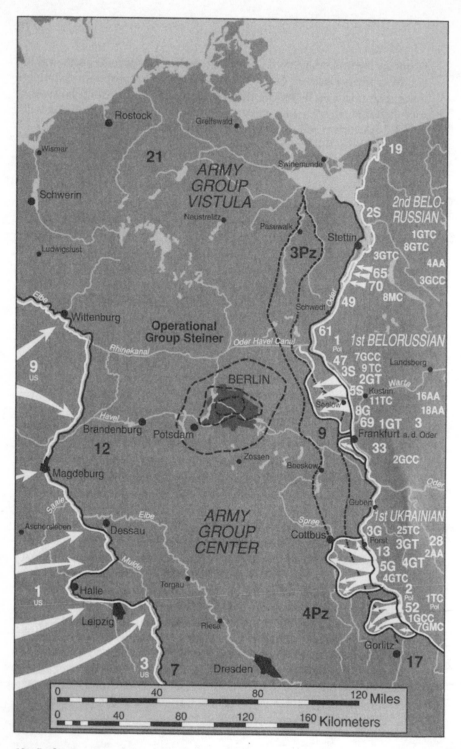

18. Berlin Operation I, 16–19 April 1945

Zhukov, who was observing the battle from the forward command post of 8th Guards Army, lost control of his iron nerve. He resorted to the type of error that had often plagued Soviet commanders in 1942–1943 (and Zhukov himself at Rzhev in November–December 1942), deciding to commit his armored exploitation forces in an effort to complete the initial penetration. Colonel General M. E. Katukov's 1st Guards and Colonel General S. I. Bogdanov's 2d Guards Tank Armies moved up but became hopelessly entangled in the artillery and supply vehicles of the assaulting infantry divisions. The 11th Tank Corps of 1st Guards Tank Army was on hand to halt a counterattack by the Panzer Division *Munchenberg*, but the two tank armies were not able to perform their deep exploitation function. Each time they attempted to move forward through the maze of fortified villages, German infantry with *Panzerfausts* ambushed them at close range. Ultimately, 1st Guards Tank's constituent brigades and corps became dispersed to support different elements of 8th Guards and 5th Shock Armies in a very slow, grinding advance.[20]

It took two days for 1st Belorussian Front forces to penetrate the Seelow Heights defenses and achieve its initial objectives. Nine understrength German divisions had opposed 8th Guards Army's penetration operation. Chuikov's attacks bogged down so badly that most of the defenders were able to extricate themselves and withdraw to the next defensive line. This withdrawal was covered by another unsuccessful German counterattack on 17 April in which three divisions attempted to cut the Berlin-Kustrin highway behind the spearheads of Katukov's tank army. The next day, Chuikov was forced to conduct a second penetration attack against the third German defensive line, which had not been identified in prebattle reconnaissance. Still, even the most determined defenders ran short of manpower and munitions. By 20 April, Lieutenant General N. E. Berzarin's 5th Shock and Chuikov's 8th Guards Armies had penetrated the fourth German defensive lines and commenced an agonizingly slow and costly advance into Berlin's eastern suburbs. Throughout the period, an impatient Stalin alternatively threatened and cajoled Zhukov on. Meanwhile, on Zhukov's right flank, Major General F. I. Perkhorovich's 47th Army and Colonel General V. I. Kuznetsov's 3d Shock Armies developed the offensive more successfully and began to envelop Berlin from the north and northwest. On the left flank, successes by Kolpakchi's 69th and Colonel General V. D. Tsvetaev's 33d Armies cut off German Ninth Army's center and right wing from Berlin and paved the way for the future envelopment of Ninth Army from the north.

Fortunately for the Soviet advance, Konev's forces on Zhukov's left flank made better progress, even though they, too, were confronted by a German defense of unexpected ferocity. Konev's 1st Ukrainian Front fired a much longer artillery preparation than Zhukov had planned but without the disastrous side effects. The guns plastered the German defenders for 40 minutes before troops began the assault crossing of the Neisse River, then conducted suppressive fire on enemy artillery for an hour during the actual crossing, and finally shelled the defenders for an additional 45 minutes after the assault elements were across the river. At the end of the first day, Konev's infantry forces, supported by 25th and 4th Guards Tank Corps and forward detachments from Rybalko's 3d and Leliushenko's 4th Guards Tank Armies, had forced the Neisse River, penetrated the German main defensive belt, and wedged 1 to 1.5 kilometers into the second belt. The following day, German counterattacks failed to blunt the Soviet advance, which penetrated to a depth of 18 kilometers. By the end of 18 April, Konev's forces had completed penetration of the Neisse defensive line and crossed the Spree River south of Berlin, creating conditions for the encirclement of Berlin from the south.[21] On the Dresden axis, Colonel General K. A. Koroteev's 52d Army continued its advance, along with Lieutenant General K. Sverchevsky's 2d Polish Army, and repelled increasingly intense German counterattacks from the Gorlitz area.[22]

Meanwhile, to the north, on 18 and 19 April, Rokossovsky's 2d Belorussian Front forces went into action by forcing the eastern channel of the Oder River and occupying jumping-off positions on river islands for subsequent forcing of the western channel.

DEATH KNELL

Given the poor progress of 1st Belorussian Front, Stalin deliberately encouraged a race between his two major *front* commanders. In dramatic telephone conversations with Zhukov and Konev late on 17 April, he amended the *Stavka* operational map by erasing the *front* boundary line between them in the vicinity of Berlin, leaving the capture of the capital to whomever got there first. As a practical matter, this action was very risky because of the danger of one unit firing at another by mistake, but it certainly encouraged the advance.[23] (See Map 19.)

On 20 April, while Zhukov's forces continued their advance, long-range artillery of 3d Shock Army's 79th Rifle Corps opened the first fire on Berlin. The following day, intermixed units of 3d Shock, 2d Guards Tank, 47th, 8th Guards, and 1st Guards Tank Armies penetrated into Berlin's suburbs and began days of difficult urban combat. In the heavily urbanized terrain of this region, the Soviet field armies had to perform many functions simultaneously: changing direction to encircle the city, bringing up supplies and artillery to sustain the attack, reorganizing assault troops

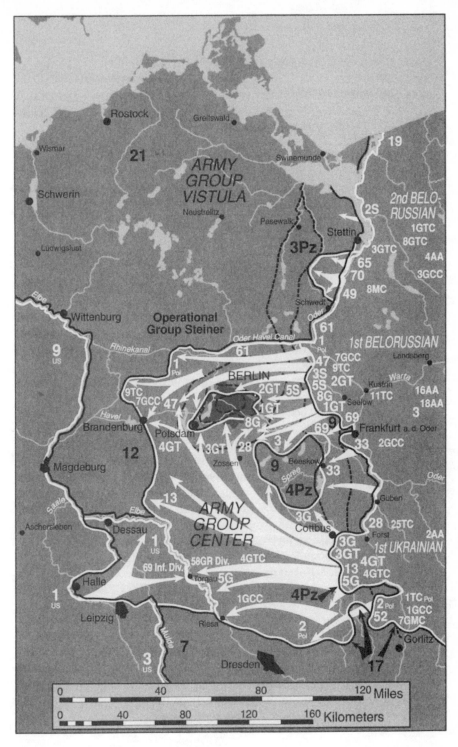

19. *Berlin Operation II, 19–25 April 1945*

into small, combined-arms teams for city fighting, and moving the bridging necessary to cross the many canals and rivers in the Berlin area. To do all this while continuing the advance against heavy opposition was a masterpiece of staff work and cooperation, an example of the sophistication achieved by Soviet forces during the Third Period of War.[24]

Meanwhile, Konev's *front* maneuvered to complete the envelopment of German Ninth Army from the south and, at the same time, reach the southern outskirts of the city. On 19–20 April, Rybalko's 3d Guards and Leliushenko's 4th Guards Tank Armies advanced 95 kilometers. The following day, elements of Rybalko's army seized the OKH headquarters at Zossen, eliminating any remaining effective control over German operations, and penetrated into the southern suburbs of Berlin, while Leliushenko's lead elements reached the southern approaches to Potsdam. The combined-arms armies of the *front's* shock group rapidly advanced westward, in the process engaging German Twelfth Army of General Walter Wenck, which the OKH had ordered eastward from the Western Front to link up with German Ninth Army and save Berlin.[25] From 20 through 26 April, 52d and 2d Polish Armies on the *front's* extended left flank repelled counterattacks from the Gorlitz region. Army Group Center had launched these attacks to break through and relieve German Ninth Army.

In the central sector, at dusk on 22 April, three forward detachments of 8th Guards Army reached the Spree River on the southern side of the German capital and achieved hasty crossings before the defenders realized their presence. On 24 April, Chuikov's 8th Guards and Katukov's 1st Guards Tank Armies linked up with Rybalko's 3d Guards Tank and Lieutenant General A. A. Luchinsky's 28th Armies southeast of Berlin, completing the encirclement of Ninth Army around Beeskow southeast of Berlin.[26] The next day, on 25 April, the Soviet 58th Guards Rifle Division of Colonel General A. S. Zhadov's 5th Guards Army linked up at Torgau on the Elbe with elements of U.S. First Army's 69th Infantry Division.[27] Soon, similar festive meetings took place along the entire front as Soviet forces advanced to the prearranged demarcation line dividing the two Allied forces.

As Allied forces linked up along the Elbe, Rokossovsky's 2d Belorussian Front forces forced the western channel of the Oder River, penetrated German defenses on its western bank, and pinned down Third Panzer Army, depriving it of the opportunity to deliver a counterblow from the north against Soviet forces encircling Berlin. This was the long-anticipated attack by so-called Group Steiner, which Hitler hoped in vain would save Berlin.

Now, even Hitler realized that the war was lost, although he continued to issue vain orders for Busse's Ninth Army (to the east), Wenck's phantom Twelfth Army (to the west), and Group Steiner (to the north) to break through to the capital (see Map 20). Any units that still had the combat power to break out of the Soviet encirclements were simply melting away, fleeing westward toward the Allies.

Lacking any effective command and control structure, the remnants of the Wehrmacht fought on like a chicken with its spinal cord severed. Zhukov began the formal assault of Berlin on 26 April, and the battle raged block by block for the next week (see Map 21). By 30 April, Soviet forces had cut the defending German force into four isolated pieces, and they set about smashing each in piecemeal fashion. The same day, Hitler committed suicide, but the carnage continued for several days. During this period, Soviet assault teams cleared the German defenders from over 300 city blocks.[28] Every house was taken by storm using task-organized assault detachments and groups made up of infantry, tanks, and artillery firing over open sights and sappers armed with explosives. Especially heavy fighting raged in the subway and in underground communications and headquarters facilities.

On 29 April, against fanatic resistance, 79th Rifle Corps troops of 1st Belorussian Front's 3d Shock Army began the symbolic struggle for the Reichstag. The following day, scouts from the 150th Rifle Division hoisted the Red Banner over the building. However, the battle for the Reichstag continued until the morning of 1 May, as Russians rooted bedraggled but stubborn groups out of the basement cellars. On 1 May 1945, forces of Kuznetsov's 3d Shock Army attacking from the north linked up just south of the Reichstag with Chuikov's 8th Guards Army troopers advancing from the south. By the evening of 2 May, German resistance had finally ceased, and remnants of the Berlin garrison, under the command of Lieutenant General Helmuth Weidling, surrendered.[29]

While the German Berlin garrison was capitulating, Konev's forces were already regrouping to prepare for an advance into Czechoslovakia along the Prague axis, while 1st Belorussian Front's combined-arms armies continued their westward advance, and on 7 May, they linked up with Allied forces on a broad front along the Elbe. The 2d Belorussian Front's forces reached the shores of the Baltic Sea and the line of the Elbe River, where they linked up with elements of British Second Army. Meanwhile, Soviet forces eliminated resisting pockets of German forces in Courland and on the Samland Peninsula, west of Konigsberg.

During the course of the Berlin operation, Soviet forces crushed the remnants of the once-vaunted Wehrmacht and captured 480,000 German troops (see Table 16-1). The cost, however, had been great; 361,367 Soviet and Polish soldiers fell in the effort.[30] The Berlin operation was prepared in a relatively short period, and its main aims—the encirclement and destruction of the German Berlin grouping and the capture of Berlin—

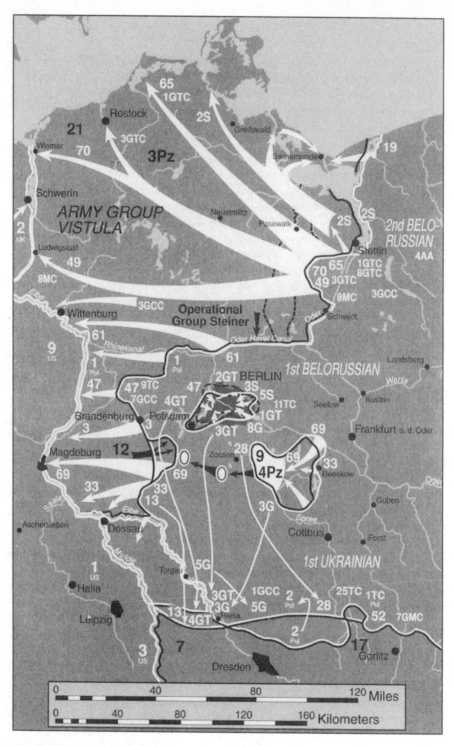

20. *Berlin Operation III, 25 April–8 May 1945*

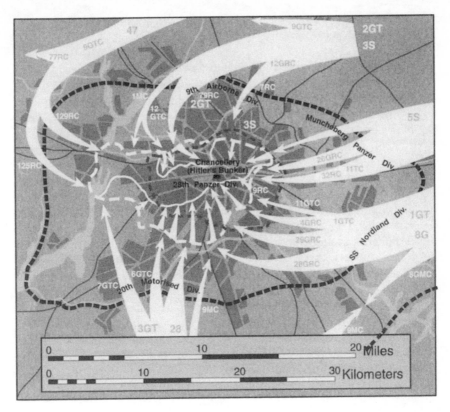

21. Assault on Berlin, 21 April–5 May 1945

Table 16-1. Count of Enemy Losses and Trophies by Soviet Fronts

Front	Killed	POWs	Tanks and Assault Guns	Guns and Mortars	Aircraft
1st Belorussian	218,691	250,534	1,806	11,680	3,426
2d Belorussian	49,770	84,234	280	2,709	1,462
1st Ukrainian	189,619	144,530	2,097	6,086	1,107
Total	458,080	479,298	4,183	20,475	4,995

Source: *Berlinskaia operatsiia 1945 goda* (Moscow: Voenizdat, 1950), 616–618.

were achieved in 17 days. The Soviets have since considered the operation to be a classic example of an offensive by a group of *fronts* conducted with decisive aims in an almost ceremonial fashion. The nearly simultaneous offensive by three *fronts* in a 300-kilometer sector with the delivery of six blows tied down German reserves, disorganized German command and control, and, in some instances, achieved operational and tactical surprise. The Berlin operation—in particular the poor performance of Zhukov's *front*—was instructive in other ways as well. As determined after the war by high level conferences held to study the operation, its nature and course were markedly different from the heavy combat the Soviets had experienced on the more open terrain further east.[31] Combat in the more heavily urban and wooded terrain near Berlin exacted a far more costly toll on the attackers than Soviet planners had anticipated. These experiences and lessons would form the basis for the postwar restructuring of the Soviet Union's armed forces.

As a reward for their performance during combat on the main axes to Berlin, six Soviet armies (3d Shock, 8th Guards, and 1st, 2d, 3d, and 4th. Guards Tank Armies) would be assigned to Soviet occupation forces in Germany. Over 40 years later, the first of these armies to enter Berlin would be the last to depart German soil.

PRAGUE

The fall of Berlin did not end the fighting. With victory in sight, Stalin and his senior commanders became more concerned than ever about the possibility that the Western Allies would play them false. At the time and long afterward, the Soviet participants took seriously the German offer to surrender to the West while continuing to fight in the East. Of course, Eisenhower insisted on total surrender on all fronts, but the Soviet leaders could not overcome their fear of treachery or, at the very least, of being cheated out of their hard-won victory.

Thus, when General Omar Bradley offered to assist in the occupation of Czechoslovakia, Stalin responded with another order to accelerate the advance. On 1 May, the *Stavka* ordered 1st Belorussian Front to relieve all elements of 1st Ukrainian Front engaged in mopping up in Berlin so that Konev could turn southwestward and, in conjunction with Marshal R. Ia. Malinovsky's 2d Ukrainian and General A. I. Eremenko's 4th Ukrainian Fronts, advance on Prague.

The Soviets' old nemesis, Army Group Center, which for over two years had been poised threateningly on the approaches to Moscow, was to become the new and last Soviet target. In May 1945, the more than 600,000 men of this Army Group, now commanded by Field Marshal Ferdinand Schoerner, awaited inevitable destruction—ironically, not in Germany but in Czechoslovakia, which had been one of Hitler's initial victims.[32]

While the Reichstag was still under assault, between 1 and 6 May, the forces under the command of Konev, Malinovsky, and Eremenko regrouped to launch an offensive of overwhelming proportions against Schoerner's force. This attack was in conjunction, if not in competition, with General George S. Patton's U.S. Third Army, which was poised to enter Czechoslovakia from Bavaria. The combined force of over 2 million Soviet and Polish soldiers planned to rely on heavy tank forces, including three tank armies and a cavalry-mechanized group, to spearhead a rapid thrust directly on the Czech capital, Prague.[33]

Konev's hastily approved plan called for Colonel General N. P. Pukhov's 13th Army and Colonel General V. N. Gordov's 3d Guards Armies to attack west of Dresden, penetrate the Erzgeberg Mountain passes in southeast Germany, and assist the subsequent commitment of Rybalko's 3d and Leliushenko's 4th Guards Tank Armies for a rapid exploitation to Prague.[34] Polish and Soviet forces would launch a supporting attack in 1st Ukrainian Front's Gorlitz sector. Simultaneously, in a wide arc covering the eastern and southern borders of Czechoslovakia, Eremenko and Malinovsky were to mount similar offensives spearheaded by tank forces.

The advance was to begin on 7 May, but at noon on 5 May, the population of Prague launched an uprising and appealed by radio for Allied help. This brief struggle with the German occupation forces cost the Czechs at least 3,000 killed and 10,000 wounded. Stalin again hurried the attack and ordered that it commence on the afternoon of 6 May.

Spurred on by Stalin's demands for haste and taking advantage of local German withdrawals, Konev struck from the north on 6 May. He launched his main attack from the Riesa area with three combined-arms armies (13th and 3d and 5th Guards) and 3d and 4th Guards Tank Armies. The next day, he launched two secondary attacks with slightly smaller forces (including 2d Polish Army) further to the east. Malinovsky's 2d Ukrainian Front struck northward from Brno toward Olomouc and Prague with four combined-arms armies (53d, 7th Guards, 9th Guards, and 46th), Colonel General A. G. Kravchenko's 6th Guards Tank Army, and Colonel General I. A. Pliev's 1st Guards Cavalry-Mechanized Group. In between Konev's and Malinovsky's forces, Eremenko's *front* pressured German defenses across its entire front.

Within two days, Konev's forces occupied Dresden, Bautzen, and Gorlitz against dwindling German resistance, and 4th Ukrainian Front seized Olomouc; a day later, it linked up with advancing 2d Ukrainian Front forces for a combined drive on Prague. To accelerate his advance, on the night of 8–9 May, Konev ordered Rybalko's and Leliushenko's tank armies to make a dash for Prague. At first light, the two tank armies, spearheaded by specially tailored forward detachments, began an 80-kilometer race, linking up in the city with forward mobile elements of 2d and 4th Ukrainian Fronts, which included Czech forces of the 1st Separate Czech Tank Brigade. During the following two days, Soviet forces liquidated or accepted the surrender of more than 600,000 remaining German forces.[35] On 11 May advanced elements of Leliushenko's tank army linked up with the forces of the U.S. Third Army east of Pilsen, ending the major wartime field operations of the Red Army.

By early May, the surviving German military leaders were more than ready to comply with Allied demands for general and unconditional surrender. Eisenhower's threat to break off negotiations and seal the front lines against refugees, in essence turning them over to the Soviets, was the final argument. Yet the Soviet representative to Eisenhower's headquarters, General I. A. Susloparov, had no instructions on the matter. When his counterpart in Moscow, Major General John Deane, inquired about coordinating the announcement of the surrender, Antonov and his staff officers again suspected that their allies were seeking to grab all the credit. Meanwhile, in Rheims the surrender ceremony had been arranged for early on 7 May, and Susloparov still had no instructions. Afraid to sign without orders, he was even more afraid to have the Soviet Union left out of the surrender. Finally, Susloparov nerved himself to sign the surrender document, annotating it with a qualifier that would allow Moscow to renegotiate later if necessary. No sooner had he reported his actions that he received a frantic telegram from the *Stavka* ordering, "Don't sign any documents!"[36]

CONCLUSIONS

The 18 months of the Third Period of War accorded a gruesome symmetry to the horrors of war on the Eastern Front. The first 18 months of war witnessed the unprecedented catastrophes that beset the Red Army and the titanic defensive battles at Moscow and Stalingrad, punctuated by periodic Soviet counteroffensive impulses. The Germans had advanced to the gates of Moscow, the banks of the Volga, and the northern slopes of the Caucasus Mountains. At a cost of over 10 million military casualties and uncounted civilian fatalities, the Red Army had halted Blitzkrieg and turned the tide of almost unending German military victories.

During the 12 months of the Second Period of War, beginning with the catastrophic German defeat on the Volga and ending with the victorious Soviet drive to the Dnepr after the equally catastrophic German defeat at

Kursk, the Red Army destroyed Blitzkreig as a viable offensive military concept. At a cost of nearly 10 million additional military casualties, the Soviets began the liberation of their territories. Unlike the First Period of War, in this period the Germans and their allies themselves suffered losses numbering in the hundreds of thousands. More devastating for the German cause was the slow realization that this process of attrition would accelerate toward inevitable and total defeat.

This process reached fruition in the Third Period of War. A seemingly unending procession of Soviet strategic victories ensued, which tore the heart out of the Wehrmacht, inexorably propelled Soviet forces into central Europe, and climaxed in the total military and political defeat of Nazi Germany. The cost to the Red Army was a final nine million casualties.

The military consequences of operations in spring 1945 were clear. The remaining forces of the once-proud and seemingly indestructible armies of Germany were crushed by the combined efforts of Allied forces assaulting from East and West. Nazi Germany, which had based its power and built its empire on the foundations of warfare of unprecedented violence and destructiveness, was felled in equally violent and decisive fashion. The colossal scope and scale of the Berlin operation, resulting in appalling Soviet casualties and equally massive destruction of the German capital, was a fitting end to a war that was so unlike previous wars. As more than one German veteran observed, war in the West was proper sport, while war in the East was unmitigated horror. This final horror eliminated the remaining 2 million men of the Wehrmacht and reduced Germany to ashes.

The political consequences of these last operations reflected a process that had been going on for over a year, which the Soviet Union's Allies had largely overlooked in their search for victory. That process now became crystal clear during the peace that followed. In the baggage of the victorious Red Army came political power in the guise of newly formed national armies for Soviet liberated states and governments to go with those armies. Two Polish, three Rumanian, and two Bulgarian armies fought and bled alongside the Red Army, together with a Czech Corps and other smaller national formations. Once returned to their liberated lands, these units cooperated with local partisan formations, many of which had also been sponsored and equipped by the Soviet Union. Under the protection of the Red Army, these armed forces and the governments-in-exile that accompanied them quickly transformed military into political power.

Slowly, in mid-May 1945, the firing died out and the war in Europe gradually came to an end. Having, at great human cost, captured Bucharest, Belgrade, Warsaw, Budapest, Vienna, Berlin, and Prague from the shattered Wehrmacht, the Soviets, by rights, had undisputed claim to the lion's share of the spoils of this victory over Nazi Germany. In Western perceptions, however, the political consequences of that victory deprived the Soviet Union of that right. Within a few short years, the horrors of war were replaced by the menace of the Cold War, and suspicions soon obscured the unprecedented suffering and triumph of the Soviet peoples.

CHAPTER 17

Conclusion

ENCORE PERFORMANCE IN MANCHURIA

While the defeat of Nazi Germany ended the Soviets' self-proclaimed "Great Patriotic War," it did not end Soviet participation in the Second World War. Just as the other Allied Powers had to turn their attention to Germany's undefeated Axis ally, Japan, the Soviet Union also looked East to eradicate a latent threat that had existed since 1941. Soviet motives for intervening in the Asian war were varied. While responding to Allied requests for assistance, the Soviet Union certainly signaled its intention to fulfill its role as an Asian power by participating in the defeat of Japan and, not coincidentally, to reap whatever spoils were possible from the ruins of the Japanese Empire. Operations in Manchuria also offered the Soviet Army the opportunity to apply skills learned in four years of combat against the Germans to battle with the Japanese.

After the undeclared war at Khalkhin-Gol in August 1939, both the Soviet Union and the Japanese Empire had turned away from their confrontation in Manchuria. In April 1941, they reached a truce that gave them some measure of reassurance against surprise attack. The truce permitted Stalin to focus his efforts against the Germans and allowed the Japanese to concentrate on conquests in China, southeast Asia, and the Pacific. Nevertheless, throughout World War II, trust never characterized Soviet-Japanese relations. Both countries reluctantly kept considerable forces facing each other in northeast Asia, while drawing off their best troops to fight elsewhere. The Japanese Kwantung Army in Manchuria, however, remained a formidable fighting force well into 1944. During the crisis periods of fall 1941 and fall 1942, the *Stavka* would have liked to have those Far Eastern divisions available for combat in the West.[1] Moreover, as Soviet intelligence probably knew, it was not until summer 1944 that the Japanese Kwantung Army's planning shifted from an offensive to a defensive orientation.[2] By that time, the best Kwantung Army units had been sucked into combat in the Pacific, and less ready garrison divisions had moved into Manchuria from China.

In August 1945, the Kwantung Army consisted of 31 infantry divisions and 12 separate brigades. All but six of these divisions had been created during the spring and summer of 1945 in a last-ditch effort to mobilize manpower that had previously been exempt or unsuited for service. These divisions had an average strength of 12,500, or about two thirds of their authorized size, and were far below their establishment in artillery and heavy weapons. Half were garrison divisions, without significant artillery or antitank capability.[3] Still, Japanese divisions were larger in numbers, if not equipment, than their Soviet counterparts. By 1945, the Soviet rifle division was authorized 11,700 men and often had less than half that number present for duty.[4]

As victory over Germany approached in 1944–1945, British and American concern over defeating the obstinate and increasingly fanatic Japanese Army increased. At the Teheran and Yalta Conferences, the Allies sounded out Stalin on Russian participation in the Pacific War and received a favorable, if vague, response. By the May 1945 Potsdam Conference, Allied concern had heightened in light of Germany's decision to fight to the end and the prospects that the more fanatical Japanese would do likewise. The atomic bomb was still an uncertain experiment, and, if losses on Okinawa were any indication, Allied troops were certain to suffer more than one million casualties if they invaded Japan proper.[5] Moreover, hundred of thousands of Japanese troops remained in China, and the still respected Kwantung Army appeared to be relatively intact in Manchuria.

Under the circumstances, the Western Allies welcomed Stalin's positive response to their request for assistance, although they did not place great confidence in it. For its part, the Soviet government wanted to eliminate the Japanese menace and gain strategic positions in the Far East. Ultimately, Moscow promised that it would attack within three months of victory in Europe—a promise Stalin kept almost to the day. In return for his participation, as had been the case in Europe, Stalin was to receive his own sphere of influence in Manchuria, northern Korea, the Kurile Islands, and Sakhalin Island. Unbeknown to the Allies, Stalin also intended to seize the Hokkaido Island portion of Japan proper.[6]

Based on the limited capacity of the Trans-Siberian Railway and the low level of activity by forward Soviet forces in the Far East, the Japanese estimated that no attack was likely in August 1945 and, in fact, before spring 1946.[7] In reality, however, the *Stavka* planned for a mid-August offensive and had carefully concealed the buildup of a force of 90 divisions, many of which crossed Siberia in their vehicles to avoid straining the railroad.[8] This was an extraordinary effort for a nation that had barely survived four years of life-or-death struggle with Germany; many of the troops rolling east were old men or boys. Ultimately, because of the United States' use of the atomic bomb on 6 August, the *Stavka* accelerated its offensive preparations and attacked on 9 August, before its forces had been fully concentrated for the attack.[9]

The terrain of Manchuria inspired Japanese confidence in its ability to defend against any attack. The province consists of a huge central plain, where almost all of the region's agriculture and industry were concentrated, surrounded on three sides by forbidding mountain and forest barriers. In particular, the Grand Khingan mountain range to the west reaches heights of 1,900 meters, with the vast, semi-desert regions of Inner Mongolia beyond the mountains. Even the few mountain passes were swampy, particularly during the summer monsoon season, when humidity, swamps, and mud made operations even more difficult. In addition to poor trafficability, the colossal scale of Manchuria should have daunted any potential attacker. The distance from the northern tip of the province to the Yellow Sea is almost equal to the distance between Normandy, France, and Minsk, Russia. Moreover, despite miracles of logistics and staff work, the Soviet forces did not have an overwhelming advantage in numbers. The overall force ratio was 1 Japanese soldier to 2.2 Soviets, and, if the puppet troops of the Manchukuo government were considered, this ratio fell to 1:1.5.[10] The Soviets did, of course, achieve a much larger superiority in tanks and artillery, but this superiority was balanced by the defender's advantages of terrain. It was not numbers but training, equipment, and tactics that produced the Soviet victory.

Based on the almost-impassible terrain to the west, the defenders of Manchuria concentrated most of their forces along the rail-lines in the east, north, and northwest. The Japanese borders in these areas were protected by massive Maginot-like border fortifications, although the Japanese 1st Area Army, headquartered at Mutanchiang, chose to hold many of its units back for a defense in depth. The 3d Area Army, responsible for the western portion of Manchuria, was scattered over a much wider area deep within Manchuria's central valley.[11]

The attackers were organized into Marshal R. Ia. Malinovsky's Transbaikal Front in the west, Colonel General M. A. Purkaev's 2d Far Eastern Front in the north, and Marshal K. A. Meretskov's 1st Far Eastern Front in the eastern parts of Manchuria. The Stavka appointed Marshal A. M. Vasilevsky to overall command, first as a Stavka representative and then, in July, as a true theater commander, a first in the war. Many of his subordinate commanders (Meretskov, Malinovsky, Kravchenko, Pliev, Krylov, Liudnikov, and others) and subordinate units were chosen to participate in the operation because of their prior experience in similar terrain.

Although the 1st Far Eastern Front had to prepare for an initial penetration attack against the Japanese fortifications in eastern Manchuria, all three *fronts* planned the campaign as if it were one huge exploitation, one

"Deep Operation" from beginning to end. In particular, the Transbaikal Front in the west controlled Kravchenko's 6th Guards Tank Army and two mixed Soviet-Mongolian cavalry-mechanized groups. The *Stavka* accepted an enormous logistical risk by concentrating these forces in the barren reaches of Mongolia. Indeed, just as in 1939, Japanese intelligence officers did not believe that the Soviets could support mechanized forces in such a remote area. The *Stavka* concept was to have these mobile organizations bypass any isolated Japanese resistance, make their way across the desert regions as rapidly as possible, and force the Grand Khingan Mountain passes before the defenders recognized the threat.

The typical Soviet military organizations were heavily task-organized for the Manchurian venture. In many instances, a rifle division had attachments that included a separate tank brigade, a self-propelled assault gun regiment, and one or more additional artillery regiments. The presence of this armor allowed every rifle division to form its own forward detachment for deep penetrations and pursuits. In effect, the typical Soviet rifle division in Manchuria was a forerunner of the 1946 organization for all rifle divisions.

Similarly, the larger mobile organizations were restructured for Manchuria based on earlier experience. The 6th Guards Tank Army, which was designated to conduct the operational-strategic penetration from the West, was completely restructured. One of its two tank corps was replaced by a second mechanized corps, and two motorized rifle divisions, remnants of the 1941 mechanized corps, were attached to the Army. In addition, two self-propelled assault gun brigades, two light artillery brigades, a motorcycle infantry regiment, and a variety of support units made the 6th Guards a much more robust, balanced force than any tank army of the German war. Ultimately, 6th Guards Tank Army consisted of 25 armored and 44 motorized rifle battalions with a total of 1,019 tanks and self-propelled guns. This structure was much closer to both the 1941 mechanized corps and the 1946 Soviet mechanized army than to the tank forces that had defeated Germany. With peace in Western Europe, the Red Army finally had enough weapons, equipment, and men to construct the ideal military units for postwar use. In essence, the *Stavka* used Manchuria as a testcase, experimenting with a variety of new organizations and concept that later became standard.[12]

The Manchurian Campaign was by no means a complete walk-over— 12,031 Soviet troops died and 24,425 were wounded in 11 days, during 9–20 August.[13] Still, the result was a masterpiece of maneuver warfare that the postwar Soviet Army studied for decades.

In western Manchuria, Colonel General A. G. Kravchenko's 6th Guards Tank Army moved across the virtually uninhabited border in the predawn hours of 9 August. In three days, it covered 450 kilometers, meeting problems of rough terrain and fuel resupply but only nominal enemy resistance. The leading element of this army, Lieutenant General M. V. Volkov's 9th Guards Mechanized Corps, found that its lend-lease Sherman tanks were ill equipped for mobility in the swampy passes of the Grand Khingan Mountains. As a result, the T-34s of Lieutenant General M. I. Savelev's 5th Guards Tank Corps assumed the lead during the final advance. The 6th Guards Tank Army was flanked by Colonel General I. I. Liudnikov's 39th Army, which bypassed and rooted out Japanese forces along the rail line from western Manchuria, and by Colonel General I. A. Pliev's Cavalry-Mechanized Group, which marched across endless expanses of deserts to emerge west of Peking. By 15 August, the spearhead armored units of 6th Guards Tank Army had penetrated the mountain barrier and raced into the central valley of Manchuria, paralyzing the remnants of Japanese 3d Area Army into inactivity. It meant nothing that, by this time, Kravchenko's advance consisted only of forward detachments supplied with fuel by air.[14] The damage was done, and all remaining bypassed Japanese forces in the west fought desperate but irrelevant battles in total isolation.

Farther to the north, Lieutenant General A. A. Luchinsky's 36th Army was not so lucky. At 0020 hours on 9 August, two rifle battalions of this army seized river crossings over the rain-swollen Argun River, scattering the Japanese security platoons in the area. By the end of the first day, 36th Army, with 205th Tank Brigade acting as its forward detachment, was closing on the fortified town of Hailar. The 36th Army Commander, Lieutenant General A. A. Luchinsky, attempted to seize the town by a sudden night attack from the march but was stopped cold by the Japanese 80th Independent Mixed Brigade. For nine days, an entire Soviet rifle corps was tied down clearing Hailar house by house, overcoming determined Japanese resistance. This resistance did not prevent Luchinsky from bypassing the town with his 2d Rifle Corps, which continued the exploitation. The 205th Tank Brigade and 2d Rifle Corps battered away at the Japanese 119th Infantry Division in the high passes of the Grand Khingans. The Soviets finally broke through into the central plains on 17 August, just as the local Japanese commanders began to obey the Emperor's cease-fire order.[15]

On the other side of Manchuria, Meretskov's 1st Far Eastern Front had a much more difficult task. To achieve surprise, the Soviets dispensed with the usual artillery preparation. Instead, the first reconnaissance battalions crossed the border in terrible thunderstorms at 0030 hours on 9 August. Half an hour later, the assault units began to cut lanes through the obstacles. By 0500 hours, the sophisticated Soviet infiltration tactics had disrupted the Japanese forward defensive scheme, and the Soviet troops shifted to the exploitation.[16] By the end of the first day, the tank brigades attached to each rifle division were up to 22 kilometers into Manchuria, leaving bypassed Japanese forts to be reduced by follow-on units.

The 5th Army Commander, Colonel General N. I. Krylov, sent a reinforced tank brigade forward in a dash toward the Japanese Army Group headquarters in the city of Mutanchiang, 60 kilometers from the border. Early on 12 August, the Japanese 135th Infantry Division checked this advance with a violent counterattack. Within hours, Krylov had brought up two rifle divisions, organized a 30-minute artillery barrage, and disrupted the Japanese defenses in a hasty attack. By 13 August, four other rifle divisions, each led by a tank brigade, were closing in on Mutanchiang. For two days, five Japanese regiments held Mutanchiang in ferocious house-to-house fighting, during which one regiment was destroyed to a man.

The advance was by no means bloodless for the Red Army. During the first three days of the campaign, the 257th Tank Brigade, which acted as the forward detachment for Colonel General A. P. Beloborodov's 1st Red Banner Army in eastern Manchuria, dwindled from an authorized strength of 65 tanks to only 19 but continued the advance.[17] If a forward detachment was halted by the defenders, the parent headquarters simply organized another such detachment and bypassed the resistance. Everywhere, the experienced Soviet commanders used maneuver and subordinate initiative in a manner that stunned the Japanese, who still retained the 1930s stereotype (reinforced by German reports) of their "clumsy" opponent.

Although Japan would undoubtedly have surrendered without Soviet intervention, the Red Army's remarkable performance against serious resistance made a significant contribution to the Pacific war. For his services, Stalin received the Kurile Islands, southern Sakhalin Island, and temporary rule over Manchuria and northern Korea. He was, however, thwarted in his plans to seize Hokkaido. On 22 August, only a day before its launch, he halted a joint airborne and amphibious operation against Hokkaido Island.[18] Japan was thus spared the postwar ordeal experienced by a divided Germany.

CONTRIBUTIONS AND COSTS

On the 50th anniversary of the Normandy invasion of 1944, a U.S. news magazine featured a cover photo of General Dwight D. Eisenhower, who was labeled the man who defeated Hitler. If any one man deserved that label, it was not Eisenhower but Zhukov, Vasilevsky, or possibly Stalin himself. More generally, the Red Army and the Soviet citizenry of many nationalities bore the lion's share of the struggle against Germany from 1941 to 1945. Only China, which suffered almost continuous Japanese attack from 1931 onward, matched the level of Soviet suffering and effort. In military terms, moreover, the Chinese participation in the war was almost insignificant in comparison with that of the Soviets, who were constantly engaged and absorbed more than half of all German forces.

From June through December 1941, only Britain shared with the Soviet Union the trials of war against the Germans. Over three million German troops fought in the East, while less than a million struggled elsewhere, attended to occupied Europe, or rested in the homeland. From December 1941 through November 1942, while over nine million troops on both sides struggled in the East, the only significant ground action in the Western Theater took place in North Africa, where relatively small British forces engaged Rommel's Afrika Corps and its Italian allies. In November 1942, the British celebrated victory over the Germans at El Alamein, defeating four German divisions and a somewhat larger Italian force, and inflicting 60,000 Axis losses. The same month, at Stalingrad, the Soviets defeated and encircled German Sixth Army, damaged Fourth Panzer Army, and smashed Rumanian Third and Fourth Armies, eradicating over 50 divisions and over 300,000 men from the Axis order of battle. By May 1943, the Allies had pursued Rommel's Afrika Corps across northern Africa and into Tunisia, where, after heavy fighting, the German and Italian force of 250,000 surrendered. Meanwhile, in the East, another German army (Second) was severely mauled, and Italian Eighth and Hungarian Second Armies were utterly destroyed, exceeding Axis losses in Tunisia.

While over two million German and Soviet troops struggled at Kursk and five million later fought on a 600-kilometer front from Smolensk to the Black Sea coast, in July 1943, Allied forces invaded Sicily, and drove 60,000 Germans from the island. In August, the Allies landed on the Italian peninsula. By October, when 2.5 million men of the Wehrmacht faced 6.6 million Soviets, the frontlines had stabilized in Italy south of Rome, as the Germans deployed a much smaller, although significant, number of troops to halt the Allied advance. (See Appendix, Table C, for relative Eastern Front strengths.)

By 1 October 1943, 2,565,000 men—representing 63 percent of the Wehrmacht's total strength—struggled in the East, together with the bulk of the 300,000 Waffen SS troops. On 1 June 1944, 239 (62 percent) of the German Army's division equivalents fought in the East. With operations in Italy at a stalemate, until June 1944, the Wehrmacht still considered the West as a semi-reserve.[19] In August 1944, after the opening of the second front, while 2.1 million Germans fought in the East, 1 million opposed Allied operations in France.

Casualty figures underscore this reality (see Appendix, Table E). From September 1939 to September 1942, the bulk of the German Army's 922,000 dead, missing, and disabled (14 percent of the total force) could be credited to combat in the East. Between 1 September 1942 and 20 November 1943, this grim count rose to 2,077,000 (30 percent of the total force), again primarily in the East. From June through November 1944, after the opening of the second front, the German Army suffered another 1,457,000 irrevocable losses. Of this number, 903,000 (62 percent) were lost in the East.[20] Finally, after losing 120,000 men to the Allies in the Battle of the Bulge, the Germans suffered another 2 million losses, two thirds at Soviet hands from 1 January to 30 April 1945.

Total Wehrmacht losses to 30 April 1945 amounted to 11,135,500, including 6,035,000 wounded. Of these, almost 9,000,000 fell in the East. German armed forces' losses to war's end numbered 13,488,000 men (75 percent of the mobilized forces and 46 percent of the 1939 male population of Germany). Of these, 10,758,000 fell or were taken prisoner in the East.[21] Today, the stark inscription "died in the East" that is carved on countless thousands of headstones in scores of German cemeteries bears mute witness to the carnage in the East, where the will and strength of the Wehrmacht perished.

The Soviets have bitterly complained since the war about the absence of a real second front before June 1944, and that issue remains a source of suspicion even in post–Cost War Russia. Yet, the Allies' reasons for deferring a second front until 1944 were valid, and Allied contributions to victories were significant. As the American debacle at the Kasserine Pass in December 1942 and the Canadian-British performance at Dieppe on 19 August 1942 indicated, Allied armies were not ready to operate in France in 1943, even if a sufficient number of landing craft had been available for the invasion, which was not the case. Even in 1944, Allied success at Normandy was a close thing and depended, in part, on major German misperceptions and mistakes. Once in France, after the breakout from the Normandy bridge-head in August, the two million Allied troops in France inflicted grievous losses on the one million defending Germans—100,000 at Falaise and a total of 400,000 by December 1944. In the subsequent Battle of the Bulge (16 December 1944–31 January 1945), the Germans lost another 120,000 men.[22] These losses in the West, combined with the over 1.2 million lost in the East during the same period, broke the back of the Wehrmacht and set the context for the final destruction of Germany in 1945.

In addition to its ground combat contribution, the Allies conducted a major strategic bombing campaign against Germany (which the Soviets could not mount) and, in 1944, drew the bulk of German operational and tactical airpower. The strategic bombing campaign did significant damage to German industrial targets, struck hard at the well-being and morale of the German civil population, and sucked into its vortex and destroyed a large part of the German fighter force, which had earlier been used effectively in a ground role in the East. Although airpower did not prove to be a war-winning weapon, and German industrial mobilization and weapons production peaked in late 1944, the air campaign seriously hindered the German war effort.

Equally disastrous for the Germans were the losses of tactical fighters in that campaign and in combat in France in 1944. So devastating were these losses that after mid-1944, the German air force was no longer a factor on the Eastern Front.

Another controversial Allied contribution to the war effort was the Lend-Lease Program to send supplies to the Soviet Union. Although Soviet accounts have routinely belittled the significance of Lend-Lease in the sustainment of the Soviet war effort, the overall importance of the assistance cannot be understated.[23] Lend-Lease aid did not arrive in sufficient quantities to make the difference between defeat and victory in 1941–1942; that achievement must be attributed solely to the Soviet people and to the iron nerve of Stalin, Zhukov, Shaposhnikov, Vasilevsky, and their subordinates. As the war continued, however, the United States and Great Britain provided many of the implements of war and strategic raw materials necessary for Soviet victory. Without Lend-Lease food, clothing, and raw materials (especially metals), the Soviet economy would have been even more heavily burdened by the war effort. Perhaps most directly, without Lend-Lease trucks, rail engines, and railroad cars, every Soviet offensive would have stalled at an earlier stage, outrunning its logistical tail in a matter of days. In turn, this would have allowed the German commanders to escape at least some encirclements, while forcing the Red Army to prepare and conduct many more deliberate penetration attacks in order to advance the same distance. Left to their own devices, Stalin and his commanders might have taken 12 to 18 months longer to finish off the Wehrmacht; the ultimate result would probably have been the same, except that Soviet soldiers could have waded at France's Atlantic beaches. Thus, while the Red Army shed the bulk of Allied blood, it would have shed more blood for longer without Allied assistance.

As indicated in Appendix, Table A, the war with Nazi Germany cost the Soviet Union at least 29 million military casualties. The exact numbers can never be established, and some revisionists have attempted to put the number as high as 50 million. Uncounted millions of civilians also perished, and wartime population dislocation in the Soviet Union was catastrophic (comparable to an enemy occupation of the United States from the Atlantic coast to beyond the Mississippi River). Millions of Soviet soldiers and civilians disappeared into German detention camps and slave labor factories. Millions more suffered permanent physical and mental damage.

Economic dislocation was equally severe. Despite the prodigious feats the Soviets accomplished in moving productive capability deep within the Soviet Union and east of the Urals and building a new industrial base in the Urals region and Siberia, the losses in resources and manufacturing capacity in western Russia and the Ukraine were catastrophic. The heavy industry of the Donbas, Leningrad, Kiev, Khar'kov, and a host of regions fell under German control, along with key mineral resource deposits and most of the Soviet Union's prime agricultural regions. Again, an equivalent degree of damage to the U.S. economy and military capability would have resulted had German armies conquered the territory from the East Coast to the Mississippi River and into the eastern Great Plains. This stark context underscores the importance of Lend-Lease shipments, and explains why "Villies," "Studabaker," and "Spam" remain familiar terms to middle-aged and older Russians.

Coming on top of World War I, the Civil War, forced collectivization and industrialization, and the purges of the 1930s, this staggering butcher's bill and economic cost left the Soviet populace and economy weakened for decades to come. Moreover, the "never again" attitude of the Soviet populace, characterized by the Soviet Union's constant repetition of the slogan, "No one will forget, nothing will be forgotten," fostered a paranoic concern with national security that would contribute, ultimately, to the bankruptcy and destruction of the state.

THE TWO ARMIES

While most historians have recognized the scope of Soviet sacrifice and achievement, stereotypes persist as to *how* the Wehrmacht and the Red Army fought. While the Red Army never slavishly copied the Germans and, in fact, followed its own traditions in matters of organization, tactics, and leadership, it did learn from its more skilled opponent. During wartime, it built upon its own rich theoretical base and implemented what theorists had ordained but had not been able to realize in the 1930s. Necessity drove that education, and the cost of that education was high. In a strange sort of reciprocity, as the war dragged on, the German Army came to resemble its 1941 opponent, while the Red Army came closer to the essence of the original Blitzkrieg, now under the rubric of the "deep operation."

In 1941, the German Army prided itself on *Auftragstaktik*, relying on all leaders to understand the commander's overall concept and to cooperate in a flexible, decentralized manner that allowed considerable scope for individual initiative. German army units, particularly the panzer forces, were already famous for their ability to reorganize as required by the situation, to bypass centers of enemy resistance, and to continue the exploitation far into the enemy rear areas. Despite the widespread infection of Nazi racist views, the German commanders, or at least the professional officers at the top, considered themselves to be trusted subordinates of the state, divorced from the Nazi Party and its ideology. If the Wehrmacht had a limitation in 1941–1942, it was in the area of logistics. The entire scope of the Russian campaign was probably beyond German capability from the start, and many of the early German offensives were halted by lack of supplies rather than by Soviet resistance.

By contrast, the 1941–1942 Red Army was a victim of Stalin's dictatorship. Its troops lacked training and equipment; it had abandoned its advanced operational and tactical tradition and concepts; its brain had been lopped off in the purges; and its officer corps had been decimated and demoralized. The German invasion caught the Red Army in transition, without coherent organizations or effective weapons. Commanders tended to ignore the terrain and the enemy situation, deploying their forces evenly across the front and failing to accomplish the most elemental coordination between infantry and artillery. The more unscrupulous political officers second-guessed tactical leaders, and summary execution awaited those officers who failed.

Stalin, stunned by the disaster of 1941, did not trust even his few competent generals and attempted to manage the war personally. On occasion, such as in the defense of Moscow, Leningrad, and Stalingrad, Stalin's stubbornness was an asset. At other times, however, his demands to counterattack at the frontiers, to defend Kiev in 1941, or to resume the offensive in May 1942 were based on a complete misunderstanding of the military situation. Even when Soviet arms achieved limited victories during the winter offensives of 1941–1942 and 1942–1943, Stalin was too ambitious, attempting to win the war in one all-out advance instead of a series of cautious offensives.

From late 1942 onward, the Wehrmacht began to lose many of its distinctive advantages and to acquire some of the weaknesses of its opponent. Continuous casualties meant a decline in training and, therefore, in tactical proficiency. Equipment wore out, and the German economy was no longer able to provide quality weapons in sufficient quantities to maintain the previous technological edge. As for leadership, Adolph Hitler began to resemble the Stalin of 1941. Having been correct to forbid withdrawals during the first Soviet winter offensive, Hitler interfered more and more in operations, both offensive and defensive. Although this interference has been exaggerated as a kind of universal German alibi for any defeat, it is true that the German forces gradually lost the flexibility and subordinate initiative that had made them so successful. A few brilliant commanders were permitted to make their own decisions as late as 1945, but, if they failed, they were soon replaced by men too timid to even request the authority to maneuver. *Führungsoffiziers*, the Nazi equivalent of political commissars, began to appear in German headquarters, and commanders who suffered defeat for any reason were lucky to escape with their lives. Under these circumstances, the German soldier's principal motivation became simple survival. At the tactical level, only the most fanatical Nazis had any faith in ultimate victory, but every German feared to surrender to a seemingly inhuman enemy.

The Red Army painfully developed effective leaders, organizations, weapons, and tactics, in the process returning to its prewar concepts of warfare. During the second period of war, from late 1942 through 1943, the army blossomed into a force that not only could halt the fabled Blitzkrieg offensive but could also conduct its own offensives in all types of weather and terrain. German accounts of overwhelming Soviet forces are really a tribute to the Soviet ability to deceive their opponents and concentrate all available forces on a narrow frontage at an unpredictable point. As a result, the Red Army was able to decimate the Wehrmacht, establishing the overall numerical superiority that characterized the last two years of the war. Even then, however, Soviet manpower was not inexhaustible, and the Soviet commanders increasingly attempted to avoid expensive frontal assaults whenever possible.[24]

Of course, Red Army commanders continued to make costly mistakes as late as the Battle of Berlin, but the officer corps became steadily more competent and trusted. Communist ideology was, in large measure, supplanted by patriotism and by the daily demands of the struggle. Political officers confined themselves to matters of morale and propaganda, and even Stalin began to trust his subordinates as professional experts. The all-powerful "representatives of the *Stavka*" gave way to separate *front* or multi-*front* headquarters and finally to decentralized authority throughout the chain of command. It is true that, during the last few campaigns of 1945, Stalin inserted himself as overall field commander in order to preserve his political status. Yet even this action was a vote of confidence in his officers. Except for key political, strategic, and operational decisions, Stalin could and did leave the conduct of these campaigns and operations to the *front* commanders and their staffs. He had enough faith in the Red Army to allow it to conclude the war, knowing that his own prestige would only be enhanced by his superbly competent subordinates.

These subordinates had developed their own procedures and techniques for conducting mechanized warfare on a massive scale. By 1944, the typical Soviet offensive was preceded by careful planning and deception measures, designed to concentrate forces at the designated breakthrough point. The attack began with a wave of reconnaissance battalions that infiltrated the German defenses and seized key positions, thereby rendering the rest of the German positions untenable. This infiltration was accompanied or followed by massive, carefully orchestrated air and artillery offensives. When the whirlwinds of artillery fire shifted from the front lines toward the German rear areas, infantry, heavy armor, and engineers conducted the conventional assault to eliminate the remaining centers of German resistance. As quickly as possible, senior Soviet commanders committed their mobile forces through the resulting gaps. Although the tank armies and separate mobile corps were large formations commanded by experienced general officers, much of their tactical success depended on the work of the young captains and majors who commanded the leading forward detachments. These highly mobile, combined-arms groups of 800 to 2,000 soldiers avoided pitched battle whenever possible, bypassing German defenders in order to establish large encirclements and seize the bridgeheads for the next offensive. Follow-on rifle forces, supported by the increasingly powerful Red Air Force, then reduced the German encirclements, while the mobile forces continued their exploitation. Throughout these offensives, the Rear Services performed prodigious feats of improvisation to keep the spearheads supplied even 400 kilometers behind enemy lines. Just as in the German offensives of 1941–1942, the later Soviet attacks were often halted by logistical overextension rather than by enemy action.

Thus, in June 1941, a preeminent law of physics experienced its ultimate test when the universally recognized irresistible force of the Wehrmacht struck the seemingly immovable Red Army. The immovable object bent and bled but did not break. In four years of combat, which consumed immense resources and energy, the Red Army survived and prevailed. In a struggle whose effects Stalin later likened to an atomic war, the irresistible force of the Wehrmacht was totally destroyed.

WAR AND THE SOVIET STATE

The Soviets' enormously sophisticated war-fighting capability redounded to the credit not only of Stalin but of his entire government. The German invasion gave the communist regime unprecedented legitimacy as the organizer of victory. Men and women who had been apathetic about that regime could not avoid physical and emotional involvement in the struggle against the invader. By emphasizing patriotism rather than Marxist purity, the Communists identified themselves with the survival of the entire nation. In the process, soldiers found it much easier to obtain membership in the Communist Party and in the Komsomol, giving the Communists a more pervasive, if less obtrusive, hold on the army and the entire country. During and even after the war, virtually the entire Soviet population was united by the drive to expel the Germans and the determination to prevent any repetition of the horrors of 1941–1942.

Yet after the war, the Soviets became in some sense prisoners of their own success. Although the Red (later Soviet) Army was scaled back, it still occupied pride of place in the Soviet government, and all postwar Soviet leaders struggled to limit both the political and the budgetary impact of the defense forces. The Soviet economy, already stunted by its wartime experiences, was forced to allocate its most valuable resources to defense.

More generally, the German invasion had reinforced the traditional and justified Russian fear of invasion. The Great Patriotic War, with its devastation and suffering, colored the strategic thinking of an entire generation of Soviet leaders. Postwar Soviet governments created an elaborate system of buffer and client states, designed to insulate the Soviet Union from any possible attack. Although the Warsaw Pact countries contributed to Soviet defense and to the Soviet economy, their rebellious populations were a recurring threat to the regime's sense of security. Outposts such as Cuba and Vietnam might appear to be useful gambits in the Cold War struggle with the West, but they represented further drains on the Soviet economy. In the long run, the Soviet government probably lost as much as it gained from the buffer and client states.

In retrospect, the determination to preserve the fruits of victory and preclude any future attack was a dangerous burden for the Moscow government. This determination, accompanied by huge military spending and ill-conceived foreign commitments, was a permanent handicap that helped doom the Soviet economy and with it the Soviet state.

Appendixes: Statistical Tables

Table A. Red Army Personnel Losses, 22 June 1941–9 May 1945

| | RED ARMY PERSONNEL LOSSES | | | |
Period	Average Strength (monthly)	Killed or Missing	Wounded and Sick	Total
1941, 3d Quarter	3,334,000	2,067,801	676,964	2,744,765
1941, 4th Quarter	2,818,500	926,002	637,327	1,563,329
Yearly Total	3,024,900	2,993,803	1,314,291	4,308,094
1942, 1st Quarter	4,186,000	619,167	1,172,274	1,791,441
1942, 2d Quarter	5,060,300	776,578	702,150	1,478,728
1942, 3d Quarter	5,664,600	1,141,991	1,276,810	2,418,801
1942, 4th Quarter	6,343,600	455,800	936,031	1,391,831
Yearly Total	5,313,600	2,993,536	4,087,265	7,080,801
1943, 1st Quarter	5,892,800	656,403	1,421,140	2,077,543
1943, 2d Quarter	6,459,800	125,172	471,724	596,896
1943, 3d Quarter	6,816,800	694,465	2,053,492	2,747,957
1943, 4th Quarter	6,387,200	501,087	1,560,164	2,061,251
Yearly Total	6,389,200	1,977,127	5,506,520	7,483,647
1944, 1st Quarter	6,268,600	470,392	1,565,431	2,035,823
1944, 2d Quarter	6,447,000	251,745	956,828	1,208,573
1944, 3d Quarter	6,714,300	430,432	1,541,965	1,972,397
1944, 4th Quarter	6,770,100	259,766	1,026,645	1,286,411
Yearly Total	6,550,000	1,412,335	5,090,869	6,503,204
1945, 1st Quarter	6,461,100	468,407	1,582,517	2,050,924
1945, 2d Quarter	6,135,300	163,226	609,231	772,457
Yearly Total	6,330,880	631,633	2,191,748	2,823,381
Wartime Totals		10,008,434	18,190,693	28,199,127

Total Armed Forces Losses by Category

	Number (%)
Irrevocable	
Killed in battle or died during evacuation	5,187,190 (17.5)
Died of wounds in hospital	1,100,327 (3.7)
Died of illness (nonbattle)	541,920 (1.8)
Missing in action or captured	4,455,620 (15.1)
Total	11,285,057 (38.1)
Sanitary	
Wounded	15,205,592 (51.3)
Sick	3,047,675 (10.3)
Frostbitten	90,881 (0.3)
Total	18,344,148 (61.9)
Total armed forces losses	29,629,205

Note: Red Army personnel losses include those of the air force.

Table B. Soviet Wartime Strength and Losses

Operation	PERSONNEL LOSSES				MATERIÉL LOSSES		
	Strength	Killed or Missing	Wounded	Total	Tanks and SP Guns	Artillery	Aircraft
First Period of War (22 June 41–8 Nov. 42)							
Baltic Defense (22 June–7 Sept. 41)	498,000	75,202	13,284	88,486	2,523	3,561	990
Defense in Belorussia (22 June–7 Sept. 41)	627,300	341,073	76,717	417,790	4,799	9,427	1,777
Defense in Ukraine (22 June–6 July 41)	864,600	172,323	69,271	241,594	4,381	5,806	1,218
Northern Defense (29 June–10 Oct. 41)	358,390	67,265	68,448	135,713	546	540	64
Kiev Defense (7 July–26 Sept. 41)	627,000	616,304	84,240	700,544	411	28,419	343
Defense in Moldavia (1 July–26 July 41)	364,700	8,519	9,374	17,893			
Leningrad Defense (10 July–30 Sept. 41)	517,000	214,078	130,848	344,926	1,492	9,885	1,702
Odessa Defense (5 Aug.–16 Oct. 41)	34,500	16,578	24,690	41,268			
Battle of Smolensk (10 July–10 Sept. 41)	581,600	214,078	130,848	344,926	1,348	9,290	903
El'nia Offensive (30 Aug.–8 Sept. 41)	103,200	10,701	21,152	31,853			

Table B. (Continued)

Operation	Strength	PERSONNEL LOSSES			MATERIÉL LOSSES		
		Killed or Missing	Wounded	Total	Tanks and SP Guns	Artillery	Aircraft
Donbas-Rostov Defense (29 Sept.–16 Nov. 41)	541,600	143,313	17,263	160,576	101	3,646	240
Tikhvin Defense (16 Oct.–18 Nov. 41)	135,700	22,743	17,846	40,589			
Crimean Defense (18 Oct.–16 Nov. 41)	235,600	48,438	15,422	63,860			
Moscow Defense (30 Sept.–5 Nov. 41)	1,250,000	514,338	143,941	658,279	2,785	3,832	293
Tikhvin Offensive (10 Nov.–30 Dec. 41)	192,950	17,924	30,977	48,901	70	2,293	82
Rostov Offensive (17 Nov.–2 Dec. 41)	349,000	15,264	17,847	33,111	42	1,017	42
Sevastopol Defense (30 Oct. 41–4 July 42)	52,000	156,800	43,601	200,481			
Moscow Offensive (5 Dec. 41–7 Jan. 42)	1,021,700	139,586	231,369	370,955	429	13,350	140
Kerch-Feodosiia Offensive (25 Dec. 41–2 Jan. 42)	82,500	32,453	9,482	41,935	35	133	39
Liuban' Offensive (7 Jan.–30 April 42)	325,700	95,064	213,303	308,367			
Demiansk Offensive (7 Jan.–20 May 42)	105,700	88,908	156,603	245,511			

Bolkhov Offensive (8 Jan.–20 April 42)	317,000	21,319	39,807	61,126			
Rzhev-Viaz'ma Offensive (8 Jan.–20 April 42)	1,059,200	272,320	504,569	776,889	957	7,296	550
Toropets-Kholm Offensive (9 Jan.–6 Feb. 42)	122,100	10,400	18,810	29,210			
Barvenkovo-Lozovaia Offensive (18 Jan.–31 Jan. 42)	204,000	11,095	29,786	40,881			
Kerch Defense (8 May–19 May 42)	249,800	162,282	14,284	176,566			
Khar'kov Offensive (12 May–29 May 42)	765,300	170,958	106,232	277,190			
Liuban' Relief (13 May–10 July 42)	231,900	54,774	39,977	94,751			
Voronezh-Vorosh Defense (28 June–24 July 42)	1,310,800	370,522	197,825	568,347	2,436	13,716	783
Stalingrad Defense (17 July–18 Nov. 42)	547,000	323,856	319,986	643,842	1,426	12,137	2,063
N. Cauc. Defense (25 July–31 Dec. 42)	603,200	192,791	181,120	373,911	990	5,049	644
Rzhev-Sychevka Offensive (30 July–23 Aug. 42)	345,100	51,482	142,201	193,683			
Siniavinsk Offensive (19 Aug.–10 Oct. 42)	190,000	40,085	73,589	113,674			
Second Period of War (19 Nov. 42–31 Dec. 43)							
Stalingrad Offensive (19 Nov. 42–2 Feb. 43)	1,143,500	154,885	330,892	485,777	2,915	3,591	706

Table B. (*Continued*)

| Operation | PERSONNEL LOSSES | | | | MATERIÉL LOSSES | | |
	Strength	Killed or Missing	Wounded	Total	Tanks and SP Guns	Artillery	Aircraft
Rzhev-Sychevka Offensive (24 Nov.–16 Dec. 42)	1,400,000	260,000	500,000	760,000	1,847	1,100	120
Velikie Luki Offensive (24 Nov. 42–20 Jan. 43)	86,700	31,674	72,348	104,022			
N. Cauc. Offensive (1 Jan.–4 Feb. 43)	1,145,300	69,627	84,912	154,539	220	895	236
Leningrad Offensive (Dec. 42–30 Jan. 43)	302,800	33,940	81,142	115,082	41	417	41
Voronezh-Khar'kov Offensive (13 Jan.–3 April 43)	502,400	55,475	98,086	53,561	1,023	2,106	307
Krasnodar Offensive (9 Feb.–24 May 43)	390,000	66,814	173,902	240,176			
Demiansk Offensive (15 Feb.–28 Feb. 43)	327,600	10,016	23,647	33,663			
Rzhev-Viaz'ma Offensive (Feb.–31 March 43)	876,000	38,862	9,715	138,577			
Khar'kov Defensive (April–25 March 43)	345,900	45,219	41,250	86,569	322	3,185	110
Kursk Defensive (May–23 July 43)	1,272,700	70,330	107,517	177,847	1,614	3,929	459
Orel Offensive (12 July–18 Aug. 43)	1,287,600	112,529	317,361	429,890	2,586	892	1,104

Operation						
Mga Offensive, Leningrad (22 July–22 Aug. 43)	253,300	20,890	59,047	79,937		
Belgorod-Khar'kov Offensive (March–23 Aug. 43)	1,144,000	71,611	183,955	255,566	1,864	423	153
Smolensk Offensive (7 Aug.–2 Oct. 43)	1,252,600	107,645	343,821	451,466	863	243	303
Donbas Offensive (13 Aug.–22 Sept. 43)	1,011,900	66,166	207,356	273,522	886	814	327
Chernigov-Poltava Offensive (26 Aug.–30 Sept. 43)	1,581,300	102,957	324,995	427,952	1,140	916	269
Briansk Offensive (1 Sept.–3 Oct. 43)	530,000	13,033	43,624	56,657		
Novorossiisk-Taman' Offensive (10 Sept.–9 Oct. 43)	317,400	14,564	50,946	65,510	111	70	240
Lower Dnepr Offensive (26 Sept.–20 Dec. 43)	1,506,400	173,201	581,191	754,392	2,639	3,125	430
Melitopol' Offensive (26 Sept.–5 Nov. 43)	555,300	42,760	155,989	198,749		
Nevel'-Gorodok Offensive (6 Oct.–31 Dec. 43)	198,000	43,551	125,351	168,902		
Zaporozhe Offensive (10 Oct.–14 Oct. 43)	150,500	3,443	14,265	17,708		
Kerch-Eltigen Offensive (31 Oct.–11 Dec. 43)	150,000	6,985	20,412	27,397		
Kiev Offensive (March–13 Nov. 43)	671,000	6,491	24,078	30,569	271	104	125
Gomel'-Rechitsa Offensive (10 Nov.–30 Nov. 43)	761,300	21,650	66,556	88,206		

Table B. (Continued)

| Operation | PERSONNEL LOSSES | | | | MATERIÉL LOSSES | | |
	Strength	Killed or Missing	Wounded	Total	Tanks and SP Guns	Artillery	Aircraft
Kiev Defensive (13 Nov.–22 Dec. 43)	730,000	26,443	61,030	87,473			
Third Period of War (1 Jan. 44–9 May 45)							
Right Bank of Ukraine Offensive (24 Dec. 43–17 April 44)	2,406,100	270,198	839,330	1,109,528	4,666	7,532	676
Zhitomir-Berdichev Offensive (24 Dec. 43–14 Jan. 44)	831,000	23,163	76,855	100,018			
Kalinkovichi-Mozyr' Offensive (8–30 Jan. 44)	232,600	12,350	43,807	56,157			
Korsen'-Shevchenkovskii Offensive (24 Jan.–17 Feb. 44)	336,700	24,286	55,902	80,188			
Rogachev-Zhlobin Offensive (21–26 Feb. 44)	232,000	7,164	24,113	31,277			
Leningrad-Novgorod Offensive (14 Jan.–1 April 44)	822,100	76,686	237,267	313,953	462	1,832	260
Crimean Offensive (8 April–12 May 44)	462,400	17,754	67,065	84,819	171	521	179
Vyborg-Petrozavodsk Offensive (10 June–9 Aug. 44)	451,500	23,674	72,701	96,375	294	489	311
Belorussian Offensive (23 June–29 Aug. 44)	2,441,600	180,040	590,848	770,888	2,957	2,447	822

Operation						
Rezekne-Dvinsk Offensive (10–27 July 44)	391,200	12,880	45,115	57,995			
Pskov-Ostrov Offensive (11–31 July 44)	258,400	7,633	25,951	33,584			
L'vov-Sandomierz Offensive (13 July–29 Aug. 44)	1,002,200	65,001	224,295	289,296	1,269	1,832	289
Madona Offensive (1–28 Aug. 44)	390,000	14,669	50,737	65,406			
Tartu Offensive (10 Aug.–6 Sept. 44)	272,800	16,292	55,514	71,806			
Iassy-Kishinev Offensive (20–29 Aug. 44)	1,314,200	13,197	53,933	67,130	75	108	111
East Carpathian Offensive (8 Sept.–28 Oct. 44)	378,000	28,473	103,437	131,910	478	962	192
Baltic Offensive (14 Sept.–24 Nov. 44)	1,546,400	61,468	218,622	280,090	522	2,593	779
Belgrade Offensive (28 Sept.–20 Oct. 44)	300,000	4,350	14,488	12,740	53	184	66
Petsamo-Kirkenes Offensive (7–29 Oct. 44)	133,500	6,084	15,149	21,233	21	40	62
Debrecen Offensive (6–28 Oct. 44)	698,200	19,713	64,297	84,010			
Goldap Offensive (16–30 Oct. 44)	377,300	16,819	62,708	79,527			
Budapest Offensive (29 Oct. 44–13 Feb. 45)	719,500	80,026	240,056	320,082	1,766	4,127	293
Vistula-Oder Offensive (12 Jan.–3 Feb. 45)	2,203,600	43,476	150,715	194,191	1,267	374	343

Table B. (Continued)

| Operation | PERSONNEL LOSSES | | | | MATERIÉL LOSSES | | | |
	Strength	Killed or Missing	Wounded	Total	Tanks and SP Guns	Artillery	Aircraft
West. Carpathian Offensive (12 Jan.–18 Feb. 45)	593,000	19,080	72,852	91,932	359	753	94
East Prussian Offensive (13 Jan.–25 April 45)	1,669,100	126,464	458,314	584,778	3,525	1,644	1,450
Lower Silesian Offensive (8–24 Feb. 45)	980,000	23,577	75,809	99,386			
East Pomerania Offensive (10 Feb.–4 April 45)	996,100	55,315	179,045	234,360	1,027	1,005	1,073
Balaton Defensive (6–15 March 45)	465,000	8,492	24,407	32,899			
Upper Silesian Offensive (15–31 March 45)	408,400	15,876	50,925	66,801			
Morava-Ostrava Offensive (10 March–5 May 45)	317,300	23,964	88,657	112,621			
Vienna Offensive (16 March–15 April 45)	745,600	41,359	136,386	177,745	603	764	614
Bratislava-Brno Offensive (25 March–5 May 45)	272,200	16,933	62,663	79,596			
Berlin Offensive (16 April–8 May 45)	2,062,100	81,116	280,251	361,367	1,997	2,108	917
Prague Offensive (6–11 May 45)	2,028,100	11,997	40,501	52,498	373	1,006	80
Manchuria Offensive (9 Aug.–2 Sept. 45)	1,685,500	12,103	24,550	36,653	78	232	62

Table C. Comparative Strengths of Combat Forces, Eastern Front, 1941–1945

Date	Soviet	Soviet Allies	Correlation	German	German Allies
22 June 1941	2,680,000 (Western MDs); 5,500,000 (overall) 12,000,000 (mobilizable)		1 : 1.4	3,050,000 (eastern Europe) 67,000 (northern Norway)	500,000 Finns, 150,000 Rumanians Total 3,767,000
11 Sept. 1941	3,463,000 (front); 7,400,000 (overall)		1 : 1.16	3,315,000 (Eastern Front) 67,000 (northern Norway)	500,000 Finns, 150,000 Rumanians Total 4,022,000
1 Nov. 1941	2,200,000 (front)		1 : 1.9	2,800,000 (Eastern Front) 67,000 (northern Norway)	500,000 Finns, 150,000 Rumanians Total 3,517,000
1 Dec. 1941	4,197,000 (front)		1.23 : 1	2,700,000 (Eastern Front) 67,000 (northern Norway)	500,000 Finns, 140,000 Rumanians Total 3,407,000
7 March 1942	4,663,697 (front); 397,978 (hospital); 9,597,802 (total)		1.34 : 1	2,500,000 (Eastern Front) 80,000 (northern Norway)	450,000 Finns, 140,000 Rumanians, 300,000 Hungarians and Italians Total 3,470,000

Table C. (Continued)

Date	Soviet	Soviet Allies	Correlation	German	German Allies
5 May 1942	5,449,898 (front); 414,400 (hospital); 8,950,000 (total)		1.52 : 1	2,550,000 (Eastern Front) 80,000 (northern Norway)	450,000 Finns, 500,000 Rumanians, Hungarians, and Italians Total 3,580,000
7 June 1942	5,313,000 (front); 383,000 (hospital); 9,350,000 (total)		1.42 : 1	2,600,000 (Eastern Front) 90,000 (northern Norway)	430,000 Finns, 600,000 Rumanians, Hungarians, and Italians Total 3,720,000
5 July 1942	5,647,000 (front); 298,480 (hospital); 9,205,000 (total)		1.50 : 1	2,600,000 (Eastern Front) 90,000 (northern Norway)	430,000 Finns, 620,000 Rumanians, Hungarians, and Italians Total 3,740,000
6 Aug. 1942	5,772,000 (front); 301,960 (hospital); 9,332,000 (total)		1.58 : 1	2,500,000 (Eastern Front) 100,000 (northern Norway)	400,000 Finns, 650,000 Rumanians, Hungarians, and Italians Total 3,650,000
7 Oct. 1942	5,912,000 (front); 476,670 (hospital); 9,254,000 (total)		1.62 : 1	2,490,000 (Eastern Front) 100,000 (northern Norway)	400,000 Finns, 648,000 Rumanians, Hungarians, and Italians Total 3,638,000

Date	German strength	Ratio	Soviet strength	Allied strength
1 Nov. 1942	6,124,000 (front); 9,300,000 (est total)	1.74 : 1	2,400,000 (Eastern Front) 100,000 (northern Norway)	400,000 Finns, 600,000 Rumanians, Hungarians, and Italians Total 3,500,000
2 Feb. 1943	6,101,000 (front); 659,000 (hospital); 9,455,000 (total)	2.03 : 1	2,200,000 (Eastern Front) 100,000 (northern Norway)	400,000 Finns, 300,000 Rumanians, Hungarians, and Italians Total 3,000,000
3 April 1943	5,792,000 (front); 674,000 (hospital); 9,486,000 (total)	1.68 : 1	2,732,000 (Eastern Front) 100,000 (northern Norway)	400,000 Finns, 200,000 Rumanians and Hungarians Total 3,432,000
9 July 1943 (20 July 1943 for the Germans, but probably pre-Kursk strength)	6,724,000 (front); 446,445 (hospital); 10,300,000 (total)	1.71 : 1	3,403,000 (Eastern Front) 80,000 (northern Norway)	400,000 Finns, 150,000 Rumanians and Hungarians Total 3,933,000
27 July 1943	6,903,000 (front); 354,500 (hospital); 10,547,000 (total)	1.86 : 1	3,064,000 (Eastern Front) 80,000 (northern Norway)	400,000 Finns, 150,000 Rumanians and Hungarians Total 3,694,000
14 Oct. 1943	6,600,000 (est-front); 10,200,000 (est total); (6,165,000 on 1 Jan. 1944)	2:15 : 1	2,498,000 (Eastern Front) 70,000 (northern Norway)	350,000 Finns, 150,000 Rumanians and Hungarians Total 3,068,000

Table C. (*Continued*)

Date	Soviet	Soviet Allies	Correlation	German	German Allies
12 March 1944 (1 April 1944 for the Germans)	6,394,000 (front); 727,000 (hospital); 9,980,000 (total)		2.20 : 1	2,336,000 (Eastern Front) 70,000 (northern Norway)	300,000 Finns, 198,000 Rumanian and Hungarians Total 2,904,000
1 May 1944	6,425,000 (23 June)		1.91 : 1	2,460,000 (Eastern Front) 60,000 (northern Norway)	300,000 Finns, 550,000 Rumanians and Hungarians Total 3,370,000
1 July 1944	6,800,000 (est-front)		2.17 : 1	1,996,000 (Eastern Front) 60,000 (northern Norway)	200,000 Finns, 774,000 Rumanians and Hungarians Total 3,130,000
1 Sept. 1944	6,600,000 (est-front)	100,000 Poles and Czechs	2.64 : 1	2,042,000 (Eastern Front) 50,000 (northern Norway)	180,000 Finns, 271,000 Hungarians Total 2,542,000
1 Oct. 1944	6,600,000 (est-front)	210,000 Poles, Rumanians, and Czechs	3.22 : 1	1,790,138	320,000 Hungarians Total 2,110,000
1 Nov. 1944	6,500,000 (est-front)	210,000 Poles, Rumanians, and Czechs	3.02 : 1	2,030,000	190,000 Hungarians Total 2,220,000
1 Jan. 1945	6,532,000	360,000 Poles, Rumanians, Bulgarians, and Czechs	2.96 : 1	2,230,000	100,000 Hungarians Total 2,330,000

Date					
1 March 1945	6,332,000	3.22 : 1	2,000,000	450,000 Poles, Rumanians, Bulgarians, and Czechs	100,000 Hungarians Total 2,100,000
1 April 1945	6,410,000	3.50 : 1	1,960,000	450,000 Poles, Rumanians, Bulgarians, and Czechs	Total 1,960,000
8 May 1945	5,700,000	4.10 : 1	1,510,000	450,000 Poles, Rumanians, Bulgarians, and Czechs	Total 1,510,000

German Sources:

Earl F. Ziemke, *From Stalingrad to Berlin: The German Defeat in the East* (Washington, D.C.: U.S. Army Center of Military History, 1968), 9, 18–19, 144, 412–413, 457, 498.

Fremde Heere Ost comparative strength reports for 1. 4. 43; 20. 7. 43; 14. 10. 43; 1. 5. 44; 1. 6. 44; 1. 8. 44; 1. 9. 44; and 1. 11. 44.

Soviet Sources:

G.F. Krivosheev, *Grif sekretnosti sniat: Poteri vooruzhennykh sil SSSR v voinakh, boevykh deistviiahk, i voennykh konfliktakh* [Losses of the armed forces of the USSR in wars, combat actions, and military conflicts] [Moscow: Voenizdat, 1993], 152–153.

Voennoe iskusstva vo vtoroi mirovoi voine (Moscow: Voenizdat, 1973), 171. Textbook, for internal use only by the Voroshilov Academy of the General Staff. Soviet strength data is accurate, but German strength is grossly inflated.

TsPA UML (Central Party Archives of the Institute of Marxism and Leninism), which include:

State Committee of Defense (GKO) Decree of 11. 9. 41 (f. 644, op. 1, d. 9).

GKO Decree of 7. 3. 42 (f. 644, op. 1, d. 23, l. 127–129).

GKO Decree of 5. 5. 42 (f. 644, op. 1, d. 33, l. 48–50).

GKO Decree of 7. 6. 42 (f. 644, op. 1, d. 39, l. 74–78, 170).

GKO Decree of 5. 7. 42 (f. 644, op. 1, d. 41, l. 163–165).

GKO Decree of 6. 8. 42 (f. 644, op. 1, d. 50, l. 71–74).

GKO Decree of 7. 10. 42 (f. 644, op. 1, d. 61, l. 88–91).

GKO Decree of 2. 2. 43 (f. 644, op. 1, d. 85, l. 95–95).

GKO Decree of 3. 4. 43 (f. 644, op. 1, d. 100, l. 117–118).

GKO Decree of 9. 6. 43 (f. 644, op. 1, d. 125, l. 35–36).

GKO Decree of 27. 7. 43 (f. 644, op. 1, d. 138, l. 205–206, 208).

GKO Decree of 12. 3. 44 (f. 644, op. 1, d. 218, l. 1, 49, 101–104).

Table D. Soviet Weapons Production, 1941–1945

Soviet Weapons Production[a]

Year	Rifles	Tanks and SP Guns	Guns and Mortars	Combat Aircraft	Combat Ships
1941	1,760,000	4,700	53,600	8,200	35
1942	5,910,000	24,500	287,000	21,700	15
1943	5,920,000	24,100	126,000	29,900	14
1944	4,860,000	29,000	47,300	33,200	4
1945 (Jan.–Apr.)	1,380,000	16,000	11,300	8,200	2
Total	19,830,000	98,300	525,200	122,100	70

Red Army Weaponry Strength 1941–1945[b]

Date	Tanks and SP Guns		Guns and Mortars (over 50 mm)		Combat Aircraft	
	Total	Field Forces	Total	Field Forces	Total	Field Forces
22 June 41	22,600	14,200	76,500	32,900	20,000	9,200
1 Jan. 42	7,700	2,200	48,600	30,000	12,000	5,400
1 Jan. 43	20,600	8,100	161,600	91,400	21,900	12,300
1 Jan. 44	24,400	5,800	244,400	101,400	32,500	13,400
1 Jan. 45	35,400	8,300	244,400	114,600	43,300	21,500
9 May 45	35,200	8,100	239,600	94,400	47,300	22,300

Red Army Weaponry Losses

Year	Tanks and SP Guns	Guns and Mortars (over 50 mm) (%)	Combat Aircraft (%)
1941	20,500 (72.7)	63,100 (59)	17,900 (34.4)
1942	15,100 (42.3)	70,300 (32)	12,100 (22.9)
1943	23,500 (49.1)	25,300 (9)	22,500 (20.4)
1944	23,700 (40.1)	43,300 (15)	24,800 (14.2)
1945	13,700 (28)	16,000 (4)	11,000 (7)
Total	96,500 (73.3)	218,000 (48)	88,300 (31.8)

[a]Source: G.F. Krivosheev, *Grif sekretnosti sniat: Poteri vooruzhennykh sil SSSR v voinakh, boevykh deistviiakh, i voennykl konfliktakh* [Losses of the armed forces of the USSR in wars, combat actions, and military conflicts] (Moscow: Voenizdat, 1993), 349.
[b]Source: Krivosheev, *Grif sekretnosti*, 350.

Table E. Wehrmacht Casualties in World War II, 1939–1945

Permanent Losses
(dead, missing, or disabled)

Sept. 1939–1 Sept. 1942	922,000 (14% of total force)*
1 Sept. 1942–20 Nov. 1943	2,077,000 (30% of total force)*
20 Nov. 1943–June 1944	1,500,000 (est.)
June–Nov. 1944	1,457,000*
Dec. 1944–30 April 1945	2,000,000**

Losses

Total to 30 April 1945	11,135,800 (including 6,035,000 wounded)**
Total armed forces losses to war's end	13,448,000, including wounded (75% of mobilized force and 46% of 1939 male population)**

Krivosheev, 391, places the Eastern Front losses of Germany's allies at 1,725,800, broken down as follows:

Nation	Dead and Missing	POWs	Total
Hungary	350,000	513,700	863,700
Italy	45,000	48,900	93,900
Rumania	480,000	201,800	681,800
Finland	84,000	2,400	86,400
Total	959,000	766,800	1,725,800

Krivosheev, 392, cites Soviet POW figures and deaths (in Soviet captivity) as follows:

Germany	2,389,600	450,600
Austria	156,000	N/A
Hungary	513,700	54,700
Rumania	201,800	40,000
Italy	48,975	N/A
Finland	2,400	N/A
Others (French, Czech, Slovak, Belgium, and Spanish in SS and auxilliary formations)	464,147	N/A
Total	3,777,290	

Sources:
*Earl F. Ziemke, *From Stalingrad to Berlin: The German Defeat in the East* (Washington D.C., U.S. Army Center of Military History, 1968), 213–214, 412.
**G. F. Krivosheev, *Grif sekretnosti sniat: Poteri vooruzhennykh sil SSSR v voinakh, boevykh deistviiakh i voennykh konfliktakh* [Losses of the armed forces of the USSR in wars, combat actions, and military conflicts] (Moscow: Voenizdat, 1993), 384–392, places German dead at 3,888,000 and POWs (including Austrians, SS, and foreign auxiliaries in the German Army) at 3,035,700.

Although a vast literature exists on the German-Soviet War, much of this work has suffered from the inaccessibility of Soviet military accounts and the lack of Soviet archival materials. Fascinating as they are, the popular memoirs of Heinz Guderian, F. W. von Mellenthin, and Erich von Manstein describe a war against a faceless enemy, a host that has no concrete form nor precise features. In short, other than sensing the size and power of their foe and the ferocity and inhumanity of combat, they knew not what they fought. Talented historians, such as Earl Ziemke, Albert Seaton, and many others, have left a legacy of superb works, but try as they did to reconstruct the Soviet face of war, much of their primary material remained German.

A few historians, through their linguistic talents or unique access to Soviet sources, have been able to expose the nature of Soviet participation in war. Foremost among this small group is John Erickson, whose massive tomes *Moscow to Stalingrad* and *Stalingrad to Berlin* will remain military classics. Yet even Erickson would admit that, although much of his work has withstood the archival test, he would have preferred to have had greater access to Soviet archives when these works were written.

Given the long-standing archival problem with Eastern Front history and the fact that Soviet archival materials are now becoming available, it is proper here to review briefly the archival materials upon which this book is based.

GERMAN ARCHIVAL MATERIALS

A vast quantity of German archival material exists upon which to construct an account of the war on the Eastern Front. Much of this material was captured by the Allied armies at war's end, and the portions captured by U.S. and British forces have been made readily accessible to historians through their respective archive systems. Materials that fell exclusively into Soviet hands, however, remain inaccessible to Western scholars. Although the extent of this material is obscure, it certainly includes the records of those military formations that were destroyed or captured by the

Red Army during the course of combat in eastern and central Europe. This includes, for example, the combat records of German Ninth and Sixth Armies, portions of which have now been shown but not released to Western scholars.

Among the most valuable German records used in the production of this book are the postwar compilations of German archival materials issued in book form and the voluminous German military unit records maintained in the National Archives, Washington, D.C. Most, but not all of these materials have been retained in the archives on microfilm; the originals have been returned to the custody of the German archives (in Freiberg). These include:

> The *OKW War Diary*, ed. Percy E. Schramm (Frankfurt a. Main: Bernard und Graefe, 1961-1965), a comprehensive chronological high-level German record of the entire war, and associated diaries by Alfred Jodl, Franz Halder, and other high-level leaders;
>
> OKH *Lage Ost* maps, showing a complete German order of battle and the intelligence assessments of the Soviet order of battle on a daily basis throughout the war. These invaluable wall-size maps have been returned to Germany without microfilm copying;
>
> National Archives Microfilm (NAM) series T-78, the records of Foreign Armies East (*Fremde Heere Ost*), which contains wartime intelligence materials and assessments of all aspects of the Soviet armed forces and military-industrial activity. Most interesting are the assessments of Soviet (and German) strength, order of battle, force composition, strategic and operational intentions, war production, and morale;
>
> NAM series T-311, the records of German Army Groups. Although incomplete, these include periodic situation maps and logs of military activities, operational and intelligence assessments, operational studies, and correspondence between major headquarters. This series also includes some of the records of subordinate armies;
>
> NAM series T-312, the records of German field armies, contains information prepared by the operations department (Ia), intelligence (Ic), quartermaster, and other staff departments subordinate to army headquarters. Large gaps exist, particularly involving the Ninth and Sixth Armies;
>
> NAM series T-313, the records of German panzer groups and armies, which are analogous to those maintained by field armies;
>
> NAM series T-314, the record of German army and panzer corps, similar to those at army level. The most valuable aspects are the war diaries (*Tagebuchen*) and associated periodic maps;

NAM series T-315, the records of German divisions, similar to records maintained at corps level; and

A host of additional archival materials superbly described in some detail in Earl F. Ziemke, *From Stalingrad to Berlin: The German Defeat in the East* (Washington, D.C.: U.S. Army Center of Military History, 1968), 507–510.

SOVIET ARCHIVAL MATERIALS

The "Archives"

The Soviet (Russian) military archives are voluminous but fragmented in nature. Besides the Central State Archives of the Soviet Army (TsGASA) located in Moscow, which contains army military records from 1918–1940, there exist numerous branch archives at other locations associated with various ministries and their subordinate entities.

The Soviet (now Russian) armed forces maintain a network of archives, which include the Central Archives of the Combined Armed Forces [TsAOVS] (formerly the Central Archives of the USSR Ministry of Defense-TsAMO), located at Podolsk, near Moscow; the Central Archives of the Navy, located at Gatchina near Leningrad; the archives of military medical records of the Military-Medical Museum located in Leningrad; and the archives of military districts, army groupings, fleets, flotillas, and military naval bases scattered across the nation.[1] The latter turn over key records to the appropriate Central Archives after a specific period of time.

The Central Archives [TsAOVS] is the largest storehouse of military documentation in Russia (and the CIS). It contains more than 18 million records, with documents from other central military command bodies: the *Stavka;* force branches; armies, special forces headquarters, operational commands, large formations and units; and military institutions, organizations, and enterprises (excluding the Navy). More than 10 million of these records deal with the period from 1941 to 1945. The Central Archives and that of the Navy also supervise the work of the remainder of the military archival system.

The recent increased flow of Soviet and Russian archival materials to the West is heartening but must be viewed in perspective. Collectively, it represents only the tip of the iceberg, and the release has been selective in nature. Some of the materials have been accurate and candid; others have been as inaccurate as some of the existing open source materials published over the past 40 years. All of this, of course, conveys the clear message that some "archival" materials are not really archival at all; instead, they are the products of the system that was so effective at managing information.

Military archival materials released thus far fall into the following categories:

General Staff studies. Prepared by the Directorate for the Study of War Experience and the Military-historical Directorate, they include the following collections:

> *Sbornik materialov po izucheniiu opyta voiny, No. 1–26* [Collection of Materials for the Study of War Experience, No. 1–26] (Moscow: Voenizdat, 1942–1948). Originally classified *sekretno* [secret]. Hereafter cited as *SMPIOV*.
>
> *Sbornik boevykh dokumentov Velikoi Otechestvennoi voiny, Vypusk 1–43* [Collection of Combat Documents of the Great Patriotic War, Issues 1–43] (Moscow: Voenizdat, 1947–1960). Originally classified *sovershenno sekretno* [absolutely secret] or *sekretno*. Hereafter cited as *SBDVOV*.
>
> *Sbornik voenno-istoricheskikh materialov Velikoi Otechestvennoi voiny, Vypusk 1–19* [Collection of Military-historical materials of the Great Patriotic War, Issues 1–19] (Moscow: Voenizdat, 1949–1968). Originally classified *sekretno*. Hereafter cited as *SVIMVOV*.
>
> *Sbornik takticheskikh primerov po opytu Otechestvennoi voiny, No's 1–23* [Collection of Tactical Examples Based on the Experience of the Patriotic War, No. 1–23] (Moscow: Voenizdat, 1942–1947). Originally classified *sekretno*. Hereafter cited as *STPPOOV*.

Studies by the Naval Staff, which to date include:

> *Sbornik materialov po opytu boevoi deiatel'nosti Voenno-Morskogo Flota SSSR, No. 1–39* [Collection of Materials Based on the Experiences of the U.S.S.R.'s Naval Fleets' Combat Activities, No. 1–39] (Moscow: Main Naval Staff, NKVMF, U.S.S.R., 1943–1950). Originally classified *sekretno*. Hereafter cited as *SMPOBDVMF*.

U.S.S.R. Ministry of Defense, Institute of Military History, which to date include:

> *Informatsionnyi biulleten', T. 1–89* [Informational bulletins, Vols. 1–89] (Moscow: Military History Institute, 1968–1988). Unclassified, but not released in the West.
>
> *Vestnik voennoi istorii. Nauchnye zapiski, T. 1–2* [Herald of Military History. Scientific Notes, Vols 1–2] (Moscow: Military History Institute, 1970–1971). Unclassified, but not released in the West.

Journals hitherto unavailable to the public, which include:

Voennaia mysl' [Military Thought] (1937–1989).
Voennaia zarubezhnik [Military Foreigner] (1921–1972).
Voina i revoliutsiia [War and Revolution] (1925–1936).
Zarubezhnoe voennoe obozrenie [Foreign Military Review] (1973–1990).
Zhurnal avtobronetankovykh voisk [Journal of Tank Forces] (June 1942–September 1946).

Books. Hitherto unavailable in the West, they include the works of such key interwar-theorists as A. M. Zaionchkovsky, A. A. Svechin, M. N. Tukhachevsky, E. A. Shilovsky, G. Isserson, and others. Most of these works were suppressed by Stalin.

Classified books. Issued in wartime by Voenizdat [the Ministry of Defense publishing house], concerning major wartime operations. Most of these were prepared under General Staff auspices. For example, see B. M. Shaposhnikov, ed., *Razgrom nemetskikh voisk pod Moskvoi, t. 1–3* [The Destruction of German Forces at Moscow, Vols. 1–3] (Moscow: Voenizdat, 1943), classified *sekretno*. Also, similar but shorter volumes on many of the lesser operations of the war, some classified and some unclassified.

Voroshilov Academy of the General Staff. Publications and lecture materials concerning wartime operations, published during and after the war. Some are classified and the remainder are available only to serving officers. They include the following series:

Istoriia voennogo iskusstva. Sbornik materialov, V. 1–5 [History of Military Art. Collection of Materials, Issues 1–5] (Moscow: Voroshilov Academy of the General Staff, 1951–1955).
Dissertations prepared by General Staff Academy students from 1946–1953.

Mobilization materials:

Voiskovaia mobilizatsiia [Force Mobilization] (Moscow: Publications of the Main Directorate of the RKKA, 1926–1930). Issues of a controlled journal published from 1926–1930.
Classified mobilization manuals of the Red Army published in 1939 and 1940 (without key appendices showing linkages between mobilization and war plans).

Frunze Academy materials. For the use of serving officers only, they include:

> *Trudy akademii* [Works of the Academy] (Moscow: 1942–1945).
> Various internal books and lectures of the academy.
> Such special classified studies on High Command conferences as *Stenogrammy vystuplenii na Voennom Soveshchanii 23–29 dekabria 1940 g.* [Stenographic speeches at a military conference, 23–29 December 1940] (Moscow: TsGASA [Central Archives of the Soviet Army], 1940).

Archival materials. Primarily documents published in Soviet and Russian journals, to include:

> *Voenno-istoricheskii zhurnal* [Military-historical journal]. See, for example, "Pervyye dni voiny v dokumentakh" [The First Days of War in Documents], *VIZh,* 5–9 (May-September 1989); "Voennye razvedchiki dokladyvali . . ." [Military intelligence reported], 2–3 (February-March 1989); and "GKO postanovliaet . . ." [The Peoples Commissariat of Defense Decrees], 2–5 (February-May 1992).
> *Izvestiia TsK KPSS* [News of the Central Committee of the Communist Party of the Soviet Union]. See, for example, the extensive series of documents published under the rubric "Iz istoriia Velikoi Otechestvennoi voiny" in nos. 1–12 (January-December 1990) and 1–8 (January-August 1991). Unfortunately, the failed coup and outlawing of the Communist Party ended the publishing life of this journal and this series of documents.

It is important to note that most of these materials, although technically archival, are in some way *processed* and that processing has often affected their content. In addition, these are *released* materials that have found their way to the West largely through commercial conduits.[2] Although release of these materials is welcome, the larger question regarding direct archival access, in the Western sense of the word, remains unanswered. Russian authorities have frequently announced that the archives are open for foreign scholars.[3] I have seen no evidence to date that this is, in fact, true. When archival access has been tested and published as in the case of the officially agreed upon United States search for POW information, the documents were brought to researchers rather than giving researchers the freedom to hunt for documents in the actual archive locations. To date, scholars who claim to have access usually have been limited to peripheral materials or have been provided selected materials on request.

ASSESSMENT OF RELEASED MATERIALS

The most accurate and useful archival materials are those series prepared by various directorates of the General Staff during the period 1942–1968. The work that went into the preparation of these series represents a genuine attempt by the General Staff to establish the truth about the course and consequences of wartime military operations and to harness that truth in the service of improving Soviet army combat performance. For the most part, comparison of these studies with German and Japanese archival records attests to their general accuracy and candor. There are, of course, topics that the General Staff could not address, including some of the most sensitive operations (such as Liuban' 1942, with its Vlasov connection) and those whose conduct raised sensitive political issues, such as the discussions and disputes between *Stavka* (Stalin) and field commanders and the political motives for military decisions. This sort of information remains in the domain of the infamous and elusive "Stalin Archives."

The earliest General Staff series, the war experience collection *SMPIOV*, is the product of a system established in 1942 to exploit the study of war experiences in the service of improving Red Army combat performance. Although earlier attempts had been made to implement such a system at *front*-level, these efforts were uneven, and only after November 1942 did the army-wide program work properly. Numbers 1 to 4 in this series, published between July 1942 and February 1943, contain random reports covering a host of unrelated subjects and are each about 200 pages in length. Subsequent volumes in this series are longer, more substantial, and essentially thematic in nature. Single volumes often cover in detail various aspects of a single major operation. These studies include the following operations: Moscow (No. 5); Stalingrad (Nos. 6–9); Voronezh-Kastornoe (No. 10); Kursk (No. 11); Dnepr River Crossings (No. 12); Mius and Crimea (No. 13); Korsun'–Shevchenkovskii (No. 14); Belorussia (Nos. 15, 17–18); Iassy-Kishinev (No. 19); Budapest (No. 21); L'vov-Sandomiercz (No. 22); Carpathia (No. 23); East Prussia (No. 24); and Vistula–Oder (No. 25). Interspersed among these major studies are several volumes containing shorter studies, cften on functional topics. The final volume, published in 1948, concerns topographical support of combat operations.

Supplementing the war-experience volumes, the even more extensive document series *SBDVOV*, contains directives and orders from *Stavka*, as well as combat documents relating to the activities of all branches and types of Soviet forces. The first 30 volumes (called issues) focus on such functional themes as offense, defense, artillery support, river crossing, engineer support, air defense, troop combat training, armored and mechanized forces, and so on. An exception is Issue 5, which contains selected *Stavka* orders. Issues 31 and 32 changed the focus, providing combat histories of the first four Soviet guards rifle divisions during the period from 22 June to 31 December 1941. These issues paved the way for an even more extensive effort by the General Staff to reconstruct, on a documentary basis, the events of the initial period of war.

The subsequent issues, numbered 33–43, are perhaps the most informative and interesting portions of the document series. These are compilations of combat orders and reports of *fronts*, armies, and corps during the period from 22 June to 5 November 1941, assembled in the fashion of force war diaries. Although their component documents are selective, the coverage is thorough, and they provide a most vivid, candid, and probably accurate portrait of combat during this difficult period. For undetermined reasons, the *SBDVOV* document collection and publication effort ended in 1960. Whether the General Staff intended to continue to re-create war diaries is also unknown. Nevertheless, it is a pity they did not continue the effort beyond November 1941.

The General Staff used the raw materials contained in these and other series, together with the full mass of other archival materials, to prepare more polished studies of major wartime operations. Some of these appeared as multivolume books (such as the Moscow study edited by Shaposhnikov 1943–1945), and others appeared as single-issue operational studies. The latter were published between 1949 and 1968 in the series *SVIMVOV*. While some of these 19 issues describe aspects of multiple operations (such as Issue 1 on the Ostorozhsk-Rossosh', East Pomeranian, and Prague operations), others are devoted to studies of single operations, such as: Iassy-Kishinev (Issue 3); Tallin (Issue 4); East Prussia (Issue 6); Upper Silesia (Issue 8); Ostrogozhsk-Rossosh' (Issue 8); Lower Silesia (Issue 10–11); Voronezh–Kastornoe (Issue 13); Odessa 1941 (Issue 14); and Carpatho–Duklin (Issue 17). Essentially, these issues tend to cover operations of lesser significance than those covered in major books.

Issues 16 and 18 depart from the usual format by including captured German documents relating to the outbreak of war and subsequent German wartime operational planning. Finally, issue 19 contains an interesting and detailed survey of Soviet formation and use of allied (Polish, Czech, Bulgarian, Rumanian, and so on) forces during wartime.

Supplementing these essentially strategic and operational series, the General Staff prepared and published the tactical series *STPPOOV*. The 23 volumes (called numbers) in this series were organized functionally by type of combat action (offense, defense, pursuit, reconnaissance, and the use of types of specialized forces). Of particular interest are the Soviet assessments of German tactics (Nos. 1, 3, 4, and 7), and the tremendous attention paid in these studies to combat actions by fortified regions [*ukreplennie raiony*].

The 39-volume Naval Staff series *SMPOBDVMF* is similar in format to the General Staff war-experience volumes. Single volumes relate in detail the wartime operations of fleets, flotillas, and naval bases, and also cover in detail major naval and amphibious operations by the Soviet submarine force. These seem as accurate and candid as their General Staff counterparts. Although not yet released, there probably exist other naval studies published in more polished book form.

Many books prepared by the General Staff appeared during wartime or during the immediate postwar years. These represent major studies on the most important wartime operations. Shaposhnikov's edited study (in three volumes) of the Moscow operation is a detailed, accurate, and fairly candid account, and its recent release will substantially alter existing historiography on that operation, which is largely based on German sources. Other published studies include major books on the Kursk and Berlin operations (criticized as being politically incorrect at the time of their publication). One hopes that the original or corrected versions will soon be released, together with other major studies the General Staff prepared. These materials, prepared and published during or immediately after the war, were all classified, and their high quality, candor, and accuracy reflected the best traditions of General Staff work. They were, in essence, utilitarian and designed to teach the Red Army how to better conduct combat operations.

Other publications by the General Staff or Ministry of Defense including wartime issues of journals (*Voennaia mysl'* [Military Thought]) and studies prepared by the Voroshilov General Staff Academy and Frunze Academy during and shortly after the war, achieved this same high quality. Interestingly enough, the content of many works published publically before 1965—such as D. Proektor's study of the Carpatho-Dukla operation (1960), V. A. Matsulenko's study of 37th Army in the Iassy-Kishinev operation (1954), K. K. Rokossovsky's Stalingrad study (1965)—closely resemble their classified counterparts. Although accurate in the main, these works leave out statistical data, in particular that relating to correlation of forces and means.

Recently released classified or restricted archival materials published after 1968 lack the substance and accuracy of their wartime and postwar counterparts. In fact, they bear many of the characteristics of open source operational and tactical literature published during the period. They are generally accurate in operational and tactical detail and in their narrative account of events. They are, however, wholly inaccurate regarding the correlation of forces, in particular enemy strength, and they cover up the worst aspects of Soviet combat performance, in particular the specific details of combat disasters. Moreover, their political content is more pervasive and strident than that of the earlier General Staff volumes. This is particularly disturbing when found in the educational materials used at the Voroshilov and Frunze Academies and may explain why many contemporary Russian officers recently have been less than enthusiastic about the study of their operational experiences. They themselves understand that what has been and is taught to them is less than the whole truth. In this sense, release of archival materials will also benefit the Russian military educational system.

Recently released archival materials about the war, originally published between 1965 and 1989, fall into three general categories: Military Institute publications and those of the Voroshilov and Frunze Academies. Undoubtedly other studies exist, but their nature remains unknown. A series of books was published during this period under the imprimatur "Institit," and the two volumes I have seen in this series are substantial. The series, however, remains unavailable outside of official circles, and I have been unable to ascertain who published it. The general characteristics of all available material in these three categories is the same; it lacks the substance, quality, accuracy, and candor of the earlier works.

The Institute of Military History, which may have sponsored the mysterious "Institut" series (but, if so, will not admit it), has published a number of shorter series under the rubrics "Bulletins" and "Notes." The former contain short articles (from 10 to 20 pages) on a wide variety of military subjects; the latter was an attempt to create an institute journal of more substance. The attempt failed after two annual issues. The articles in both of these publications in no way compare with the more substantive work of earlier years, for they are sketchy in detail and more highly politicized in content.

Voroshilov Academy publications, issued in a variety of formats under the imprimatur *VAGSh*, include texts, studies, analytical works, and lectures delivered at the academy. Some of these are multivolume surveys of the history of war and military art, such as a two-volume work edited by the eminent military historian I. E. Shavrov, which were published in revised versions every few years. The most interesting and valuable are the wartime volumes and the collections (*Sborniki*) of wartime materials. In general, the Voroshilov materials are more scholarly in nature and, hence, less inaccurate and political. The studies and lectures from the period after 1968, however, contain the same inaccuracies that are found in other Soviet publications. Frunze Academy publications, which have not been released in as great a number as the Voroshilov materials, share the same characteristics of their Voroshilov counterparts.

Particularly interesting are several special publications released by the Central Archives of the Soviet Army. The first of these are the mobilization regulations [*Ustav*], issued in the years immediately preceding the war and the Red Army's mobilization journal. Although these records cast considerable light on Soviet mobilization capabilities and procedures, the critical appendices linking mobilization and war plans have been removed. The second striking document is the transcript of proceedings of the controversial December 1941 Conference of the High Command. Release of this lengthy document ends years of speculation regarding what was said and by whom at this critical session, which followed the completion of the last major Soviet war games before the German attack in June 1941.

Finally, the collections of selective documents published in recent journals seem to be authentic and represent a genuine effort to begin an increased flow of released archival materials. By their very nature, however, they are selective, and the flow of materials has noticeably decreased since the downfall of Gorbachev and the collapse of the Soviet Union. It remains to be seen whether this trend will be reversed.

CONCLUSIONS

Compared with the past state of Soviet historiographic work on the subject of Eastern Front operations, what has transpired in recent years regarding release of archival materials has been revolutionary. But, just as the new Soviet (Russian) Revolution is in its infancy, so also is the revolution in historiography. The archival materials that have been released thus far appear prodigious compared with the meager amount previously available through captured German records. They are, however, very limited compared with what certainly exists behind still closed doors. Thus, while there is much to celebrate, there is also much to anticipate.

We can call the Russian (Soviet) archives open only when the archival flow is complete and when scholars (Western and Russian alike) have physical access to the archival repositories themselves. Clearly there remain certain limits on what can be seen and used, just as there are in the West. But these limits should be well defined and understood. In particular, access can be judged as adequate only when the records of *Stavka* and operating *fronts*, armies, corps, and other military organizations are made available to scholars. The task of negotiating this access has only just begun.

Notes

Introduction

1. For example, the ever-popular memoirs of Heinz Guderian (*Panzer Leader* [New York: E. P. Dutton, 1952]), F. W. von Mellenthin (*Panzer Battles* [Norman: University of Oklahoma Press, 1956]), and Erich von Manstein (*Lost Victories* [Novato, Calif.: Presidio Press, 1982]) were written from memory, usually without benefit of archival materials of any kind. More general studies such as Albert Seaton's *The Russo-German War* (London: Arthur Baker, 1971), military histories such as Earl Ziemke's *From Stalingrad to Berlin: The German Defeat in the East* (Washington, D.C.: U.S. Army Center for Military History, 1968), and popular narratives such as *Hitler Moves East* (New York: Ballantine, 1973) by Paul Carrell use Russian works in English translation, but these are few in number and superficial in content. The best survey history of the Red Army by Malcolm MacIntosh (*Juggernaut: A History of the Soviet Armed Forces* [New York: Macmillan, 1968]) was a pioneering effort in the field, but now requires major revision. The monumental works of John Erickson (*The Road to Stalingrad: Stalin's War with Germany*, vol. 1 [New York: Harper & Row, 1979] and *The Road to Berlin* [Boulder Colo.: Westview Press, 1983]) have withstood the rigors of time; however they are virtually impenetrable to the lay reader.

2. A notable exception is the extensive, multivolume study by Colonel General Gotthard Heinrici, the noted German defensive specialist, which has just been unearthed and is being prepared for publication.

1. The Red Army

1. B. I. Kuznetsov, "Eshelonnaia voina" [Echelon war], *Sovetskaia voennaia entsiklopediia, T. 8* [Soviet military encyclopedia, vol. 8] (Moscow: Voenizdat, 1980), 619.

2. A. Ekimovskiy and A. Tonkikh, "Red Army Tactics in the Civil War," translated from *Voyenni vestnik* [Military Herald] 1 (January 1967): 9–15 (hereafter cited as *VV*, with appropriate volume and date). See also K. A. Meretskov, *Serving the People* (Moscow: Progress Publishers, 1971), 36–45. Soviet success with employing large cavalry forces led to the creation of a 2d Cavalry Army in 1920 and to Soviet fixation on the importance of cavalry as a key maneuver element in the postwar years. Stalin's close Civil War association with 1st Cavalry Army veterans (S. M. Budenny, K. E. Voroshilov, and others) gave birth to the Stalinist clique of favorite officers that would dominate the Soviet High Command well into World War II.

3. In 1925 the Red Army consisted of 41 regular-cadre divisions (31 rifle and 10 cavalry), 46 territorial rifle divisions, and 8 territorial cavalry brigades, plus several smaller nationality formations. In wartime these divisions would produce a total of 140 divisions. For details, see David M. Glantz, *The Military Strategy of the Soviet Union: A History* (London: Frank Cass & Co., Ltd., 1992), 46–53.

4. Hans W. Gatzke, "Russo-German Military Collaboration During the Weimar Republic," *American Historical Review* 63:3 (April 1958): 565–597. Extensive Russian sources include A. Zdanovich, "Sekretnye laboratorii reikhsvera v Rossii" [Secret laboratories of the Reichswehr in Russia], *Armiia* 1 (January 1992): 62–68; 2 (January 1992): 59–64; 3–4 (February 1992): 67–71; 6 (March 1992): 67–71; and S. A. Gorlov, "Voennoe sotrudnichestvo SSSR i Germanii v 20-e gody" [Military cooperation of the USSR and Germany in the 1920s], *Voenno-istoricheskii zhurnal* [Military-historical journal] 9 (September 1991): 4–11. Hereafter cited as *VIZh*, with appropriate volume and date.

5. As implied by Frunze's use of the term, "doctrine" referred to highly abstract concepts about the state's use of military power in warfare. By contrast, Western soldiers tend to use the same term to mean more specific principles for the application of military force at all levels of war. Because of this difference in terminology, the ensuing discussion treats such Soviet terminology as "strategic," "operational," and "tactical concepts and theories" as distinct from higher-level Soviet "doctrine," but analogous to Western "doctrine."

6. R. Savushkin, "K voprosu o zarozhdenii teorii posledovatel'nykh nastupatel'nykh operatsiii, 1921–1929 gg." [On the question of the origin of the theory of successive operations, 1921–1929], *VIZh* 5 (May 1983): 77–83.

7. A. A. Svechin, "Strategiia" [Strategy], quoted in *Voprosy strategii i operativnogo iskusstva v sovetskikh voennykh trudakh, 1917–1940 gg* [Questions of strategy and operational art in Soviet military works, 1917–1940] (Moscow: Voenizdat, 1965), 238. For a full explanation of the relationship of strategy, operational art, and tactics, see A. A. Svechin, *Strategiia* [Strategy] (Moscow: Voenizdat, 1926).

8. Quoted in A. Riazansky, "The Creation and Development of Tank-Troop Tactics in the Pre-War Period," *VV* 11 (November 1966): 25–32.

9. Tanks were echeloned into direct infantry support [*neposredstvennoi podderzhki pekhoty*-NPP], long-range support [*dal'nei podderzhka pekhoty*-DPP], and long-range action [*dal'nego deistviia*-DD] groups. The latter, depending on their size, soon became forward detachments [*peredovye otriady*] and mobile groups [*podvizhnye gruppy*] designated to conduct tactical and operational maneuvers in the service of corps, armies, and *fronts*. The mobile group was the descendant of the more modern operational maneuver group (OMG).

10. Among many articles detailing weapons developments, see A. Iovlev, "Tekhnicheskoe perevooruzhenie Krasnoi Armii v gody pervoi piatiletki" [The technical rearmament of the Red Army during the first five-year plan], *VIZh* 12 (December 1964): 4–13.

11. The Soviets had formed the 3d Tank Regiment in Moscow in October 1924, but the following year abolished the regiment and replaced it with two separate

tank battalions. The new 1927 regiment (the 1st) also contained six armored car battalions and about 30 armored trains. See A. Ryzhakov, "K voprosy o stroitel'stve bronetankovykh voisk Krasnoi Armii v 30-e gody" [Concerning the formation of Red Army armored forces in the 1930s] *VIZh* 8 (August 1968): 105; and David M. Glantz, *The Motor-Mechanization Program of the Red Army in the Interwar Years* (Fort Leavenworth, Kan.: Soviet Army Studies Office, 1990).

12. Ryzhakov, "K voprosy o stroitel'stve" 106. The new brigade consisted of 4,700 men, 119 tanks, 100 tankettes (small machine-gun tanks), 15 armored cars, and a variety of supporting weaponry. In addition, three tank regiments were added to the force structure.

13. The two new corps, created on the basis of the 11th and 45th Rifle Divisions in the Leningrad and Ukrainian Military Districts, consisted of 490 tanks, 200 vehicles, and about 10,000 men each.

14. The shift from territorial/cadre system to full cadre system began in 1937 and ended 1 January 1939. The change was prompted by Moscow's appreciation of new European threats, especially the rise of Nazi Germany. During this period, 35 territorial divisions converted to cadre status. Red Army strength increased from 1.5 million (96 rifle divisions) on 1 September 1939, to 2.3 million (170 rifle divisions) on 1 December 1939, 4.5 million (161 rifle divisions) on 1 February 1940, and finally to 5 million (196 rifle divisions) in June 1941. See S. A. Tiushkevich, ed., *Sovetskie vooruzhennye sily* [The Soviet armed forces] (Moscow: Voenizdat, 1978), 236; and A. A. Volkov, *Kriticheskii prolog* [Critical prologue] (Moscow: Aviar, 1992), 27.

15. Dimitri Volkogonov, *Stalin: Triumph and Tragedy*, trans. and ed. Harold Shukman (Rocklin, Calif.: Prima Publishing, 1992), 47, 250–252, 319–324.

16. O. F. Suvenirov, "Vsearmeiskaia tragediia" [An army-wide tragedy], *VIZh* 3 (March, 1989): 42. Numerous recent Russian accounts document the scope and impact of the military purges. These confirm the judgments of detailed contemporary U.S. Army evaluations of the purges, which have been reproduced as "Attache Assessments of the Impact of the 1930s Purges on the Red Army," *Journal of Soviet Military Studies* 2:3 (September 1989): 417–436. They also confirm judgments in older Western works, such as Malcolm MacIntosh, *Juggernaut: A History of the Soviet Armed Forces* (New York: Macmillan, n.d.), 93.

17. S. S. Biriuzov, *Sovetskii soldat na Balkanakh* (Moscow, 1963), 137–43; For the English translation, see Seweryn Bialer, ed., *Stalin and his Generals: Soviet Military Memoirs of World War II* (Boulder, Colo.: Westview Press, 1984), 84–86.

18. David M. Glantz, "Vatutin," *Stalin's Generals*, ed., H. Shukman (London: Weidenfeld & Nicolson, 1993), 289. All three became key *Stavka* or *front* staff officers.

19. Only three typescript copies of Tukhachevsky's landmark 1928 work *Budushchaia voina* [Future war] survived, buried deep in the archives. When released recently, its carefully controlled cover sheet showing access to the document contained only 13 signatures, all since 1955.

20. The Soviet General Staff journal *Voennaia mysl'* [Military thought] and *VIZh* published numerous articles in the late 1930s on experiences in Spain that

reflected such Soviet indecision regarding the feasibility of conducting deep operations. See also David M. Glantz, "Observing the Soviets: U.S. Military Attaches in Eastern Europe During the 1930s," *The Journal of Military History* 5:2 (April 1991): 153–183.

21. See Ryzhakov, 105–111, and Glantz, "Observing the Soviets," 43–45 for the commission's decision and the structure of subsequent motorized forces.

22. For specifics, see I. F. Kuz'min, *Na strazhe mirnogo truda (1918–1940 gg.)* [On guard for peaceful work] (Moscow: Voenizdat, 1959); and V. Ezhakov, "The Battles at Lake Khasan (On the 30th Anniversary of the Defeat of the Japanese Troops)," *VIZh* 7 (July 1968): 124–128. Losses provided in G. F. Krivosheev, ed., *Grif sekretnosti sniat: Poteri vooruzhennykh sil SSSR v voinakh, boevykh deistviiakh i voennykh konfliktakh* [Losses of the armed forces of the USSR in wars, combat actions, and military conflicts] (Moscow: Voenizdat, 1993), 71–73.

23. The best short study on Khalkhin-Gol remains Edward J. Drea's *Nomonhan: Japanese-Soviet Tactical Combat, 1939*. Leavenworth Papers, no. 2, (Fort Leavenworth, Kans.: U.S. Army Command and General Staff College, 1981.) Alvin D. Coox, *Nomonhan: Japan Against Russia, 1939*, 2 vols. (Stanford, Calif.: Stanford University Press, 1985) is an exhaustive study, but it is told almost entirely from the Japanese perspective. Number of losses taken from Krivosheev, *Grif sekretnosti*, 77–85.

2. Armed Truce

1. For Soviet military preparations, see David M. Glantz, *The Military Strategy of the Soviet Union: A History* (London: Frank Cass & Co., 1992), 69–72.

2. Numerous Russian archival sources now document the contents of this agreement, including the secret protocols, whose existence the Soviets have long denied. See, for example, A. Chubar'ian, "V preddverii vtoroi mirovoi voiny" [On the threshold of the Second World War], *Kommunist* 14 (September 1988): 102–112; D. A. Volkogonov, "Drama reshenii 1939 goda" [Drama of the 1939 decision], *Novaia i noveishaia istoriia* [New and newest history] 4 (July–August 1989): 3–26; and "Na rokovom poroge (iz arkhivnykh materialov 1939 goda)" [On a fateful threshold (from archival materials of 1939)], *Voprosy istorii* [Questions of history] 11 (December 1989): 87–112 and 3 (March 1990): 13–39.

3. S. M. Shtemenko, *The General Staff at War, 1941–1945*, vol. 1 (Moscow: Progress Publishers, 1985), 15–18. For details on mobilization and subsequent operations, see *Istorii voin, voennogo iskusstva i voennoi nauki: Uchebnik dlia voennoi akademii general'nogo shtaba vooruzhennykh sil SSSR* [A history of warfare, military art, and military science: Textbook for the Military Academy of the General Staff of the Armed Forces of the USSR] (Moscow: Voroshilov Academy of the General Staff, 1977), 520–553. This section was translated by Harold Orenstein and published in *JSMS* 6:1 (March 1993): 86–141.

4. The Belorussian Front's mobile cavalry-mechanized group, commanded by Corps Commander I. V. Boldin, consisted of 15th Tank Corps and 3d and 6th

Cavalry Corps and the Ukrainian Front's cavalry-mechanized group of 25th Tank Corps and 4th and 5th Cavalry Corps. See *Istorii voin*, 107–108.

5. Andrei I. Eremenko, *The Arduous Beginning* (Moscow: Progress Publishers, 1974), 15–19.

6. Alexander Werth, *Russia at War, 1941–1945* (New York: E. P. Dutton & Co., 1964), 63–64. Losses provided in G. F. Krivosheev, ed., *Grif sekretnosti sniat: Poteri vooruzhennykh sil SSSR v voinakh, boevykh deistviiakh i voennykh konfliktakh* [Losses of the armed forces of the USSR in wars, combat actions, and military conflicts] (Moscow: Voenizdat, 1993) 85–90. The Soviets committed 466,516 troops to the operation.

7. Dimitri Volkogonov, *Stalin: Triumph and Tragedy*, trans. and ed. by Harold Shukman (Rocklin, Calif.: Prima Publishing, 1992) 359–360. The Yeltsin government has provided full documentation on the tragedy to the Polish government, which subsequently released the documents. The collection of four top secret documents relating to the matter, named *Paketa N1* [Packet Number 1], were released and signed by P. G. Pikhov, Main State Archives of the Russian Federation.

8. Among the many accounts of Soviet occupation of the Baltic States, see "Dopustit' razmeshchenie voisk . . . (O vvode chastei Krasnoi Armii na territorii Litvy, Latvii, Estonii v 1939–1940 gg.)" [Permit stationing of troops . . . (Concerning the introduction of Red Army forces in the territory of Lithuania, Latvia, and Estonia in 1939–1940)], *VIZh* 4 (April 1990): 31–39.

9. Ibid.

10. For details, see *Istorii voin*, 116–118.

11. Malcolm MacIntosh, *Juggernaut: A History of the Soviet Armed Forces* (New York: Macmillan, n.d.) 113–116. See also Eloise Engle and Lauri Paananen, *The Winter War: The Russo-Finnish Conflict, 1939–40* (New York, 1973). Krivosheev, *Grif sekretnosti*, 93–105, cites initial Finnish strength as 600,000 men with 7 infantry divisions, 4 separate infantry and 1 cavalry brigade, and several separate infantry battalions supported by 270 combat aircraft deployed on the Karelian isthmus and specialized detachments deployed further north. *Istorii voin*, 126, cites Finnish operating strength at 500,000 organized into a total of 12 infantry divisions, 5 infantry brigades, 5 separate infantry regiments, 22 rifle and partisan battalions, and 1 cavalry brigade. Initially, they were faced by four Soviet armies (14th, 9th, 8th, and 7th) numbering 21 rifle divisions, 1 tank corps, and 3 tank brigades with a strength on 1 January 1940 of 550,757 men. By 1 March, total Soviet strength rose to 916,613.

12. MacIntosh, *Juggernaut*, 116–117. For a detailed account of 9th Army operations see O. A. Dudorova, "Neizvestnye stranitsy 'zimnei voiny' [Little-known pages of the "Winter War"], *VIZh* 9 (September 1991): 12–23.

13. Military Intelligence Division, U.S. Army, *Soviet-Finnish War: Operations from November 30, 1939, to January 7, 1940* (U.S. Army: January 10, 1940). Reprinted in Jonathan M. House, ed., *Selected Readings in Military History: Soviet Military History*, vol. 1 of *The Red Army, 1918–1945* (Fort Leavenworth, Kan.: Combat Studies Institute, 1984), 125–134. For more details, see *Istorii voin*, 520–553.

14. For gruesome details of the disaster, see Dudorava, *"Neizvestnye,"* 12–23, which contains the war diary of the ill-fated unit. Between 1 and 7 January, the 44th Rifle Division lost 4,756 men (1,001 killed, 1,430 wounded, 82 frozen, and 2,243 unaccounted for) and virtually all of its weaponry.

15. Shtemenko, *The General Staff at War,* 24–25.

16. Werth, *Russia at War,* 79. Krivosheev, *Grif sekretnosti,* however, places Soviet losses at 333,084 men (65,384 killed, 19,610 missing, 186,584 wounded, 9,614 frost-bitten, and 51,892 sick).

17. Volkogonov, *Stalin: Triumph and Tragedy,* 367 ff.

18. See David M. Glantz, *Soviet Military Operational Art: In Pursuit of Deep Battle* (London: Frank Cass & Co., 1991), 96, and Glantz, *The Motor-Mechanization Program of the Red Army in the Interwar Years* (Fort Leavensworth, Kan.: Soviet Army Studies Office, 1990) 45–48, for variations in the strength of these mechanized forces and others created during the period of the Timoshenko reforms.

19. Volkogonov, *Stalin: Triumph and Tragedy,* 369.

20. Transcripts of the proceedings of this conference are now public. For example, see S. K. Timoshenko, *Zakliuchitel'naia rech' narodnogo komissara oborony soiuza SSSR 1940 geroia i marshala Sovetskogo Soiuza S. K. Timoshenko na voennom soveshchanii, 31 dekabria 1940g.* [Concluding speech of the People's Commissar of Defense of the USSR, Hero and Marshal of the Soviet Union S. K. Timoshenko at a military conference, 31 December 1941] (Moscow: Voenizdat, 1941). Complete analysis of the conference and ensuing war game are found in M. V. Zakharov, *General'nyi shtab v predvoennye gody* [The General Staff in the prewar years] (Moscow: Voenizdat, 1989), 239–250.

21. Eremenko, *Arduous Beginning,* 22–43. Numerous articles now document parlous Soviet preparedness. For example see Iu.G. Perechnev, "O nekotorykh problemakh podgotovki strany i Vooruzhennykh Sil k otrazheniiu fashistskoi agressii" [Concerning some problems in preparing the country and the armed forces to repel fascist aggression], *VIZh* 4 (April 1988): 42–50.

22. For details on the war game, see Glantz, *Military Strategy,* 81–86.

23. For an excellent exposition of the Pripiat' problem, see A. Filippi, *Pripiatskaia problema* [The Pripiat' problem], (Moscow: Izdatel'stvo inostrannnoi literatury [Foreign Language Publishing House], 1959).

24. Zakharov, *General'nyi shtab,* 125–128, provides the details of defensive planning. See also Glantz, *Military Strategy,* 55–82.

25. Zakharov, *General'nyi shtab,* 248–250. See also David M. Glantz, "Soviet Mobilization in Peace and War," *The Journal of Soviet Military Studies* 5:3 (September 1992): 236–239.

26. Among the best of many recent Soviet articles on the intelligence picture prior to Barbarossa is "Nakanune voiny, 1940–41 gg.: O podgotovka germanii k napadeniiu na SSSR" [On the eve of war, 1940–41: Concerning the preparations of Germany for the attack on the USSR], *Izvestiia TsK KPPS* [News of the Central Committee of the Communist Party of the Soviet Union] 4 (April 1990): 251–264. It provides a staggering number of intelligence reports from the military and NKVD archives.

27. See Glantz, *Military Strategy*, 306–312; and Zakharov, *General'nyi shtab*, 258–262.

28. Zakharov, *General'nyi shtab*, 259, and A. G. Khor'kov, "Nekotorye voprosy strategicheskogo razvertivaniia Sovetskikh Vooruzhennykh Sil v nachale Velikoi Otechestvennoi voiny" [Some questions concerning the strategic deployment of the Soviet armed forces in the beginning of the Great Patriotic War], *VIZh* 1 (January 1986): 11–12.

29. Within the past two years, the argument has emerged that in May 1941, in light of German mobilization and obvious German offensive intentions, the Soviet Union was planning to launch a "preventative war" against Hitler. Fueled by reevaluation of a 15 May 1941 proposal [*predlozhenie*] to that effect by Zhukov, which was published in fragmentary form in a number of Soviet journals, the Soviet émigré V. Rezun, writing under the pen name of Victor Suvorov, has published two books categorically accusing Stalin of planning such a war. Rezun's views have gained wide acceptance, for understandable reasons, in the German historical community. They are now being accepted, primarily for political reasons, by a growing circle of Russian scholars, most of whom are reformers who accept as true anything that discredits the former regime.

In short, Rezun has interpreted all the military measures undertaken by Stalin between the late 1930s and June 1941 as being consciously offensive and geared to the summer 1941 launching of a strike against Germany. The Zhukov proposal, which called for such an offensive in July, rests at the heart of Rezun's arguments. This proposal is probably authentic, although it is likely that there were many such proposals, since contingency planning is the job of any general staff. In addition, Rezun vividly portrays a huge Soviet military machine, with imposing and sinister capabilities, poised to strike in 1941.

While one can accept the fact that Stalin well understood that future war between Germany and the Soviet Union was likely, it is clear from existing evidence that he did not wish that war to occur before 1942 at the earliest. It is also clear from every indicator of subsequent Soviet combat performance and, in particular, from existing Soviet and German archival materials, that the supposedly imposing Red Army was neither imposing nor ready for war in 1941.

Even if Rezun's claims are correct, German offensive planning predated Soviet offensive planning, and the earliest the Soviets could have launched Zhukov's offensive would have been late July, long after the German offensive war scheduled to occur. This offensive was originally planned for May but was delayed until 22 June. (See chapter 3 for Zhukov's plan.)

3. Opposing Armies

1. For a discussion of German organization and doctrine, see Jonathan M. House, *Towards Combined Arms Warfare: A Survey of 20th-Century Tactics, Doctrine, and Organization* (Fort Leavenworth, Kan.: Combat Studies Institute, 1984), 81–83 and 96–97. See also F. W. von Senger und Etterlin, *Die Panzergrenadiere: Geschichte und Gestalt der mechanisierten Infanterie 1930–1960*

[The history and form of mechanized infantry 1930–1960] (Munich: J. F. Lehmanns Verlag, 1961), 72–77.

2. In early 1943, motorized corps were redesignated as panzer corps, and motorized infantry divisions became panzer-grenadier divisions.

3. Timothy A. Wray, *Standing Fast: German Defensive Doctrine on the Russian Front During World War II; Prewar to March 1943* (Fort Leavenworth, Kan.: Combat Studies Institute, 1986), 1–21.

4. Earl F. Ziemke and Magna E. Bauer, *Moscow to Stalingrad: Decision in the East* (Washington, D.C.: U.S. Army Center of Military History, 1987), 14.

5. Robert M. Kennedy, *The German Campaign in Poland, 1939* (Washington, D.C.: Office of the Chief of Military History, 1956), 120. On the centralized maintenance system, see for example Kenneth Macksey, "The German Army in 1941," in *The Initial Period of War on the Eastern Front, 22 June–August 1941. Proceedings of the 4th Art of War Symposium*, ed. David M. Glantz (London: Frank Cass and Co., Ltd., 1993), 64–65.

6. Klaus Reinhardt, *Moscow—The Turning Point: The Failure of Hitler's Strategy in the Winter of 1941–1942*, trans. Karl B. Keenan (Oxford and Providence: Berg Publishers, 1992), 26–28.

7. The complete Barbarossa directive is included as Appendix XXII to Heinz Guderian, *Panzer Leader* (New York: E. P. Dutton, 1952), 513–516.

8. Franz Halder, *The Halder War Diaries, 1939–1942*. eds. Charles Burdick and Hans–Adolf Jacobsen (Novato, Calif.: Presidio Press, 1988), 294.

9. The actual numbers involved in the 1941 campaign remain the subject of some debate, due largely to differences in counting units in Norway and in second echelon or reserve forces within Germany. The figures given here are intended to reflect the entire theater of war, as described in Ziemke and Bauer, *Moscow to Stalingrad*, 7–8, and David M. Glantz, *The Military Strategy of the Soviet Union: A History* (London: Frank Cass & Co., 1992) 91–98.

10. Malcolm MacIntosh, *Juggernaut: A History of the Soviet Armed Forces* (New York: Macmillan, n.d.), 137–139; and Glantz, *The Initial Period of War*, 185–187.

11. In some cases the Germans failed to detect these bases and they became valuable sources of weaponry for partisan bands.

12. O. A. Losik, ed., *Stroitel'stvo i boevoe primenenie sovetskikh tankovykh voisk v gody Velikoi Otechestvennoi voiny* [The formation and combat use of Soviet tank forces in the years of the Great Patriotic War] (Moscow: Voenizdat, 1979), 44. Soviet force structure in 1941 is detailed in Glantz, *Soviet Military Operational Art*, 93–97.

13. Glantz, *The Initial Period of War*, 34, provides figures for all mechanized corps. The most exact figures are found in Steven Zaloga, "Technological Surprise and the Initial Period of War: The Case of the T-34 Tank," *JSMS* 6:4 (December 1994): 634–646. Zaloga's figures are gleaned from three recently declassified archival volumes that contain the June 1941 war diaries of the three Soviet forward *fronts*.

14. MacIntosh, *Juggernaut*, 132; Konstantin K. Rokossovsky, *A Soldier's Duty* (Moscow: Progress Publishers, 1985), 12–15.

15. Zaloga, "Technological Surprise." Of the 1,861 new tanks, 1,475 (508 KVs and 967 T-34s) were assigned to formations in the western military districts. These, however, outnumbered and outgunned the 1,449 Mk-III and 517 Mk-IV medium tanks available to German forces.

16. S. Alferov, "Strategicheskoe razvertyvanie sovetskikh voisk na Zapadnom TVD v 1941 gody" [The strategic deployment of Soviet forces in the western TVD in 1941], *VIZh* 6 (June 1981): 31.

17. For further details on tank construction, see V. Mostovenko, "Razvitie sovetskikh tankov v gody Velikoi Otechestvennoi voiny" [The development of Soviet tanks in the Great Patriotic War], *VIZh* 9 (September 1961): 33–45.

18. Zaloga, "Technological Surprise." For a detailed discussion of German armor at this stage of the war, see I. S. O. Playfair, F. C. Flynn, C. J. C. Molony, and S. E. Toomer, *The Mediterranean and the Middle East, Vol. II: The Germans Come to the Help of Their Ally, 1941* (London: H.M.S.O., 1956), 13–14, 173–175, and 341–345.

19. Williamson Murray, *Luftwaffe* (Baltimore, Md.: Nautical and Aviation Publishing Co. of America, 1985), 79, 83.

20. Van Hardesty, *Red Phoenix: The Rise of Soviet Air Power, 1941–1945* (Washington, D.C.: Smithsonian Institution Press, 1982), 21 and 54–55. For accurate figures on Soviet aircraft strength, see M. I. Mel'tiukhov, "22 iiunia 1941 g.: Tsifri svidetel'stvuiut" [22 June 1941: Numbers bear witness], *Istoriia SSSR* 3 (March 1991): 16–28.

21. Alexander Werth, *Russia at War, 1941–1945* (New York: E. P. Dutton, 1964), 139. Dimitri Volkogonov, *Stalin: Triumph and Tragedy*, trans. and ed. Harold Shukman, 375.

22. For details of these Soviet plans, see Glantz, *Soviet Military Strategy*, 78–81, and Volkogonov, *Triumph and Tragedy* (Rocklin, Calif.: Prima Publishing, 1992), 396–398.

23. This section is based largely on Ziemke and Bauer, *Moscow to Stalingrad*, 18–22, which cites S. P. Ivanov, *Nachalnyi period voiny* [The initial period of war] (Moscow: Voenizdat, 1974). See also Glantz, *Soviet Military Strategy*, 95–98, and Iu. Ia. Kirshin and N. M. Ramanichev, "Nakanune 22 iiunia 1941 g. (po materialam voennykh arkhivov)" [On the eve of 22 June 1941 (according to military archival materials)], *Novaia i noveishaia istoriia* [New and newest history] 3 (March–April 1991): 3–19.

24. Ivanov, *Nachalnyi period*, 101, 106–107, 204. Shtemenko, *The General Staff At War*, vol. 1, 33.

25. V. Karpov, "Zhukov," *Kommunist vooruzhennykh sil* [Communist of the armed forces] 5 (May 1990): 67–68.

26. This section is based primarily on Barton Whaley, *Codeword Barbarossa*, (Cambridge, Mass.: M.I.T. Press, 1973). See also Robert Savushkin, "In the Tracks of a Tragedy: On the 50th Anniversary of the Start of the Great Patriotic War." *JSMS* 4:2 (June 1991): 213–251; and A. G. Khorkov, *Nakanune groznykh sobitii* [On the eve of threatening events], *VIZh* 5 (May 1988): 42–49.

27. Werth, *Russia At War*, 113.

28. Whaley, *Codeword Barbarossa*, 193–196.

29. The text of this message is reproduced in Savushkin, "In the Tracks of a Tragedy," 221–222.

4. German Onslaught

1. From "A Collection of Combat Documents Covering Soviet Western Front Operations: 24–30 June 1941," trans. Harold S. Orenstein, *JSMS* 4:2 (June 1991): 334. Full collection of documents in "Dokumenty po boevym deistviiam voisk Zapadnogo fronta s 22 iiunia po 5 iiulia 1941 g." [Documents on combat operations of Western Front forces from 22 June through 5 July 1941], *Sbornik boevykh dokumentov Velikoi Otechestvennoi voiny, No. 1* [Collection of combat documents of the Great Patriotic War, No. 1] (Moscow: Voenizdat, 1947); henceforth abbreviated as *SBDVOV*. Classified secret; declassified 1964. Similar volumes cover *fronts*, armies, corps, and in some cases *Stavka* documents for the period 15 June through October and early November 1941. Unfortunately, this series of document collections seems to have terminated in 1960 with No. 43. Hereafter cited as *SBDVOV*, with appropriate volume and date.

2. Van Hardesty, *Red Phoenix: The Rise of Soviet Air Power, 1941–1945* (Washington, D.C.: Smithsonian Institution Press, 1982), 11.

3. "A Collection of Combat Documents," 329ff; Werth, *Russia At War, 1941–1945* (New York: Dutton, 1964), 151–155. A harrowing account of the first few days of war is provided in I. V. Boldin, *Strasnitsy zhizni* [Pages of a life] (Moscow: Voenizdat 1961). The best memoir account of Western Front operations in the initial days of war is found in L. M. Sandalov, "Stoiali nasmert' " [Stand to the death], *VIZh* 10 (October 1988): 3–13; 11 (November 1988): 3–10; 12 (December 1988): 13–22; 2 (February 1989): 32–41; and 6 (June 1989): 8–15. Sandalov was the chief of staff of the 4th Army.

4. On Directive No. 3, see John Erickson, *The Road to Stalingrad: Stalin's War with Germany*, vol. 1 (New York: Harper & Row, 1979), 132; S. M. Shtemenko, *The Soviet General Staff At War*, vol. 1 (Moscow: Progress Publishers, 1985), 37–40.

5. For a harrowing account of 6th Panzer Division's encounter with the new tanks of Soviet 2d Tank Division at the town of Raseinai, see David M. Glantz, ed., *The Initial Period of War on the Eastern Front*, 22 June–August 1941. Proceedings of the 4th Art of War Symposium (London: Frank Cass & Co., Ltd., 1993) 93–96, 112–119.

6. Glantz, *The Initial Period of War*, 87–100.

7. Erich von Manstein, *Lost Victories* (Novato, Calif. Presidio Press, 1982), 178–185.

8. "A Collection of Combat Documents," 31–339, 343.

9. Quoted in "A Collection of Combat Documents," 344.

10. For the sordid tale of Pavlov's summary execution, see "Delo No. P-24000 generala Pavlova Dmitriia Grigor'evicha" [Case No. P-24000 of General Pavlov, Dmitri Grigr'evich], *Kommunist vooruzhennykh sil* [Communist of the armed

forces] 8 (April 1991): 70–75; 9 (May 1991): 68–73; 11 (June 1991): 54–60; 13 (July 1991): 63–68; and 14 (July 1991): 57–67. Considered by Stalin to have been a traitor, Pavlov's reputation is now being cleansed a bit.

11. G. F. Krivosheev, *Grif sekretnosti: Poteri Vooruzhennykh sil SSSR V voinakh, boevykh deistviiakh i voennykh konfliktakh* [Losses of the armed forces of the USSR in wars, combat actions, and military conflicts] (Moscow: Voenizdat, 1993), 162, cites Soviet losses of 417,790 out of a total Western Front initial combat strength of 627,300 during the period 22 June to 9 July 1941. By contrast, Northwestern Front lost 88,486 out of 498,00 soldiers during the same period.

12. Franz Halder, *The Halder War, 1939–1942*, Charles Burdick and Hans-Adolf Jacobsen eds. (Novato, Calif.: Presidio Press, 1988), 432–435. German intelligence had almost completely failed to detect the many mechanized corps in the forward area. They detected only the corps in the Kaunus region because their agent network was still active there. See Glantz, *The Initial Period of War*, 83.

13. The best Soviet sources for action in the Southwestern Front's sector are A. Vladimirsky, "Nekotorye voprosy provedeniia kontrudapov voiskami Iugo-Zapadnogo fronta 23 iiunia-2 iiulia 1941 goda" [Some aspects of the conduct of counterstrokes by Southwestern Front forces between 23 June and 2 July 1941], *VIZh* 7 (July 1981): 21–28; A. A. Gurov, "Boevye deistviia sovetskikh voisk na iugo-zapadnom napravlenii v nachal'nom periode voiny" [Combat actions of Soviet forces on the southwestern direction in the initial period of war], *VIZh* 8 (August 1988): 32–41; and A.V. Vladimirsky, *Na kievskom napravlenii* [On the Kiev axis] (Moscow: Voenizdat, 1989). See also K. Rokossovsky, *A Soldier's Duty* (Moscow: Progress Publishing, 1985), 14–24 (reprinted in unexpurgated form in *VIZh* from April 1989 through March 1992); and Glantz, *The Initial Period of War*, 248–344. For documents, see *SBDVOV*, No. 36 (Moscow: Voenizdat, 1959).

14. Krivosheev, *Grif sekretnosti*, 164. The Southwestern Front lost 241,594 soldiers out of an initial strength of 864,600 during the period 22 June to 6 July 1941.

15. Heinz Guderian, *Panzer Leader*, (Washington, D.C.: Zenger Publishing Co., 1979), 152.

16. Omer Bartov, *The Eastern Front, 1941–45; German Troops and the Barbarisation of Warfare*. (New York: St. Martin's Press, 1986), 51, 66.

17. Ibid., 109. On the atrocity issue, see also Werth, *Russia At War*, 208, 373–376, 700–709.

18. Bartov, *The Eastern Front*, 153.

19. Ibid., 111; Reinhardt, *Moscow—The Turning Point*, 41, 262–263.

20. Halder, *The Halder War Diaries*, 446.

21. Initially, Lieutenant General M.F. Lukin's 16th Army fielded only two rifle divisions.

22. Additionally, 29th, 30th, 31st, 32d, and 33d Armies, formed primarily from NKVD border guards forces and peoples militia from the Moscow region, mobilized and deployed into positions from Staraia Russa to south of Viaz'ma to cover the approaches to Moscow. See A. I. Evseev, "Manevr strategicheskimi rezervami v pervom periode Velikoi Otechestvennoi voiny" [Maneuver of strategic reserves in the first period of the Great Patriotic War], *VIZh* 3 (March 1986): 9–20.

23. V. Butkov, "Kontrudar 5-iu mekhanizirovannogo korpusa na lepel'skom napravlenii (6-11 iiulia 1941 goda)" [The counterstroke of 5th Mechanized Corps on the Lepel axis (6–11 July 1941], *VIZh* 9 (September 1971): 59–65. See also *SBDVOV*, No. 37 (Moscow: Voenizdat, 1959).

24. The stubborn defense of Mogilev was used by Soviet propagandists to create a mystique associated with heroic city defenses. This would pay dividends in the future.

25. For details of this battle, see Guderian, *Panzer Leader*, 167–174; P.A. Kurochkin, "Battle of Smolensk," *Soviet Military Review* 4 (April 1968): 41–44; K. Cheremukhin, "Na smolenskom-moskovskom strategicheskom napravlenii letom 1941 goda" [On the Smolensk-Moscow strategic direction in summer 1941], *VIZh* 10 (October 1966): 3–18; and Bryan Fugate, *Operation Barbarossa*, (Novato, Calif.: Presidio Press, 1984), 137–142.

26. Imposing on paper, the counterattacking divisions were woefully under-strength or remnants of divisions already wrecked in earlier battles.

27. Bartov, *The Eastern Front*, 20.

28. To support the hastily fielded and largely unprepared new reserve armies, the *Stavka* converted tank divisions from mechanized corps in the internal military districts that had avoided destruction in the first several weeks of war into a new 100-series of tank divisions. Some of these, like the 101st, 102d, 104th, 105th, 108th, and 107th, were simply renumbered existing divisions (the 52d and 56th from 26th Mechanized Corps, the 9th and 53d of 27th Mechanized Corps, 23d Mechanized Corps' 51st Tank Division, and the separate 69th Mechanized Division from the Far East). Others, like the 111th and 112th, were formed in the Far East from local units and disbanded units of 30th Mechanized Corps. Still others were formed from reserve tank cadres and surviving elements of previously damaged mechanized corps. Creation of the new tank divisions represented a stop-gap measure to provide a modicum of armored support to hard-pressed rifle forces. The strength of these divisions was ad hoc. Tank divisions from the mechanized corps in the internal military districts had their own armor plus whatever armor the *Stavka* could provide from equipment reserves and recent production. Other divisions were manned with whatever local resources were available.

For this transformation of division numerals, see "Operativniai svodka shtab zapadnogo fronta No. 50 ot 21 iiulia 1941 g. o boevkh deistviiakh voisk fronta" [Operational summary No. 50 of the Western Front staff, dated 21 July 1941, about combat operations of *front* forces], *SBDVOV* 37:99 and sequential reports in the same documents series from the Reserve Front, such as "Operativnaia svodka shtab fronta reservnykh armii No. 9 k 20 chasam 16 iiulia 1941 g. o polozhenii voisk fronta' [Operational summary 9, dated 16 July 1941, about the situation of *front* forces], *SBDVOV* 37:141–142, and "Boevoi prikaz komanduiushchego voiskami 24-i armii No. 05/op ot 17 iiulia 1941 g. o perepodchinenii i peregruppirovke voisk armii" [Combat order 5/op of the 24th Army commander, dated 17 July 1941, about the resubordination and regrouping of army forces], *SBDVOV* 37:316.

One of the few existing open-source explanations of the origins of the 100-series tank divisions is found in O. A. Losik, *Stroitel'stvo i boevoe primenenie sovetskikh tankovykh voisk v gody Velikoi Otechestvennoi voiny* [The formation and combat use of Soviet tank forces during the Great Patriotic War] (Moscow: Voenizdat, 1979), 46. Losik states, "At this time [mid-July 1941] 10 tank divisions were formed from mechanized corps located in the internal military districts." Archival materials clearly support Losik's claim.

29. See V. Shevchuk, "Deistviia operativnykh grupp voisk v Smolenskom srazhenii (10 iiulia-10 sentiabria 1941 g.) [The actions of operational groups of forces in the battle of Smolensk (10 July–10 September 1941)], *VIZh* 12 (December 1979): 10–13. Documents in *SBDVOV*, No. 36.

30. Kurochkin, "Battle of Smolensk," 43–44; Rokossovsky, *A Soldier's Duty*, 25–39.

31. Indicative of the intense fighting at and around Smolensk, from 10 July to 10 September, Western Front lost 469,584 soldiers out of 579,400 engaged. The Reserve and Central Front together lost an additional 210,372 during their defense and major counterstrokes (Initial *front* strength unknown). Yet by 1 October, the strength of Western Front had risen to 558,0000 effectives, and a new Reserve Front covering Moscow counted another 448,000 troops, thus attesting to the massive human resources available to the *Stavka*. See Krivosheev, *Grif sekretnosti*, 168–171.

5. Soviet Response

1. On the many changes in this organization, see V. D. Danilov, *Stavka VGK, 1941–1945* [Stavka of the Supreme High Command, 1941–1945] (Moscow: "Znanie," 1991); and in English, Stephen J. Cimbala, "Intelligence, C3, and the Initial Period of War," *JSMS* 4:3 (September 1991): 397–447.

2. John Erickson, *The Road to Stalingrad* (New York: Harper and Row, 1975), 172–173.

3. S. P. Ivanov, N. Shekhovtsov, "Opyt raboty glavnykh komandovanii na teatrakh voennykh deistvii" [Experience of the work of main commands in theaters of military operations], *VIZh* 9 (September 1981): 11–18; and V. D. Danilov, "Glavnye komandovaniia napravlenii v Velikoi Otechestvennoi voine" [Main commands of directions in the Great Patriotic War], *VIZh* 9 (September 1987): 17–23. The Northwestern Direction lasted until 27 August 1941; the Western Direction until 27 September 1941 and again from 1 February until 5 May 1942; the Southwestern Direction until 21 June 1942; and the North Caucasus Direction, formed on 21 April 1942, endured until 19 May 1942.

4. For example, former chief of staff and *front* commander K. A. Meretskov was imprisoned, interrogated by the NKVD in Moscow in late summer 1941, and later returned to *front* command.

5. Alexander Werth, *Russia at War, 1941–1945* (New York: E. P. Dutton, 1964), 168–169, 227–228; Dimitri Volkogonov, *Stalin: Triumph and Tragedy*, trans. and ed., Harold Shukman (Rocklin, Calif.: Prima Publishing, 1992), 423, 427.

6. These problems are candidly addressed in General Staff war experience studies in the archival series *SMPIOV* (*Sbornik materialov po izuchenie opyta voiny* [Collection of materials, for the study of war experience]) and in more

general terms in the numerous open-source, formerly classified studies of operational art and tactics. For example, see A. A. Strokov, *Istoriia voennogo iskusstva* [History of military art], (Moscow: Voenizdat, 1966), 388–392.

7. The contents of this circular and the changes it mandated are found in the Frunze Academy publication, Iu. P. Babich and A. G. Baier, *Razvitie vooruzheniia i organizatsii sovetskikh sukhoputnykh voisk v gody Velikoi Otechestvennoi voiny* [Development of the armament and organization of the Soviet ground forces in the Great Patriotic War], (Moscow: Izdanie Akademii, 1990).

8. By 31 December 1941, only 6 of 62 rifle corps remained.

9. James M. Goff, "Evolving Soviet Force Structure, 1941–1945: Process and Impact." *JSMS* 5:3, (September 1992): 381–382.

10. Tank brigades formed in late August numbered 93 tanks, but due to a shortage of tanks this number was soon reduced to 46. By December 1941, the Soviets possessed 79 tank brigades. Numerous separate tank battalions fielded 29 tanks each.

11. *History of the Great Patriotic War*, Vol. II (Washington, D.C.: Office of the Chief of Military History), p. 62, an OCMH translation of Vol. II of *Istoriia Velikoi Otechestvenunoi voiny*, 4 vols. (Moscow: Voenizdat, 1962–1964).

12. F. Utenkov, "Dokumenty sovetskogo komandovaniia po bor'be s tankami protivnika" [Documents of the Soviet commands concerning combat with enemy tanks], *VIZh* 8 (August 1976): 65–68. For the contents of this and other important Soviet wartime documents concerning antitank warfare, see *Sbornik boevykh dokumentov Velikoi Otechestvennoi voiny (SBDVOV), vypusk* 16 [Collection of combat documents of the Great Patriotic War, Issue 16] (Moscow: Voenizdat, 1952), 5–72. Classified secret; declassified in 1964.

13. David M. Glantz, "Soviet Mobilization in Peace and War, 1924–42: A Survey." *JSMS* Vol. 5, No. 3 (September 1992), 351.

14. Glantz, "Soviet Mobilization," 345.

15. Glantz, "Soviet Mobilization," 352. See also A. I. Evseev, "Manevr strategicheskimi rezervami v pervom periode Velikoi Otechestvennoi voiny" [Maneuver of strategic reserves during the first period of the Great Patriotic War], *VIZh* 3 (March 1986): 11–13; and V. Golubovich, "Sozdanie strategicheskikh reservov" [The creation of strategic reserves], *VIZh* 4 (April 1977): 12–19.

16. *History of the Great Patriotic War*, Vol. II, p. 139, 142; OCMH translation, 150, 156. Volkogonov, *Stalin: Triumph and Tragedy*, 415, 418.

17. *History of the Great Patriotic War*, Vol. II, 144–148; OCMH translation, 158–167. See also A. Nikitin, "Perestroika raboty promyshlennosti SSSR v pervom periode Velikoi Otechestvennoi voiny" [Rebuilding the work of military industry of the USSR during the first period of the Great Patriotic War], *VIZh* 2 (February 1963): 11–20.

18. Reinhardt, *Moscow — The Turning Point*, 32, 146–147.

6. To Moscow

1. By way of contrast, from 22 June to 30 September, the Red Army and Fleet lost a total of 2,129,677 soldiers: 236,372 were killed, 40,680 died of wounds,

153,526 died from illness and other noncombat causes, and 1,699,099 were missing and prisoners of war. Another 687,626 soldiers were wounded sufficiently to cause hospitalization. All told, the casualty figure equals more than 50 percent of the armed forces' prewar strength. For further details, see Krivosheev, *Grif sekretnosti*, 146–153.

2. Klaus Reinhardt, *Moscow—The Turning Point: The Failure of Hitler's Strategy in the Winter of 1941–1942*, trans. Karl B. Keenan (Oxford and Providence, R.I.: Berg Publishers, 1992) 26–27.

3. Franz Halder, *The Halder War Diaries, 1939–1942*, eds. Charles Burdick and Hans-Adolf Jacobsen (Novato, Calif.: Presidio Press, 1988) 480, 487–495. Hitler was unaware that OKH had already authorized the release of these engines.

4. Halder, *The Halder Diaries*, 506.

5. Heinz Guderian, *Panzer Leader* (Washington, D.C.: Zenger Publishing, 1979), 190.

6. The Germans were forced to abandon the El'nia bridgehead. The costly Soviet counterstroke at Staraia Russa, conducted between 12 and 23 August, caused some anxious moments for German Army Group North but resulted in heavy Soviet losses and, according to current Russian analysis, placed Leningrad in greater jeopardy. Soviet forces involved in the operation (11th, 34th, and 27th Armies) lost 198,549 of 327,098 soldiers and considerable scarce equipment. The 34th Army, the main Soviet shock force, lost 60 percent of its 54,912 men, 74 of its 83 supporting tanks, and 628 of its 748 artillery pieces. The 48th Army, which was encircled in the operation, emerged from encirclement on 25 August with but 7,000 survivors. For details, see A. A. Volkov, *Kriticheskii prolog: nezavershennye frontovye nastupatel'nye operatsii pervykh kampanii Velikoi Otechestvennoi voiny* [Critical prologue: Incompleted *front* offensive operations during the first campaigns of the Great Patriotic War] (Moscow: Aviar, 1992), 65–70.

7. Halder, *The Halder Diaries*, 508–524; Guderian, *Panzer Leader*, 189–214. In fact, the *Stavka* was already planning a counterstroke in this region by Eremenko's new Briansk Front.

8. Earl F. Ziemke and Magna E. Bauer, *Moscow to Stalingrad: Decision in the East* (Washington, D.C.: U. S. Army Center of Military History, 1987) 33–34; John Erickson, *The Road to Stalingrad: Stalin's War with Germany* (New York: Harper and Row, 1979) 202; and Volkov, *Kriticheskii prolog*, 73–76. Although Eremenko was promoted to Colonel General and ordered to renew his futile attacks on 12 September, the "Soviet Guderian," so-named because of his supposed expertise in armored warfare, failed to halt Guderian's advance.

9. *History of the Great Patriotic War*, Vol. II, 104–109, OCMH translation 76–86; Werth, *Russia at War*, 205–206. For documentary evidence of the agonies of Kirponos, see the war diary entries of Southwestern Front forces in "Dokumentov po boevym deistviiam voisk Iugo-Zapadnogo napravleniia na pravoberezhnoi i levoberezhnoi Ukraine s 6 avgusta po 25 sentiabria 1941 g." [Documents on the combat activities of southwestern direction forces on the Right Bank and Left Bank of the Ukraine from 6 August to 25 September 1941], *SBDVOV, vypusk 40* [Issue 40] (Moscow: Voenizdat, 1960). Classified secret; declassified in 1964.

10. Volkov, *Kriticheskii prolog*, 76. Overall Southwestern Front losses from 7 July through 26 September were 585,598 out of 627,000 engaged. Central Front's 21st Army lost 35,585 in the operation, and Southern Front's 6th and 12th Armies lost another 79,220 in the Uman' encirclement. See Krivosheev, 166–167. See also A. Rakitsky, "Kievskaia oboronitel'naia operatsiia" [The Kiev defensive operation], *VIZh* 8 (August 1976): 124–128.

11. Soviet losses in the Donbas-Rostov strategic defensive operation were 160,567 of 541,600 engaged. During the counteroffensive phase, Soviet forces lost 33,111 out of 349,000. Krivosheev, 170–173.

12. *History of the Great Patriotic War*, Vol. II, 80–91, OCMH translation 35–56. In early September, Stalin sent K. A. Meretskov (recently released from prison), N. A. Bulganin, and L. Z. Mekhlis to Leningrad to restore the situation. On 10 September, G. K. Zhukov took command of the Leningrad Front after his dispute with Stalin over strategy on the western direction. Fortunately for the Soviets, the Finnish Army, which had joined the German assault in the north, prudently halted its advance at the 1939 Soviet-Finnish borders.

13. For a Soviet version of this engagement, see M. F. Lukin, "V Viazemskoi operatsii" [In the Viaz'ma Operation], *VIZh* 9, (September 1981): 30–37. Lieutenant General M. F. Lukin commanded 19th Army and the encircled forces at Viaz'ma. Some Soviet sources recognize that German tank strength was considerably less than 1,700. See "Proval nastupleniia nemetsko-fashistkoi armii na Moskvu" (Iz dnevnika nachal'nika germanskogo shtaba za period s 30 avgusta po 4 noiabria 1941 goda) [Defeat of the German-Fascist Army's offensive on Moscow (From the diary of the chief of the German Army General Staff for the period from 30 August to 4 November 1941)], *VIZh* 11 (November 1961): 71, which quotes Halder's diary entry that on 1 October 1941, Second Panzer Group was at 50 percent strength, First and Third Panzer Groups were at 70 to 80 percent strength, and First Panzer Group was near full strength.

14. *History of the Great Patriotic War*, Vol. II, 235–236, OCMH translation 114–115; I. Konev, "Nachalo Moskovskoi bitvy" [The beginning of the Battle of Moscow], *VIZh* 10 (October 1966): 56–67. According to Krivosheev, *Grif Sekretnosti*, 171, Soviet personnel strength on the Moscow axis on 30 September was 1,250,000, comprising 84 rifle divisions, 1 tank division, 2 motorized rifle divisions, 9 cavalry divisions, 1 rifle brigade, 13 tank brigades, and 2 fortified regions. Of these, Western Front counted 558,000, Reserve Front 448,000, and Briansk Front 244,000.

15. The Viaz'ma encirclement contained four field army headquarters (19th, 20th, 24th, and 32d); and 37 divisions, 9 tank brigades, and 31 High Command reserve artillery regiments assigned to 22d, 30th, 19th, 16th, 20th, 24th, 43d, 31st, 32d, 49th Armies and Operational Group Boldin. Personnel losses were heavy. For example, only 681 soldiers of 19th Army's 248th Rifle Division escaped encirclement. See B. I. Nevzorov, "Pylaiushchee Podmoskov'e" [The blazing approaches to Moscow], *VIZh* 11 (November 1991): 18–25. Krivosheev, *Grif Sekretnosti*, 171, places Western Front's personnel losses at 310,240 and Reserve Front's at 188,761.

16. Colonel General Eremenko's Briansk Front, consisting of 3d, 13th, and 50th Armies, and an operational group under Major General A. N. Ermakov, defended from Briansk southward to south of Glukhov.

17. Erickson, *The Road to Stalingrad*, 215; Guderian, *Panzer Leader*, 230–232.

18. The Briansk encirclement contained three army headquarters (3d, 50th, and 13th), 27 divisions, 2 tank brigades, and 19 High Command reserve artillery regiments. In the Viaz'ma and Briansk battles, the Soviets lost 252,600 soldiers killed or wounded, 673,000 captured, and another 94,800 requiring hospitalization. German casualties are cited as 145,000 killed or wounded. See Nevzorov, *Pylaiuschee*, 24.

19. Guderian, *Panzer Leader*, 232–235; *History of the Great Patriotic War*, Vol. II, 239–240, OCMH translation 122–124; D. Leliushenko, "Boi pod Mtsenskom" [The battle at Mtsensk], *VIZh* 12 (December 1960): 34–44. Krivosheev, *Grif Sekretnosti*, 171, cites Briansk Front personnel losses of 109,915.

20. Erickson, *The Road to Stalingrad*, 216–221; S. M. Shtemenko, *The Soviet General Staff at War*, Vol. I, (Moscow: Progress Publishers, 1985) 49–50; Werth, *Russia at War*, 234–241.

21. Ziemke and Bauer, *Moscow to Stalingrad*, 42–46.

22. Halder, *The Halder War Diaries*, 437.

23. The conversation between Zhukov and Stalin relating to these attacks is found in G. Zhukov, "V bitve za stolitsy" [In the battle for the capital], *VIZh* 9 (September 1966): 61–62. The two attacks were near Volokolamsk (16th Army) and Serpukhov (Group Belov).

24. This attack was conducted by an operational group commanded by Major General P. A. Belov, consisting of Belov's 2d Cavalry Corps, Colonel A. L. Getman's 112th Tank Division, and 173d Rifle Division, as a result of which "The enemy were forced to throw into Serpukhov part of its reserve to repel the counterattack of our forces." See A. Getman, "112-ia tankovaia diviziia v bitve pod Moskvoi" [The 112th Tank Division in the Battle of Moscow], *VIZh* 11 (November 1981): 49; and B. M. Shaposhnikov, ed., *Razgrom nemetskikh voisk pod moskvoi (moskovskaia operatsiia zapadnogo fronta 16 noiabria 1941 g.-31 ianvaria 1942 g.) 3 chastei* [The destruction of German forces at Moscow (The Moscow operation of Western Front 16 November 1941–31 January 1942)], (Moscow: Voenizdat, 1943). Classified secret, declassified 1965. In Part 1, 113, Shaposhnikov wrote that the 112th Tank Division also suffered heavy casualties.

25. Although this incident sounds apocryphal, it is not. According to A. Ia. Soshnikov, ed., *Sovetskaia kavaleriia* [Soviet cavalry] (Moscow: Voenizdat, 1984), "On 16 November, as a result of combat with units of 35th Infantry and 2d Panzer divisions, [44th Cavalry] suffered serious losses and withdrew to new defensive positions." These actions were part of a larger 16th Army counterattack conducted by Major General L. M. Dovator's Cavalry Group and the 17th, 24th, 44th Cavalry, 58th Tank, and 126th Rifle Divisions.

26. Soviets place German strength opposite Western Front at 233,000 men, 1,880 guns, 1,300 tanks, and 600–800 aircraft. German concentration accorded them marked superiority on offensive axes until the tide of battle turned in the

Soviet's favor. Then, given the arrival of fresh reserves, the reverse was true. For immense and accurate detail on the conduct of all stages of the operation, see Shaposhnikov, *Razgrom*.

27. Erickson, *The Road to Stalingrad*, 257–258; Ziemke and Bauer, *Moscow to Stalingrad*, 49–53.

28. P. A. Rotmistrov, "Bronetankovye voiska" [Armored Troops], *VIZh* 1 (January 1982): 23.

29. Guderian, *Panzer Leader*, 242–256.

30. F. Gaivoronsky, "Razvitie operativnogo iskusstva" [Development of operational art], *VIZh* 12 (December 1981): 24–29; M. Sidorov, "Boevoe primenenie rodov voisk v bitva pod Moskvoi; Artilleriia" [Combat use of types of forces in the Battle of Moscow: The Artillery], *VIZh* 1 (January 1982): 11–17.

31. P. A. Belov, *Za nami Moskva* [Behind us Moscow], (Moscow: Voenizdat, 1963). Belov's force initially consisted of 129 tanks, mostly light. Shaposhnikov, *Razgrom*, Part 1, 117–119, identifies 9th Tank Brigade as cooperating with Belov's force.

32. Shaposhnikov, *Razgrom*, Part 1, 91–95.

33. Ibid., 7–8. Average Moscow temperatures in winter 1941–1942 were: November, −5 degrees celsius; December, −12 degrees; and January, −19 degrees; as opposed to normal −3, −8, and −11 degrees, respectively. On several occasions in January, temperatures fell to between −35 and −40 degrees. Snow cover reached a depth of 50 to 65 centimeters.

34. See "Moskovskaia bitva 1941–42" *Velikaia Otechestvennaia voina 1941–1945: entsiklopediia* [The Great Patriotic War 1941–1945: An encyclopedia] (Moscow: "Sovetskaia entsiklopediia, 1985), 465. According to Krivosheev, *Grif Sekretnosti*, 174, however, Soviet strength at Moscow was 1,021,700 soldiers, including: Western Front, 748,000; Kalinin Front, 192,200; and the right wing of Southwestern Front, 80,800. Shaposhnikov, *Razgrom*, Part 1, 5, places Western Front's combat strength at 388,000 troops, 4,865 guns and mortars, 550 tanks, and 750 aircraft facing 240,000 troops, 4,760 guns and mortars, 900 tanks, and 600 aircraft of Army Group Center.

35. According to Shaposhnikov, *Razgrom*, Part 1, 72, the Western Front's right wing consisted of 152,000 men, 2,295 guns and mortars, 360 AT guns, and 270 tanks. German forces numbered 75,000 men, 1410 guns and mortars, 470 AT guns, and 380 tanks.

36. For details, see A. A. Zabaluev, S. G. Goriachev, *Kalininskaia nastupatel'naia operatsiia* [The Kalinin offensive operation], (Moscow: Voroshilov Higher Military Academy, 1942), and "Operativnye itogi razgroma nemtsev pod Moskvoi" [Operational results of the destruction of the Germans at Moscow], *SMPIOV* No. 5., (Moscow: Voenizdat, 1943), 3–22. Classified secret; declassified in 1964.

37. Shaposhnikov, *Razgram*, Part 2, 57–60. Katukov's 4th Tank Brigade performed similar heroics in operations against Klin and Volokolamsk.

38. Near Elets on Southwestern Front's right flank, between 6 and 19 December, 13th Army and a *front* operational group under command of General F. Ia.

Kostenko struck at overextended German forces at Elets. Soviet forces numbered 40,000 men, 245 guns and mortars, and 16 tanks against the German's 31,500 men, 470 guns, and 30–40 tanks. Through artful use of a mobile group formed around the nucleus of 5th Cavalry Corps and 129th Tank Brigade, the operation inflicted heavy losses on the Germans (16,257 killed and captured). Soviet casualties were approximately 6,000 killed and 10,000 wounded. See I. V. Parot'kin, *Eletskaia operatsiia (6–16 dekabria 1941 g.)* (Moscow: Voenizdat, 1943). Prepared by the Military-historical Section of the Red Army General Staff. Classified secret, declassified in 1964.

According to Krivosheev, *Grif sekretnosti*, 174–175, overall Soviet casualties during the first phase of the Moscow counteroffensive (5 December 1941–7 January 1942) were 370,955 (139,586 killed or missing and 231,369 wounded) out of the initial 1,021,700 engaged. Classified Soviet accounts place German losses opposite Western Front at over 85,000 killed and 1,434 tanks destroyed in the period 16 November through 10 December.

39. Halder, *The Halder Diaries*, 571–574, 586–592.

40. Guderian, *Panzer Leader*, 262–271.

41. These offensives would involve the Volkhov Front south of Leningrad, the Northwestern Front toward Staraia Russa, the Kalinin and Western Front toward Viaz'ma and Smolensk, the Briansk Front toward Orel, the Southwestern Front toward Khar'kov, and the Transcaucasus Front toward Sevastopol'.

42. E. Klimchuk, "Vtoraia udarnaia i Vlasov ili pochemu odin predal, a v predateli popala vsia armiia" [The 2d Shock Army and Vlasov, or why, because of one traitor, the blame was laid on the whole army], *Sovetskii voin* 2 (February 1989): 76–81. Translated in the English-language edition of *Soviet Soldier* 4 (April 1990): 35–39.

43. The details of the Vlasov "matter" have now been revealed, and the sordid context in which Vlasov's "crime" occurred has been clarified. See P. Pal'chikov, "Iz sekretnykh arkhivov: Delo N-1713" [From the secret archives: Case No. 1713], *Voennye znaniia* [Military knowledge] 1 (January 1990): 6–7.

44. See Kalinin Front order No. 057 and Western Front orders No. 0141 and 0152 in Shaposhnikov, *Razgrom*, Part 3, 4–5. This volume contains a thorough unvarnished account of the operations.

45. Krivosheev, 176, cites total Western and Kalinin Front strength of 1,052,200 (346,000 Kalinin and 713,100 Western). Actual combat strengths were considerably lower. For example, Shaposhnikov, *Razgrom*, Part 3, 85, shows 123,450 men of 49th, 50th, and 10th Armies facing 44,500 Germans. A. V. Vasil'ev, *Rzhevsko-Viazemskaia operatsiia kalininskogo i zapadnogo frontov (ianvar'-fevral' 1942 g.)* [The Rzhev-Viaz'ma operation of the Kalinin and Western Fronts (January-February 1942)] (Moscow: Voroshilov Higher Military Academy, 1949), secret, declassified 1964, shows the Kalinin Front with 348,300 (85,000 combat infantry) soldiers and 107 tanks facing 65,000 Germans and the Western Front with 168,000 combat infantry and 174 tanks facing 150,000 Germans and 200 tanks. Whatever numbers are correct, it is clear that Soviet forces outnumbered the Germans by at least two to one in manpower, while the Germans had a clear superiority in armor.

46. Efremov died on 19 April, leading his troops in a vain attempt to break out to Soviet lines.

47. In the Demiansk operation, Northwestern Front's 11th, 1st Shock, and 34th Armies, with an initial strength of 105,700 men, lost 88,908 killed and captured and 156,603 wounded from 7 January to 20 May 1942. Northwestern Front's 3d and 4th Shock Armies, while conducting the Toropets-Kholm' operation from 9 January to 6 February, lost 10,400 killed and captured and 18,810 wounded out of an initial strength of 122,100 soldiers. See Krivosheev, *Grif sekretnosti*, 224.

48. In the little-known Bolkhov offensive operation (8 January to 20 April 1942), Briansk Front's 61st, 13th, and 3d Armies, with a strength of 317,000 men (210,103 engaged), and 54 tanks, attacked 150,000 Germans supported by 145 tanks. Attrition by 1 February had reduced the strengths of the two sides to 93,081 and 115,000 respectively. The 3d Army's 287th Rifle Division alone lost 82 percent of its strength in nine days of combat. By 1 April, Briansk Front's total strength was 232,830, making it the weakest Soviet *front* (Karelian Front was the next weakest with 285,000). See Krivosheev, *Grif sekrenosti*, 224, and Volkov, *Kriticheskii prolog*, 122–127.

49. According to Krivosheev, *Grif sekretnosti*, 225, 204,000 Soviet soldiers participated in the Barvenkovo-Lozovaia operation. Of the number the Soviets suffered 40,881 casualties, including 11,095 killed and missing, and 29,786 wounded. The Soviets had an initial superiority of almost 2 to 1 over their opponents.

50. Krivosheev, *Grif sekretnosti*, 175, cites a combined Soviet naval-ground force strength of 82,500 in the Kerch-Feodosiia operation. Almost half (41,935) of this number became casualties, including 32,453 killed and missing and 9,482 wounded. Initial Soviet force superiority was more than 2 to 1.

51. For details on this and other Soviet winter airborne operations and available archival materials, see David M. Glantz, *A History of Soviet Airborne Forces* (London: Frank Cass and Co., 1994).

52. Ultimately, in late June, Belov's combined command of cavalry, airborne, and remnants of 33d Army broke through German lines near Kirov, after a hegira of several hundred kilometers.

7. *Rasputitsa*

1. By one estimate, the Allies delivered 600 antitank guns, 1,000 antiaircraft guns, 2,600 armored vehicles, and 4,700 aircraft between October 1941 and May 1942. Very few of these weapons, however, were of first-line design. Klaus Reinhardt, *Moscow — The Turning Point: The Failure of Hitler's Strategy in the Winter of 1941–1942*, trans. Karl B. Keenan (Oxford and Providence, R.I.: Berg Publishers, 1992), 129.

2. A. Razdievsky, "Proryv oborony v pervom periode voiny" [Penetration of a defense in the first period of war], *VIZh* 3 (March 1972): 11–21. Actual order in *SVDVOV*, No. 5 (Moscow: Voenizdat, 1947), 8–11. Classified secret; declassified in 1964.

3. G. Peredel'sky, "Artilleriiskoe nastuplenie v armeiskikh operatsiiakh" [The artillery offensive in army operations], *VIZh*, No. 11 (November 1976), 13–14.

4. Iu. P. Babich and A. G. Baier, *Razvitie vooruzheniia i organizatsii sovietskikh sukhoputnykh voisk v gody Velikoi Otechestvennoi voiny* [Development of the armament and organization of the Soviet ground forces in the Great Patriotic War] (Moscow: Izdanie akademii, 1990) 42–43.

5. See O. A. Losik, ed., *Stroitel'stvo i boevoe primenenie sovetskikh tankovykh voisk v gody Velikoi Otechestvennoi voiny* [The formation and combat use of Soviet tank forces in the years of the Great Patriotic War] (Moscow: Voenizdat, 1979), for Soviet development of tank and mechanized forces, in particular the tank and mechanized corps and tank armies. Corps formed in 1942 included four in April (1st, 2d, 3d, 4th), nine in May (5th through 8th, 10th, and 21st through 24th), six in May (9th, and 11th through 15th), four in June (16th through 18th, and 27th), three in July (25th, 26th, and 28th), and two in December (19th and 20th).

6. Babich and Baier, *Razvitie vooruzheniia*, 44–45.

7. Ibid., 46. Ideally, the rifle divisions conducted the penetration of enemy defenses, the tank corps conducted the exploitation, and the cavalry corps screened the tank corps flanks. To coordinate the operations of footbound infantry with tracked vehicles and horse cavalry was difficult, if not impossible, as the combat record of these formations soon indicated.

8. At Zhukov's suggestion, Order No. 308, dated 18 September 1941, created the first four guards divisions (1st through 4th, based on the 100th, 127th, 153d, and 161st Rifle Divisions that had distinguished themselves at El'na). These divisions received special pay and other priorities, and were used as shock troops throughout the war. By 1945, the guards designation had been given to 11 rifle and 6 tank armies; a cavalry-mechanized group; 40 rifle, 7 cavalry, 12 tank, and 9 mechanized corps; 117 rifle, 9 airborne, 17 cavalry, 6 artillery, 7 guards mortar, and 5 air-defense artillery divisions; 13 motorized rifle, 3 airborne, 66 tank, 28 mechanized, 3 self-propelled artillery, 63 artillery, 1 mortar, 40 guards mortar, 6 engineer, and 1 railroad brigade; and 1 fortified region. See S. I. Isaev, "Rozhdennaia v boiakh" [Born in battle], *VIZh* 9 (September 1986): 78–83; and Volkogonov, *Stalin: Triumph and Tragedy*, 431.

9. Reinhardt, *Moscow—The Turning Point*, 369. Soviet open source estimates of German losses until recently have been routinely and grossly inflated. New archival materials are correcting this error.

10. Ibid., 213–263, 381; Omar Bartov, *The Eastern Front, 1941-1945: German Troops and the Barbarization of Warfare* (New York: St. Martin's Press, 1986), 110–111.

11. Reinhardt, *Moscow—The Turning Point*, 395–396; Albert Speer, *Inside the Third Reich*, 25n, 193–213; Williamson Murray, *Luftwaffe* (Baltimore, Md.: Nautical and Aviation, 1985), 133–134.

12. Bartov, *The Eastern Front*, 75–99.

13. "Operatsiia 'Kreml'" [Operation Kremlin], *VIZh* 8 (August 1961): 79–90, contains a full set of German planning documents for the deception.

14. For Soviet spring planning, see I. Kh. Bagramian, *Tak shli my k pobede* [As we went on to victory] (Moscow: Voenizdat, 1977), 47–88; S. K. Moskalenko, *Na iugo-zapadnom napravlenii, T. 1* [On the southwestern direction, Vol. 1], (Moscow: "Nauka," 1969), 172–191; and S. F. Begunov, A. V. Litvinchuk, and V. A. Sutulov, "Vot gde pravda, Nikita Sergeevich!" [Where is the truth, Nikita Sergeevich], *VIZh* 12 (December 1989): 12–21; 1 (January 1990): 9–18; and 2 (February 1990): 35–46. The latter series contains declassified planning documents and correspondence related to strategic planning for early 1942.

15. Ziemke and Bauer, *Moscow to Stalingrad*, 225–231 and A. Zheltov, "Na pravom flange" [On the right flank], *VIZh* 1 (January 1980): 47–54.

8. Operation Blau

1. This section is based primarily on George E. Blau, *The German Campaign in Russia: Planning and Operations, 1940–1942* (Washington, D.C.: OCMH, 1955; reprinted 1988), 109–142.

2. Ibid., 121–128.

3. Erich von Manstein, *Lost Victories* (Chicago: Henry Regnery Co., 1958), 291–293.

4. This section is based primarily on a previously classified study by the Soviet General Staff contained in *Sbornik voenno-istoricheskikh materialov Velikoi Otechestvennoi voiny, vypusk 5* [Collection of military-historical materials of the Great Patriotic War, Issue 5] (Moscow: Voenizdat 1951), 3–89. This study is translated by Harold S. Orenstein and published in two installments as "The Khar'kov Operation, May 1942: from the Archives, Part I" and "Part II" in *JSMS* 5:3 (September 1992): 451–493; and 4 (December 1992): 611–686. See also the map study that accompanies Part I of this translation, in *JSMS* 5:3 (September 1992): 494–510. For the German side, see A. F. von Bechtolzheim, *The Battle of Kharkov, MS # L-023* (Headquarters United States Army, Europe Historical Division, 1956). The Soviets referred to this as the Khar'kov Offensive Operation.

5. The overall offensive was directed by Marshal Timoshenko's Southwestern Direction headquarters. For planning details and disputes over its conduct, see I. Kh. Bagramian, *Tak shli my k pobeda* [How we went on to victory] (Moscow: Voenizdat, 1977), 47–141; K. S. Moskalenko, *Na iugo-zapadnom napravlenii* [On the southwestern direction] (Moscow: "Nauka," 1969), 132–218; and the more recent series by S. F. Begunov, A. V. Litvinchuk, and V. A. Sutulov, "Vot gde pravda, Nikita Sergeevich" [Where is the truth, Nikita Sergeevich], *VIZh* 12 (December 1989): 12–21; 1 (January 1990): 9–18; 2 (February 1990): 35–45. The latter details the political machinations associated with the defeat. Nikita S. Khrushchev was Southwestern Front commissar.

6. Earl F. Ziemke and Magna E. Bauer, *Moscow to Stalingrad: Decision in the East* (Washington, D.C.: U.S. Army Center of Military History, 1987) 272–276.

7. Out of an initial strength of 765,300 men the Soviets lost 277,190 (170,958 killed, seriously wounded, and missing and 106,232 sanitary casualties), 18 to 20 divisions, 4,934 guns and mortars, and 652 tanks. The southern encirclement itself

swallowed up over 207,000 Soviet soldiers and 6th Army (with Group Bobkin) alone lost most of its senior commanders, 148,325 men, and 468 tanks. See G. F. Krivosheev, *Grif sekretnosti sniat: poteri vooruzhennykh sil SSSR v voinakh, boevykh deistviiakh i voennykh konfliktakh* [Losses of the armed forces of the USSR in wars, combat actions, and military conflicts] (Moscow: Voenizdat, 1993) 225.

8. For details, see the exposé by B. N. Nevzorov, "Mai 1942-go: Ak Monai, Enikale" [May 1942: Ak Monai, Enikale], *VIZh* 8 (August 1992): 32–42. According to Nevzorov, during the February-April offensive, the Soviets lost 226,370 men; and during the May catastrophe, more than 150,000 men, 4,646 guns and mortars, 496 tanks, and 417 aircraft were lost. During the harrowing withdrawal, 140,000 troops were evacuated or swam across the Kerch Straits to the Taman Peninsula. Krivosheev, *Grif sekretnosti*, 225, places Soviet losses in May at 176,566 out of a total force of 249,800, 162,282 of which were irrevocably lost.

9. von Manstein, *Lost Victories*, 233–257; Blau, *The German Campaign in Russia*, 140–141.

10. See A. M. Vasilevsky, *Delo vsei zhizni* [A Lifelong Cause] (Moscow: Voenizdat, 1983), 197, and Moskalenko, 214–245. For a full discussion of Soviet strategic assessments and the role of intelligence in their formulation, see David M. Glantz, *Soviet Military Intelligence in War*, (London: Frank Cass, 1990), 61–72.

11. Ziemke and Bauer, *Moscow to Stalingrad*, 342–343; Shtemenko, *The Soviet General Staff at War*, Vol. 2, 79–84. "Combat Operations of Briansk and Voronezh Front Forces in Summer 1942 on the Voronezh Axis," *JSMS* 6:2 (June 1993): 300–340, which is a translation of the same Russian title in *SVIMVOV*, Vol. 15 (Moscow: Voenizdat, 1955), 115–146; classified secret. See also M. Kazakov, "Na voronezhkom napravlenii letom 1942 goda" [On the Voronezh axis in summer 1942], *VIZh* 10 (October 1964): 27–44. Kazakov cites 5th Tank Army's tank strength as 600 against half as many German tanks on the same axis.

12. For a detailed assessment of this hitherto obscure Soviet failure see "Nekotorie vyvody po operatsiiam levogo kryla Zapadnogo fronta" [Some conclusions concerning the operations of the Western Front's left wing], *SMPIOV* No. 5 (Moscow: Voenizdat, 1943), 60–75. Classified secret.

13. Ziemke and Bauer, *Moscow to Stalingrad*, 346–348.

14. Blau, *German Campaign in Russia*, 145–149, 155.

15. Ibid., 150. Ziemke and Bauer provide an extended discussion/conjecture (340–343) about the Soviet counterattacks and decision to retreat. Similar discussions are found in Vasilevsky, *Delo vsei zhizni*, 201–202, and Shtemenko, *The Soviet General Staff at War*, 88–91. Soviet losses in the so-called Voronezh-Voroshilovgrad strategic defensive operation (28 June–24 July) were 568,347 of 1,310,800 engaged, broken down as follows:

Force	Strength	Unreturned	Sanitary	Total
Briansk Front	169,400	36,883	29,329	66,212
Southwestern Front	610,000	161,465	71,276	232,741
Southern Front	522,500	128,460	64,753	193,213

Voronezh Front		43,687	32,442	76,129
Azov Flotilla	8,900	27	25	52
Total	1,310,800	370,522	197,825	568,347

16. For German strategic debates, see V. E. Tarrant, *Stalingrad* (New York: Hippocrone, 1992), 37–38.

17. The Southwestern Strategic Direction headquarters was abolished on 21 June 1942, in part because of its and Timoshenko's dismal performance. Henceforth the *Stavka* worked through the General Staff and individual *front* headquarters, often using *Stavka* representatives to coordinate major strategic operations.

18. Ziemke and Bauer, *Moscow to Stalingrad*, 357–358; Shtemenko, *The Soviet General Staff at War*, Vol. 2, 87–90. For details on the operations of 62d, 64th, 1st Tank, and 4th Tank Armies, see A. Vasilevsky, "Nezabyvaemye dhi" [Unforgettable days], *VIZh* 10 (October 1965): 13–25, who places the tank armies' respective strengths at 160 and 80; and F. Utenkov, "Nekotorye voprosy oboronitel'nogo srazheniia na dal'nikh podstupakh k Stalingrady" [Some questions concerning the battles on the distant approaches to Stalingrad], *VIZh* 9 (September 1962): 34–48. For a classified account, see "Srazheniia za Stalingrad" [The Battle for Stalingrad], *SMPIOV* No. 6 (Moscow: Voenizdat, 1943), 22–37. Classified secret.

19. The 4th Tank Army was later renumbered as 65th Army. Its new commander, General Batov, relates that when he assumed command, the army was referred to derisively as the "4-tank army," reflecting its parlous state at the time.

20. Volkogonov, *Stalin: Triumph and Tragedy*, 458–460. Order No. 227 is reproduced in full in "Dokumenty i materialy" [Documents and materials], *VIZh* 8 (August 1988): 73–75.

21. On the Stalingrad Battle, see V. I. Chuikov, *Srazheniia veka* [Battle of the century] (Moscow: Voenizdat, 1875); K. K. Rokossovsky, ed., *Velikaia pobeda na volga* [Great victory on the Volga] (Moscow: Voenizdat, 1965); and A. M. Samsonov, *Stalingradskaia bitva* [The Battle of Stalingrad] (Moscow: Voenizdat, 1982). Archival materials closely match the details in these books. From the German viewpoint, Edwin P. Hoyt, *199 Days: The Battle of Stalingrad* (New York, 1993), provides fascinating details.

22. Selected casualty figures for the Stalingrad defense were as follows: 95th Rifle Division arrived in late September 1942 with approximately 7,000 men; strength on 8 October, 3,075 men; evacuated on 14 October with approximately 500 men. The 193d Rifle Division arrived on the night of 27–28 September with 5,000 men; strength on 8 October, 350 men. The 112th Rifle Division was present from the beginning of battle (September) with a strength of approximately 7,000 men; strength on 29 September, 250 men organized into a composite battalion; evacuated on 14 October. The 37th Guards Rifle Division arrived on the night of 2–3 October with 7,000 men; fought at Tractor Factory; evacuated on 15 October with 250 men. The 13th Guards Rifle Division (187th Rifle Division), commanded by Major General Rodimtsev, arrived on the night of 15–16 September with over

10,000 men, fought at Mamaev Kurgon and Tractor Factory; strength of several hundred on 15 October.

23. Blau, *German Campaign in Russia*, 168–175. According to Krivosheev, *Grif sekretnosti*, 197, Soviet casualties during the Stalingrad Strategic Defensive Operation (17 July–18 November) were 643,842 (323,856 irrevocable and 319,986 sanitary). Initial Soviet strength was 547,000 troops.

9. Operation Uranus

1. For a clear picture of how the *Stavka* and General Staff functioned, see the two volumes by S. M. Shtemenko, *The Soviet General Staff at War*, 2 vols. (Moscow: Progress Publishers, 1985).

2. For a complete description of the operations of the *Stavka* and its representatives, see V. D. Danilov, *Stavka VGK, 1941–1945* [*Stavka* of the Supreme High Command, 1941–1945] (Moscow: "Znanie," 1991).

3. Dimitri Volkogonov, *Stalin: Triumph and Tragedy*, trans. and ed., Harold Shuhman (Rocklin, Calif.: Prima Publishing, 1992), 461–463. See also S. Mikhalev, "O razrabotke zamysla i planirovanii kontranastupleniia pod Stalingradom" [About the concept and planning of the counteroffensive at Stalingrad], *Vestnik voennoi informatsii* [Herald of military information] 8 (August 1992): 1–5, which discusses offensive variants developed by the *Stavka* between July and October 1942.

4. N. F. Vatutin, described as the ultimate staff planner, had served on the staff of the Special Kiev Military District as chief of staff of the Northwestern Front and as troubleshooter for the *Stavka* and A. M. Vasilevsky. All the while he hankered for *front* command, which he finally received during the perilous days before Stalingrad. Thereafter, he earned a reputation as one of the most audacious *front* commanders, before he perished at the hands of Ukrainian partisans in April 1944.

5. For details, see K. K. Rokossovsky, ed., *Velikaia pobeda na Volga*, [Great Victory on the Volga] (Moscow: Voenizdat, 1965) and the formerly classified archival accounts "Flangovye udary Krasnoi Armii v Stalingradskom srazhenii" [Flank strikes in the Stalingrad battle], and "Deistviia podvizhnoi gruppy 5 tankovoi armii v proryve" [Actions of 5th Tank Army in the penetration], *SMPIOV* 6 (April–May 1943): 37–62.

6. Van Hardesty, *Red Phoenix: The Rise of Soviet Air Power, 1941–1945* (Washington, D.C.: Smithsonian Institution Press, 1982), 83–85, 94–95, 104.

7. George E. Blau, *The German Campaign in Russia: Planning and Operations, 1940–1942* (Washington, D.C.: OCMH, 1955), 161, 171–172.

8. For example, from 31 July–23 August, the Kalinin and Western Fronts conducted the Rzhev-Sychevka operation against Army Group Center but recorded only limited gains. In the Leningrad region, the Volkhov and Leningrad Fronts launched the Siniavinsk operation from 20 August to early September but failed to relieve the siege of the city.

9. M. Kozlov, "Razvitie strategie i operativnogo iskusstva" [Development of strategy and operational art], *VIZh* 11 (November 1982): 12; Blau, *German*

Campaign in Russia, 173. For a full account of Soviet deception planning, see David M. Glantz, *Soviet Military Deception in the Second World War* (London: Frank Cass, 1989), 105–119.

10. According to G. F. Krivosheev, *Grif sekretosti sniat: Poteri vooruzhennykh sil SSSR v voinakh, boevykh deistviiakh, i voennykh konfliktakh* [Losses of the armed forces of the USSR in war, combat actions, and military conflicts (Moscow: Voenizdat, 1965), 181–182, and Rokossovsky, *Velikaia pobeda*, 254–258, German (and allied) forces in the Stalingrad region numbered about 600,000 men, 500 tanks, and 400 aircraft. These included Sixth Army force of about 300,000; Third and Fourth Rumanian Armies, with about 200,000; and elements of Fourth Panzer Army, with about 100,000. The Eighth Italian Army, with 100,000 troops, was not subjected to attack in November. About 100,000 troops of the Soviet Southwestern Front were also not directly involved in the November operation.

11. Fortuitously for the Soviets, near Kalach was a German training area where Soviet vehicles were used in tactical exercises. Apparently, the German sentries presumed that Filippov's tanks were associated with this training area. The Germans did retake the town for a time, but the Soviets held the key bridges until the main body of 26th Tank Corps had arrived.

12. O. Losik, "Boevoe primenenie bronetankovykh i mekhanizirovannykh voisk" [Combat employment of armored and mechanized forces [at Stalingrad], *VIZh* 11 (November 1982): 45–47.

13. These reserves included Lieutenant General R. Ia. Malinovsky's powerful 2d Guards Army, which the Germans did not know existed and which would soon make its presence known.

14. Hardesty, *Red Phoenix*, 107–119.

15. For a limited view of the *Stavka* plan, see G. K. Zhukov, *Reminiscences and Reflections*, Vol. 2 (Moscow: Progress Publishers, 1989), 129–131. M. D. Solomatin, *Krasnogradtsy* [The Krasnograds] (Moscow: Voenizdat, 1963), 5–44, confirms Zhukov's description and provides considerable detail on the role of 1st Mechanized Corps and 6th Rifle Corps in the operation. M. E. Katukov, *Na ostrie glavnogo udara* [At the point of the main attack] (Moscow: Voenizdat, 1976), 182–184, refers to the operation as the Rzhev-Sychevka operation and emphasizes its importance. All these studies were written in the early 1960s, when Soviet historiography was briefly noted for its candor. Before and since that time, Soviet sources have said virtually nothing about this operation, except to claim that it was a diversion for Stalingrad.

16. For confirmation of the importance the Germans accord to the operation, see David Kahn, "An Intelligence Case History: The Defense of Osuga, 1942," *Aerospace Historian* 28:4 (Winter 1981): 243–254. Kahn's judgments regarding the operation's intended significance are likely correct. Soviet force concentrations during late November 1942 underscore the seriousness of Operation Mars. The three Soviet *fronts* (Southwestern, Don, and Stalingrad) participating in Operation Uranus at Stalingrad contained 1,103,000 men; 15,501 guns and mortars; 1,463 tanks; and 928 combat aircraft. At the same time, the Kalinin and Western Fronts and Moscow Defense Zone numbered 1,890,000 men; 24,682 guns and

mortars; 3,375 tanks; and 1,170 aircraft. Main attack armies in the sector from Belyi to Viaz'ma (41st, 20th, 33d, 5th, and perhaps 3d Tank) were as strong as or stronger than their counterparts in the Stalingrad region (63d, 5th Tank, 21th, and 57th), and mobile forces were just as imposing. Forces concentrated for Operation Mars constituted 31 percent of the personnel, 32 percent of the artillery, 45 percent of the tanks, and almost 39 percent of the aircraft of the entire Red Army, while commensurate percentages for Operation Uranus were 18 percent personnel, 20 percent artillery, 20 percent tanks, and 30 percent aircraft. See G. F. Krivosheev, *Grif sekretnosti sniat: poteri vooruzhennykh sil SSSR v voinakh, boevykh deistviiakh, i voennykh konfliktakh* [Classification secret removed: Losses of the armed forces of the USSR in wars, combat actions, and military conflicts] (Moscow: Voenizdat, 1993), 181–182, and A. A. Grechko, ed., *Istoriia vtoroi mirovoi voiny 1939–1945, T. 6* [A history of the Second World War, Vol. 6] (Moscow: Voenizdat, 1976), 35. For complete Soviet order of battle, and in particular the combat composition and strength of all armies in Operations Uranus and Mars, see *Boevoi sostav Sovetskoi armii, chast' 2* [The combat composition of the Soviet Army, Part 2] (Moscow: Voenizdat, 1966). Prepared by the Military-Scientific Directorate of the Soviet Army General Staff, this classified study leaves no doubt about the power and intent of Operation Mars and its aborted follow-on operation.

17. The most thorough German account of the operation, together with a complete Soviet order of battle, is found in "Feindnachrichtenblatt" Nrs. 138, 139, 140, and 141, *Armeeoberkommando 9 Ic/A.O., 3134/12 geh.*, A.H.Qu., 30.11.42, 3 March 1942, and 15 December 1942, with appendices and daily maps in NAM T-312. According to these documents, Solomatin's and Povetkin's corps were destroyed, Katukov's corps suffered 75 to 85 percent losses, and Konev's two armies and several mobile corps were also decimated in the November-December battles. The Germans counted 195 tanks destroyed in the initial three days of combat on Konev's *front*, as the Soviets committed their armor prematurely and in piecemeal fashion. By German estimates, between 24 November and 14 December, the Soviets lost a total of 1,655 tanks and more than 15,000 dead. Krivosheev, *Grif sekretnosti*, 225, is silent about Soviet losses in this operation, although he shows a figure of 104,022 lost at Velikie Luki and 86,700 men initially engaged. On the other hand, the Germans lost almost the entire 7,000-man garrison at Velikie Luki after rescue attempts failed. The Soviet defeat, particularly in 20th Army's sector, resulted in part from the premature commitment of massive armored forces into a confined penetration sector. The crush of forces and resulting confusion were so great that supporting artillery could not be brought up. Deprived of artillery support and immobilized on crowded roads, Soviet mobile forces and infantry perished in staggering numbers. Interestingly enough, Zhukov would repeat this pattern in April 1945 when his forces assaulted the Seelow Heights east of Berlin, but with less disastrous consequences.

18. The Soviets lost almost one half million men in the operation. Casualties in individual formations were appalling: the 20th Army's after action report recorded 58,524 lost out of 114,176 committed to action. The 20th Army's 8th Guards Rifle corps lost 6,058 in five days of combat and its 148th and 150th Rifle Brigades emerged with

74 and 110 surviving riflemen, respectively. The 6th Tank Corps lost its entire strength of 170 tanks twice over, 1st Mechanized Corps with its 15,200 men and 224 tanks was destroyed, and 5th Tank Corps lost all of its tanks in just three days of combat.

19. For details, see M. Shaposhnikov, "Boevye deistviia 5-go mekhanizirovan-nogo korpusa zapadnee Surovokino v dekabre 1942 goda" [Combat operations of 5th Mechanized Corps west of Surokovino in December 1942], *VIZh* 10 (October 1982): 32–37. Interestingly, 5th Mechanized Corps was equipped with 193 tanks, the bulk of which were Matilda and Valentine lend-lease tanks with 40-mm guns, which had weak armor-piercing capability. See also H. Schneider, "Breakthrough Attack by the V Russian Mechanized Corps on the Chir River from 10–16 December 1942," *Small Unit Tactics, Tactics of Individual Arms: Project No. 48, MS # P-060 f, Part II* (Historical Division, U.S. Army European Command: Foreign Military Studies Branch, undated), Appendix 3.

20. For details on the Tatsinskaia raid, see David M. Glantz, *From the Don to the Dnepr: Soviet Offensive Operations, December 1942–August 1943* (London: Frank Cass, 1991), 65–69.

21. Earl F. Ziemke and Magna E. Bauer, *Moscow to Stalingrad: Decision in the East* (Washington, D.C.: U.S. Army Center of Military History, 1987), 501. According to V.E. Tarrant, *Stalingrad* (New York: Hippocrene Books, 1992), 230, German and Rumanian forces surrounded at Stalingrad numbered 267,000, of which 36,000 were evacuated by air, 140,000 were killed, and 91,000 surrendered. Another 15,000 Germans in Sixth Army were killed in the counteroffensive (19–23 November) for a total of 241,000 dead in Sixth Army. In addition, some 300,000 Rumanian, Italian, and Hungarian forces were lost at Stalingrad and in associated operations.

22. See Ziemke and Bauer, *Moscow to Stalingrad*, 74. The new Tiger tanks went into action in support of SS *Viking* Motorized Division.

23. For details on this operation, see "Ostrogozhsko-Rossoshanskaia nas-tupatel'naia operatsiia voisk voronezhskogo fronta" [The Ostrogozhsk-Rossosh' offensive operation of Voronezh Front forces], *SVIMVOV*, Issue 9 (Moscow: Voenizdat, 1953), 1–121; classified secret.

24. For an account of the Voronezh-Kastornoe operation, see "Voronezhsko-kastornenskaia nastupatel'naia operatsiia voisk voronezhskogo i levogo kryla brianskogo frontov" [The Voronezh-Kastornoe offensive operation of forces of the Voronezh and left wing of the Briansk Fronts], *SVIMVOV*, Issue 13 (Moscow: Voenizdat, 1954); classified secret.

25. For details on operations Star and Gallop, see Glantz, *From the Don to the Dnepr*, 82–215. No formerly classified accounts of these two operations have been released by the Russians.

26. Erich von Manstein, *Lost Victories* (Chicago: Henry Regnery Co., 1958), 422–423.

27. The original concept of operation is in A. M. Vasilevsky, *Delo vsei zhizni* [A lifelong cause] (Minsk: "Belarus," 1984), 278–279. Other details are offered in David M. Glantz, "Prelude to Kursk: Soviet Strategic Operations, February-March 1943," to be published in a forthcoming volume by the German Military History Office, Freiburg, Germany.

28. For details on Central Front Operations, see K. Rokossovsky, *A Soldier's Duty* (Moscow: Progress Publishers, 1985), 174–178. Other memoirs, including those of P. I. Batov (65th Army) and I. M. Chistiakov (21st Army), and unit histories such as 21st Army's, contain fragmentary materials on the operation.

29. For details of Lieutenant General Bagramian's failure, see I. Kh. Bagramian, *Tak shli my k pobeda* [As we went on to victory] (Moscow: Voenizdat, 1988), 371–378.

30. A particularly good account of 2d Tank Army's role is found in F. E. Vysotsky, et al., *Gvardeiskaia tankovaia* [Guards tank] (Moscow: Voenizdat, 1963), 15–23.

31. These operations are especially impressive in light of the relative weakness of forces involved. For example, Popov's mobile group numbered only 212 tanks initially and 25 tanks on 20 February. On 6 February 7th and 11th Panzer Divisions possessed only 35 tanks and 16 tanks, respectively. During von Manstein's counter-stroke 17th Panzer Division of XXXXVIII Panzer Corps numbered only 8 tanks and 11 self-propelled guns. On the other hand, Soviet 25th and 1st Guards Tank Corps totaled 300 tanks, as did the two SS panzer divisions.

32. von Manstein, *Lost Victories*, 431–433. German records show Soviet losses as 23,200 dead, 9,071 captured, and 615 tanks destroyed. Krivosheev, *Grif sekretnosti*, is silent on Soviet losses in this operation and in Rokossovsky's operation.

33. Russian archival sources released to date generally say nothing about the Khar'kov defensive operation and the Central Front offensive in February and March, nor does Krivosheev, *Grif sekretnosti*, provide casualties. In fact, no reference is made to the Central Front during the entire period.

10. Rasputitsa and Operational Pause

1. George E. Blau, *The German Campaign in Russia: Planning and Operations, 1940–1942* (Washington, D.C.: OCMH, 1955), 153, 156, 162. Heinz Guderian, *Panzer Leader* (Washington, D.C.: Zenger Publishing Co., 1979), 310.

2. Blau, *German Campaign in Russia*, 169.

3. Williamson Murray, *Luftwaffe* (Baltimore, Md.: Nautical and Aviation Publishing Co. of America, 1985), 158.

4. Ibid. 144 (Table 31).

5. Brian Moynahan, *Claws of the Bear* (Boston: Houghton Mifflin, 1989), 129. Moynahan provides a good brief summary of Lend-Lease aid on pp. 127–129. For the uranium oxide incident, see Steven J. Zaloga, *Target America: The Soviet Union and the Strategic Arms Race, 1945–1965* (Novato, Calif.: Presidio Press, 1993), 18–19. For the first candid Russian appreciation of the scope and impact of Allied Lend-Lease, see B. V. Sokolov, "The Role of Lend-Lease in Soviet Military Efforts, 1941–1945," *JSMS* 7:3 (September 1994): 567–586.

6. On P-39s in the Kuban, see Van Hardesty, *Red Phoenix: The Rise of Soviet Air Power, 1941–1945* (Washington, D.C.: Smithsonian Institution Press, 1982), 139–142.

7. German strength from "Kraftegegenubersrellung Stand: 1.4.43" *Anlage 4b zu Abt. Fr.H.Ost(I), No. 80/43 g. Kdos vom 17.10.43* NAM T-78, Roll 552. The

Germans assessed Soviet strength at 5,152,000 troops, 6,040 tanks, and 20,683 artillery pieces. Based on data from GKO files of the Central Party Archives (TsPA) UML, fond 644, op. 1, d.100, on 3 April 1943, Soviet strength was as follows: ration strength (army), 9,486,000; hospital strength (army), 1,066,000; operating *fronts* and armies, 5,792,000; nonoperating forces (Transcaucasus and Far East), 1,469,000; internal military districts, 2,225,000; fleet, 400,000; NKVD troops, 471,000; and GKO subordination, 718,000.

8. Timothy A. Wray, *Standing Fast: German Defensive Doctrine on the Eastern Front During World War II: Prewar to March 1943* (Fort Leavenworth, Kan.: Combat Studies Institute, 1986), 113. This discussion of German defensive organization and doctrine is based on pp. 112–172.

9. Earl F. Ziemke and Magna E. Bauer, *Moscow to Stalingrad: Decision in the East* (Washington, D.C.: U.S. Army Center of Military History, 1987), 325.

10. Erich von Manstein claims to have protested this matter to Hitler at his promotion ceremony in October 1942. See von Manstein, *Lost Victories* (Chicago: Henry Regnery Co., 1958), 268–269, 280.

11. Wray, *Standing Fast*, 118–123.

12. Blau, *German Campaign in Russia*, 166–167; Guderian, *Panzer Leader*, 275.

13. Guderian, *Panzer Leader*, 287–300.

14. For a good description of this process, see P. A. Kurochkin, *Obshchevoiskovaia armiia na nastuplenii* [The combined-arms army on the offensive] (Moscow: Voenizdat, 1966); and Iu. P. Babich and A. G. Baier, *Razvitie vooruzheniia i organizatsii sovetskikh sukhoputnykh voisk v gody Velikoi otechestvennoi voiny* [The development of equipment and the organization of Soviet ground forces during the Great Patriotic War] (Moscow: "Akademii," 1990)

15. These indices of depth increased steadily from 50 km in summer 1943 to more than 200 km in summer 1944 and 1945.

16. Tank armies were formed in accordance with GKO Order No. 2791, dated 28 January 1943. See Babich and Baier, *Razvitie vooruzheniia*, 46.

17. For detail, on the 9 October decree, see Ziemke and Bauer, *Moscow to Stalingrad*, 438–439. In addition, since 1941, soldiers had been allowed to join the Communist Party and Komsomol with few, if any, formalities, spreading the party's network within troop units.

18. Numerous Soviet studies and unit histories document this fact, as do extensive holdings in German *Fremde Heere Ost* files.

19. Guderian, *Panzer Leader*, 306–309. See also Bryan Perrett, *Knights of the Black Cross: Hitler's Panzerwaffe and Its Leaders* (New York: St. Martin's, 1986), 161–163.

20. G. Zhukov, "Na Kurskoi duge," [In the Kursk Bulge], *VIZh* 8 (August 1967): 73, 76. Vatutin was among those who argued for an earlier offensive.

21. A. M. Vasilevsky, *Delo vsei zhizni* [A lifelong cause] (Minsk: "Belarus," 1984), 288–306; G. K. Zhukov, *Reminiscences and Reflections*, Vol. 2 (Moscow: Progress Publishers, 1989), 144–182; S. M. Shtemenko, *The Soviet General Staff at War*, Vol. 1 (Moscow: Progress Publishers, 1985), 211–234.

11. Kursk to the Dnepr

1. For the German order of battle and preparations, see Bryan Perrett, *Knights of the Black Cross: Hitler's Panzer Waffe and Its Leaders* (New York: St. Martin's Press, 1986), 163–164.

2. Heinz Guderian, *Panzer Leader* (Washington, D.C.: Zenger Publishing Co., 1979), 299.

3. Perrett, *Knights of the Black Cross*, 156–158; and Iu. P. Babich and A. G. Baier, *Razvitie vooruzheniia i organizatsii sovetskikh sukhoputnykh voisk v gody Velikoi otechestvennoi voiny* [The development of equipment and the organization of Soviet ground forces during the Great Patriotic War] (Moscow: "Akademii," 1990), 12, 91. The principal antitank weapons remained the 45mm antitank and 76mm regimental gun, supplemented by the 57mm gun later in 1943. For the development of SP and antitank guns and units, see M. Popov, "Razvitie samokhodnoi artillerii" [The development of self-propelled artillery], *VIZh* 1 (January 1977) 27–31; and V. Budur, "Razvitie protivotankovoi artillerii gody Velikoi Otechestvennoi voiny" [The development of antitank artillery in the Great Patriotic War], *VIZh* 6 (June 1973) 79–84.

4. David M. Glantz, "Soviet Operational Intelligence in the Kursk Operation, July 1943" in *Intelligence and National Security* 5:1 (January 1990), 8–15, and David M. Glantz, *Soviet Military Intelligence in War* (London: Frank Cass and Co., 1990), 184–283. For an example of Soviet order-of-battle analysis, see "Report of the Voronezh Front to the Chief of Staff," April 12, 1943, reprinted in *The Battle of Kursk*, ed. Ivan Parotkin (Moscow: Progress Publishers, 1974), 346.

5. David M. Glantz, *Soviet Defensive Tactics at Kursk, CSI Report No. 11* (Fort Leavenworth, Kan.: Combat Studies Institute, 1986).

6. For full details on the Battle of Kursk from the Soviet viewpoint, including complete order of battle and operational and tactical detail, see the formerly classified "Kurskaia bitva" [The Battle of Kursk], *SMPIOV*, No. 11 (Moscow: Voenizdat, 1964).

7. According to V. N. Simbolikov, *Kurskaia bitva, 1943* [The Battle of Kursk, 1943] (Moscow: Voroshilov Academy of the General Staff, 1950), classified secret, total Soviet strength, including noncombat units, was: Central Front, 711,575; Voronezh Front, 625,591; and Steppe Front, 573,195, for a total Soviet strength of 1,920,361. See G. Koltunov, "Kurskaia bitva v tsifrakh" [The Battle of Kursk in numbers], *VIZh* 6 (June 1968): 58–68.

8. R. A. Savuskhin, ed., *Razvitie Sovetskikh vooruzhennykh sil i voennogo iskusstva v Velikoi Otechestvennoi voine 1941–1945 gg.* [The development of the Soviet Armed Forces and military art in the Great Patriotic War, 1941–1945] (Moscow: VPA, 1988), 65. These figures include forces along the entire strategic front from Orel to Khar'kov.

9. In fact, German intelligence failed to detect the presence of the majority of Soviet strategic reserves. See David M. Glantz, *Soviet Military Intelligence in War* (London: Frank Cass and Co., 1990), 267–279.

10. F. W. von Mellenthin, *Panzer Battles*, trans. H. Betzler (Norman, Okla. University of Oklahoma Press, 1956), 218–225.

11. For a thorough account of this tank battle, see P. A. Rotmistrov, *Stal'naia gvardiia* [Steel guards] (Moscow: Voenizdat, 1988). Precise tank strength on both sides has been unclear and controversial. Accordingly to formerly classified Soviet sources, II SS Panzer Corps numbered 600 tanks, including 100 Tigers and Ferdinands, of which 500 were engaged at Prokhorovka. Rotmistrov's 5th Guards Tank Army numbered 793, including 501 T-34s, 261 light T-70s, and 31 English Churchills. Of the 793 tanks, 100 were in 2d Guards Tank Corps, operating south of Prokhorovka. See Simbolikov, *Kurskaia bitva, 1943.*

12. Among the best Soviet accounts of the Orel operation are: "Proryv oborony na flange orlovskoi gruppirovki nemtsev" [Penetration of defenses on the flank of the enemy Orel group], *SMPIOV* 10 (Moscow: Voenizdat, 1944), 4–48; L. Sandalov, "Brianskii front v orlovskoi operatsii" [The Briansk Front in the Orel operation], *VIZh* 8 (August 1963): 62–72; and I. Bagramian, "Flangovi udar 11-i gvardeiskoi armii" [The flank attack of 11th Guards Army], *VIZh* 7 (July 1963): 83–95. According to G. F. Krivosheev, *Grif sekretnosti sniat: Poleri vooruzhennykh sil SSSR v voinakh, boevykh deistviiakh, i voennykh konfliktakh* [Losses of the armed forces of the USSR in wars, combat actions, and military conflicts] (Moscow: Voenizdat, 1993), 189, 1,287,600 Russian troops took part in the operation (Western Front, 233,300; Briansk Front, 409,000; and Central Front, 645,300).

13. The offensives along the Mius and Northern Donets River, launched by Southern and Southwestern Fronts on 17 July, were spectacularly unsuccessful. Although they did fulfill their purpose of diverting significant forces from the Khar'kov region, the *Stavka* probably wished they could have accomplished even more. The best Soviet account of these operations is A. G. Ershov, *Osvobozhdenie donbassa* [Liberation of the Donbas] (Moscow: Voenizdat, 1973). Deception aspects of the operation are found in David M. Glantz, *Soviet Military Deception in the Second World War* (London: Frank Cass and Co., 1989), 146–182.

14. For details on the Belgorod-Khar'kov operation, see David M. Glantz, *From the Don to the Dnepr Soviet Offensive Operations, December 1942 to August 1943* (London: Frank Cass and Co., 1991), 215–366, and Glantz, *Soviet Military Deception*, 174–179.

15. According to Krivosheev, *Grif sekretnosti*, 190, Soviet strength in the Belgorod-Khar'kov operation was 1,144,000 (Voronezh Front, 739,000; Steppe Front, 464,600) opposed by about 350,000 Germans. Soviet losses were 255,566, including 71,611 killed or missing and 183,955 wounded.

16. See Glantz, *Soviet Military Deception*, 186–202. The best Soviet account is found in V. P. Istomin, *Smolenskaia nastupatel'naia operatsiia (1943 g.)* [The Smolensk offensive operation, 1943] (Moscow: Voenizdat, 1975). According to Krivosheev, *Grif sekretnosti*, 191, Soviet strength in Operation Suvorov totaled 1,252,600 men (Kalinin Front, 428,400; Western Front, 824,200), and from 7 August through 2 October the Soviets suffered 451,466 casualties, including 107,645 killed or missing and 343,821 wounded. The multistaged offensive propelled Soviet forces forward by early October to the eastern approaches to Vitebsk and Orsha in Belorussia.

17. Rokossovsky threw 579,600 men into the effort, known as the Chernigov-Pripiat' operation. According to Krivosheev, *Grif sekretnosti*, 183, Soviet losses totaled 141,401 killed or missing and 107,878 wounded. For a brief account of the operation, see Glantz, *Soviet Military Deception*, 208–216.

18. According to Krivosheev, *Grif sekretnosti*, 226, Popov's *front* numbered 530,000 men and lost 56,657, including 13,033 killed or missing, during the Briansk operation.

19. For details, see Ershov, *Osvobozhdenie*. According to Krivosheev, *Grif sekretnosti*, 192, Malinovsky and Tolbukhin committed 564,200 and 446,700 troops, respectively, to battle during these operations and suffered combined losses of 273,522 (66,166 killed or missing and 207,356 wounded).

20. Vatutin's and Konev's operations, in reality a continuation of the Belgorod-Khar'kov operation, are known as the Sumy-Priluki and Poltava operations. Together with Rokossovsky's Chernigov-Pripiat' operation, they constitute the Chernigov-Poltava strategic offensive operation.

21. A. P. Riiazansky, *V ogne tankovykh srazhenii* [In the fire of tank battles] (Moscow: Nauka, 1975), 95.

22. For details on the Bukrin airborne drop, see David M. Glantz, *A History of Soviet Airborne Forces* (London: Frank Cass and Co., 1994).

23. See Ershov, *Osvobozhdenie*, for details on Tolbukhin's Melitopol' operation. Krivosheev, *Grif sekretnosti*, 226, cites his strength as 555,300 men and places his losses at 198,749, including 42,760 killed or missing.

24. On 20 October 1943, the Voronezh, Steppe, Southwestern, and Southern Fronts were renamed the 1st, 2d, 3d, and 4th Ukrainian Fronts, respectively. At the same time, the Central and Briansk Fronts merged to become the Belorussian Front and the Kalinin Front became the Baltic Front. Shortly thereafter, the Baltic Front split into the 1st and 2d Baltic Fronts, and on 20 November, the Northwestern Front was inactivated.

25. Among the many accounts of the Kiev operation, see K. Krainiukov, "Osvobozhdenie Kieva" [The liberation of Kiev], *VIZh* 10 (October 1963): 67–79; and G. Utkin, *Shturm 'Vostochnogo vala'* [Storm of the "Eastern Wall"] (Moscow: Voenizdat, 1967). Krainiukov was commissar for 1st Ukrainian Front. According to Krivosheev, *Grif sekretnosti*, 196, Vatutin fielded 671,000 men in the operation, and because of the surprise he achieved, his *front* suffered relatively light losses totaling 30,569 (6,491 killed or missing and 24,078 wounded.)

26. According to Krivosheev, *Grif sekretnosti*, 226, Rokossovsky's Belorussian Front committed 761,300 troops in the Gomel'-Rechitsa operation, losing 88,206 in the process (21,650 killed or missing and 60,556 wounded). Eremenko's 1st Baltic Front fielded 198,000 men and lost 168,900 men in more than two months of heavy fighting north of Vitebsk. Operations by Sokolovsky's Western Front against Vitebsk and Orsha have been ignored by Soviet historians. According to M. A. Gareev, "Prichiny i uroki neudachnykh nastupatel'nykh operatsii Zapadnogo fronta zimoi 1943–1944 goda" [Causes and lessons of unsuccessful Western Front offensive operations in winter 1943–1944], *Voennaia mysl'* [Military thought] 2 (February 1994): 50–58, the Western Front launched

four distinct offensives along the Orsha axis between 12 October and December 1943, suffering 104,064 casualties in the process. Gareev blames poor command procedures and excessive *Stavka* ambitiousness for the failures. German archival materials vividly underscore Soviet intentions and the futility of these attacks.

27. Timothy Wray, *Stand Fast: German Defensive Doctrine on the Eastern Front During World War II; Prewar to March 1943* (Fort Leavenworth, Kan.: Combat Studies Institute, 1986), 114, 150.

28. The immense casualties had a direct impact on combat results. For example, during fall 1943, Western Front rifle divisions numbered between 2,500 and 3,000 men each. Although this was the case in a less active sector, even along main axes Soviet divisions contained less than 6,000 men.

12. Third Winter of the War

1. Heinz Guderian, *Panzer Leader* (Washington, D.C.: Zenger Publishing Co., 1979), 314.

2. Fritz Stoeckli, "Wartime Casualty Rates: Soviet and German Loss Rates During the Second World War, the Price of Victory," *JSMS* 3:4 (December 1990): 649. Soviet regiments leading the attack in main attack sectors routinely lost 50 percent of their strength during an initial penetration operation (1 to 3 days).

3. By early 1944, the Soviets had fielded 10 Guards armies (numbered 1 through 8 and 10 and 11, with number 9, a special airborne army, appearing in October 1944) and 5 Shock armies (numbered 1–5). Three tank armies (1st, 3d, and 5th) plus a host of corps, divisions, and lesser units had received Guards designation.

4. *Polevoi ustav krasnoi armii 1944 (PU-44)* [Field Regulations of the Red Army, 1944] (Moscow: Voenizdat, 1944); translated by the Office of the Assistant Chief of Staff, G2, U.S. Army, p. 9.

5. This section draws upon those measures prescribed by the 1944 regulations, the collected volumes of war experiences (*SMPIOV*), memoir literature, and detailed interviews with 25 veterans who served as Soviet officers during the wartime operations.

6. German intelligence collected fragmentary evidence about the existence of two additional tank armies, the 7th and 8th, in the Ukraine in late 1944. Given that after the war these armies were stationed in Poland and in the Carpathian Military District (now known as the 7th and 8th Mechanized Armies, as tank armies were designated in 1945) it is likely these reports were correct. It is clear that the Soviets did not employ these armies during the war but rather held them back to deal with certain strategic eventualities, such as conflict with Allied forces at war's end.

7. At times a habitual relationship developed between a brigade serving as forward detachment and its parent tank army. For example, 1st and 3d Guards Tank Armies often employed 1st Guards and 91st Separate Tank Brigades for that

purpose. The Soviets exploited this pattern to deceive the Germans regarding their offensive intentions.

8. For German strength, see "Kraftegegenüberstellung," *Abt. Fr. H. Ost (1) No. 80/43 gkdes vom 17.10.43.* The Germans estimated Soviet troop strength on 1 January 1944 at 5,512,000 men, 8,400 tanks, and 20,770 guns and mortars. Official Soviet archival reports contained in data from the GKO files of the Central Party Archives (TsPA) IML, font. 644, op. 1, d. 218, ll. 101–102, 103–104, show the following Soviet strength on 12 March 1944: ration strength (army), 9,980,000; hospital strength (army), 1,255,000; *fronts* and armies in the field, 6,394,500; nonoperating forces (Trans-Baikal and Far East), 1,338,500; internal military districts, 2,247,000; fleets, 423,000; NKVD, 540,000; and GKO subordination, 860,000.

G. F. Krivosheev, *Grif sekretnosti sniat: Poteri vooruzhnnykh sil SSSR v. voinakh, boevykh deistviiakh i voennykh konfliktakh* [Losses of the armed forces of the USSR in wars, combat actions, and military conflicts] (Moscow: Voenizdat, 1993), 162, 350, places average monthly strength of the armies in the field at 6,343,600 for the third quarter 1943; 5,892,800 for the first quarter 1944; and 6,459,800 for the second quarter 1944. He provides the following equipment strength for armies in the field on 1 January 1944: 5,800 tanks and SP guns, 101,400 guns and mortars, and 13,400 combat aircraft.

9. For the planning of these operations, see A. M. Shtemenko, *General'nyi shtab v gody voiny* [The general staff in the war years] (Moscow: Voenizdat, 1968). Documents found in the classified volumes of *SBDVOV* verify much of Shtemenko's claims, as they do Zhukov's and Vasilesky's memoirs, which are also valuable sources for aspects of *Stavka* planning. See G. K. Zhukov, *Reminiscences and Reflections*, Vol. 2 (Moscow: Progress Publishers, 1989) and A. M. Vasilesky, *Delo vsei zhizni* [A lifelong cause] (Minsk: "Belarus," 1984). The five operations that constituted the first phase of the winter campaign are as follows: the Zhitomir-Berdichev operation (1st Ukrainian Front), 24 December 1943–14 January 1944; the Kirovograd operation (2d Ukrainian Front), 5–16 January 1944; the Korsun'-Shevchenkovskii operation (1st and 2d Ukrainian Fronts), 24 January–17 February 1944; the Rovno-Lutsk operation (1st Ukrainian Front), 29 January–11 February 1944; and the Nikopol'-Krivoi Rog operation (3d and 4th Ukrainian Fronts), 30 January–29 February 1944.

10. According to Krivosheev, *Grif sekretnosti*, 227, 1st Ukrainian Front's strength in the Zhitomir-Berdichev operation was 831,000 men, of which 100,018 were lost (23,163 killed or missing and 76,855 wounded). Konev's 2d Ukrainian Front fielded 550,000 men in the Kirovograd operation. Among the best accounts of both operations is A. M. Grylev, *Dnepr-karpaty-krym: Osvobozhdenie prav-oberezhnoi ukrainy i kryma v 1944 gody* [Dnepr–Carpathia–Crimea: The liberation of the right bank of Ukraine in 1944] (Moscow: "Nauka," 1970).

11. See "Korsun'-Shevchenkovskaia operatsiia" [The Korsun'-Shevchenkovskii operation], *SMPIOV*, No. 14 (Moscow: Voenizdat, 1945), 3–65, classified secret; and David M. Glantz, *Soviet Military Deception in the Second World War* (London: Frank Cass and Co., 1989), 314–322. For the German version, see U.S.

Department of the Army, *Historical Studies: Operations of Encircled Forces; German Experiences in Russia*, Pamphlet 20–234 (Washington D.C.: OCMH, 1952), 15–42.

12. Krivosheev, *Grif sekretnosti*, 227, places Vatutin's and Konev's combined force strength at 336,700, including reinforcements received during the operation, which included elements of 1st and 2d Tank Armies dispatched from other front sectors to help block German relief forces. Overall German strength was about 130,000. Soviet losses were 80,188, including 24,286 killed or missing.

13. For details on the Rovno-Lutsk operation, see I. M. Belkin, *13 armiia v Lutsko-Rovenskoi operatsii 1944 g.* [13th Army in the Rovno-Lutsk operation 1944] (Moscow: Voenizdat, 1960).

14. These included the Proskurov-Chernovtsy operation (1st Ukrainian Front), 4 March–17 April; the Uman'-Botoshany operation (2d Ukrainian Front), 5 March–17 April; the Bereznegovataia-Snigirevka operation (3d Ukrainian Front), 6–18 March; the Odessa operation (3d Ukrainian Front), 26 March–14 April; and the Crimean operation (4th Ukrainian Front), 8 April–12 May. The *Stavka* committed the four Ukrainian *fronts* and the 2d Belorussian Front (formed on 15 March in the Kovel' sector) to carry out these operations, which are known collectively as the Dnepr-Carpathian strategic offensive operation. According to Krivosheev, *Grif sekretnosti*, 197–198, 2,406,100 troops participated and Soviet losses were 1,109,528, including 270,198 killed or missing. The best overall account is found in Grylev, *Dnepr-karpaty-krym*.

15. For details, see Grylev, *Dnepr-karpaty-krym*, 137–160.

16. According to Krivosheev, *Grif sekretnosti*, 197, Zhukov's force numbered about 700,000 troops. His losses during the operation were in excess of 150,000.

17. Grylev, *Dnepr-karpaty-krym*, 160–178, and "Umanskaia nastupatel'naia operatsiia voisk 2-go Ukrainskogo fronta vo vtopom udare" [The Uman' offensive operation of 2d Ukrainian Front forces during the second blow], *SMIMVOV*, Issue 15 (Moscow: Voenizdat, 1955), 1–116, classified secret.

18. The 2d Ukrainian Front's initial strength was about 500,000, with losses of less than 100,000. See Krivosheev, *Grif sekretnosti*, 198.

19. Grylev, *Dnepr-kerpaty-krym*, 179–200; and I. A. Pliev, *Pod gvardeiskim znamenem* [Under the guards banner] (Ordzhonikidze: Izdatel'stvo "IR," 1976), 100–110.

20. Krivosheev, *Grif sekretnosti*, 197–198, provides strength figures for the entire Dnepr-Carpathian strategic offensive operation (liberation of the right bank of the Ukraine), which included all operations conducted by the four Ukrainian *fronts* from 24 December 1943 to 17 April 1944. He cites an overall strength of 2,406,100 men committed in the operations and losses of 1,109,528, including 270,198 killed or missing. German records cite German strength in Army Groups South and A in late fall at 700,000 and 253,000, respectively, plus 50,000 Rumanians. The same German reports estimate opposing Soviet strength, including reserves, at 2.5 million, which is fairly accurate. See "Kraftegegenüberstellung, Stand: 14.10.43," *Anlage 4c zu Abt. Fr. H. Ost(1) No. 80/43 g.kdos vom 17.10.43.*

21. For details, see "Krymskaia operatsiia voisk 4-go Ukrainskogo fronta, 1944 g." [The Crimean operation of 4th Ukrainian Front forces, 1944], *SMPIOV*, No. 13 (Moscow: Voenizdat, 1944), 3–69; classified secret.

22. For details of the German defense, see Earl F. Ziemke, *From Stalingrad to Berlin: The German Defeat in the East* (Washington, D.C.: U.S. Army Center of Military History, 1968), 290–295. Ziemke places original Axis strength at 152,216, including 63,537 Rumanians. After losing 30,783 men during the first 10 days of the operation and a significant number thereafter, on 5 May, 64,700 remained. Of these, 26,700 were "left on the beach." The Soviets' claim of 100,000 German losses, including 61,580 prisoners, is close to the mark. According to Krivosheev, *Grif sekretnosti*, 200–201, Soviet forces numbered 462,400 men, with total losses of 84,819 (17,754 killed and wounded).

23. John Erickson, *The Road to Berlin* (Boulder, Colo.: Westview Press, 1983), 187–188.

24. The Novgorod-Luga operation was but one phase of a longer operation the Soviets called the Leningrad-Novgorod strategic offensive operation, in which the 2d Baltic Front joined forces with the Leningrad and Volkhov Fronts. Conducted between 14 January and 1 March, it involved a total of 822,100 troops in four distinct operations across a front of 600 kilometers. The 313,953 Soviet casualties attests to the severity of the fighting. The best account of the operation is found in S. P. Platonov, ed., *Bitva za Leningrad 1941–1944* [The battle of Leningrad, 1941–1944] (Moscow: Voenizdat, 1964). See also, I. T. Korovnikov, *Novgorodsko-luzhkom operatsiia: nastuplenie voisk 59-i armii, ianvar'-fevral' 1944 g.* [The Leningrad-Luga operation: The offensive of 59th Army forces, January–February 1944] (Moscow: Voenizdat, 1960).

25. Erickson, *The Road to Berlin*, 172–177.

26. Ibid., 174–176.

27. These lesser known operations include the 1st Baltic Front's Gorodok operation (13–31 December 1943), the Belorussian Front's Kalinkovichi-Mozyr operation (8–30 January 1944), the Rogachev-Zhlobin operation (21–26 February 1944), and seven Western Front operations against Orsha, Vitebsk, and Bogushevsk. For emerging details on the latter, see M. A. Gareev, "O neudachnykh nastupatel'nykh operatsiiakh Sovetskikh voisk v Velikoi Otechestvennoi voine" [Concerning unsuccessful offensive operations of Soviet forces in the Great Patriotic War], *Novaia i noveishaia istoriia* [New and Newest History] 1 (January 1994): 3–29. Because of Western Front's failures, Sokolovsky and many of his staff and subordinates, including Lieutenant General V. N. Gordov, commander of 33d Army, were removed from command and reassigned. The Western Front was then subdivided into 2d and 3d Belorussian Fronts.

13. Operation Bagration

1. For details on this strategic debate, see S. M. Shtemenko, *The Soviet General Staff at War*, Vol. 1 (Moscow: Progress Publishers 1985), 200–202, and S.

Shtemenko, "Pered udarom v Belorussii" [Before the blow in Belorussia], *VIZh* 9 (September 1965): 45–71.

2. John Erickson, *The Road to Berlin* (Boulder, Colo.: Westview Press, 1983), 197, 199.

3. For Vasilevsky's and Zhukov's roles in the operation, see A. M. Vasilevsky, *Delo vsei zhizni* [A lifelong cause] (Minsk: "Belarus," 1984), 388–389, and G. K. Zhukov, *Reminiscences and Reflections*, Vol. 2 (Moscow: Progress Publishers, 1989), 516–518.

4. A. Matsulenko, *Operativnaia maskirovka voisk* [Operational *maskirovka* of forces] (Moscow: Voenizdat, 1975), 113. The scale of necessary redeployments is covered in detail in N. Iakovlev, "Operativnye peregruppirovka voisk pri podgotovka Belorusskoi operatsii" [The operational regrouping of forces during the preparation for the Belorussian operation], *VIZh* 9 (September 1975), 91–97.

5. Shtemenko, "Pered udarom," 56; K. Rokossovsky, "Dva glavnykh udara" [Two main attacks], *VIZh* 6 (June 1965): 13–17.

6. Erickson, *Road to Berlin*, 206–207; I. S. Konev, *Zapiski komanduiushchego frontam 1943–1945* [Notes of a *front* commander 1943–1945] (Moscow: "Nauka," 1972), 231–323.

7. N. Antipenko, "Voprosy tylovogo obespecheniia Belorusskoi operatsii" [Questions of logistical support for the Belorussian operation], *VIZh* 6 (June 1964): 36–51; David M. Glantz, *Soviet Military Deception in the Second World War* (London: Frank Cass and Co., 1989), 360–378.

8. For Soviet strength in the operation, see *Razgrom nemetsko-fashistskikh voisk v Belorussii v 1944 gody, tom pervyi, Podgotovka Belorusskoi operatsii 1944 goda* [The destruction of German-Fascist forces in Belorussia in 1944, Vol. 1, Preparation for the 1944 Belorussian operation] (Moscow: Academy of the General Staff, 1959), 39. Classified secret. This agrees with data in "Belorusskaia operatsiia v tsifrakh" [The Belorussian operation in numbers] *VIZh* 6 (June 1964): 74–77. G. F. Krivosheev, *Grif sekretnosti sniat: Poteri vooruzhennykh sil SSSR v voinakh, boevykh deistviiakh i voennykh konfliktakh* [Losses of the armed forces of the USSR in wars, combat actions, and military conflicts] (Moscow: Voenizdat, 1993), 203, cites a total strength for the four Soviet *fronts* for the duration of the operation at 2,411,600 troops, including the almost 80,000-man Polish army. German strength opposite the four Soviet *fronts* and north of the Pripiat' River was 888,000 men, supported by 996 tanks and assault guns and about 3,000 artillery pieces. Another 200,000 men faced 1st Belorussian Front's left wing south of the Pripiat'. At the time, the Germans estimated Soviet strength opposite Army Group Center at about 1,230,000 troops, supported by 1,100 tanks and SP-guns and 5,000 guns and mortars. See "Kraftegegenüberstellung, Stand: Siehe Fussnote (1.5–1.6. 44)," *Fremde Heere Ost (ic), Pruf No. 1551*.

9. According to Krivosheev, *Grif sekretnesti*, 102–203, and other Soviet sources, Soviet strength in the operation was 451,000 troops (Leningrad Front, 202,300; Karelian Front, 188,800; and Baltic Fleet, 60,400), 10,000 artillery pieces and mortars, and 800 tanks opposed to 268,000 Finns with 1,930 guns and 110 tanks and assault guns. Soviet losses in the operation were 23,674 personnel killed or missing

and 72,701 wounded, and 294 tanks and 489 artillery pieces destroyed. For operational details, see S. P. Platonov, ed., *Bitva za Leningrad 1941–1945* [The battle for Leningrad 1941–1945] (Moscow: Voenizdat, 1964), 428–430; A. Novikov, "Na Karel'skom peresheike" [On the Karelian peninsula], *VIZh* 7 (July 1969): 62–73, and "Inzhernernoe obespechenie proryva oborony finnov na Karel'skom peresheike" [Engineer support for the penetration of the Finnish defense on the Karelian peninsula], *SMPIOV*, No. 14, (Moscow: Voenizdat, 1945), 180–194, classified secret.

10. For details on German-Finnish negotiations, see Earl F. Ziemke, *Stalingrad to Berlin: The German Defeat in the East* (Washington, D.C.: U.S. Army Center of Military History, 1968), 300–301.

11. David M. Glantz, *Soviet Military Deception in the Second World War* (London: Frank Cass and Co., 1989). 370, 407–408.

12. Hans von Ness, "Study of the Destruction of Army Group Center during the Summer of 1944 as Seen from the Point of View of Military Intelligence," in *1985 Art of War Symposium, From the Dnepr to the Vistula: Soviet Offensive Operations, November 1943–August 1944*, ed. David M. Glantz (Carlisle Barracks, Pa.: U.S. Army War College, 1985), 251, 278.

13. Georg Lemm, "Defense of Mogilev by the 12th Infantry Division," *1985 Art of War Symposium*, 366–67. Lemm commanded the 12th Infantry Division and escaped with his battalion from Mogilev.

14. Among the many articles and books on partisan operations, see B. Chertok, "Vzaimodeistvie partisan voiskami 65-i armii pri osvobozhdenii belorussii [Cooperation of partisans with 65th Army during the liberation of Belorussia], *VIZh* 7 (July 1984): 85–89.

15. P. Biriukov, "Osobennosti primeneniia inzhenernykh voisk Belorusskoi operatsii" [Peculiarities in the employment of engineer forces in the Belorussian operation], *VIZh* 6 (June 1984): 34–40; V. Mikhailkin, "Boevoe primenenie artillerii v Belorusskoi operatsii" [Combat use of artillery in the Belorussian operation], *VIZh* 6 (June 1984): 25–33; O. Losik, "Primenie bronetankovykh i mekhanizirovannykh voisk v Belorusskoi operatsii" [Employment of armored and mechanized forces in the Belorussian operation], *VIZh* 6 (June 1984): 20–24. For detailed accounts of the entire operation, see A. M. Samsonov, ed. *Osvobozhdenie Belorussii, 1944* [The liberation of Belorussia, 1944] (Moscow: "Nauka," 1974), and *Razgrom nemetsko-fashistkikh voisk v Belorussii v 1944 godu* [The destruction of German-Fascist forces in Belorussia in 1944], *SMPIOV*, No. 18 (Moscow: Voenizdat, 1945). The latter is classified secret.

16. Lemm, "Defense of Mogilev," 372, 376–77.

17. Biriukov, "Peculiarities in the employment of engineer forces," 35–36; A. Luchinsky, "28-ia armiia v Bobruiskoi operatsii" [The 28th Army in the Bobruisk operation] *VIZh* 2 (February 1969): 66–75.

18. K. Telegin, "V boiakh za osvobozhdenie Belorussii" [In battles for the liberation of Belorussia], *VIZh* 6 (June 1969): 88; A. Tsikin, "Aviatsiia 16-i vozdushnoi armii pri razgrome gruppirovka protivnika pod Bobruiskom" [The aviation of 16th Air Army in the destruction of the enemy grouping at Bobruisk], *VIZh* 7 (July 1962): 22–23.

19. A. A. Sidorenko, *Na mogilevskom napravlenii* [On the Mogilev axis] (Moscow: Voenizdat, 1958).

20. Lemm, "Defense of Mogilev," 374–75, 427.

21. The 5th Panzer Division's defense is covered in A. D. von Plato, *Die Geschichte der 5. Panzerdivision 1938 bis 1945* [The History of 5th Panzer Division, 1938–1945 (Regensburg: Walhalla u Praetoria Verlag KG Georg Zwichenpflug, 1978). A shorter account is found in von Plato, "Defensive Combat of 5th Panzer Division," *1985 Art of War Symposium*, 385–418. Von Plato was the Ia (operations officer) for 5th Panzer Division.

22. Rotmistrov's tank losses were high during the advance to Minsk, particularly from German tank ambushes. Later, his army would suffer even higher losses in the battle for Vilnius. Rotmistrov began the operation with 524 tanks and SP-guns and had 307 serviceable tanks and SP-guns on 5 July, after the fall of Minsk. By 16 July, after the fall of Vilnius, the army was down to about 50 tanks and had to be withdrawn from combat for refitting. See *Razgrom nemetsko-fashistskikh* vorsk (1959) 168–169, 195, 286.

23. A. Belousov, "4-ia gvardeiskaia tankovaia brigada v boiakh za Minsk" [The 4th Guards Tank Brigade in the battles for Minsk], *VIZh* 7 (July 1974): 45–49; A. Karavan, "Na minskom napravlenii" [On the Minsk axis], *VIZh* 6 (June 1969): 52–57.

24. The reduction of the encircled German Fourth Army is covered in *Razgrom nemetsko-fashistskikh vorsk* (1959), 114–118.

25. Quoted by Gerd Niepold in, "The Defense of 12th Panzer Division," *1985 Art of War Symposium*, 432. Niepold, the Ia of 12th Panzer Division, has written the best recent assessment from the German side: *Battle for White Russia: The Destruction of Army Group Center, June 1944*, trans. Richard Simpkin (London: Brassey's, 1987).

26. Niepold 12th Panzer Div., 442–443.

27. S. Poplavsky, "K 20-letiiu osvobozhdeniia Vil'niusa" [On the 20th Anniversary of the liberation of Vilnius], *VIZh* 7 (July 1964): 42–46.

28. I. Bagramian, "Nastuplenie voisk 1-go Pribaltiiskogo fronta v Belorusskoi operatsii" [The offensive of 1st Baltic Front forces during the Belorussian operation], *VIZh* 4 (April 1961): 12–27; 5 (May 1961): 15–31.

29. Rotmistrov was replaced by Lieutenant General M. D. Solomatin, the successful commander of 1st Mechanized Corps, on 8 August. After Solomatin was wounded by a German mine while moving his tank army to Siauliai, he was replaced by Vol'sky. While only a novel about the life of Cherniakhovsky mentions the reasons for Rotmistrov's removal as army commander, 5th Guards Tank Army's losses are well documented. Rotmistrov, himself, died before finishing his memoirs, and they only cover the period to February 1944.

30. For detailed classified accounts of what was originally called the L'vov-Peremyshl' operation, see "L'vovsko-Peremyshl'skaia operatsiia 1-go Ukrainskogo fronta, Iiul'-avgust 1944 g." [The L'vov-Peremyshl' operation of the 1st Ukrainian Front, July–August 1944], *SMPIOV*, No. 22 (Moscow: Voenizdat, 1946), 3–91; and "Okruzhenie i razgrom brodskoi gruppirovka nemtsev, iiul' 1944 g.," *SMPIOV*, No. 17 (Moscow: Voenizdat, 1945), 31–43.

31. Krivosheev, *Grif sekretnosti*, 204–205, and M. Polushkin, "L'vovsko-Sandomirskaia nastupatel'naia operatsiia 1-go Ukrainskogo fronta v tsifrakh" [The L'vov-Sandomirsk operation of the 1st Ukrainian Front in numbers], *VIZH* 8 (August 1969): 58, state that Konev fielded 1,002,200 troops (843,772 combat) throughout the duration of the operation, supported by 2,206 tanks and SP-guns, and 13,825 guns and mortars. "Kraftegegenüberstellung, Stand: Siehe Fussnote (1.5–1.6. 44)," cites opposing German strength at 430,000 German and 196,000 Hungarian troops, supported by 811 tanks and assault guns and 1,100 artillery pieces. The Hungarian forces covered the southern flank of the operation and were scarcely engaged.

32. S. Petrov, "Dostizhenie vnezapnost' v L'vovsko-Sandomirskoi operatsii" [The achievement of surprise in the L'vov-Sandomirsk operation], *VIZh* 7 (July 1974): 31; and Glantz, *Soviet Military Deception*, 379–399.

33. P. Kurochkin, "Proryv oborony na L'vovskom napravlenii" [Penetration of the enemy defense on the L'vov exis], *VIZh* 7 (July 1964): 22–30; and I. Konev, "Zavershenie osvibozhdeniia sovetskoi Ukrainy i vykhod na Vislu," [The completion of the liberation of Soviet Ukraine and the advance to the Vistula], *VIZh* 7 (July 1964); 3–21.

34. A. Zhadov, "Boevye deistviia na Sandomirskom platsdarme," [Combat operations in the Sandomirsk bridgehead], *VIZh* 7 (July 1975): 50–59.

35. According to *Razgrom nemetsko-fashistkikh voisk* (1959) 267, Rokossovsky's left wing numbered 410,162 troops, supported by 1,654 tanks and SP guns and 8,742 guns and mortars, facing an estimated 84,175 Germans, supported by 214 tanks and assault guns and 1,530 guns and mortars.

36. B. Petrov, "O sozdanii udarnoi gruppirovki voisk v Liublinsko-Brestskoi nastupatel'noi operatsii" [Concerning the creation of a shock group in the Lublin-Brest offensive operation], *VIZh* 3 (March 1978): 83–89, writes about the early stages of the operation. A. Radzievsky, "Na puti k Varshave" [On the path to Warsaw], *VIZh* 10 (October 1971): 68–77, recounts the exploitation to Warsaw. German Ninth Army and Second Army records substantiate his account and the damage done to his army by the German counterattack.

37. Ibid; and Ziemke, *Stalingrad to Berlin*, 341.

38. Ziemke, *Stalingrad to Berlin*, 340–341, 344–345. For a recent Russian account, see Iu. V. Ivanov and I. N. Kosenko, "Kto kogo predal" [Who betrayed whom], *VIZh* 3 (March 1993): 16–24; 4 (April 1993): 13–21, which contains newly released formerly classified documents.

39. R. Nazarevich, "Varshavskoe vostanie 1944 g.," *Novaia i noveishchaia istoriia* [New and recent history] 2 (January 1989), 186–210, translated from the Polish.

40. Ziemke, *Stalingrad to Berlin*, 345.

41. "Kraftegegenüberstellung, Stand: Siehe Fussnote (1.7–1.8. 44)," *Fremde Heere Ost (IIc), Pruf Nr. 1058;* and Ziemke, *Stalingrad to Berlin*, 340.

42. Krivosheev, *Grif sekretnosti*, 203–205, 371.

43. "Kraftegegenüberstellung, Stand: Siehe Fussnote (1.7–1.8. 44)," "Kraftegegenüberstellung, Stand: 1.9.44.," *Fremde Heere Ost (IIc), Pruf Nr. 1859*, and "Kraftegegenüberstellung, Stand: 1.11.44" (handwritten changes), *Fremde Heere*

Ost (lic), Pruf Nr. 1904; and Krivosheev, *Grif sekretnosti,* 350–358. For Soviet strength on 12 March 1944, see "Postanovlenie GKO 12 Morta 1944 g." [Decree of the GKO of 12 March 1944], TsPA. IMA [Central Party Archives of the Institute of Marxism and Leninism], f. 644, op.1, g. 218, l. 100–101.

14. Clearing the Flanks

1. Earl F. Ziemke, *Stalingrad to Berlin: The German Defeat in the East* (Washington, D.C.: U.S. Army Center of Military History, 1968), 335.

2. Hermann von Trotha, "German Defensive Measures in Army Group South Ukraine, August 1944," *1985 Art of War Symposium, From the Dneper to the Vistula: Soviet Offensive Operations, November 1943–August 1944,* ed. David M. Glantz (Carlisle, Pa.: U.S. Army War College, 1985), 465.

3. G. F. Krivosheev, *Grif sekretnosti sniat: Poteri vooruzhnnykh sil SSSR v voinakh, boevykh deistviiakh i voennykh konfliktakh* [Losses of the armed forces of the USSR in wars, combat actions, and military conflicts] (Moscow: Voenizdat, 1993), 205–206, and other Russian sources place Soviet strength at 771,200 for 2d Ukrainian Front, 523,000 for 3d Ukrainian Front, and the 20,000 troops of the Black Sea Fleet and Danube River Flotilla, supported by 14,851 guns and mortars and 1,874 tanks and SP guns. Of the over 1.3 million troops, 886,491 were combat soldiers. Axis strength is derived from *Fremde Heere Ost* strength returns of 1 July, adjusted downward to accommodate transfers to other front sectors.

4. A multitude of Soviet divisional histories refer to this problem. Divisions often numbered between 2,500 and 5,000 men, and only elite formations (such as some guards divisions, a select few regular divisions, and guards airborne divisions) exceeded 5,000 men. Numerous *Fremde Heere Ost* reports and analyses of Soviet divisions underscore this problem and note the high proportion of ethnic soldiers (central Asians, and so on) and young and old soldiers in these units. Women were not uncommon in some combat units.

5. Planning and conduct of the operation are covered in detail in "Iassko-Kishinevskaia operatsiia" [The Iassy-Kishinev operation], *SMPIOV,* No. 19 (Moscow: Voenizdat, 1945); "Boevye deistviia konno-tankovoi gruppy v Iassko-Kishinevskoi operatsii" [Combat actions of a cavalry-tank group in the Iassy-Kishinev operation] and "Nastuplenie 104-go strelkovogo korpusa s proryvom podgotovlennoi oborony protivniki severo-zapadnee Iassy" [The offensive of the 104th Rifle Corps with a penetration of a prepared enemy defense northwest of Iassy], *SVIMVOV,* Issue 3 (Moscow: Voenizdat, 1950), 55–119, classified secret. Among the best of many articles is V. Matsulenko, "Nekotorye osobennosti voennogo iskusstva v Iassko-Kishinevskoi operatsii" [Some features of military art in the Iassy-Kishinev operation], *VIZh* 8 (August 1969): 12–30. Operational and planning documents are found in V. P. Krikunov, "Razgrom gruppy armii 'Iuzhnaia Ukraina' " [The destruction of Army Group South Ukraine], *VIZh* 10 (October 1989): 7–19.

6. The thorough deception operation is covered in David M. Glantz, *Soviet Military Deception in the Second World War* (London: Frank Cass and Co., 1989), 409–421.

7. I. Shinkarev, "Razgrom nemetsko-fashistkikh voisk v Rumynii" [The destruction of German-Fascist forces in Rumania], *VIZh* 10 (October 1981): 65–72. On 6 September 1944, the entire Rumanian field army was placed under the operational control of the 2d Ukrainian Front. It included the 138,073 men of the 1st and 4th Rumanian Armies, the 4th Independent Army Corps, and the 1st Air Corps.

8. See detailed reports from the *front* commands in Krikunov, "Razgrom gruppy," 15–17, and the comments on inter-*front* command and control problems in M. Zakharov, "Molnienosnaia operatsiia" [A lightning operation], *VIZh* 8 (August 1964): 15–28.

9. Soviet documents cite enemy losses in excess of 200,000 men killed or missing, 208,600 taken prisoner, and 830 tanks and assault guns and 3,500 guns and mortars destroyed or captured. See Krikunov, "Razgrom gruppy," 13. Krivosheev, *Grif sekretnosti*, 206, places Soviet losses at 67,130 (13,197 killed or missing and 53,933 wounded), 75 tanks and SP guns, and 108 guns and mortars.

10. "Kraftegegenüberstellung, Stand: 1.9.44." *Fremde Heere Ost (IIc) Pruf Nr. 1859.*

11. The best overall sources on the Soviet war in the Balkans, including operations in Bulgaria, is M. V. Zakharov, ed., *Osvobozhdenie iugo-vostochnoi i tsentral'noi evropy voiskami 2-go i 3-go ukrainskikh frontov, 1944–1945* [The liberation of southeastern and central Europe by forces of the 2d and 3d Ukrainian Fronts, 1944–1945] (Moscow: "Nauka," 1970); and M. M. Minasian, *Osvobozhdenie narodov iugo-vostochnoi evropy* [The liberation of the peoples of southeastern Europe] (Moscow; Voenizdat, 1967). Operations in Bulgaria are covered in detail in A. Zheltov, "Osvobozhdenie Bolgarii" [The liberation of Bulgaria], *VIZh* 9 (September 1969): 59–69.

12. A. Zheltov, "Osvobozhdenie Vengrii" [The liberation of Hungary], *VIZh* 10 (October 1974), 44–50, and Krivosheev, *Grif sekretnosti*, 211. In late October, Malinovsky's *front* fielded just over 700,000 men, supported by 750 tanks and SP guns and 10,200 guns and mortars. Included in the force were 22 Rumanian divisions. Combined German and Hungarian forces numbered almost 250,000 men, with 300 tanks and assault guns and 3,500 artillery pieces.

13. Ziemke, *Stalingrad to Berlin*, 360.

14. The best short account of this operation is P. Varakhin, "6-ia gvardeiskaia tankovaia armiia v Debretsenskoi operatsii" [6th Guards Tank Army in the Debrecen operation] *VIZh* 11 (November 1975): 69–75. Krivosheev, *Grif sekretnosti*, 227, places Malinovsky's overall strength in the operation at 698,200 troops and about 500 tanks. According to Varakhin, "6-ia gvardeiskaia," 71, 6th Guards Tank Army numbered 34,494 men, 188 tanks and SP guns, and 982 guns and mortars. The 2d Ukrainian Front's losses in the operation were 84,010 men, including 19,713 killed or missing, and 64,297 wounded, and several hundred tanks.

15. Thorough classified accounts of the Budapest operation include "Budapeshtskaia operatsiia" [The Budapest operation], *SMPIOV*, No. 21 (Moscow: Voenizdat). Krivosheev, *Grif sekretnosti*, 211–212, 370, cites Soviet strength in the operation at 719,500 troops (including the Danube Flotilla) but does not break the totals down between 2d and 3d Ukrainian Fronts. He places Soviet losses throughout the duration of the operation at 320,082 (80,026 killed or missing and 240,056 wounded) divided roughly evenly between the two *fronts*. Armored losses amounted to 1,766 tanks and SP guns. German and Hungarian strength during the operation rose from 250,000 in late October to over 440,000 (330,000 Germans and 110,000 Hungarians) in December, with the arrival in Hungary of large German reinforcements. German armored strength rose correspondingly to over 400 tanks and assault guns. This shifting correlation of forces contributed to the decreased speed of the Soviet advance.

16. The 3d Ukrainian Front's operations are covered by S. Alferov, "Nastuplenie 4-i gvardeiskoi armii v Budapeshtskoi operatsii" [4th Guards Army's offensive in the Budapest operation], *VIZh* 9 (September 1982): 13–19; and M. Sharokhin, V. Petrukhin, "Forsirovanie Dunaia voiskami 57-i armii i zakhvat operativnogo platsdarma v raione Batiny" [57th Army's forcing of the Danube River and the seizure of an operational bridgehead at Batina], *VIZh* 2 (February 1960): 25–36.

17. Ziemke, *Stalingrad to Berlin*, 383.

18. Alferov, "Nastuplenie 4-i gvardeiskoi," 17–19; N. Biriukov, "Na podstupakh k Budapeshtu" [On the approaches to Budapest], *VIZh* 3 (March 1965): 94.

19. Ziemke, *Stalingrad to Berlin*, 383–386. Zheltov, in "The liberation of Hungary," claims that 188,000 Germans and Hungarians were encircled in Budapest and that 138,000 ultimately surrendered on 13 February 1945.

20. For details, see "Operations in Hungary, January–March 1945," in David M. Glantz, ed., *1986 Art of War Symposium, From the Vistula to the Oder: Soviet Offensive Operations, October 1944–March 1945* (Carlisle, Pa.: U.S. Army War College, 1986), 665–788.

21. For details, see "Karpatsko-Duklinskaia operatsiia" [The Carpathian-Dukla operation], *SVIMVOV*, Issue 17 (Moscow: Voenizdat, 1956), classified secret; and the unclassified version, D. M. Proektor, *Cherez Duklinskii pereval* [Through the Dukla Pass] (Moscow: Voenizdat, 1960). Krivosheev, *Grif sekretnosti*, 206, credits 38th Army and its supporting units with a strength of 99,100 troops, but he does not provide armored strength. K. S. Moskalenko probably fielded up to 300 tanks and SP guns. His losses in the operation, 62,014 men (13,264 killed or missing and 48,750 wounded), attest to the ferocity of the fighting.

22. The 1st Guards Cavalry Corps escaped from encirclement but lost most of its equipment in the process.

23. For details, see "Karpatskaia operatsiia 4-go Ukrainskogo fronta, sentiabr'–oktiabr' 1944 g." [The Carpathian operation of the 4th Ukrainian Front, September–October 1944], *SMPIOV* 23 (March–June 1946): 3–95. The 4th Ukrainian Front numbered 264,000 men, supported by about 100 tanks and SP guns. No

German strength figures are available for the two Carpathian operations. The Soviets probably outnumbered their foes by between 2.5 and 3:1.

24. The best accounts of the so-called Siauliai-Mtava operation, which began on 5 July 1944, are I. Bagramian, "Shauliaisko-Mitavskaia operatsiia voisk 1-go Baltiiskogo fronta" [The Siauliai-Mtava operation of the 1st Baltic Front], *VIZh* 10 (October 1962): 3–23; and I. Bagramian, "Na zavershaiushchem etape Shia-uliaiskoi operatsii" [In the final stage of the Siauliai operation], *VIZh* 5 (May 1976): 51–61. According to Krivosheev, *Grif sekretnost*, 203, 1st Baltic Front numbered 395,500 troops. *Razgrom nemetsko-fashistskikh voisk v Belorussii* (1959), 173, cites an armored strength of 358 serviceable tanks and SP guns (and 230 requiring repair). These figures do not count 5th Guards Tank Army or 19th Tank Corps, which joined the *front* in mid-August.

25. Ziemke, *Stalingrad to Berlin*, 342–343.

26. For details on the Soviet defense, see Bagramian, "In the final stage," and I. Strel'bitsky, "Podvig artilleristiv pod Shiauliaem" [The heroism of artillerymen at Siauliai], *VIZh* 1 (January 1970): 52–59. Soviet sources claim German armored strength was 500 tanks and assault guns and place their own strength at about 400. They place their own losses at 67,606 (of which 15,900 were killed, captured, or missing), and German losses at 67,000 (60,000 killed and wounded and 7,000 captured) and 300 tanks destroyed.

27. Among the many articles, see M. Kazakov, "V boakh za sovetskuiu Pri-baltiku" [In battles for the Soviet Baltic], *VIZh* 2 (February 1967): 62–75. Krivosheev, *Grif sekretnosti*, 207–208, cites a total Soviet strength in the over two-month operation of 1,546,400 troops, of which 280,090 were lost (61,468 killed or missing and 218,622 wounded). Armor played primarily an infantry support role in the operations. According to *Fremde Heere Ost* documents, German strength fell from 510,000 (plus 45,000 allies) on 1 September to 400,000 (and 20,000 allies) on 1 November. See "Kraftegegenüberstellung, Stand: 1.9.44," *Fremde Heere Ost (IIc), Prüf 1859*, and "Kraftegegenüberstellung, Stand: 1.11.44," *Fremde Heere Ost (IIc), Prüf 1904*.

28. Ziemke, *Stalingrad to Berlin*, 403–407.

29. Among the many sources, see D. Muriev, "Nekotorye kharakternye cherty frontovykh i armeiskikh operatsii, provedennykh v Pribaltiiskoi strategicheskoi operatsii 1944 goda" [Some characteristic features of *front* and army operations, conducted in the 1944 Baltic strategic operation], *VIZh* 9 (September 1984): 22–28.

30. Glantz, *Soviet Military Deception*, 433–440.

31. Ziemke, *Stalingrad to Berlin*, 407, documents the German surprise.

32. Although Krivosheev, *Grif sekretnosti*, does not provide specific strength figures for the Memel' operation, after the regrouping, the 1st Baltic Front's strength probably exceeded 600,000 men and 400 tanks and SP guns, providing an overwhelming superiority of up to 5:1 over Third Panzer Army.

33. Ziemke, *Stalingrad to Berlin*, 409.

34. This operation has been overlooked in most histories because it took place after major Soviet strategic victories in Belorussia and the Baltic, and because it

failed. Its importance rests on how it affected Soviet offensive preparations in January 1945. For one of the few articles on the operation, see M. Alekseev, "Nachalo boev v Vostochnoi Prussii" [The beginning of combat in East Prussia], *VIZh* 10 (October 1964): 11–22. Krivosheev, *Grif sekretnosti*, 227, who refers to it as the "Goldap operation," cites Colonel General I. D. Cherniakhovsky's strength as 377,300 troops, of which 79,527 were lost (16,819 killed or missing and 62,708 wounded). Soviet tank strength was probably around 300. Alekseev places total German armor strength, with reinforcements, at 500, but it was probably closer to half that amount.

35. Ziemke, *Stalingrad to Berlin*, 390.

36. The most thorough analysis of the Petsamo-Kirkenes operation is James F. Gebhardt, *The Petsamo-Kirkenes Operation: Soviet Breakthrough and Pursuit in the Arctic, October 1944. Leavenworth Paper No. 17* (Fort Leavenworth, Kan.: Combat Studies Institute, 1989).

37. Krivosheev, *Grif sekretnosti*, 210, cites Soviet strength of 133,500, including 20,300 men of the Northern Fleet, and places Soviet losses at 21,233 (6,084 killed or missing and 15,149 wounded). Kh. Khudalov, "Petsamo-Kirkenesskaia operatsiia" [The Petsamo-Kirkenes operation], *VIZh* 10 (October 1969): 116, claims German losses totaling 18,000 killed and 713 prisoners.

38. Ziemke, *Stalingrad to Berlin*, 412–413. *Fremde Heere Ost* documents on German and Soviet strength present an equally grim picture.

15. Battles in the Snow

1. Among the many sources on the siege, see S. P. Ivanov, "K 40-letiiu Budapeshtskoi operatsii" [On the 40th anniversary of the Budapest operation], *VIZh* 11 (November 1984): 18–19.

2. Heinz Guderian, *Panzer Leader* (Washington, D.C., Zenger Publishing Co., 1979), 384. Soviet intelligence detected the movement of the German corps from Poland to Hungary but seems to have lost its precise location when the force reached Hungary. While Soviet radio-intercept and decoding capabilities did well against most German units, for some reason it was less able to track the movement of SS forces, which used separate codes and communications nets. See David M. Glantz, *Soviet Military Deception in the Second World War* (London: Frank Cass and Co., 1989), 466–467.

3. John Erickson, *The Road to Berlin* (Boulder, Colo.: Westview Press, 1983), 439–441. For day-to-day details on the fighting from both the Soviet and German perspectives, see David M. Glantz, ed., *1986 Art of War Symposium, From the Vistula to the Oder: Soviet Offensive Operations—October 1944–March 1945* (Carlisle, Pa.: U.S. Army War College, 1986), 663–789. German armored strength during the initial counterattacks (1–10 January) amounted to about 260 tanks in IV SS Panzer Corps and 146 tanks in III Panzer Corps. These were opposed initially by about 30 tanks of 18th Tank Corps' lead brigade, and then by the corps' remaining armor (about 100 tanks) and the over 150 tanks of 2d Guards Mechanized Corps. On 20 January, IV SS Panzer Corps and III Panzer Corps together

numbered about 200 tanks and assault guns. In this and subsequent night attacks, the Germans employed a crude, experimental version of infra-red night fighting devices. The surprise use of this new technology resulted in the decimation of 18th Tank Corps' armored force, and frenetic attempts by the Soviets to counter the new technology. In the end, however, day battles and Soviet strength negated this temporary German advantage.

4. Erickson, *The Road to Berlin*, 441–444. See also Ivanov, "K 40-letiiu Budapeshtkoi," 18.

5. Erickson, *The Road to Berlin*, 422. For thorough classified assessments of conditions on the Eastern Front and for immense detail on the preparation and conduct of the Vistula-Oder operation, see *SMPIOV*, No. 25 (Voenizdat, 1947), and A. V. Vasil'ev, *Visla-oderskaia operatiia* [The Vistula-Oder operation] (Moscow: Voroshilov Academy of the General Staff, 1948). These sources cite German army strength on 1 January 1945 at 338 division equivalents, with 228 division equivalents (188 divisions, 50 separate regiments, and 180 separate battalions) on the Eastern Front (two thirds of the total force), 73 divisions on the Western Front, 18 in northern Italy, and 9 in Norway and Denmark. *Fremde Heere Ost* records dated 1 November show German Eastern Front strength at 2,030,000 men with 190,000 allied forces. Replacements raised this figure slightly after 1 January 1945. Soviet open sources have traditionally inflated this number to 3.1 million by including *Volkssturm* [Home Guards] and irregular units to improve perceptions of Red Army performance. According to G. F. Krivosheev, *Grif sekretnosti sniat: Poteri vooruzhennykh sil SSSR v voinakh, boevykh deistviiakh i voennykh konfliktakh* [Losses of the armed forces of the USSR in wars, combat actions, and military conflicts] (Moscow: Voenizdat, 1993) 73, the average operating strength of the Red Army during the first quarter of 1945 was 6,461,000 men. Therefore, Soviet strategic superiority in manpower was about 3:1 over German forces. Soviet superiority in armor and artillery was even more pronounced.

6. According to Krivosheev, *Grif sekretnosti*, 213, and other classified Soviet sources, total Soviet strength in the operation was 2,112,700 troops (1,565,000 combat), 7,042 tanks and SP-guns, and more than 33,500 guns and mortars, supplemented by 90,900 Polish troops. *Fremde Heere Ost* records (an interpolation of the 1 November reports cited earlier) place German estimated strength at 400,000 men (and about 40,000 *Volkssturm*), 800 tanks and assault guns (reinforced to 1,136 during the operation), and 4,103 artillery pieces.

7. With Soviet concentration of forces on main attack axes and economy of force measures in secondary sectors, this 5:1 Soviet strategic superiority became 10:1 at the operational level (in each bridgehead sector) and up to 13:1 in tactical (corps and division) sectors. Soviet superiority in supporting arms (tanks, SP-guns, and artillery) was even more pronounced. On the other hand, in some sectors (up to 30 percent of the front occupied by fortified regions), German forces outnumbered their Soviet foes.

8. For more details on German planning and force redeployment controversies, see Earl F. Ziemke, *Stalingrad to Berlin: The German Defeat in the East* (Washington, D.C.: U.S. Army Center of Military History, 1968), 410–419.

9. Ibid., 411–414.

10. Guderian, *Panzer Leader,* 385–395.

11. For details on combat operations from both the German and Soviet side, see Glantz, ed., *1986 Art of War Symposium,* 497–663. Among many excellent Soviet classified accounts are *SMPIOV,* No. 25; A. D. Bagreev, *Visla-oderskaia operatsiia: Razgrom nemetsko-fashistskikh voisk v Pol'she sovetskimi voiskami v ianvare 1945 goda* [The Vistula-Oder operation: the destruction of German-Fascist forces in Poland by Soviet forces in 1945] (Moscow: Voroshilov Academy of the General Staff, 1957); N. A. Antonov, *Proryv oborony protivnika voiskami 1-go Belorusskogo fronta v vislo-oderskoi operatsii (ianvar' 1945)* [Penetration of the enemy defenses by 1st Belorussian Front forces in the Vistula-Oder operation, January 1945] (Moscow: Voroshilov Academy of the General Staff, 1980); and A. P. Snegov, *Voennoe iskusstvo v Vislo-Oderskoi operatsii* [Military art in the Vistula-Oder operation] (Moscow: Lenin Military-Political Academy, 1979).

12. For details on the intracacies of tank army operations, see I. M. Kravchenko, *Boevye deistviia voisk 3 gvardeiskoi tankovoi armii v khode Vislo-oderskoi operatsii* [Combat operations of 3d Guards Tank Army during the Vistula-Oder operation] (Voroshilov Academy of the General Staff, 1978); classified secret. See also the unit history of 3d Guards Tank Army and the memoirs of Rybalko, the army's commander. Air-ground coordination is covered in A. Efrimov, "Primenenie aviatsii provedenii operatsii v vysokikh tempakh i na bol'shuiu glubinu" [The employment of aviation during the conduct of high tempo operations to great depth], *VIZh* 1 (January 1985): 22–29.

13. For an excellent German personal view of XXIV Panzer Corps operations, see H. G. Liebisch, "17th Panzer Division operations to 27 January," in *1986 Art of War Symposium, From the Vistula to the Oder: Soviet Offensive Operations, October 1944–March 1945* (Carlisle, Pa.: U.S. Army War College, 1986) 609–626. Liebisch was one of the few battalion commanders in the division to escape with his battalion. This and subsequent information on the techniques of Soviet armored forward detachments are based in part on extensive interviews conducted by the author in Moscow (June 1989) with I. I. Gusakovsky, commander, 44th Guards Tank Brigade, 11th Guards Tank Corps, 1st Guards Tank Army; A. F. Smirnov, executive officer, 100th Tank Brigade, 31st Tank Corps; B. P. Ivanov, battalion commander, 40th Guards Tank Brigade, 11th Guards Tank Corps, 1st Guards Tank Army; D. A. Dragunsky, commander, 55th Guards Tank Brigade, 7th Guards Tank Corps, 3d Guards Tank Army; and A. A. Dement'ev, commander, 93d Separate Tank Brigade, 4th Guards Tank Army.

14. H. G. Liebisch, "Second Phase of 17th Panzer Division Retrograde Operations East of the Oder River," *1986 Art of War Symposium,* 639–642.

15. Kravchenko, *"Boevye deistviia,"* 41–55.

16. Among the many works on Zhukov's penetration operation, see A. P. Snegov, *Organizatsiia i osushchestvlenie proryv podgotovlennoi oborony protivnika soedineniami 32-go strelkovogo korpusa 5-go udarnoi armii v Vislo-oderskoi operatsii* [The organization and realization of a penetration of prepared enemy

defenses by formations of the 1st Belorussian Front's 5th Shock Army's 32d Rifle Corps in the Vistula-Oder operation] (Moscow: Lenin Military-Political Academy, 1980).

17. The Polish role in the capture of Warsaw is covered in S. Poplavsky, "1-ia armiia voisk Pol'skogo v boiakh za Varshavu" [The 1st Polish Army in the battles for Warsaw], *VIZh* 1 (January 1965): 47–53. Poplavsky was the army's commander.

18. For details on this grueling experience, see W. Hartelt, "Battle Report of a Panther Tank Company of Panzer Division 'Hermann Goering,' " *1986 Art of War Symposium*, 627–638.

19. These escaped units had to be recommitted to combat to stop the advance of 4th Tank Army, which, along with 13th Army, had seized a sizable bridgehead over the Oder near Keben. Only the use of these forces prevented further Soviet advance.

20. The Soviets employed special stay-behind forces to irradiate bypassed German units. These included elements of 33d and 3d Guards Armies, and 7th Guards Mechanized Corps. For details on the latter's operations, see D. Barinov and G. Nekhonov, "Unichtozhenie bluzhdaiushchei' gruppirovki protivnika" [The destruction of "floating" enemy groups], *VIZh* 3 (March 1965): 62–68. Barinov was the corps' chief of staff.

21. Ziemke, *Stalingrad to Berlin*, 423, 427.

22. For a glimpse of actions at Posnan, see G. Khlopin, "Shturm forta 'Raukh' " [Assault on Fort "Rauch"], *Voennyi vestnik* [Military herald] 6 (June 1988): 15–17.

23. Details on the Soviet seizure and subsequent battles for Oder bridgeheads are found in F. Bokov, "Pylaiushchii platsdarm" [Flaming bridgehead], *VIZh* 5 (May 1972): 49–55; and A. M. Sokolov, "Zakreplenie i rasshirenie platsdarmov v Vislo-Oderskoi operatsii" [The fortification and expansion of bridgeheads in the Vistula-Oder operation], *VIZh* 4 (April 1986): 32–38. Krivosheev, *Grif sekretnosti*, 213, cites 193,125 Soviet losses in the operation (43,251 killed or missing and 149,874 wounded). According to Vasil'ev, "Vislo-Oderskoi operatsii," 58, 76, 1st Belorussian Front counted 130,000 German dead, 37,300 prisoners, 614 tanks and assault guns destroyed and 617 captured between 14 and 22 January. By 4 February, this total had risen to 216,970 German dead, 60,308 prisoners, 1,237 tanks and assault guns destroyed and 1,119 captured. The 1st Ukrainian Front's total count was significant, but somewhat less. Total German losses exceeded 300,000 men.

24. Among the many accounts of the East Prussian operation, see Glantz, *1986 Art of War Symposium*, 279–486; *SMPIOV*, No. 22 (Moscow: Voenizdat, 1946), 91–120; *SMPIOV*, No. 23 (Moscow: Voenizdat, 1947), 131–160; *SMPIOV*, No. 24 (Moscow: Voenizdat, 1947); and "Proryv nepriiatel'skoi oborony 28-i armiei v vostochnoi prussii (ianvar' 1945 g.)" [Penetration of the enemy defense by 28th Army in East Prussia (January 1945)], *SVIMVOV*, Issue 6 (Moscow: Voenizdat, 1952). All are classified secret.

25. According to Krivosheev, *Grif sekretnosti*, 215–216, other classified Soviet sources, and *Fremde Heere Ost* records, Soviet strength in the operation was

1,669,100 troops (1,220,000 combat), 3,859 tanks and SP guns, and 25,426 guns and mortars facing 580,000 German troops (plus 200,000 *Volkssturm*), 700 tanks and assault guns, and 8,200 artillery pieces.

26. For an excellent account of 7th Panzer Division operations, see J. Condne, "Employment of 7th Panzer Division with Emphasis on its Armored Group," *1986 Art of War Symposium*, 451–486. Condne was a panzer battalion commander in the division.

27. According to Krivosheev, *Grif sekretnosti*, 215–216, Soviet losses in the operation were 584,778 (126,464 killed or missing and 458,314 wounded). Although there is no good source for German losses, they must have exceeded 100,000; over 300,000 troops were bottled up in Konigsberg and the Heilsberg Fortified Region.

28. For details on the changing Soviet intelligence assessment, see D. M. Glantz, *Soviet Military Intelligence in War* (London: Frank Cass and Co., 1990), 335–346.

29. Ibid. Details on German activity along the Oder in early February are found in Ziemke, *Stalingrad to Berlin*, 426–428, 439–444; and H. Liebeskind, "Operations of 21st Panzer Division in the Kuestrin Area and Between the Oder and Neisse Rivers," *1986 Art of War Symposium*, 643–653. Liebeskind commanded two heavy companies of the division's 2d Battalion, Panzer Grenadier Regiment 125.

30. These orders, together with a detailed account of the Lower Silesian Operation are found in "Nizhne-silezskaia nastupatel'naia operatsiia voisk 1-go Ukrianskogo fronta" [The Lower Silesian offensive operation of the 1st Ukrainian Front], *SVIMVOV*, Issues 10–11 (Moscow: Voenizdat, 1953); classified secret. A subsequent 10 February 1945 proposal by Zhukov to Stalin to continue the advance on Berlin is published in Marshal G. K. Zhukov: ". . . Nastuplenie Na Berlinmogy nachat" 19–20.2.45" [Marshal G. K. Zhukov: ". . . the offensive on Berlin can begin in 19–20.2.45"] *VIZh* 2 (March–April 1995), 4–6.

31. Examination of existing Soviet documents indicates that the decision was most likely made shortly before 16 February, when intelligence indicators concerning German offensive intent in Pomerania became clear.

32. Since the early 1960s, a debate has raged in the open Soviet press concerning the wisdom of a Soviet February advance on Berlin. The debate pitted Zhukov and some of his supporters against Chuikov and others. The debate also reflected internal struggles over Zhukov's reputation and political debates between Khrushchev and other Soviet political factions.

33. Details provided in *SVIMVOV*, Issues 10–11. Krivosheev, *Grif sekretnosti*, 227, and other sources cite Soviet strength in the operation as 980,800 troops.

34. Krivosheev, *Grif sekretnosti*, 227, lists Soviet losses in the operation as 99,386 (23,577 killed or missing and 75,809 wounded).

35. For detailed coverage, see A. S. Zav'ialov and T. E. Kaliadin, *Vostochnaia-Pomeranskaia nastupatel'naia operatsiia Sovetskikh voisk, fevral'-mart 1945* [The Eastern Pomeranian offensive operation of Soviet forces, February–March 1945] (Moscow: Voenizdat, 1960). Krivosheev, *Grif sekretnosti*, 216, 372, lists Soviet strength in the operation (including 1st Polish Army) at 996,100 troops. Soviet losses

were 225,692 (52,740 killed or missing and 172,952 wounded), and 1,027 tanks and SP guns and 1,005 guns and mortars damaged or destroyed. Precise German strength figures are not available but probably did not exceed 200,000 men.

36. For details, see *Shturm Kenigsberga* [The storm of Konigsberg] (Kaliningrad, Izdatel'stvo Kaliningrada, 1973); I. Bagramian, "Shturm Kenigsberga" [The storm of Konigsberg], *VIZh* 8 (August 1976): 56–64, and 9 (September 1976): 47–57; N. Krylov, "Razgrom zemlandskoi gruppirovki protivnika" [Destruction of the Zemland enemy group], *VIZh* 4 (April 1972): 52–58; and B. Arushanian, "Na Zemlandskom poluostrove" [On the Zemland Peninsula], *VIZh* 4 (April 1970): 80–88.

37. "Kenigsbergskaia operatsiia 1945," [The Konigsberg operation 1945], in *Velikaia Otechestvennaia voina 1941–1945, entsiklopediia* [The Great Patriotic War 1941–1945, an encyclopedia] (Moscow: "Sovetskaia entsiklopediia," 1985), 329. Hereafter cited as *VOV*. Over 300,000 Soviet troops took part in the siege, supported by 538 tanks and SP guns and 5,200 guns and mortars.

38. "Zemlandskaia operatsiia 1945" [The Zemland operation 1945], *VOV*, 288, states that 111,000 Soviet troops took part in the operation, supported by 324 tanks and SP guns and 5,200 guns and mortars. This source places German strength on the peninsula at 65,000 men, 166 tanks and assault guns, and 1,200 artillery pieces, but these figures are probably inflated.

39. Erickson, *The Road to Berlin*, 520–521.

40. For details, see "Verkhne-Silezskaia nastupatel'naia operatsiia voisk 1-go Ukrainskogo fronta, 15–31 marta 1945 g." [The Upper Silesian offensive operation of the 1st Ukrainian Front, 15–31 March 1945], *SVIMVOV*, Issue 6 (Moscow: Voenizdat, 1952), 3–80; classified secret. Krivosheev, *Grif sekretnosti*, 228, and other sources cite Soviet strength in the operation as 408,400 troops, supported by 988 tanks and SP guns and 5,640 guns and mortars.

41. Krivosheev, *Grif sekretnosti*, 228, cites Soviet losses of 66,801 (15,876 killed or missing and 66,801 wounded). German losses are listed in "Verkhne-silezskaia operatsiia 1945" [The Upper Silesian operation 1945], *VOV*, 126, as 40,000 troops destroyed and 14,000 captured.

42. Planning for the Vienna operation is covered in P. Ia. Malinovsky, *Budapesht-Vena-Praga* [Budapest-Vienna-Prague] (Moscow: "Nauka," 1965); and A. Rakitsky, "Ot Budapeshta do Veny" [From Budapest to Vienna], *VIZh* 4 (April 1975): 119–123.

43. For details on intelligence and deception in the operation, see Glantz, *Soviet Military Deception*, 515–520. German planning and Sixth SS Panzer Army's role in the operation is covered in A. Werncke, "The Employment of 6th SS Panzer Army in Hungary and Austria from February to May 1945," *1986 Art of War Symposium*, 771–787. Werncke was deputy logistical officer for the army.

44. For details on combat operations, see D. M. Glantz, "An Overview of Operations in Hungary, 1 January–16 March 1945," *1986 Art of War Symposium*, 665–756; and R. Stoves, "Comments on German Counterattacks in Hungary," *1986 Art of War Symposium*, 761–770. Stoves commanded a panzer company in 1st Panzer Division and has since written extensively on his division, and armor in general, in the war. Soviet accounts include, "Oboronitel'nye boi 64-go strelkovogo

korpusa iuzhnee ozera Balaton v marte 1945 g." [The defensive battles of 64th Rifle Corps south of Lake Balaton in March 1945], *SVIMVOV*, Issue 9 (Moscow: Voenizdat, 1953), 121–166 (classified secret); and "Sryv kontranastupleniia nemetsko-fashistkikh voisk u ozera Balaton" [Disruption of the counteroffensive of German-Fascist forces at Lake Balaton], *VIZh* 3 (March 1969): 14–29. Krivosheev, *Grif sekretnosti*, 228, and other Soviet sources cite the strength of Soviet forces in the Balaton operation at 465,000 troops, supported by 407 tanks and SP guns (less 6th Guards Tank Army), and 6,889 guns and mortars. This includes only the defending forces of 3d Ukrainian Front. To this must be added the 101,500 troops and almost 400 tanks and SP guns of 2d Ukrainian Front west of Budapest and the over 100,000 troops of 9th Guards Army in reserve east of Budapest. German strength in the attack is obscure. However, along the entire front from southern Slovakia to south of Lake Balaton, Army Group South fielded about 430,000 men, supported by 900 tanks and assault guns. The bulk of this armor, 807 pieces by Soviet estimation, was employed in the Balaton counterstroke.

45. Krivosheev, *Grif sekretnosti*, 228, cites Soviet losses in the Balaton operation as being 32,899 (8,492 killed or missing and 24,407 wounded). Raditsky's claim (119) that the Germans lost 40,000 men, 500 tanks and assault guns, and 300 guns and mortars in the attack seems reasonable.

46. Krivosheev, *Grif sekretnosti*, 218, places Soviet strength in the Vienna operation at 745,600 troops, including 100,900 Bulgarians, supported by an estimated 400 tanks and SP guns. This includes 46th Army and supporting units from 2d Ukrainian Front. The remaining 272,200 men (plus over 100,000 Rumanians) of Malinovsky's 2d Ukrainian Front, supported by 300 tanks and SP guns, conducted the Bratislava-Brno operation in Slovakia and in Hungary north of the Danube, beginning on 25 March. Although the Soviets treat Malinovsky's operation as distinct from the Vienna operation, German Army Group South had to contend with both Soviet *fronts* simultaneously. After their Balaton losses, Army Group South forces numbered less than 400,000 men, supported by about 400 tanks and assault guns.

47. According to Krivosheev, *Grif sekretnosti*, 218, Soviet losses in the Vienna operation were 167,940 (38,661 killed or missing and 129,279 wounded). The Bulgarian 1st Army suffered 9,805 casualties (2,698 killed or missing and 7,107 wounded). The 2d Ukrainian Front suffered 79,596 casualties in the Bratislava-Brno operation (16,933 killed or missing and 62,663 wounded).

48. According to Krivosheev, *Grif sekretnosti*, 153, Soviet losses during the period 1 October through 31 December 1944 were 259,766 killed or missing and 1,026,645 wounded and during the period 1 January–31 March 1945, 468,407 killed or missing and 1,582,517 wounded. German strengths and losses during January and February are from Ziemke, *Stalingrad to Berlin*, 457.

16. End Game

1. Detailed Soviet military operational studies, classified or published openly, in particular those written before 1968, were generally candid and detailed insofar

as they went. This had to be the case if they were to suit the purposes for which they were intended, which was the proper education of the Soviet Army in the conduct of war and military operations. There were always some operations, however, which for political reasons could not be examined or discussed. This included many military failures, such as the Mars operation of November–December 1942, the defeats in February–March 1943, and the failures in Belorussia from November 1943 to February 1944, as well as politically sensitive issues, such as the failure of the Soviets to help the Warsaw Poles in August–September 1944. For details on these works, see Archival Sources.

2. For a complete German order of battle on the Berlin axis, see *Berlinskaia operatsiia 1945 goda* [The Berlin operation 1945] (Moscow: Voenizdat, 1950), 1–44. This classified work, prepared by the Main Military-Scientific Directorate of the Soviet Army General Staff, is the most compete study of all details of the Berlin operation yet made available. See also, W. Willemer, *The German Defense of Berlin*, MS # P-136 (Historical Division, Headquarters United States Army, Europe, 1953). Compiled by German veterans of the battle, this study provides an excellent description of German defenses around and in Berlin.

3. V. Chuikov, *The End of the Third Reich*, (Moscow: Progress Publishers, 1978), 166–169. This is an honest translation of Chuikov's multivolume autobiography, which fully underscores his disagreements with Zhukov and the general historical controversies associated with the 1945 operations. See also, Earl F. Ziemke, *From Stalingrad to Berlin: The German Defeat in the East* (Washington, D.C.: U.S. Army Center for Military History, 1968), 463, for Hitler's changing assessment of Soviet intentions.

4. Chuikov, *End of the Third Reich*, 166–169; Ziemke, *Stalingrad to Berlin*, 464–465.

5. Chuikov, *End of the Third Reich*.

6. For a glimpse of Soviet suspicions, see V. Pozniak, "Zavershaiushchie udary po vragu" [The final blow against the enemy], *VIZh* 5 (May 1965): 26. Virtually all of Shtemenko's numerous accounts express the same suspicions.

7. See, *Berlinskaia operatsiia*, 1–44, which places German strength in and forward of Berlin at 766,750 men, supported by 1,519 tanks and assault guns, and 9,303 artillery pieces. Other Soviet sources have credited the Germans with one million men, including 200 *Volkssturm* battalions totaling 200,000. These estimates include all of Army Group Vistula and the Twelfth Army from the West. Actual German strength on the Eastern Front in April 1945, based upon surrender figures, appear to be: Army Group Vistula, 550,000; Army Group Center, 500,000 (of which 150,000 were involved in the Berlin operation); Army Group South, 450,000; Army Group North (in Courland), 300,000; and the Berlin Garrison, 120,000.

8. Willemer, *German Defense of Berlin*, 25–39.

9. Chuikov, *End of the Third Reich*, 166, 175.

10. Ibid.; V. A. Matsulenko, *Voennoe iskusstvo v Berlinskoi operatsii* [Military art in the Berlin operation] (Moscow: Voroshilov Academy of the General Staff, 1983), 7–20.

11. See complete planning details in *Berlinskaia operatsiia*, and Matsulenko, *Voennoe iskusstvo*.

12. G. Zhukov, "Na berlinskom napravlenii" [On the Berlin axis], *VIZh* 6 (June 1965): 12–22. Soviet armored strength is found in V. I. Gan'shin, *Tankovye i mekhanizirovannye voiska v Berlinskoi operatsii* [Tanks and mechanized forces in the Berlin operation] (Moscow: Voroshilov Academy of the General Staff, 1948), classified secret; and *Berlinskaia operatsiia*, 173–188.

13. I. S. Konev, *Year of Victory* (Moscow: Progress Publishers, 1984), 315–316. This is a good translation of *God pobedy* [Year of Victory] (Moscow: Voenizdat, 1966).

14. K. Rokossovsky, "Severnee Berlina" [North of Berlin], *VIZh* 5 (May 1965): 36–41.

15. See G. F. Krivosheev, *Grif sekretnosti sniat: Poteri vooruzhennykh sil SSSR v voinakh, boevykh deistviiakh i voennykh konfliktakh* [Losses of the armed forces of the USSR in wars, combat actions, and military conflicts] (Moscow: Voenizdat, 1993), 219–220.

16. N. M. Ramanichev, "Iz opyta peregruppirovki armii pri podgotovke Berlinskoi operatsii" [From the experience of regrouping an army during the preparation of the Berlin operation], *VIZh* 8 (August 1979): 9–16; "Kombinirovannyi marsh 47-go strelkovogo korpusa 70-i armii pri peregruppirovke voisk 2-go Belorusskogo fronta s dantsigskogo na shtettinskoe napravlenie (aprel' 1945 g.)" [The combined march of 70th Army's 47th Rifle Corps during the regrouping of 2d Belorussian Front forces from the Danzig to the Stettin axis], *SVIMVOV*, No. 7 (Moscow: Voenizdat, 1952), 97–118; classified secret.

17. For complete planning figures, see *Berlinskaia operatsiia* text and figures. Details of air-ground cooperation are found in "O primenenii aviatsii v Berlinskoi operatsii" [Concerning the employment of aviation in the Berlin operation], *VIZh* 4 (April 1985): 18–26, which consists of an interview with S. I. Rudenko, 16th Air Army commander in the operation.

18. Chuikov, *End of the Third Reich*, 177–181. Full details on engineer support are also found in S. Kh. Agonov, "Inzhenernye voiska v Berlinskoi operatsii" [Engineer forces in the Berlin operation], *VIZh* 4 (April 1985): 36–40.

19. For details on the problems and resulting carnage, see *Berlinskaia operatsii*, 493–550.

20. As an indicator of the intensity of combat, during the penetration battle between 16 and 19 April, 1st Belorussian Front lost 727 tanks, representing 23 percent of its initial tank strength. During the entire operation, 1st Guards Tank Army lost 431 of its 706 tanks and SP guns, including 104 in Berlin street fighting; 232 of these were irretrievable combat losses. See Gan'shin, *Tankovye i mekhanizirovannye*, 40.

21. See also Konev, *Years of Victory*, 317–325; D. Leliushenko, "Pered nami Berlin!" [Before us Berlin], *VIZh* 6 (June 1970): 65–72.

22. For the Polish role in the operation, see E. Dymkovsky, "2-ia armiia Voiska Pol'skogo v Berlinskoi i Prazhskoi operatsiiakh" [Polish 2d Army in the Berlin and Prague operations], *VIZh* 6 (June 1975): 41–45; E. Bordzilovsky, "Uchastie 1-i

armii Voiska Pol'skogo v Berlinskoi operatsii" [The participation of 1st Polish Army in the Berlin operation], *VIZh* 10 (October 1963): 15–29.

23. Chuikov, *The End of the Third Reich*, 189; Pozniak, "Zavershaiushchie udary," 31. For details on the "race for Berlin" between Zhukov and Konev, see (forthcoming) O. A. Rzheshevsky, "The Race for Berlin," *Journal of Slavic Military Studies* 8 (September 1995).

24. Of the many descriptions of this complex fighting, see Chuikov, *The End of the Third Reich*, 18; V. Makarevsky, "17-ia motoinzhenernaia brigada v Berlinskoi operratsii" [The 17th Motorized Engineer Brigade in the Berlin operation], *VIZh* 4 (April 1976): 61–65; and I. Sinenko, "Organizatsiia i vedenie boia 164-m strelkovym polkom za Batslov pod Berlinom" [The organization and conduct of combat for Batslow near Berlin by the 164th Rifle Regiment], *VIZh* 4 (April 1976): 65–70. The engineer brigade supported 1st Guards Tank Army, and the rifle regiment was in 3d Shock Army.

25. Ziemke, *Stalingrad to Berlin*, 479–485, writes of Hitler's attempts to organize relief for Berlin.

26. In addition to the classified works, see A. Luchinsky, "Na Berlin!" [On to Berlin!], *VIZh* 5 (May 1965): 81–91.

27. Among the works describing the link up of Soviet and Allied troops, see A. Faizulin, P. Dobrovol'sky, "Vstrecha na El'be" [Meeting on the Elbe], *VIZh* 4 (April 1979): 51–53, which contains documentary reports; and G. Nekhonov, "Vstrecha na El'be" [Meeting on the Elbe], *VIZh* 4 (April 1965): 119–121. The meeting on 25 April at Torgau was between a patrol of the U.S. 69th Infantry Division and the 2d Battalion, 173d Guards Rifle Regiment, 58th Guards Rifle Division, 5th Guards Army. Later the same day, elements of the 15th Guards Rifle Division (5th Guards Army) linked up with the 69th Division near Riesa, and on the next day, elements of the 121st Guards Rifle Division (13th Army) met advanced elements of U.S. 9th Infantry Division near Wittenberg. Further north, on 2 May, lead elements of Soviet 70th Army (2d Belorussian Front) met American troops of XVIII Airborne Corps (under British Second Army command) near Schwerin.

28. Among the many accounts on fighting in Berlin, see V. S. Antonov, "Poslednie dni voiny" [The final days of war], *VIZh* 7 (July 1987): 70–75; and S. Neustroev, "Shturm reikhstaga" [Assault on the Reichstag], *VIZh* 5 (May 1960): 42–51.

29. For details on the surrender of Berlin, together with appropriate documents, see V. G. Kuznetsov and V. P. Modlinsky, "Agoniia" [Agony], *VIZh* 6–7 (June–July 1992): 4–12.

30. According to Krivosheev, *Grif sekretnosti*, 219–220, Soviet casualties in the Berlin operation totaled 78,291 killed or missing and 274,184 wounded. Polish casualties amounted to 2,825 killed or missing and 6,067 wounded. The Soviets also lost 1,997 tanks and SP guns, 2,108 artillery pieces, and 917 aircraft in the operation. Soviet classified figures on German losses are found in *Berlinskaia operatsiia*, 616–618.

31. These conferences were held at the headquarters of the Group of Soviet Forces in Germany (GSFS) and the Central Group of Forces (CGF) from February through April 1945. Two of the conference reports were later published as "Iz

doklada komanduiushchego bronetankovymi i mekhanizirovannymi voiskami Gruppy sovetskikh voisk v Germanii marshala bronetankovykh voisk P. A. Rotmistrova na voenno-nauchnoi konferentsii po izucheniiu Berlinskoi operatsii" [From the report of the commander of armored and mechanized forces of the Group of Soviet Forces in Germany, Marshal P. A. Rotmistrov, at a military-scientific conference on the study of the Berlin operation], *VIZh* 9 (September 1985): 43–50; and "Iz vystupleniia Marshala Sovetskogo Soiuza I. S. Koneva na voenno-nauchnoi konferentsii vysshego komandnogo sostava Tsentral'noi gruppy voisk po izucheniiu opyta Berlinskoi i Prazhskoi operatsii" [From a presentation of Marshal of the Soviet Union I. S. Konev at a military-scientific conference of the higher command staff of the Central Group of Forces on the study of the experience of the Berlin and Prague operations], *VIZh* 4 (April 1985): 53–59. The reports conclude that terrain considerations in the central European region and the changing nature of combat required an alteration of the army force structure away from the tank-heavy formations prevelant during the war to a more balanced combined-arms mixture. As a result, in 1946 and 1947 the Soviet abolished the tank armies and the tank and mechanized corps, replacing them with mechanized armies and tank and mechanized divisions, each with an increased complement of infantry and supporting arms. At the same time, rifle divisions were beefed up in firepower and supporting arms and were slowly motorized.

32. According I. Vyrodov and V. Gurkin, "Prazhskaia nastupatel'nia operatsiia: fakty i tsifry" [The Prague operation: facts and figures], *VIZh* 5 (May 1972): 126, German strength in the Prague operation was 900,000 men, 1,900 tanks and assault guns, 9,700 guns and mortars, and 1,000 aircraft. This included Army Group Center and over half of Army Group Austria (former Army Group South). Ziemke, *Stalingrad to Berlin*, 498, places German strength on 8 May at 600,000 for Army Group Center and 430,000 for Army Group Austria (Ostmark). Thus, the two sources essentially agree.

33. Krivosheev, *Grif sekretnosti*, 221, and Vyrodov and Gurkin, "Prazhskaia," 126, agree on Soviet strength in the Prague operation: 2,028,100 troops, 1,960 tanks and SP guns, 30,452 guns and mortars, and 3,014 aircraft.

34. For details on operational planning and conduct of the operation, see S. M. Shtemenko, *The Last Six Months: Russia's Final Battles with Hitler's Armies in World War II* (Garden City, N.Y.: Doubleday and Co., 1977), 393–396. For the best Russian-language account, see A. N. Grylev, V. P. Morozov, A. F. Ryzhakov, and V. V. Gurkin, *Za osvobozhdenie Chekhoslovakii* [For the liberation of Czechoslovakia] (Moscow: Voenizdat, 1965). See also, R. Malinovsky, "2-i Ukrianskii Front v bor'be za osvobozhdenie Chekhoslovakii" [The 2d Ukrainian Front in the struggle for the liberation of Czechoslovakia], *VIZh* 5 (May 1960): 11–25.

35. Krivosheev, *Grif sekretnosti*, 221, places Soviet, Bulgarian, Rumanian, and Czech losses in the operation at 52,498, including 11,997 killed or missing and 40,501 wounded. Matérial losses were 373 tanks and SP guns, 1,006 guns and mortars, and 80 aircraft.

36. Shtemenko, *The Last Six Months*, 401–410.

17. Conclusion

1. Soviet strength in the Far East on 22 June 1941 included 24 rifle, motorized rifle, and cavalry divisions; 8 tank and mechanized divisions; and 13 fortified regions. The *Stavka* drew heavily on its forces in the Far East and Trans-Baikal Military Districts in 1941 as it halted the German offensive at Moscow and conducted its Moscow counteroffensive. What many authors have referred to as "Siberian" divisions were, in fact, primarily from the Far Eastern and Trans-Baikal Military Districts (such as A. P. Beloborodov's famous 78th Rifle Division). Subsequently, Soviet strength in Manchuria ranged from just over 30 divisions and 14 fortified regions on 1 January 1942 to 47 divisions and 19 fortified regions on 1 January 1945. This total increased to 80 divisions, 4 tank and mechanized corps, and 21 fortified regions on 9 August 1945.

2. Japanese wartime planning for the Kwantung Army is covered in U.S. Army Military History Section, "Japanese Preparations for Operations in Manchuria, January 1943–August 1945," *Japanese Monograph No. 138* (U.S. Army Forces Far East, 1951), 90–110, 141–151.

3. The Japanese garrison divisions were structured for occupational duties and not for field combat. They had four regiments rather than three, and no antitank or artillery capability. Even the regular field divisions, organized into three regiments, had virtually no antitank capability since the Japanese discounted the Soviet's ability to introduce tanks into Manchuria, and combat in the Pacific had not required the Japanese to develop and employ modern antitank guns. Therefore, in Manchuria the Japanese added a "raiding" battalion to each of its field divisions. Personnel of the raiding battalions carried explosive charges to use against enemy tanks in human-bomb fashion. After the Soviet offensive began, these suicide attacks proved ineffective because the explosive charges were too weak. In response, the Japanese command doubled the size of the charges. Most Soviet tank losses came at the hands of these suicide attacks, called by the Russians "*smertniki*" [deathniks].

4. Japanese divisions numbered from 9,000 to 18,000 men. Soviet divisions averaged about 5,000 men, with some as low as 3,000.

5. For information on the diplomatic background to Soviet participation, in addition to Soviet sources, see Herbert Feis, *The Atomic Bomb and the End of World War II* (Princeton, N.J.: Princeton University Press, 1966); Charles L. Mee, *Meeting at Potsdam* (New York: M. Evans, 1975).

6. For details on planning for the Hokkaido operation, see V. P. Galitsky and V. P. Zimonin, "Desant na Khokkaido otmenit' " [Descent on Hokkaido countermanded], *VIZh* 3 (March 1994): 5–10, which includes correspondence between Stalin and Vasilevsky regarding the operation.

7. For information on Japanese intelligence, see David M. Glantz, *Soviet Military Deception in the Second World War*, (London: Frank Cass and Co., 1989), 544–555; and E. J. Drea, "Missing Intentions: Japanese Intelligence and the Soviet Invasion of Manchuria, 1945," *Military Affairs* (April 1984): 67–70.

8. For details on the extensive regrouping effort, see N. V. Eronin, *Strategicheskaia peregruppirovka sovetskikh vooruzhennkh sil (pri podgotovka Dal'*

nevostochnoi kampanii 1945 goda [Strategic regrouping of the Soviet armed forces (during preparations for the 1945 Far Eastern Campaign] (Moscow: Voroshilov Academy of the General Staff, 1980); classified secret. From 1 January to 9 August 1945, Soviet personnel strength in the Far East rose from 1,010,400 to 1,577,700. While this source is accurate concerning Soviet strength and preparations, it woefully overstates Japanese strength in Manchuria.

9. For details on these changes in Soviet plans and on the conduct of the operation, see David M. Glantz, *August Storm: The Soviet 1945 Strategic Offensive in Manchuria*, Leavenworth Papers No. 7 (Fort Leavenworth, Kan.: Combat Studies Institute, 1983); David M. Glantz, *August Storm: Soviet Tactical and Operational Combat in Manchuria, 1945*, Leavenworth Papers No. 8 (Fort Leavenworth, Kan.: Combat Studies Institute, 1983).

10. According to G. F. Krivosheev, *Grif sekretnosti sniat: Poteri vooruzhennykh sil SSSR v voinakh, boevykh deistviiakh i voennykh konfliktakh* [Losses of the armed forces of the USSR in wars, combat actions, and military conflicts] (Moscow: Voenizdat, 1993), 222–223, the Soviets committed 1,669,500 men to Far Eastern operations, including action in Manchuria, Korea, and on Sakhalin Island and the Kurile Islands. The Mongolians committed another 16,000 men as part of Pliev's cavalry-mechanized force. In Manchuria proper, the Soviets fielded 1,577,725 troops supported by 5,556 tanks and SP guns, 27,086 guns and mortars, and 3,721 aircraft against the 713,000-man Kwantung Army (and 170,000 Manchukuoan and 44,000 inner Mongolian forces, most of which refused to fight or were ineffective). An additional 280,000 Japanese were stationed in Korea, on Sakhalin Island, and in the Kuriles. While the Japanese had considerable artillery strength located in fortresses and under army command, they had virtually no modern tanks. See Glantz, *August Storm* (No. 7), 25–47.

11. The Japanese adopted Fabian tactics designed to draw Soviet forces into Manchuria and then destroy them as they reached the end of their logistical tether. The final battle was to be in the formidable Japanese defensive redoubt in southern Manchuria along the Korean border. Rapid Soviet operations simply preempted these Japanese plans.

12. Based on experiences in Europe (principally at Berlin) and conscious experimentation in Manchuria, the Soviet postwar force reorganization added greater mobility, sustainability, and firepower to all Soviet military formations. For details on Soviet force structure in Manchuria and the postwar restructuring, see Glantz, *August Storm* (No. 7), 47–58, 163–182.

13. Krivosheev, *Grif sekretnosti*, 222–223, 373. In addition, the Soviets lost 78 tanks and SP guns (most to "*smertniks*") and 232 guns and mortars. The Mongolians lost 72 killed or missing and 125 wounded. Krivosheev, 391, places Japanese losses at 83,700 killed and 609,400 captured (plus 16,100 Chinese, 10,300 Korean, 3,600 Mongolian, and 700 Manchukoan prisoners). Japanese prisoners went into long-term captivity in Siberia and the Far East, where they worked on reconstruction of the Soviet economy. Like German prisoners, many perished and were not repatriated to Japan.

14. Details on 6th Guards Tank Army operations appear in I. Krupchenko, "6-ia gvardeiskaia tankovaia armiia v Khingano-Mukdenskoi operatsii" [The 6th Guards Tank Army in the Khingan-Mukden operation], *VIZh* 12 (December 1962): 15–30.

15. Among the many articles on 36th Army's operations, see A. A. Luchinsky, "Zabaikal'tsy na sopkakh Man'chzhurii" [Trans-Baikal troops in the hills of Manchuria], *VIZh* 8 (August 1971): 67–74.

16. For details on 5th Army's operations, see N. I. Krylov, N. I. Alekseev, I. G. Dragan, *Navstrechu pobede: boevoi put' 5-i armii, oktiabr 1941g.- avgust 1945g.* [Toward victory: the combat path of 5th Army, October 1941–August 1945] (Moscow: "Nauka," 1970).

17. Details on 257th Tank Brigade's operations are found in A. Beloborodov, "Na sopkakh Man'chzhurii" [In the hills of Manchuria], *VIZh* 12 (December 1980): 30–35; and 1 (January 1981): 45–51. Beloborodov has written several superb accounts about operations of his 1st Red Banner Army.

18. Galitsky and Zimonin, "Destination Khokkaido," 9.

19. Earl F. Ziemke, *From Stalingrad to Berlin: The German Defeat in the East* (Washington, D.C.: U.S. Army Center of Military History, 1968), 412.

20. Ibid., 213. See also Appendix, Table E, in this book on German wartime losses.

21. Ziemke, *Stalingrad to Berlin*, 213–214, 412, places total German dead at between 3 and 3.5 million. The author estimates that about 88 percent fell in the East. Krivosheev, *Grif sekretnosti*, 384–392, places German dead at 3,888,000 and POWs (including Austrians, SS, and foreign auxiliaries in the German Army) at 3,035,700.

22. For German strength and losses in the West, see Frank P. Chambers, *This Age of Conflict* (New York: Harcourt, Brace & World, 1962), 589–596.

23. Sokolov, "The Role of Lend-Lease," convincingly expresses Russian revisionist views on the importance of Lend-Lease to the Soviet war effort.

24. Based on interviews conducted by the author with Soviet war veterans in July 1989, it is apparent that Soviet infantry casualties remained high throughout the war, in particular, in first-echelon assault units. For example, when asked what the normal losses were in a first-echelon regiment on the main attack axis during the penetration phase of an operation, a former regimental commander of 97th Guards Rifle Division stated *"pochti polovina"* [almost half] of the regiment's strength. He went on to state that such was the case to the very end of the war.

Archival Sources

1. For a more detailed explanation of the Soviet (Russian) archives system, see Colonel I. N. Venkov, "Military Archives in the U.S.S.R.," unpublished 1989 manuscript held by the Foreign Military Studies Office, Combined Arms Command, Fort Leavenworth, Kan.; and Colonel V. V. Mukhin, "Problemy voennykh arkhivov" [Problems of Military Archives], Voenno-istoricheskii zhurnal, 6–7 (June–July 1992).

2. A virtual monopoly on released archival materials has been arranged by the U.S. firm East View Publications. In this sense, the idea of market economics has taken firm hold.

3. For example, in April 1990, a new Russian firm named MITEK announced that it was the sole organization governing archival access. Whether this organization survived the subsequent revolution is unknown.

About the Authors

Colonel David M. Glantz, U.S. Army, Retired, has been described as the West's foremost expert on the Red Army's performance in the Great Patriotic War. A graduate of the Virginia Military Institute and the University of North Carolina, his military career included both service in Vietnam and teaching at a variety of U.S. Army schools. He retired in 1993 as director of the U.S. Army's Foreign Army Studies Office, Fort Leavenworth, Kansas, and remains the editor of the *Journal of Slavic Military Studies* and a member of the Academy of Sciences of the Russian Federation. Colonel Glantz's many publications include *Soviet Military Deception in the Second World War, From the Don to the Dnepr: Soviet Offensive Operations December 1942 to August 1943, The Military Strategy of the Soviet Union*, and his most recent work, *A History of Soviet Airborne Forces*.

Lieutenant Colonel Jonathan M. House is associate professor of history at Gordon College, Barnesville, Georgia. A graduate of Hamilton College, he received his doctorate in history at the University of Michigan. His active-duty service included command and staff positions in the United States and in Korea, as well as instructional assignments at various U.S. Army service schools. Lieutenant Colonel House is the author of *Towards Combined Arms Warfare: A Survey of 20th-Century Tactics, Doctrine, and Organization*, and *Military Intelligence, 1870-1991: A Research Guide*.

Index